HANDBOOK OF SPECIALTY ELEMENTS IN ARCHITECTURE

HANDBOOK OF SPECIALTY ELEMENTS IN ARCHITECTURE

Andrew Alpern, AIA

EDITOR IN CHIEF

McGRAW-HILL BOOK COMPANY

New York   St. Louis   San Francisco   Auckland   Bogotá   Hamburg
Johannesburg   London   Madrid   Mexico   Montreal   New Delhi
Panama   Paris   São Paulo   Singapore   Sydney   Tokyo   Toronto

Library of Congress Cataloging in Publication Data

Main entry under title:

Handbook of specialty elements in architecture.

   Includes bibliographies and index.
   1. Architecture — Miscellanea. 2. Landscape
architecture. 3. Art. 4. Recreation centers.
4. Playgrounds. 5. Fountains. 6. Lighting,
Architectural and decorative. 7. Signs and symbols
in architecture. 8. Architecture and the physically
handicapped. I. Alpern, Andrew.
NA2540.H32   720   81-8417
                 AACR2

ISBN 0-07-001360-8

1 2 3 4 5 6 7 8 9 0 HDHD 8 9 8 7 6 5 4 3 2 1

The editors for this book were Harold B. Crawford, Patricia
Allen-Browne, Virginia Blair, and Ann Gray; the designer was
Elliot Epstein; and the production supervisor was Sally Fliess. It
was set in Souvenir by University Graphics, Inc. It was printed
and bound by Halliday Lithograph.

To working architects, everywhere

CONTENTS

Preface

The professions of architecture and interior design often demand of their practitioners a significant amount of knowledge in specialized fields beyond the normal realm of practice. Obtaining this knowledge for the infrequent projects that require it can mean timeconsuming research and the tracking-down and acquisition of an extensive library of reference books and manufacturers' catalogues.

This handbook obviates all that. It gathers together in one convenient volume the essentials of twelve specialty areas of concern to architects and designers. Presented in twelve chapters, this material gives the reader a sound general understanding of each subject specialty as well as offering a wealth of specific working data. From the information supplied, the design professional will be able to handle most situations unaided. For more complex projects the reader will gain sufficient working knowledge to interact productively with consultant specialists who may need to be retained.

The chapter subjects have been selected to encompass those specialty areas that are encountered sufficiently often to make this handbook one to which designers will regularly refer. The material complements other commonly used reference works, filling in the gaps where coverage has been thin or nonexistent. Each chapter is written from the point of view of the working designer, and presents its subject matter in readily understood terms.

Chapter 1, "Audiovisual Communications," presents the theory and practical application of integrating audiovisual communications and presentations facilities into interior architecture in a manner that makes the medium totally subservient to the message, and that enables the person presenting that message to concentrate on the presentation content rather than on its mechanics.

Chapter 2, "Exterior Plantings," presents a simplified approach to exterior plantings that relate closely to buildings, and includes specification data and good photographs of effectively executed plantings.

Chapter 3, "Trees and Plants for Interior Design," presents a similarly easy-to-understand approach to interior plantings for buildings, and includes a very extensive encyclopedia of suitable plants, giving photographs, characteristics, environmental requirements, and specification data.

Chapter 4, "Sculpture," presents an approach to working with a sculptor and integrating sculpture and architecture. It includes data on pertinent characteristics of various commonly used sculpture materials and also includes a suggested form of agreement for commissioning a sculptor, as well as numerous photographs of sculptures used in conjunction with buildings and architectural interiors.

Chapter 5, "Interior Art," describes the types of art that are suitable for commercial interiors and discusses framing, lighting, insurance, and different ways of obtaining art. The chapter includes information about working with a professional art consultant, and is profusely illustrated.

Chapter 6, "Adult Outdoor Recreation Facilities," presents a theory of adult recreation and discusses the factors that must be considered in designing recreational facilities for adults. Data is given on construction materials that can be used, and planning and construction drawings are included for most commonly played varieties of recreational games.

Chapter 7, "Juvenile Play Areas," presents the essential background on how and why children play. It shows how the designer can create an environment conducive to play and discusses materials, construction techniques, and safety. Data on play environments for children of different ages are included.

Chapter 8, "Decorative Pools and Fountains," tells how the use of decorative pools and fountains can enhance architecture and the built environment. It shows how water features can be integrated with a building design and presents the technical data necessary to understand the design of a pool or a fountain. Included is a detailed case history of the development of a major public fountain display, complete with drawings and photographs.

Chapter 9, "Exterior Lighting," presents a simplified approach to designing the kinds of outdoor lighting such as would commonly be encountered by architects. The chapter discusses how lighting can be used as a creative tool for making the built environment more usable and enjoyable, and includes data and discussion of various light sources and how to use them. Costs, maintenance, suitability, and other pertinent factors are covered.

Chapter 10, "Flagpoles," tells you everything you ever wanted to know about flagpoles, in one conveniently usable chapter. Included are the types available, materials, costs, maintenance, sizing, construction details, and specifications.

Chapter 11, "Signage," presents the theory of signage and instant information communication. It shows how to plan a signage program for one or more buildings, both external and internal, and tells about the various types of signs available and when to use which. Detailed specifications for lettering sizes, sign materials, and construction details are given.

Chapter 12, "Designing for the Disabled," tells about the different forms of human disability and shows how the designer can compensate for them. It presents specific detailed drawings showing how various common architectural situations can be modified to suit the needs of the disabled.

The authors of these chapters are professionals in their respective fields, and have drawn on their many years of experience and practical knowledge in preparing their material. The pragmatic information they present offers a useful support to an architectural or interior design practice and can serve as a constant ready-reference source of help and advice.

We have developed an excellent professional handbook, but of course we welcome suggestions for improvement. Letters offering comments or proposals for additional chapters will be well received by the editor in care of the publisher.

Andrew Alpern, AIA

New York
May 1981

ACKNOWLEDGMENTS

Thanks are owed to Jeremy Robinson who conceived of this handbook and helped bring it to fruition. Thanks also to Harold B. Crawford and his colleagues at McGraw-Hill who patiently encouraged the book's development and saw it through the laborious production process. And of course the lion's share of thanks goes to the contributors, without whom the project could not have become a reality. The cooperation of others who provided material is appreciated.

ABOUT THE CONTRIBUTORS

ANDREW ALPERN (editor in chief) is an architect, registered in five states and nationally certified. Educated at Columbia University, he has lectured at the City University of New York, the Institute for Architecture and Urban Studies, and the Grolier Club. Mr. Alpern is the author of *Apartments for the Affluent: A Historical Survey of Buildings in New York,* and *Alpern's Architectural Aphorisms,* both published by McGraw-Hill. He is a member of the American Institute of Architects, the Real Estate Board of New York, the Society of Architectural Historians, and a number of other professional organizations, and he serves as an arbitrator for the construction industry at the American Arbitration Association. Mr. Alpern is the editor of the McGraw-Hill periodical, *Legal Briefs for Architects, Engineers, and Contractors.* Other current projects include several books on architectural subjects. (Photo credit: Gil Amiaga.)

JAMES E. COANE (Chapter 10, "Flagpoles") was associated with the American Flagpole Company for fifteen years before leaving the post of president in 1979 to become head of planning and operations for that company's parent organization, Kearney-National, Inc. A Phi Beta Kappa graduate in economics of Duke University, Mr. Coane has been active in the flagpole industry for many years, holding the posts of director and chairman of the Flagpole Division of the National Association of American Metal Manufacturers. He is a member of the Construction Specifications Institute and has worked closely with architects to achieve an appropriate integration of flagpoles with all types of architecture.

EVERETT LAWSON CONKLIN (Chapter 3, "Trees and Plants for Interior Design") is founder and president of the international series of companies that bear his name. These firms provide both indoor and outdoor landscape and plant services throughout the world. Mr. Conklin and his firm have received almost 200 awards, and he has been honored at the White House for his horticultural work by three different administrations. Mr. Conklin is past-president of seven professional organizations, has served other industrywide organizations in other capacities, and has been a program advisor to the United States Department of Agriculture. He has written several articles on plants and landscaping and has lectured extensively at colleges and universities offering courses in horticulture or landscape architecture. (Photo credit: White Studio.)

Landscape architect and urban designer M. PAUL FRIEDBERG (Chapter 7, "Juvenile Play Areas"; Chapter 8, "Decorative Pools and Fountains") heads his own firm which has a worldwide practice and has garnered more than thirty awards, the most recent of which is the 1980 Medal from the American Institute of Architects. Mr. Friedberg is a Fellow of the American Society of Landscape Architects, a trustee of the American Academy in Rome, and has served as New York City's Commissioner of Fine Arts. A graduate of Cornell University, he is the founder and director of the urban landscape architecture program at the City University of New York, and has taught at Columbia University, Pratt Institute, and the University of Pennsylvania. Mr. Friedberg is the author of the books *Playgrounds for City Children, Play and Interplay,* and *Handcrafted Playgrounds,* as well as numerous articles.

Following a 26-year affiliation with Olmsted Associates, the oldest landscape firm in the United States, JOSEPH G. HUDAK (Chapter 2, "Exterior Plantings") is now in private practice as a landscape architect in New England. He has taught at the Graduate School of Design of Harvard University for twenty years, as well as at the Radcliffe Seminars Program, and regularly lectures in the United States and abroad. Mr. Hudak has held several important posts at the American Society of Landscape Architects, and has published numerous articles in both the professional and the popular press. He is the author of the 1976 book *Gardening with Perennials Month by Month,* and McGraw-Hill published his 1980 book *Trees for Every Purpose.* Current projects include a second book for McGraw-Hill on plants and shrubs. (Photo credit: George McLean.)

xvi

FRED T. KNOWLES (Chapter 11, "Signage"), a graduate of the Duke University School of Civil Engineering and a member of the Society of Environmental Graphic Designers, has spent more than twenty years studying and analyzing architectural signage and its effect upon people and the environment. In 1969 Mr. Knowles founded Architectural Graphics, Inc., of Norfolk, Virginia, where he serves as president and chairman of the board. In order to alleviate the blight caused by thoughtless signing, he established a corporate philosophy of "undersigning." Mr. Knowles is responsible for developing important application of fiber-reinforced plastic as a sign material offering many new design options. Architectural Graphics Inc. has developed and produced comprehensive signage programs for many of the nation's performing arts and sports centers, convention centers, hospital complexes, corporate offices, and other architectural facilities where signage is an important consideration in the efficient movement of people.

SUSAN KORNER (Chapter 3, "Trees and Plants for Interior Design") is an interior landscape designer who has worked for many years to expand the awareness of interior designers and architects to the design possibilities of plants. She has lectured, given short training courses, and mounted special presentations to this end. Ms. Korner received a masters degree from Cornell University in Interior Design and Ornamental Horticulture after having earned a Bachelor of Fine Arts degree in Photography and Advertising from the University of North Carolina. (Photo credit: Raymond Kostyn.)

JEROME MENELL (Chapter 1, "Audiovisual Communications") is a specialist in audiovisual communication, having developed over a twenty-five-year period his basic concepts of making the medium and the machinery completely subservient to the message and the person delivering it. President of his own company, Mr. Menell serves as its chief consultant and design engineer for the firm's corporate and government clients. He has designed and engineered AV communications systems for business, industry, educational institutions, and government installations, as well as for exhibits and museums. A member of the National Academy of Television Arts and Sciences, the National Audio-Visual Association, and the Society of Motion Picture and Television Engineers, Mr. Menell has lectured at the American Management Association and at Indiana University, and has published articles in the professional press. (Photo credit: Standard Studios.)

LOUIS G. REDSTONE (Chapter 4, "Sculpture") is a Fellow of the American Institute of Architects and a Fellow of the Engineering Society of Detroit, as well as the chairman of his own architectural firm which is engaged in a wide range of projects in which sculpture is an integral part. Mr. Redstone is the recipient of many professional awards and honors, including the 1969 Gold Medal of the Detroit chapter of the AIA, the 1971 Award of Merit from the Michigan chapter of the National Society of Interior Designers, and the 1977 Patron Award of the Michigan Foundation for the Arts. In 1978 he was awarded the Gold Medal of the Michigan Society of Architects, in 1979 elected Honorary Fellow of the Royal Academy of Fine Arts of the Netherlands, and in 1980 he was elected corresponding member, Royal Academy of Fine Arts of San Fernando. Mr. Redstone is the editor of *Hospitals and Health Care Facilities* (1978), and *Institutional Buildings* (1980), and is the author of *Art in Architecture* (1968), *New Dimensions in Shopping Centers and Stores* (1973), *The New Downtowns* (1976), and *Public Art: New Directions* (1980), all published by McGraw-Hill. (Photo credit: Joe Clark, HBSS.)

CYNTHIA RICE (Chapter 8, "Decorative Pools and Fountains") is a registered landscape architect with degrees in both landscape architecture and the history of art and architecture. She has been involved with the master plan studies for two major parks in New York City, as well as the Delacorte Fountain in City Hall Park in New York, and with other public-oriented landscape design projects. Ms. Rice is the author of several articles on landscape architecture and energy efficiency in site design, and she is currently an urban designer and landscape architect with Quennell Rothschild Associates in New York. (Photo credit: Gil Amiaga.)

JOHN M. ROBERTS (Chapter 6, "Adult Outdoor Recreation Facilities") is a registered landscape architect and a professor in the Department of Landscape Architecture at Iowa State University. Prior to relocating to Iowa, Mr. Roberts taught at California State Polytechnic University and practiced landscape architecture in that state. Mr. Roberts has published several articles and papers, including a chapter on sports facilities for a handbook published by the American Society of Landscape Architects, a chapter on water systems and irrigation for the same handbook, an article on continuing education for landscape architects, and papers on recreation facilities for the U.S. Forest Service.

JUDITH SELKOWITZ (Chapter 5, "Interior Art") is a professional art consultant and head of her own firm serving corporate clients and the design professions. The holder of a degree from Smith College for major studies in art history and architecture, she was the recipient of a Fulbright scholarship for additional studies in Rome. Prior to forming Judith Selkowitz Fine Art Inc. in 1970, Ms. Selkowitz worked as an art researcher for the Smithsonian Institution and served as an independent curator to private art collectors. She has lectured at the Graduate School of Design of Harvard University and at the Institute for Business Designers, and is a member of several professional organizations. (Photo credit: dacotahkromes.)

ROBERT JAMES SORENSEN (Chapter 12, "Designing for the Disabled"), a practicing architect registered in five states and nationally certified, received his Bachelor of Arts degree from the University of Minnesota and his architectural degree from the University of Illinois. He has designed patient housing for a major medical center, a school for physically handicapped children, and a group home for the physically disabled. Mr. Sorensen is the author of *Design for Accessibility* published by McGraw-Hill in 1979, and is currently at work on projects to provide access for the handicapped in existing buildings.

ERNEST WOTTON (Chapter 9, "Exterior Lighting") is a lighting designer and consultant practicing primarily in Canada. The holder of a degree in electrical engineering from the University of London, he has undertaken lighting research, designed lighting equipment, and has patented a number of special lighting devices. Mr. Wotton publishes regularly in various scientific and professional journals, and has taught at the University of Toronto, the University of Michigan, the State University of New York, the University of Virginia, and Yale University. He is a licensed professional engineer and is a Fellow of several professional organizations including the Institute of Electrical Engineers, the Chartered Institution of Building Services, and the Illuminating Engineering Societies of North America and Great Britain. He is currently a member of a number of professional committees concerned with lighting in Canada, the United States, and Great Britain. (Photo credit: Roger Jowett.)

HANDBOOK OF SPECIALTY ELEMENTS IN ARCHITECTURE

CHAPTER ONE
AUDIOVISUAL COMMUNICATIONS
Jerome Menell

INTRODUCTION

Audiovisual communications, commonly called A-V, is a simple way of referring to the variety of means for transmitting information via sight and sound. A-V systems can be as basic as a schoolteacher's talking while drawing a picture on a chalkboard, or they may be as complex as a sophisticated multimedia presentation using side-by-side image comparison, sound-synchronized slide shows with random access capability, front access and remote overhead projectors, videotape programs with projected images, and remote control with complete automation. Such systems can be part of a management communications center, an audiovisual facility, a presentation auditorium, a classroom, or just a simple conference room.

The range of problems that can be solved through the use of audiovisual communications is very broad, and solutions can be varied and complex. A-V facilities are capable of conveying ideas efficiently and effectively if they are designed, engineered, and installed utilizing a thorough knowledge of the available options and the capabilities of each. The increasing use of such facilities by educators and business people with little or no technical knowledge has produced a requirement that the systems' operation be logical, uncomplicated, and virtually foolproof. The equally increasing sophistication of those to whom audiovisual presentations are made calls for a level of quality in the presentation methods and material that is well beyond what was considered satisfactory only a short time ago.

It has now been recognized that the components of a well-designed facility include, not only the A-V systems' functional elements, but also the physical accommodations and arrangement for the viewers. Architectural design considerations and technical sophistication are not the sole components of a successful audiovisual system. Equally important is the human element. It is people who initiate the presentations and people who are the recipients of the information they are designed to convey. Regardless of the type of information being presented or the manner in which it is transmitted, the entire process must be people-oriented, with the technical aspects manipulated to suit the human needs, rather than such needs being maneuvered to match technical considerations.

In order to accomplish this goal, there must be careful implementation of a well-ordered plan that is the result of a realistic communications program. The goals and design parameters must be established at the exploratory stage. These include:

- Identification and analysis of immediate and long-range communication objectives
- Investigation of architectural possibilities and physical constraints
- Comparative analysis of alternative design approaches
- Determination of cost and establishment of budgets

The use of a programmatic approach to the problem makes it easier to define the goals and to realize them; a cost-effective system will be the outcome. Facilities developed in this manner will enable the full communication potential of every presentation to be utilized. As a result, the system becomes an extension of the person making the presentation, enhancing the transmission of his or her ideas for greater clarity and impact than would be possible unaided. In order to fulfill its purpose, the system must be able to respond to the objectives and needs of the presenter with ease and convenience, while at the same time maintaining a consistently high level of quality in both the sound and sight aspects of the facility.

CRITERIA FOR A-V FACILITIES

Generally, the visualizing capability is of primary importance with the audio capability playing a supportive role.

The most critical elements are picture quality and operational simplicity. Picture quality is affected by the visual material, optics of projection equipment, projection distance in relation to picture size, and the centering integrity of projector optics with the projection screen.

The standard viewing distance factors are based on minimum artwork standards briefly described in this chapter. Assuming adherence to these minimum standards, the recommended viewing distance can be estimated by multiplying a factor by the largest dimension of a projected image. The factors are 6 for front projection and 7.5 for rear projection.

Naturally, high-quality optics is essential in achieving an acceptable image. However, most people are not in a position to test for resolution, sharpness and edge-to-edge brightness of projection devices. While there are various modifications to slide and motion-picture equipment optics that also affect the quality of the projected images, they are outside the scope of this chapter. There are, however, physical arrangements that affect this important aspect of projected images. Although all these factors affect both rear and front projection, they are more critical with respect to rear projection.

The next most important projection-system design consideration is projection distance. This single element affects sharpness, angle of view, and apparent light falloff. All projectors project pictures in which the center is brighter than the top, bottom, and sides. Depending on the projection format, falloff varies from 80 to 50 percent of center brightness—or worse. System design should diminish this built-in falloff characteristic by careful equipment selection and the engineering of a system that provides a ratio of greater than 2 to 1 between the projection distance and the picture size. This is a minimum suggested standard. Of course, the longer the projection distance, the better the picture.

Operational simplicity is important in assuring a low frustration factor and a high usage ratio. Systems that require a trained technician are costly in terms of long-term personnel requirements as well as cost effectiveness of the system investment.

A system should be easily operable by anyone familiar with the individual projection equipment or audiovideo tape devices. This stipulation requires a human engineering approach to all system requirements. For example, the person who can operate a Kodak Carousel slide projector at home or in the office should be able to operate it in a projection system.

This means, of course, that equipment must be in position and ready for use—not on a castered stand that must be moved into position and aligned with the screen. Having to remove a projection device to realign another in its place is an even worse distraction.

The aim is to get people to be comfortable with the system so that it will be used to its fullest extent with or without an operator. Not only does this ease of use improve communications by permitting smooth integration of various media—it does so without the continued expense of a large technical staff. Of course, an operator, when desired, can function in this atmosphere with less chance of error.

THE FIRST PHASE

Determining Communication Goals

Before an A-V solution to a communication need can be developed, the problems must be identified. There are three major areas to be investigated:

What sort of audience is expected, and how big will it be?

What kinds of information are to be transmitted to that audience, and in what form do they originate?

What are the contemplated mode and style of presentation?

These areas must be fully studied well in advance of any design engineering, space allocation, or system selection. Carefully worded questions should elicit complete answers, and these data need detailed analysis. An A-V designer should be able to ask the right questions and evaluate the answers in a manner that will establish the goals and presentation modes and determine the appropriate design approaches. The designer's preliminary studies should facilitate the establishment of presentation techniques that will assure a smoothly functioning, highly effective system at a realistic cost.

Here are some of the questions that might be asked in order to determine the communication goals and develop the design parameters:

How large do you expect the audience at a typical meeting to be? Is the anticipated size subject to change now or in the future?

What kinds of information will be presented?

How easily do you expect the audience to understand what is being presented?

What are the purposes of the presentations, in order of importance?

What type of person will customarily make the presentations?

Will the presentations be in the form of lectures or discussion groups?

How long will they last?

How many days each week will the A-V facility be used?

How many hours will it be used each day?

Is the material being presented simple and easy to display, or is it complex, requiring sophisticated communications techniques?

Will the facility have to accommodate film screenings and fixed displays as well as lectures and conferences?

Will it be necessary for the presentation to reach people in locations remote from the A-V facility?

Will a central television system or a computer data access terminal be utilized in connection with the A-V system?

Who will produce or obtain the presentation materials?

Is graphic art support available?

Will the presenter want to use writing surfaces, flip charts, or other display techniques and facilities?

Who will maintain the A-V facility?

Who will operate it?

Who will store presentation materials?

Who will plan the presentations?

Preliminary System Design

The determination of the communication goals will enable the overall design parameters to be developed. These parameters will include:

- A detailed plan for the A-V communications program
- The optical and electromechanical systems
- The shape of the viewing space and its seating arrangement

These preliminary parameters are presented for discussion and detailed evaluation. They are treated as flexible and subject to change as their implications are assessed. The first of these parameters to be fixed is the basic communications concept. Based on that concept, the system can be evaluated in terms of functional efficiency, operational simplicity, viewing characteristics, and acoustical qualities.

During this stage, the effect of each aspect on the others will be investigated. The presentation requirements and audience size will influence the room dimensions, for example. On the other hand, architectural considerations may impose limitations on the room dimensions, which in turn will affect the seating arrangements and possibly some aspects of the system. When all these factors have been evaluated, the ideal balance can be achieved and the scope and basic form of the A-V facility fixed.

Budgeting

The most valid form of economy in the purchase of any equipment, be it an assortment of tools or an audiovisual communications facility, is to buy just enough of the right sorts of things to achieve the desired objectives: no more, no less. The complexity of the design process and the variety of equipment options should make apparent the need for a careful, professional approach. Only by relying on such a method can the A-V user be assured of an efficiently planned system that will meet the design criteria set for it at a cost that can be estimated on a realistic basis. An unsuitable setup can be excessively expensive or deceptively low-cost. In either case, the buyer is not spending money wisely.

The positive effects of a good A-V system are often evident in a number of tangible ways; however, it is hard to place a dollar value on these results. On the other hand, a system that is underutilized because its functional characteristics do not meet the needs of the users is a loss in terms of both money spent needlessly and communications objectives unmet.

DESIGNING THE SYSTEM

The formulation of a communications program is based on the functional requirements delineated in the feasibility study. The presentation modes to be utilized are a part of such a program. They might include slides, films, videotape, and a sound-recording and playback system. The detailed design of the facility includes the selection of basic equipment, possible modification of that equipment, and provision for additional optical elements, as well as the engineering of the electrical control circuitry and the design of the electromechanical devices that may be needed.

The implementation of a proposed A-V system is not merely an exercise in mechanical assembly. It is a highly complex process of logistics that involves providing specific functional requirements within architectural and economic constraints. Careful engineering and balancing of the alternatives available will generally achieve optimum results.

A large number of variables is encountered in every A-V design problem. As an example, the dimensions of the presentation room have a significant effect on the audience size, the acoustic characteristics, the size of the projected image, the choice of equipment, and the location and the interrelationship of the components.

The A-V consultant who is responsible for the program planning, the design, and the engineering of this complex, multifaceted discipline should be intimately familiar with the problems of fabrication, installation, and operation of such systems. This knowledge will enable the consultant to plan a facility whose execution will not create difficulties and whose construction and operation can be effected without costly changes. However, even when the consultant has experience as an adviser to members of the architectural and engineering professions, the creation of a well-integrated facility is not necessarily assured. His or her work and the completed facilities should be viewed and evaluated.

Optical Aspects

It is of critical importance for an A-V system to have the ability to display bright, sharp images to all viewers and to maintain the stability and consistency of those images in a simple and straightforward manner. The picture quality is a function of a number of factors requiring careful attention during all phases of the project. These include:

- The quality of the original photography or artwork

- The density, contrast, and sharpness of the actual material being projected
- The output intensity of the projector light source
- The optical characteristics of each projection unit
- The optical characteristics of the integrated system
- The ratio of the projection distance to the image size
- The centering integrity of the light path from the material being projected to its image on the screen
- The characteristics of the projection screen or other viewing surface

Projection Engineering

Room size Ideally, the dimensions of the viewing room should be an outgrowth of the estimate of the audience size that was established in the original A-V study. In many cases, however, the A-V design engineer must utilize a predetermined space. Given the characteristics of that space, the designer can determine the ideal audience size for each type of seating arrangement, and also ascertain whether a front or rear projection mode is feasible and what the image size should be.

The type of relationship that is desired between the person making the presentation and the audience will determine the seating configuration: theatre, lecture, or conference format. That configuration will in turn dictate the number of viewers that can be comfortably seated for optimum viewing (Figure 1-1).

As an illustration, a room 20 feet by 32 feet can accommodate about 49 people in a theatre configuration (Figure 1-2); in a lecture arrangement, the audience size would be 24 (Figure 1-3); a U-shaped table would seat 18 (Figure 1-4); and 15 people could fit comfortably at a conference table (Figure 1-5). Circular and multiuse arrangements (Figures 1-6 and 1-7) are additional examples of the relationship of seating configuration and audience size.

Other seating configurations have been devised for other types of communication program modes, each with a direct relationship between room size and audience size. The audience size is also affected by the angle of view between each member of the audience and the screen (Figure 1-1).

Whenever the A-V design engineer has the opportunity of establishing the dimensions of the presentation room, he or she should be aware of the important fact that a longer projection throw for a particular image size results in more even light distribution and sharpness as well as a better angle of view. Consequently a larger audience can be accommodated than would be possible using a system with a short projection distance and a narrower angle of view. This question of projection distance applies to both front and rear projection systems. However, as the throw is normally quite short when a rear projection screen is used, this factor of design in rear projection facilities is an extremely critical planning element.

Distortion, sometimes called "keystoning," will result if the viewing surface is not precisely parallel to the plane of the image being projected. Therefore, the light path, which is usually perpendicular to the projected material, must be carefully controlled in relation to the projector and the screen. The size of the audience and the room, as well as the mode of projection, will determine whether the screen will be vertical or at an angle (Figure 1-8). Normally, a rear projection screen will permit a vertical viewing surface.

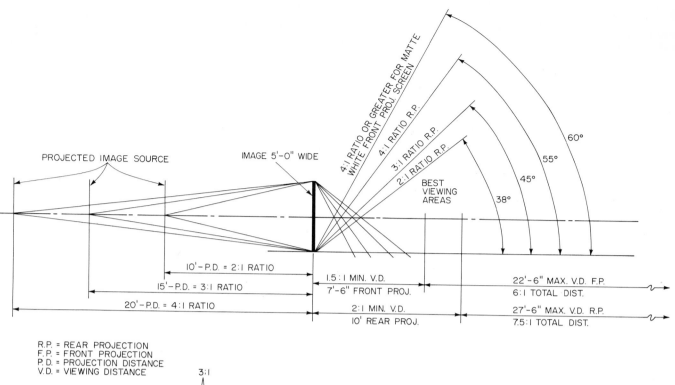

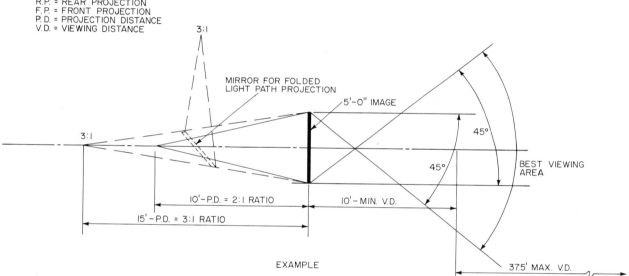

EXAMPLE

R.P. = REAR PROJECTION
F.P. = FRONT PROJECTION
P.D. = PROJECTION DISTANCE
V.D. = VIEWING DISTANCE

Fig. 1-1   The interrelationship of projection distance, image size, and viewing area.

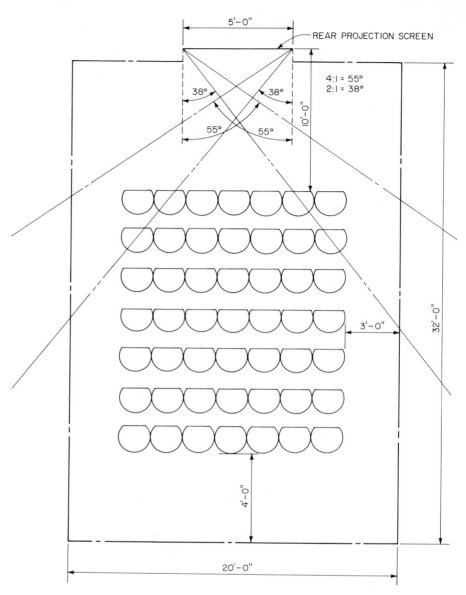

**Fig. 1-2   A room 20 feet by 32 feet, seating 49
people in theatre style.**

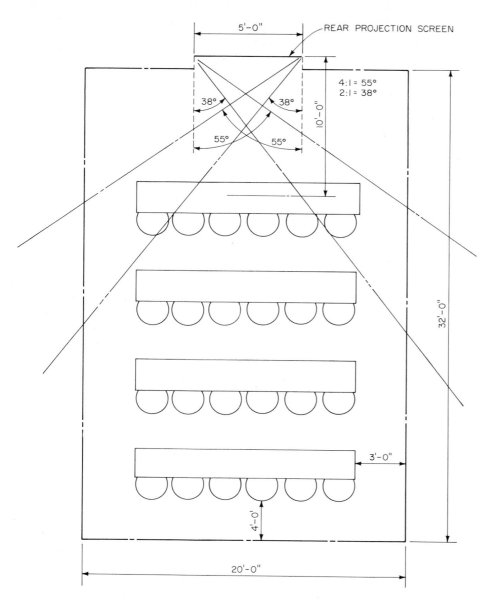

Fig. 1-3 A room 20 feet by 32 feet, seating 24 people in lecture style.

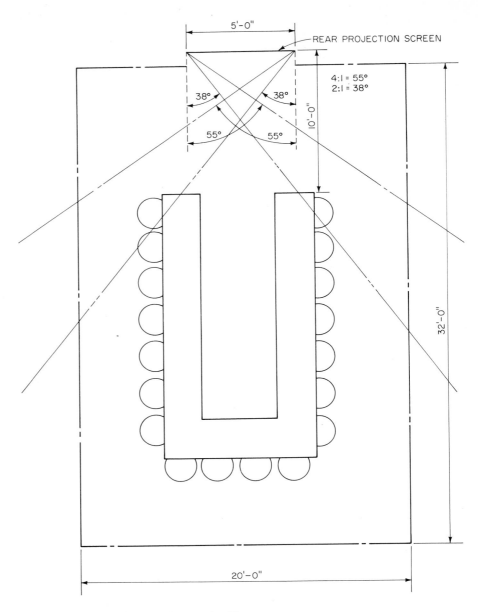

**Fig. 1-4 A room 20 feet by 32 feet, seating 18
people at a U-shaped table.**

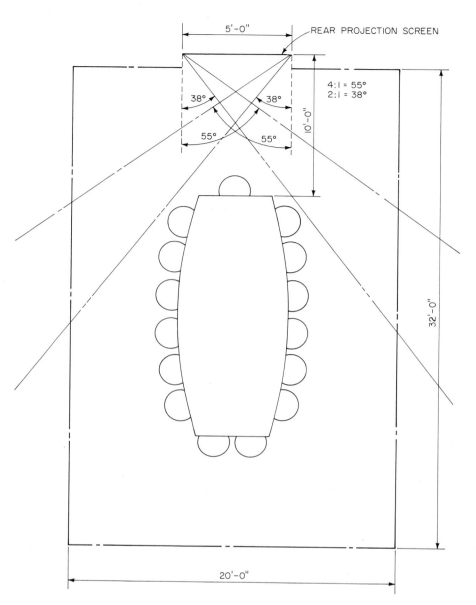

5'-0"

REAR PROJECTION SCREEN

4:1 = 55°
2:1 = 38°

38°   38°

55°   55°

10'-0"

32'-0"

20'-0"

Fig. 1-5   A room 20 feet by 32 feet, seating 15 people at a boat-shaped conference table.

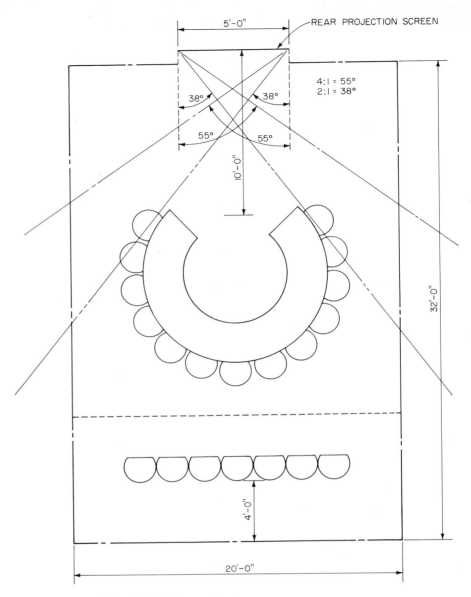

Fig. 1-6 A room 20 feet by 24 feet, seating 13 people at a circular table. With the depth increased to 32 feet, from 7 to 14 observers can also be accommodated.

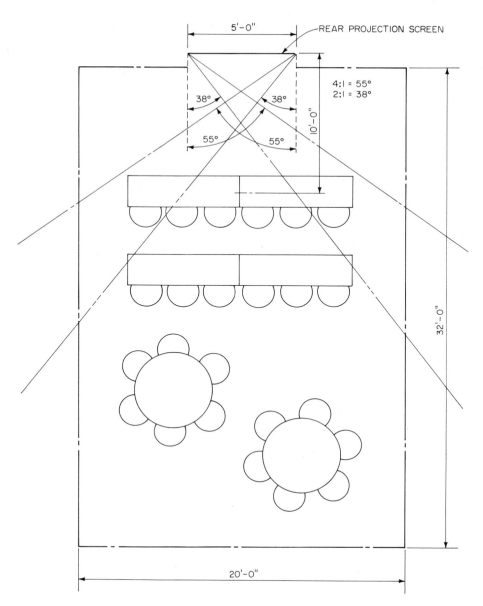

**Fig. 1-7 A modified classroom arrangement
including both lecture and separate tables.**

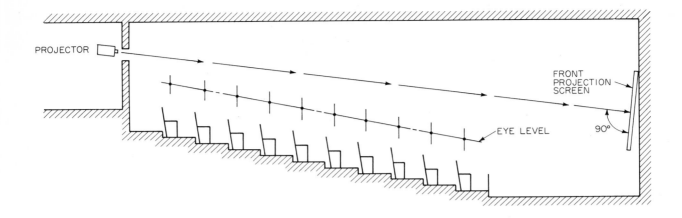

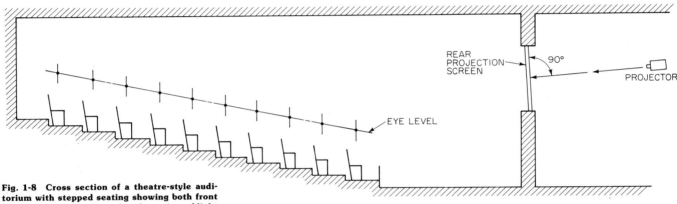

Fig. 1-8 Cross section of a theatre-style auditorium with stepped seating showing both front and rear projection. Note that the projected light beam is perpendicular to the screen in both cases.

Screen image area   The most useful screen is one that is square, as it will permit both vertical and horizontal images, as well as square ones, of course (Figure 1-9). A single image format will need one such screen, while a dual format will have a viewing surface that is the width of two images placed side by side (Figures 1-9 and 1-10).

It is an easy matter to determine the minimum image size necessary for a room of a given size. For a front projection screen the minimum size is the distance between it and the farthest viewer divided by 6. For a rear projection screen, the division factor is 7.5. As illustration: When the distance between the front projection screen and the last row of viewers, is 45 feet, the minimum image size would be 7.5 feet; with a rear projection screen, the minimum image should be 6 feet. These calculations assume that the original artwork from which the projection materials are made meets the generally accepted basic minimum standards.

Front projection   The projector in a front projection system transmits the image in the form of a light beam to an opaque screen where it is reflected back to the viewers, creating the image. As the screen reflects any light falling on its surface, the general light level in the room during a presentation must be extremely low. If the full color and contrast of the projected image is to be retained, the ambient light should be no greater than 0.3 percent of the average screen brightness.

Projectors are generally noisy and should be separated from the audience to avoid distractions. If the space is available, a separate projection booth can be built behind

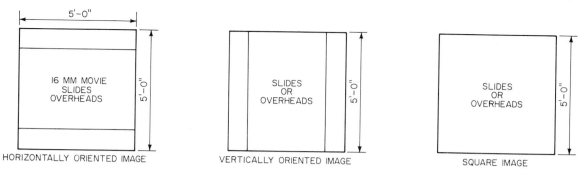

HORIZONTALLY ORIENTED IMAGE

VERTICALLY ORIENTED IMAGE

SQUARE IMAGE

Fig. 1-9 A square screen will permit horizontal, vertical, and square images to be shown.

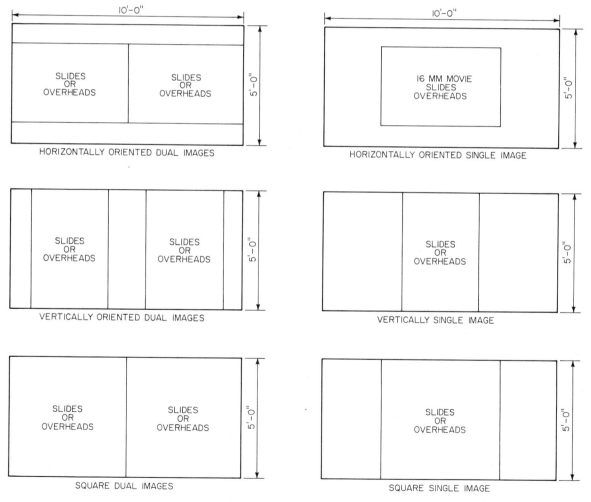

HORIZONTALLY ORIENTED DUAL IMAGES

HORIZONTALLY ORIENTED SINGLE IMAGE

VERTICALLY ORIENTED DUAL IMAGES

VERTICALLY SINGLE IMAGE

SQUARE DUAL IMAGES

SQUARE SINGLE IMAGE

Fig. 1-10 A dual-image format uses a screen that is a double square—giving the same flexibility of image shape for each of the two images or for a single central image.

15

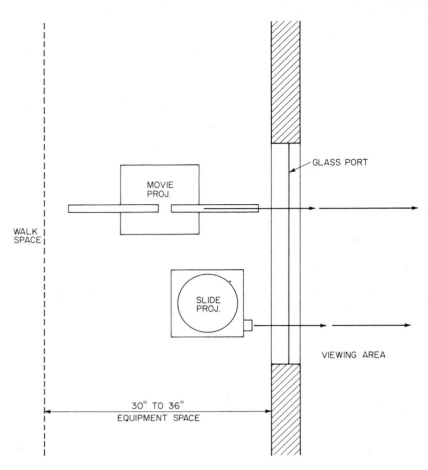

Fig. 1-11 A typical rear-access equipment arrangement for front projection.

the room's rear wall. Besides insulating the viewers from unwanted sound and light spill, this arrangement provides the opportunity for equipment to remain in place ready for use. There are other possible arrangements when space is constricted (Figures 1-11, 1-12, and 1-13).

Creating an A-V front projection system that is both aesthetically pleasing and functionally efficient requires a high level of technical expertise and design skill. The results of such a combination can be effective yet unobtrusive. Figure 1-14 provides an example of a multimedia front projection system that is compatible with the decor of the room and its formalized seating arrangement.

Rear projection The image in a rear projection system is focused on the back of a translucent screen and is visible to the audience on the other side. Since the light passes through the screen rather than being reflected off its front surface, there can be a reasonable light level in the viewing room during the presentation without affecting the quality of the image. It is only in the immediate vicinity of the screen that the room lights need be dimmed.

As is the case with all projection systems, for minimum distractions the equipment should be separated from the audience. This can be effected by means of a separate projection booth or by an enclosed cabinet within the viewing room (Figures 1-15, 1-

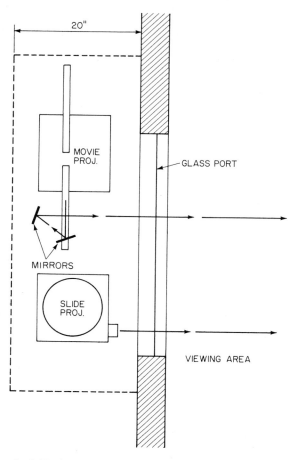

Fig. 1-12 A rear-access reduced-depth arrangement of equipment for front projection.

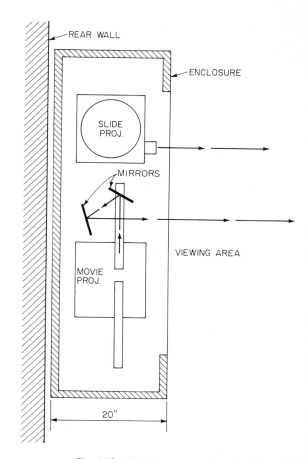

Fig. 1-13 A front-access equipment cabinet for front projection.

16, and 1-17). A separate room usually requires more space, but it may be the best solution for a particular situation. A cabinet within the viewing room permits front access to the projectors, enabling the presenter to load the equipment without assistance.

While technical expertise and design skill are needed for the creation of a front projection A-V system, they are even more important for a system intended for rear projection, as a rear-mode arrangement has more inherent problems to overcome.

A rear projection system utilizing the indirect deep method in a separate projection booth requires a considerable amount of space. In addition, if more than one projector is used in such a system, either the projectors must be optically aligned each time a change is made (as there is only one true screen axis), or they are permanently positioned a little off axis, resulting in a slight "keystone" or distortion effect in the projected image (Figure 1-18).

For good image clarity, the distance between the image source and the screen must be at least twice the picture size. To achieve this clarity within a limited amount of space, the folded light-path method can be used (Figures 1-19 and 1-20). As the name implies, the light path from the projector is "folded" by means of a large mirror, usually placed some distance away. This arrangement has the advantage of reducing the depth required behind the screen while retaining an adequate projection

17

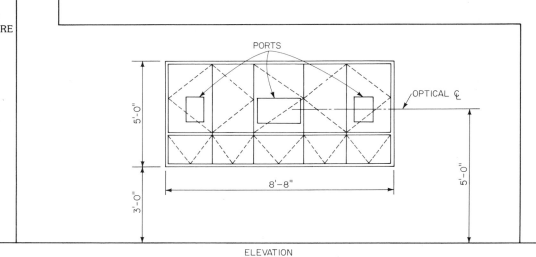

PORTS

OPTICAL ℄

5'-0"

3'-0"

8'-8"

5'-0"

ELEVATION

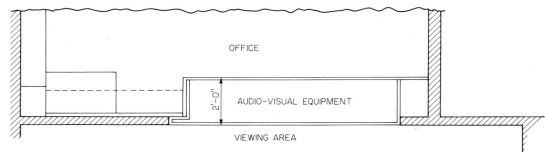

OFFICE

AUDIO-VISUAL EQUIPMENT

2'-0"

VIEWING AREA

Fig. 1-14 A custom-designed recessed front-access equipment cabinet for a multi-image front projection system.

Fig. 1-15 A front-access, rear-projection, multimedia presentation facility. *Photograph credit: Gil Amiaga.*

Fig. 1-16 A front-access presentation facility, not in use. *Photograph credit: Gil Amiaga.*

Fig. 1-17 A front-access presentation facility, completely open. *Photograph credit: Gil Amiaga.*

distance. As a further advantage, several projectors can be aligned in optically true positions by the use of a movable mirror with preset position stops.

The use of the folded light-path method of projection and a movable mirror can also be engineered in a cabinet that is directly accessible from the presentation room for "hands-on" operation by the person making the presentation. Both single-image and side-by-side dual-image systems can be designed in this manner (Figures 1-21 and 1-22).

A great number of variations are possible using the same basic engineering concepts. These variations can accommodate different functional requirements, spatial

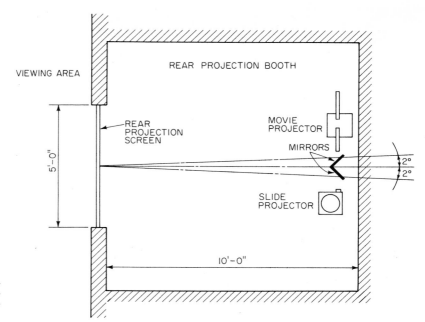

Fig. 1-18 A deep, indirect-method, rear projection arrangement using the minimum recommended ratio of 2 to 1 between projection distance and image size.

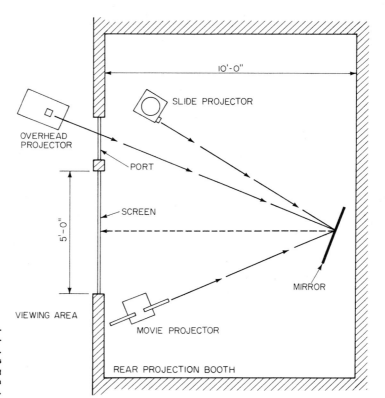

Fig. 1-19 An indirect rear projection arrangement using the folded-light-path method, resulting in a ratio of 3.5 to 1 within the same depth. This improves the image quality and increases the possible viewing angle as well as allowing rear projection of overhead transparencies with the overhead projector in the presentation room.

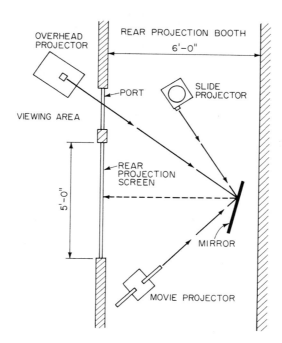

Fig. 1-20 An indirect rear projection arrangement using the folded-light-path method and the minimum recommended 2 to 1 ratio of projection distance to image size. This permits a flexible equipment arrangement within tight space limitations.

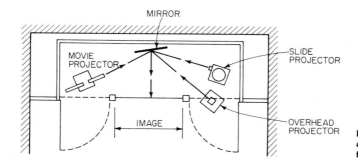

Fig. 1-21 A front-access rear projection arrangement using the folded-light-path method for single-image presentations.

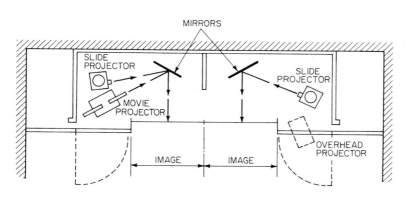

Fig. 1-22 A front-access rear projection arrangement using the folded-light-path method for dual-image presentations.

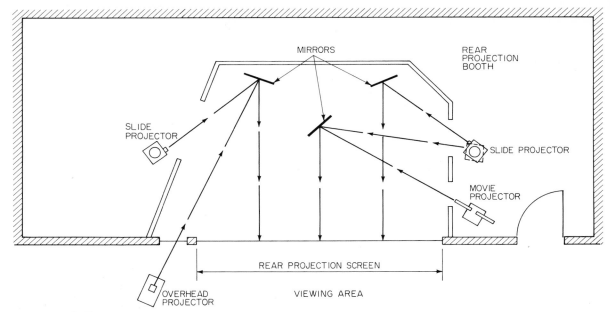

Fig. 1-23 A rear-access rear projection arrangement using the folded-light-path method for dual-image or single central-image presentations.

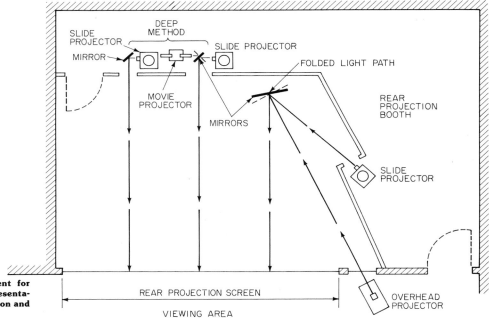

Fig. 1-24 A rear projection arrangement for dual-image and single central-image presentations utilizing both deep indirect projection and the folded-light-path method.

limitations, and image-quality parameters. Figures 1-23, 1-24, and 1-25 illustrate some of the possible arrangements. User requirements and job conditions will guide the A-V engineer in the design of a specific system.

The Optical Design Factor

A projection system—of whatever nature—is only as good as the quality of the image on the screen. The clarity, sharpness, resolution, and angle of view that can

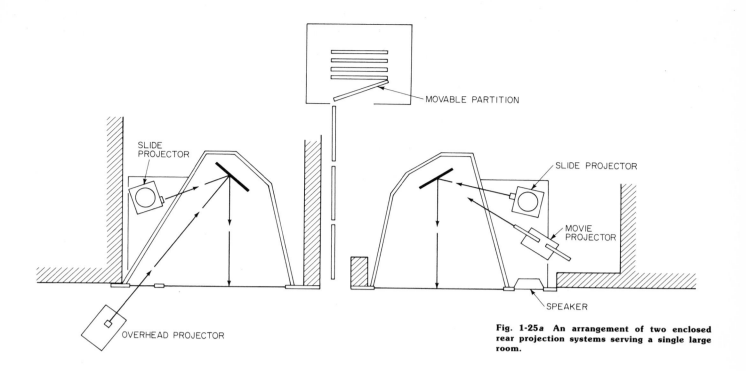

SLIDE
PROJECTOR

MOVABLE PARTITION

SLIDE PROJECTOR

MOVIE
PROJECTOR

SPEAKER

OVERHEAD PROJECTOR

Fig. 1-25a An arrangement of two enclosed rear projection systems serving a single large room.

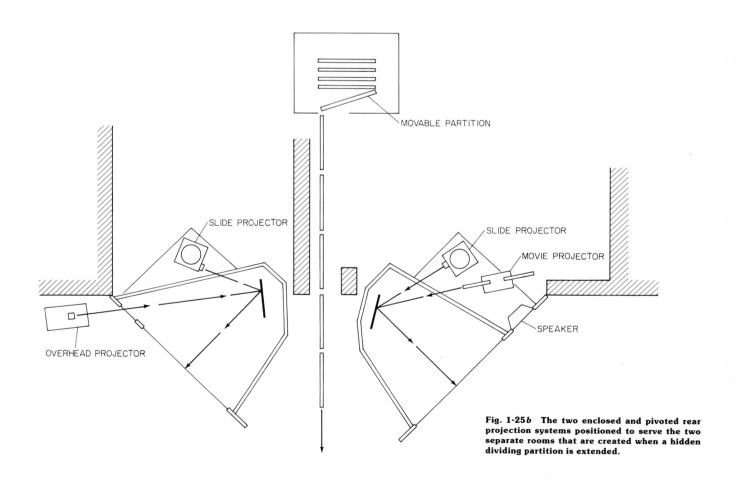

MOVABLE PARTITION

SLIDE PROJECTOR

SLIDE PROJECTOR

MOVIE PROJECTOR

SPEAKER

OVERHEAD PROJECTOR

Fig. 1-25b The two enclosed and pivoted rear projection systems positioned to serve the two separate rooms that are created when a hidden dividing partition is extended.

be expected are a direct result of the thought and care that go into the optical design of the system. The more complex the system becomes, the more critical is the system optics. The need for larger images, sharper images, multiple images, multiple image sources and the existence of physically constraining parameters all add to the conflicting requirements that must be satisfied. And they must be satisfied if an acceptable image quality is to be achieved.

The Sound System

The quality and the functional characteristics of the sound system that is part of an audiovisual facility are as important as the quality and functional characteristics of the optical system. The two aspects of a facility are mutually complementary and the one should not be neglected in relation to the other if the goal of an effective and useful facility is to be attained.

The quality of the sound, as perceived by the listener, will be influenced by such factors as:

> The sensitivity of the controls
>
> The quality of the amplifiers
>
> The quality of the speakers
>
> The location of the speakers
>
> The elimination of extraneous sounds
>
> The overall acoustical characteristics of the space

The design factors that govern the functional characteristics of the sound system might include the following:

- Sound sources:
  Voice
  Movie soundtrack
  Videotape
  Audiotape

- Telecommunication facilities for outside sound program sources

- Mixing and control requirements

- Quantity and placement of speakers

- Room size and function:
  Conference room
  Classroom
  Auditorium

- Provision for flexibility and future expansion

The Remote-Control System

Most people who make informational presentations are not audiovisual specialists. Their primary concern is with the material they are presenting and not with the mechanics of how it is to be presented. As a result, any control devices they may be required to operate should be simple and logical. The presenter should be asked to make only a minimum of effort to determine how to manipulate the controls in order to achieve a desired result. The fewer operations necessary to reach a particular goal, the better. For example, in order for a change to be made from one presentation mode to another, it may be necessary to alter the ambient room lighting, reposition a mirror, turn one machine off and then another on. If all these things can be accomplished merely by flipping one clearly marked switch, the presenter is freed from mechanical distractions and can concentrate full attention on the message being delivered. The location and spacing of the various switches on the panel, as well as the use of nomenclature unmistakable to a nontechnical person, are important parts of the design of a remote-control system that will aid the presenter in the use of the audiovisual facility (Figures 1-26 and 1-27).

Other considerations that may affect the design of a remote-control system include:

Fig. 1-26 Control panel for a front-access presentation facility. *Photograph credit: Gil Amiaga.*

The seating configuration

The room lighting

The number of control points required

The use of a lectern incorporating a control module

The number and type of functions to be controlled

The degree of automation required to meet system objectives

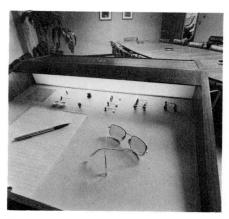

Fig. 1-27 Remote-control panel built into a lectern. *Photograph credit: Gil Amiaga.*

SUMMARY

An audiovisual presentation facility is made up of many components and subsystems which are interdependent and must perform as an integrated unit. Regardless of its size or scope, the A-V system must be conceived, designed, and installed to function as a totality—as a single entity that works with optimum efficiency and effectiveness in an unobtrusive manner.

In order to achieve this goal—that of developing a logical and workable solution to any particular communication problem—careful and detailed preliminary investigations must be made. These will determine the functional requirements that make up the design program. From this program, the space needs for the equipment and for the audience can be established early enough in the development of the project to avoid undesirable procrustean solutions later. The selection, adaptation, manufacture, assembly, and installation of equipment and components should be carefully coordinated to ensure their functional integrity and performance.

Ultimately, a successful audiovisual system is one that serves as a logical and natural extension of the human capabilities of the person using it. It should respond easily and unobtrusively to the communicator's needs, and it should reproduce the material being communicated with the highest possible degree of fidelity.

RECAP

Front Projection

1. Viewing distance factor is 6. (E.g.: If image size is 5 feet the alphanumerics would be clear at a maximum distance of 30 feet to a viewer with a 20/40 vision if characters are ³⁄₁₆ inch on 6- by 9-inch original copy area.)

2. Advantages

    a. Good angle of view

    b. Good for checking laboratory quality of all projectuals

    c. Virtually no apparent falloff to the sides

3. Disadvantages

    a. High ceilings are required to utilize a square screen to accommodate vertical as well as horizontal images.

    b. Distraction occurs when the presenter or viewers interrupt the light beam.

    c. Any ambient light adversely affects image quality. The room must be relatively dark to achieve the desired picture contrast.

    d. An overhead projector cannot be used most effectively.

Rear Projection (rigid or flexible material)

1. Viewing distance factor is 7.5. (E.g.: If image size is 5 feet, the maximum viewing distance would be 37.5 feet.)

2. Advantages

    a. A 20 percent smaller image than is required by front projection permits minimum standards to be met in low-ceilinged rooms.

    b. Can be used in higher ambient light conditions.

    c. No distracting light beam. (Presenter can more comfortably point at details.)

    d. In a brighter room, the presenter easily maintains eye contact.

    e. An overhead projector can be used, so that neither it nor the presenter blocks the image from the viewers.

3. Disadvantages

    a. The inherent grain and directional quality of the rear screen eliminate it as a viewing medium to determine laboratory quality of projectuals.

    b. The projection system must be designed to overcome apparent illumination falloff at the sides and improve the angle of view.

    c. Mirrored image is required for proper use.

    d. More space is required than with front projection.

    e. Usually costs more.

Seating

(Plan should permit several arrangements.)

1. A U- or V-table layout provides for best viewing and viewer/presenter interaction (lowest audience capacity).

2. Conference table (boat-shape or oval) provides good interaction for conferences but not so good as the U- or V-table layout for audiovisual communication.

3. Random seating style (usually with writing tablets) is frequently selected for high-level visitor presentations. It permits larger capacity and creates a more luxurious atmosphere than the two arrangements above.

4. Classroom style (shallow tables parallel to front wall with chairs behind) is the next best method but less conducive to student interraction.

    a. Stepped, curved seating (lecture hall) provides unobstructed viewing.

    b. When classroom style is contemplated, study and programmed-learning carrels should be considered.

5. Auditorium style provides the largest capacity seating and is generally used for large group-orientation and overview types of presentation.

Rear Projection System Factors

1. The physical center of all projector lenses must be in perfect alignment with the physical center of the screen to eliminate any "keystone" effect. (For dissolve mode, 2° off center vertically is permitted.)

2. A front-surface mirror should be used to reverse the image so the equipment can be loaded much as it is for front projection; slides in magazines need not be reversed, and special reversed prints are not needed for motion pictures. The use of a mirror can also extend the projection distance appreciably by folding the light path. Remember, the longer the projection distance, the better the viewing angle. Minimum projection distance should be at least 2 times the image size.

3. The screen-image area should be considered to be square to accommodate vertical and horizontal images unless the system is to be used for a special, limited requirement.

4. Apparent light falloff at the sides can be diminished or eliminated by increasing the projection distance and projector illumination. Another minor contributor is slide density. A dense or underexposed slide reduces the amount of light transmission. This condition increases apparent light falloff.

CHECKLIST FOR PLANNING AUDIOVISUAL FACILITIES

The checklist represents the basic form of investigation. From the answers to it, new questions should develop that will further define important parameters.

1. What is its purpose?
    ____ Presentations   ____ Screenings
    ____ Fixed displays   ____ All-purpose
    ____ Conferences

2. If it serves more than one purpose, what is the primary function?

3. Who will use it?
    ____ Top management   ____ Middle management

_____ Staff   _____ Public
_____ Clients   _____ Others
_____ Stockholders

4. How large an audience will it serve?

_____ 1 to 25   _____ 100 to 200
_____ 25 to 50   _____ 200 to 300
_____ 50 to 100   _____ Over 300

5. What type of seating will be used?

_____ Theatre style with or without writing tablets
_____ Lecture style
_____ Conference style

6. What type of information will be communicated?

_____ Technical   _____ Recruiting
_____ Sales training   _____ Planning
_____ Committee reports   _____ Others
_____ Financial

7. How will information be presented?

_____ Easels or flip charts   _____ Writing surfaces
_____ Movable displays   _____ Projection techniques
_____ Static displays   _____ Others

8. What communication techniques will be used?

_____ 16mm movie   _____ 8mm movie
_____ 35mm slide   _____ 35mm filmstrip
_____ Overhead transparencies   _____ Audiotape
_____ Videotape   _____ Stereo sound
_____ Dissolve   _____ Random access
_____ Multi-image

9. Special considerations

_____ Recording of proceedings   _____ Participation through telephone
_____ Security precautions   _____ Voice reinforcements

10. Budgeting

How many departments are participating? _____

What existing equipment can be used? _____

_____

11. Planned or existing room information

Height_____   Length_____   Width_____

Windows: Yes_____   No_____.   If yes, exposure_____

12. Planned or existing booth information

Height_____   Length_____   Width_____

Windows: Yes_____   No_____.   If yes, exposure_____

CHAPTER TWO
EXTERIOR PLANTINGS
Joseph G. Hudak

INTRODUCTION

Plants serve two primary functions for mankind: necessity and pleasure. Whether enjoyed as the towering canopy of trees, the understory of shrubs, or as groundcover, vegetation is both essential and useful for our welfare. When viewed primarily as necessary elements in the landscape, plants offer shelter from wind, shade from sunlight, protection of soil from erosion, food for the table, fibers for clothing, and materials for housing, along with valuable sustenance for wildlife. Colonists in a new land always valued these foremost.

When primitive societies advanced from cultivating plant materials only to meet physical needs, plants logically altered into sensory attractions providing an aesthetic experience of beauty, comfort, and convenience (Figure 2-1). These appeals remain with us today when we arrange complementary silhouettes for architectural settings; blend form, texture, and color for pleasurable ends in themselves; insert plant movement and fragrance; and generally improve our daily living with pleasing landscape changes. Happily, plants also cooperate in these ventures if treated as partners.

The basic requirements for stimulating response from plants remain constant: light, water, air, nourishment, and a fixed temperature range for durability. Plants are unique as the only landscape element that continually enlarges with time, and each planting site needs our keen evaluation beforehand if plants are to reach their intended maturity in good condition.

We need to be aware that negative environmental modifications, such as pollution of the air and waterways, additional shading from other plants or from structures, increased exposure to wind, heat or cold, major alterations in soil alkalinity or acidity, soil compaction, or undue competition from volunteer seedlings of other plants can have detrimental effects on the survival of any plant normally reliable for a local growing area.

TYPES OF PLANTS

Nature has provided us with several major plant types having flowers and seeds (ferns are nonflowering plants). To generalize, the permanent ones are *woody peren-*

Fig. 2-1 An aesthetic experience of planted beauty at Isola Bella, an Italian island. *Photograph credit: Joseph Hudak.*

nials and maintain persistent stems, (Figure 2-2). These are mainly trees and shrubs with potentially great size and durability for generations, but there are also many vines and groundcovers with similar but less dominant stems. Foliage persistence divides woody plants into deciduous (all leaves dropping at the end of one season) and evergreen (most leaves remaining a year or longer), with the evergreen types further subdivided into broadleaf and needle (including scale leaves) from the shape of the leaf outline (Figures 2-3 through 2-7).

Next come the *herbaceous perennials* (including the hardy bulbs) with most stems and leaves withering to ground level at the end of a growing season while retaining living roots and below-ground buds that reappear the following year in a continuing cycle often stretching for decades (Figures 2-8 and 2-9). Further along are the *biennials,* producing stems and leaves the first season but delaying their flowering and seed production until the second year, when the entire plant then dies. Lastly come the *annuals,* whose life span runs only through one growing season (Figure 2-10).

HOW PLANTS GROW

Plants expand from the necessary interaction of roots, stems, and leaves. Roots are generally the hidden, underground portion (although some vines also carry aerial or climbing roots for stem support) and have several important functions: absorption of water and dissolved minerals from the soil, anchoring the plant, storing nutrients, and potential reproduction. The two main root types are *tap* and *fibrous*. A tap-rooted plant—like carrot, dandelion, or sassafras—has a downward-reaching, thick main root that is difficult to relocate unless taken intact. Fortunately, most plants carry fibrous root systems and transplant far more easily because their roots are numerous, horizontal, finely elongated, and shallow-set around the entire stem of a plant.

Surprisingly, only the minute growing tip of a root absorbs water and nutrients from the soil. This vital process is adroitly managed for even the largest plant by vast numbers of microscopic root hairs with a life span of only several days but with a known capacity for constant replacement by an active, healthy plant. Such quick-repair ability is a valuable aid in recovery after transplanting.

Fig. 2-2 **A contemporary blend of woody plant types from groundcovers to trees.** *Photograph credit: Joseph Hudak.*

Fig. 2-3 **Conspicuous blossoms of the broadleaf evergreen** *Rhododendron catawbiense. Photograph credit: Joseph Hudak.*

Fig. 2-4 A splendid collection of various textures and colorings from needled evergreens. *Photograph credit: Joseph Hudak.*

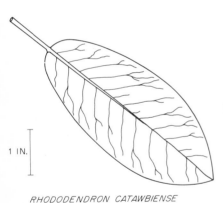

RHODODENDRON CATAWBIENSE
BROADLEAF EVERGREEN

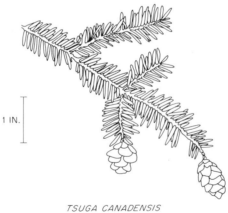

TSUGA CANADENSIS
NEEDLE EVERGREEN

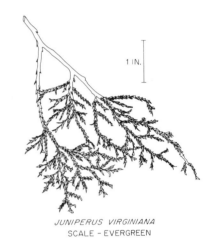

JUNIPERUS VIRGINIANA
SCALE - EVERGREEN

Fig. 2-5 *Rhododendron catawbiense* broadleaf evergreen. *Credit: Artemas Richardson.*

Fig. 2-6 *Tsuga canadensis* needle evergreen. *Credit: Artemas Richardson.*

Fig. 2-7 *Juniperus Virginiana* scale evergreen. *Credit: Artemas Richardson.*

Fig. 2-8 Spring crocus start the perennial bulb parade. *Photograph credit: Joseph Hudak.*

Fig. 2-9 **Perennial daylilies highlight summer borders.** *Photograph credit: Joseph Hudak.*

Fig. 2-10 **Flowering annuals provide months of color accent.** *Photograph credit: Joseph Hudak.*

The majority of these "feeding" roots generally exist near the surface to a depth of about 1 foot on woody plants, and they are easily harmed by heavy compaction or deep cultivation of the soil above them. They roam freely in search of food and water, but they concentrate usually around the main spread of the stems. Because transplanting necessarily severs roots, careful handling of the root ball and replanting quickly in well-prepared and moist soil, plus regular watering, are necessary for an early restoration of these vital root-hair colonies. Since air exposure, wind, and bright sunlight dehydrate dug roots easily, all delays in transplanting should be avoided and the roots should always be adequately shielded while they are above ground.

Roots continue to expand in temperate climates as long as the soil—not the air—temperature remains above 32°F (0°C). When root activity stops normally, and the entire plant is inactive for a period called dormancy, transplanting woody materials can be done with a good margin for success (Figure 2-11). This dormant time usually comes in temperate areas at late autumn and lasts until mid-spring. Tropical plants pause, too, but their resting time is far shorter.

While plant stems are usually the upright parts of the plant, some are partially or wholly underground, as in the iris and tulip. All of them support the leaves, flowers, or fruit, and their main function is as a conduit for transferring water and nutrients from the roots through the entire plant. Woody plants have a thin layer of dead cells, called bark, on the outer portion of the stem (Figure 2-12) for deflecting wind, heat, cold, and insects (and some vandals) from disrupting the vital plumbing mechanism which exists just behind the bark layer in a band of cells called sapwood. The darkened, center portion of a woody plant is the heartwood, a collection of empty cells that supply sturdiness to an enlarging trunk but that also rot easily if exposed to air from deep wounds in the stem.

All plant stems have tiny breathing pores, called lenticels, spread generously along their lengths from the ground level to the topmost foliage. These act as vents for an essential exchange of gases. Soil piled excessively high against a stem—even temporarily—can interfere enough with this "breathing" function to cause quick or

Fig. 2-11 **Transplanting dormant balled-and-burlapped holly trees in early spring.** *Photograph credit: Joseph Hudak.*

33

Fig. 2-12 Contrasted bark of an American elm (left) with shagbark hickory. *Photograph credit: Joseph Hudak.*

Fig. 2-13 Excessive fill against the trunk of the terrace maple caused its slow death. *Photograph credit: Joseph Hudak.*

lingering death to the whole plant (Figure 2-13). In transplanting or in regrading around existing plants, this stem ventilation has to be fully maintained for continued plant survival.

Many plants carry thorns or prickles along their stems as protection for their development. While useful as barrier plantings, they can be hazardous to humans and ought to be kept from areas where children will normally play.

Woody plants have two periods and types of growth enlargement. Springtime energies force the outward expansion of the long-dormant buds on each stem into new leaves and more stem growth in the "crown" or "head" of a plant. Bud production for the following year begins at midsummer and plant elongation then stops. By late summer the trunk next swells and expands, causing the bark noticeably to split, crack, or fold into the textural lines of age. This stem increase is known as the expansion of trunk caliper. Caliper, or diameter, is used commercially as a standard measurement for sizing large trees. Smaller trees and shrubs are sold mainly by height or spread of the branches.

Leaves are importantly involved in photosynthesis, a mystifyingly complex conversion of light and carbon dioxide into energy and carbohydrates essential for plant enlargement. Leaf blades, the conspicuous part of a whole leaf, have the ability to move toward the direction of the highest light intensity by means of a slender, flexible support called a petiole. Excessive leaning toward the light can force normally erect stems to be lopsided; this condition is evident in trees growing on narrow city streets lined with tall buildings. Trees crowded by nature (or people) tend to become abnormally slender and stretch tall to reach the sun. Recent studies have also shown that deciduous trees and high shrubs installed in areas illuminated by high-intensity night lighting continue growing far beyond their normal span and suffer delayed leaf drop, with a further likelihood of winter damage to ill-formed buds and immature stems. Light is essential for leaves but not at all times.

Both evergreen and deciduous leaves can be simple or compound in form, with the compound group also divided into palmate and pinnate shapes (Figures 2-14 through 2-18). Leaves provide useful shading for tender, new growth and also cool

Fig. 2-14 The simple leaves of a variegated Hosta. *Photograph credit: Joseph Hudak.*

Fig. 2-15 Pinnately compound leaves surround this spectacular tree peony flower. *Photograph credit: Joseph Hudak.*

1/2 IN.

QUERCUS PALUSTRIS
SIMPLE – LOBED

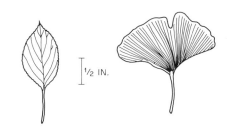

1/2 IN.

MALUS BACCATA
SIMPLE – ENTIRE

GINKGO BILOBA
SIMPLE – UNIQUE

Fig. 2-16 Quercus palustris, simple and lobed; Malus baccata, simple and entire; Ginkgo biloba, simple and unique. *Credit: Artemas Richardson.*

1/2 IN.

AESCULUS HIPPOCASTANUM
PALMATELY COMPOUND

Fig. 2-17 Aesculus hippocastanum, palmately compound. *Credit: Artemas Richardson.*

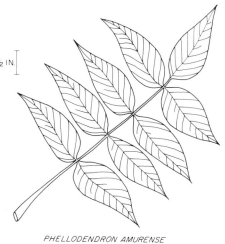

1/2 IN.

PHELLODENDRON AMURENSE
PINNATELY COMPOUND

Fig. 2-18 Phellodendron amurense, pinnately compound. *Credit: Artemas Richardson.*

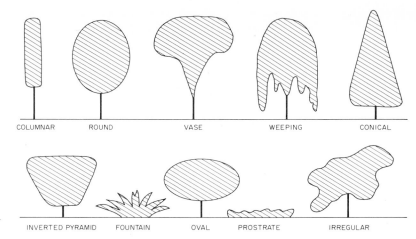

Fig. 2-19 Basic forms of plant silhouettes. *Photograph credit: Artemas Richardson.*

Fig. 2-20 Silhouettes offer double value when a reflecting pool is nearby. *Photograph credit: Joseph Hudak.*

the air by expelling oxygen and water vapor from myriad openings, called stomata, on the underside of each leaf blade. Since these venting devices do not fully close, any coupling of consistent high wind, excessive heat, or soil drought will cause abnormal water loss from the leaves and the subsequent drooping or wilting of the foliage. Prolonged dryness of both the air and soil may even lead to early leaf drop and a general debilitation of the entire plant. Because an average-sized tree can disperse up to 60 gallons of water daily during the growing season, the availability of consistent replacement moisture in the soil has a great bearing on total plant vigor and health. When artificial watering is needed to combat drought, deep penetration is best, since shallow irrigation tends to bring feeder roots harmfully closer to the surface.

PLANT FORMS

Plant silhouettes are varied enough to offer challenging opportunities for their landscape design use. The general categories of form are many: round, oval, vase-shaped, columnar, weeping, conical, inverted pyramid, fountainlike, prostrate, and irregular (Figures 2-19 and 2-20).

Added plant appeal comes as well from the vast number of variations in bark, flowers, fruit, and foliage (too many, unfortunately, to cover here). These compelling combinations of texture and colorings offer continued plant interest throughout the year. There is always much to notice in the plant kingdom (Figures 2-21 and 2-22).

PLANT HARDINESS

Hardiness in plants is primarily related to a satisfactory adjustment toward cold temperatures for prolonged periods. As useful guides to this range of low-temperature zones, maps of both North America and Europe are now available showing "zones of hardiness" on a scale of 1 (below $-50°$F or $-10°$C) to 10 ($+40°$F or $+5°$C) as a range of temperature tolerances. Most of the desirable landscape plants for temperate zones exist comfortably in zones 3 through 8. So does most of the world's population.

Many nursery catalogs and most plant identification books usually provide these hardiness data for each plant listed. As a further guideline: Plants grown in any part of the same zone can be transferred either west or east within that zone satisfactorily—provided moisture and soil conditions remain the same. Plants shipped northward generally adjust well to only one additional zone, but plants taken south are usually able to flourish in two additional zones. Microclimate areas also exist in all landscapes where sheltering buildings, fences, or other plants can raise wintertime temperatures enough to support plant life from a higher-numbered hardiness zone satisfactorily; yet microclimate sections can also refer to especially exposed sites that lower a plant's cold tolerance (Figure 2-23).

Nevertheless, this helpful temperature focus reflects only a part of successful plant adaptation, since enduring drought, excess soil moisture, great heat, constant wind, and severe alterations in light intensity markedly affect any plant's durability. One should learn what a plant naturally prefers before using it, and then earnestly attempt to supply those needs. An understanding of this valuable detail will assure greater planting response while automatically reducing total maintenance requirements.

Fig. 2-21 **Noticeable fruit clusters are a tea viburnum trait.** *Photograph credit: Joseph Hudak.*

Fig. 2-22 **A matured cone of white pine.** *Photograph credit: Joseph Hudak.*

Fig. 2-23 **A brightly painted and sturdy fence created a warmer microclimate for tender plants here.** *Photograph credit: Joseph Hudak.*

37

Fig. 2-24 The sizable daisy family *(Compositae)* includes the generous May flowering of *Doronicum caucasicum. Photograph credit: Joseph Hudak.*

Fig. 2-25 July-blooming *Senicio cineraria* is a shy member of the daisy family. *Photograph credit: Joseph Hudak.*

Fig. 2-26 The flamboyant *Rudbeckia speciosa* of August is also from the daisy clan. *Photograph credit: Joseph Hudak.*

Fig. 2-27 Seemingly unrelated *Artemesia albula* has daisylike flowers too. *Photograph credit: Joseph Hudak.*

Fig. 2-28 Fall asters easily show their kinship to the daisy group. *Photograph credit: Joseph Hudak.*

NAMING PLANTS

Official labels for plants are organized botanically into a system of scientific and common names, now adopted worldwide, which was developed by Linnaeus, an eighteenth-century botanist and taxonomist. With his cataloging, the composition of the flower parts is the key to individual placement in a major category, so that plants with similarly structured flowers are first assigned to a family (such as the *Rosaceae* or rose family) (Figures 2-24 through 2-28). Every plant in each family gains a genus identification (such as *Acer* for maple) plus a species name (such as *rubrum* for red) which separates it from other plants of the same genus by importantly altered characteristics such as leaf shape or flower color. Some plants occasionally expand into varieties or cultivars, names that further divide a species having significant variations worth noting. Using the full scientific name for a plant is essential for clarity as well as for time-saving when discussing or ordering plants.

SOIL AND FERTILIZER

Soil is the loose layer of the earth in which plants grow, and it is composed of minerals, humus, water, air, pieces of rock, and minute animal life mixed harmoniously together. The three dominant soil types are sand, silt, and clay, with the most plant-productive type being a balanced mixture of all three.

Soil is found in layers of varying thickness. The uppermost, topsoil (or loam), usually has a dark color from decayed animal and vegetable life called humus, contains the most nutrients, and is reasonably uniform and open in its composition. Its depth encourages rapid plant growth. The next level is subsoil, a denser, often rock-strewn layer acting as a reservoir of soil moisture and additional nutrients (Figure 2-29). Below this may lie gravel, clay hardpan, pure sand, or ledges of bedrock. How quickly and how deeply gravitational water drains through the top layers determines root penetration and endurance. Standing surface water or sluggish drainage lower down alters the soil's oxygen content and affects root activity appreciably, too.

Soil can be improved by either physical or chemical means. Mixing coarse sand with clay soil aerates its heaviness and improves drainage, while adding manure, peat moss, compost, or leaf mold to sandy soil increases its water-holding qualities (Figure 2-30). Soil should not be handled, however, when muddy or frozen, since these conditions can substantially modify its texture as well as the plant's response to it. Any soil that has been heavily compacted by trucking or earth-moving equipment requires well-managed restoration prior to final grading or planting.

Chemical analysis of soil for mineral content is a laboratory exercise where basic testing procedures determine the presence and amount of the three essential nutrients for plant growth: nitrogen for stems and foliage, phosphorus for roots, and potassium for flowers and fruit. It is further considered useful nowadays to test also for the trace elements such as iron, boron, magnesium, and copper, since these minor ingredients have proved influential in growth.

Soil-test recommendations for adding balanced fertilizer compounds—whether from quick-acting chemical or slow-release organic sources—mean incorporating them evenly into the topsoil before planting begins. The manufacturer's suggested

Fig. 2-29 Cultivated ground requires the removal of rock debris from the subsoil layer. *Photograph credit: Joseph Hudak.*

Fig. 2-30 New plantings benefit from careful soil preparation. *Photograph credit: Joseph Hudak.*

dosage and method of application should always be carefully followed for all fertilizers, keeping in mind that if a little is good, a lot is not necessarily better. Concentrations of fertilizer can easily damage roots, especially on small plants. Several light applications each season are often more productive for sustained growth than one heavy dose, a recognized method in lawn care and vegetable growing. One should program at least an annual fertilizing for all landscape developments, especially as growth starts in spring.

Sick or weak plants cannot always be nursed to good health only by booster applications of fertilizer nutrients — and if used, diluted solutions are preferred — since lackadaisical growth can be brought about by physical causes, too. The soil composition, drainage, and exposure conditions should be investigated before relying on fertilizer to be a cure-all.

SOIL ACIDITY

The degree of soil acidity or alkalinity also influences planting response in noticeable ways. Acid-preferring azaleas (Figure 2-31) and rhododendrons may have pallid foliage and weak stems if grown in heavily limed soils, while ground cover beds of the alkaline-favoring periwinkle expand only reluctantly in very acid soils. Lawn grasses generally favor high alkalinity and benefit from several light spreadings of ground limestone annually on acid terrain (Figure 2-32). In general, sandy soil is acid, while chalky soil is alkaline.

Soil acidity is measured scientifically by testing field samples for the potential of hydrogen ions — pH — using a scale calibrated from 1 (very acid) to 14 (very alkaline), with 7 used as a neutral balance. Most landscape plants appear to grow contentedly in a range between 4 and 7. Since the difference of one full point on this scale means the soil sample is 10 times as acid as its neighbor, such variation may prove technically difficult to adjust satisfactorily toward a preferred pH.

Adjusting imbalances in soil pH is handled by applying dry dosages of ground limestone for acid conditions and sulphur for alkaline ones. Both act only as catalysts, since neither directly enters into the chemical reaction-releasing soil nutrients but

Fig. 2-31 Azaleas prefer acid soils for their best performance. *Photograph credit: Joseph Hudak.*

Fig. 2-32 Lawn grasses thrive on alkaline soil conditions. *Photograph credit: Joseph Hudak.*

serves to promote the reaction. In any event, neither treatment should be considered as a substitute for proper fertilizing programs.

These two modifiers condition best when scratched or watered into the soil when applied, but owing to possibly negative chemical reactions, both should be spread one or two weeks ahead of intended fertilizing.

TRANSPLANTING PROCEDURES

Moving plants from one location to another involves one of three methods of handling: balled-and-burlapped (or balled-and-plastic-covered), bare-rooted, or containerized. With grass grown commercially for lawn, thin layers of sod are cut into conveniently sized strips and then rolled or piled back to back for transport.

All dug plants must be kept consistently moist and out of wind and heat until replanted. Evergreen material is never moved bare-rooted except as nursery seedlings, and all woody plants are better treated when moved in dormancy. Containerized nursery stock, which today includes small-sized trees, shrubs, herbaceous perennials, bulbs, and annuals, offers valuable convenience and safety in handling all through the growing season.

Roots wrapped for transplanting in natural vegetative material, such as burlap, can be installed with the covering left in place because it disintegrates readily (Figure 2-33). Those in plastic covers, even porous-weave ones, should have the wrapping carefully removed at planting time, since it may decay too slowly to allow for proper root development. Any container-grown material is simply knocked or cut from the pot and installed where wanted. Grass sod is laid snugly on a previously fine-graded and fertilized plot, tamped or rolled lightly to secure the roots to the soil, and then watered heavily and regularly until established and ready for mowing. Lawn seeding follows similar procedures.

Planting may be installed either individually in pits or grouped in beds uniformly prepared beforehand with conditioned topsoil. In both instances, the hole should be fully adequate to accommodate the depth and spread of all roots. Extraneous mate-

Fig. 2-33 Awaiting new homes, the burlapped plants on the grass were obviously worth transplanting during site renovations. *Photograph credit: Joseph Hudak.*

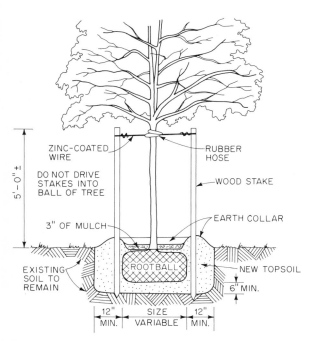

Fig. 2-34 Detail for double-staking trees with trunk diameter less than 3 inches. *Credit: Artemas Richardson.*

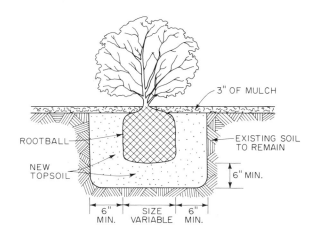

Fig. 2-35 Detail for planting shrubs in pits. *Credit: Artemas Richardson.*

rial uncovered in this digging, such as construction debris, rocks, hardpan, tree branches, and sod clumps, should be discarded as restrictive to normal growth. Tree pits ought to be dug at least 24 inches wider and 6 inches deeper than the root ball (Figure 2-34) for ease in maneuvering the plant as well as for encouraging quick rerooting in the loose backfill. Shrubs generally need less excavation (Figure 2-35).

Before installing a plant, a cushion of conditioned topsoil should be spread over the bottom of the hole. Next, the plant should be carefully deposited at a finish-grade level identical with its original growing condition. To allow for expected settlement of large plants, they should be placed slightly higher in the pit. Then the rest of the hole should be backfilled with more humus-enriched topsoil while the soil layers are judiciously tamped to remove any detrimental air pockets near the roots. Each installation should always be followed with generous watering.

Plants that settle too low or out of plumb should be reset immediately or they will continue to develop as planted. The planting of trees and shrubs of large size is completed by the addition of an earthen collar at the limits of the pit to retain and focus water toward the root ball. Slope plantings especially benefit from having this water-holding saucer.

Most large trees and shrubs require support staking or guying to hold them erect against buffeting winds. Wood or metal stakes are usual for single-trunked trees up to 3 inches in caliper and provide better support if used in pairs. Guy wiring with turnbuckles is used for anchoring large plant materials, and guy placement ordinarily follows either a triangular or rectangular pattern around the main stems (Figure 2-36). Both types of support require regular inspection for proper tautness—up to a year for woody plants—and quick repair if damaged to prevent the plant's shifting out of plumb and perhaps tearing the new roots. All wiring should be shielded with either rubber or plastic hosing buffers where it contacts the stems to avoid bark damage and the creation of an entryway for insects and diseases into the trunk. A wire collar should never be left in place beyond its original need, since normal stem enlargement will engulf it and permanently damage the vital interior plumbing system.

MULCHING

To forestall weed invasions and to preserve soil moisture, the entire planting area of trees and shrubs should be covered with at least 3 inches of a light, porous, inert

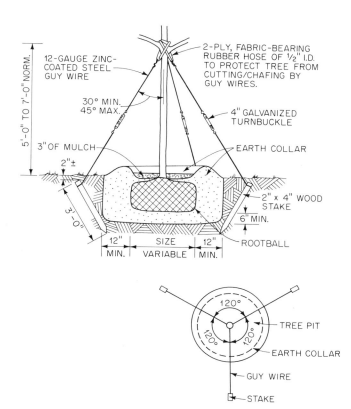

Fig. 2-36 Details for guying trees having a trunk diameter greater than 3 inches. *Note:* **If tree to be guyed is planted on a slope, place 2 stakes uphill from tree in a line parallel to contours.** *Credit: Artemas Richardson.*

Fig. 2-37 Shredded bark surrounds this pool planting for easier access as well as for less weeding. *Photograph credit: Joseph Hudak.*

vegetative product, such as pine bark, chunky wood chips, granular peat moss, peanut or buckwheat hulls, spent licorice stems, sugarcane debris, or any other locally used mulching material (Figure 2-37). Annual and herbaceous perennial beds, along with low-growing woody materials, suffice with 2 inches of mulch. Broken stone is unsuitable for mulching in full sun since it holds summer heat longer than other mulches and may harm immature growth. Soil cultivation is not needed with proper mulching, but the mulch depth should be restored occasionally, since it naturally disintegrates with time. Excessively deep mulch, however, can create soft stem tissue that will be susceptible to both insect-borer damage and winter-kill. As in all other planting recommendations, moderation is a preferred approach to use.

A currently popular weed-control item, originally developed for agricultural crops, is black plastic film placed as continuous sheeting and then pegged in place. Its appearance in landscape paintings is visually troublesome and may call for having it masked with a thin layer of decorative mulching. Its slick surface, however, allows rain and wind to winnow the loose mulch easily. High winds tend to lift the plastic end-flaps unattractively and to create a nuisance of repair. The outcome can be higher maintenance than was intended. Using adequate mulch in direct contact with the ground, plus hand weeding, is a more valid procedure.

Weed plants take moisture and nutrients away from desirable plants and should be uprooted quickly before becoming entrenched and able to produce seed. While proper mulching curtails most weed growth, reducing some weed crops may require the use of herbicides, those chemical sprays or granules manufactured for destroying unwanted plant growth with a minimum of labor cost. Although herbicides are often created for specific plant elimination, all can damage adjacent, preferred plants if used carelessly. It is wise to avoid applying any herbicide on a windy day and giving an overdosage that may collect and drain toward the roots of wanted plants. Soil contamination by herbicidal concentrations is long-lasting and so persistently toxic that it may sterilize the soil.

PRUNING TECHNIQUES

Trimming stems to create special effects or to repair storm damage is one of the most used landscape efforts. The key is to prevent plant health problems by the removal of dead, diseased, broken, cracked, or rubbing branches as found, as well as to thin out excess stems for greater air circulation and light penetration. Pruning is also important to control unwanted growth, to forestall interference with other plants, and to reshape for personal needs. All pruning, however, should continually maintain the natural shape and habit of the plant.

After a break or cut occurs in the stem of a woody plant, natural healing for this wound comes from an existing, triple-cell layer called cambium (Figure 2-38). It quickly adds replacement bark tissue for sealing in plant moisture. Because these repair cells grow best on flat, smooth surfaces, pruning should never result in stub ends but should leave all cuts flush with a main stem union. Stubs eventually rot, too, allowing easy passage for insects and diseases into the trunk.

Small twig removal is usually managed with well-honed clippers for natural shaping and with hedge shears for formal shearing; larger branch removal requires sawing either with a sharp, especially toothed pruning saw or a powered chain saw. Using a carpenter's saw is wearying and inefficient.

The preferred technique for branch removal is first to undercut the limb about 1 foot from the main branch and then to make a top incision another foot beyond it so that the falling piece will crack at the undercut and not rip into the important repair mechanism of the bark (Figure 2-39). No pruning should create additional problems.

The work should be finished by neatly removing the branch stub and painting the open wound. Some recent scientific studies on pruned trees, however, now suggest that treating a wound with asphalt-based tree paint is more cosmetic than helpful for bark repair, but this evidence has not yet been awarded international acceptance.

Because evergreens have less sap flow than deciduous plants when growing or dormant, they can be safely pruned in almost any season. Many deciduous trees, such as maple and birch, however, pump sap excessively from any wounds made in spring and are better pruned in late summer or autumn. All new planting brought to a site should be pruned only after arrival—not at the nursery—since some breakage is likely in handling and shipping (Figure 2-40).

Root pruning of existing plants may be required where underground utility connections, new building and roadway construction, or major regrading changes are necessary. Removal of large portions of the anchoring and feeding roots, though, will cause a setback to growth or even a loss of stability. A careful evaluation of the potential damage to all plants is recommended before such pruning work is authorized.

Specialized pruning of woody plants into ornamental—but unnatural—shapes is

Fig. 2-38 Cambium repairs are well in hand on this pruned trunk of a Bradford pear. *Photograph credit: Joseph Hudak.*

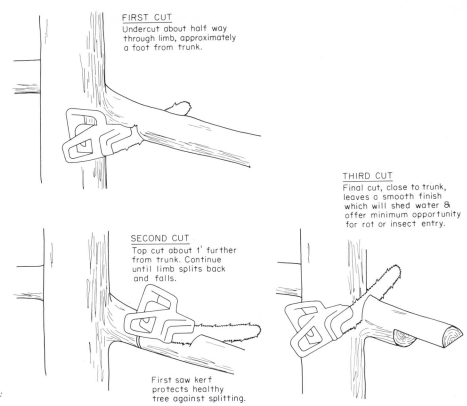

FIRST CUT
Undercut about half way
through limb, approximately
a foot from trunk.

SECOND CUT
Top cut about 1' further
from trunk. Continue
until limb splits back
and falls.

First saw kerf
protects healthy
tree against splitting.

THIRD CUT
Final cut, close to trunk,
leaves a smooth finish
which will shed water &
offer minimum opportunity
for rot or insect entry.

Fig. 2-39 Three-step cutting for pruning. *Credit:
Artemas Richardson.*

**Fig. 2-40 Logical removal of broken or dead
branching is part of systematic pruning.** *Photograph credit: Joseph Hudak.*

called topiary (Figures 2-41, 2-42, and 2-43). While visually arresting, these sculptural forms are high in maintenance needs whether arranged as clipped hedges, wall decorations of espaliers, pleached allées, or plant standards. Most require professional assistance to create and maintain, and, once begun, demand annual upkeep indefinitely.

A much-practiced but disheartening form of topiary is that which eliminates all

Fig. 2-41 Sheared holly and beech hedging is popular in England. *Photograph credit: Joseph Hudak.*

Fig. 2-42 Fanciful topiary with yew is common in Europe. *Photograph credit: Joseph Hudak.*

Fig. 2-43 Fruiting apples arranged in a flat cordon of crossing stems. *Photograph credit: Joseph Hudak.*

natural gracefulness by the constant barbering of trees and shrubs for personal whim, especially to control size (Figure 2-44). The basic errors here, besides creating high maintenance costs in time and money, are in the original plant selection and its placement. To abuse a plant's natural exuberance by constant pruning because it was chosen and placed improperly is to be insensitive to the inherent beauty of plants. Slow-growing, dwarfed, and compact plant forms are available to fit any design layout intentions, and all usually need only some touch-up pruning to maintain ongoing, neat proportions.

PLANT CONTAINERS

Planters, tubs, pots, boxes, or any other outdoor containers for plants artificially isolate woody material from natural contact with the earth and pose a curious dilemma: Each is largely dependent on human beings to survive. No potted plant flourishes as it would in nature, and all containerized material must eventually be replaced (Figure 2-45). No matter how well prepared and maintained, planters require more attention because the soil ages and dries out more quickly, roots exhaust the size limits of the container at some point and then often turn to girdling themselves harmfully, while matted balls of roots continually absorb all soil humus and nutrients to the exclusion of reserve water and nourishment.

Because containers are normally elevated from the flooring on which they rest, their exposed sides also bring the roots into closer contact with drying winds and increased warmth in all seasons, especially if the adjacent pavement is heat-absorbing and reflective. Container-held plantings of spring bulbs and summer annuals do not usually present a problem here as much as woody plants do; yet, all potted plants require additional waterings because of quickened evaporation from their raised position and small soil area (Figure 2-46).

Outdoor containers must have sufficient drainage holes to keep excess water from accumulating detrimentally. To aerate roots, the bottom of a large container may be lined with at least 3 inches of coarse, broken stone; and to restrain soil from filtering out the drainage holes, a porous mat like fiberglass may be laid over the stone base. The rest of the planter should be filled to within 3 inches of the top with nutrient-fortified and humus-conditioned topsoil. After the plant is installed, it should be given a thorough watering, additional soil as needed, and a 3-inch, porous cover of mulch.

Trees or tall shrubs requiring guy wires need secure anchor loops built into the sides of the container; these should be part of the initial construction planning.

PESTS AND DISEASES

Insect pests and plant diseases are a normal part of every environment, and while there is supposedly a natural predator and a cure for each ailment, they do not usually arrive on schedule. Drastic insect defoliation or disease disfigurement of any plant is a severe shock to its current health and future growth, so preventing and isolating the damage with the use of chemical control measures are sensible and necessary. As with fertilizing and killing weeds, spray programs for insect and disease management should follow the manufacturer's instructions explicitly. Since these control mixtures are usually diluted with water, their application in damp or threatening weather will risk their being less than fully effective. All are poisonous to some degree

Fig. 2-44 Vigorous evergreens are graceless and high in maintenance cost when sheared continually. *Photograph credit: Joseph Hudak.*

Fig. 2-45 Containerized planting is wholly dependent on human concern for good growth. *Photograph credit: Joseph Hudak.*

Fig. 2-46 Only a generously sized planter with proper drainage can support a large planting mix attractively. *Photograph credit: Joseph Hudak.*

49

Fig. 2-47 Evergreen trees can quickly dominate any nearby planting in the use of water and space. *Photograph credit: Joseph Hudak.*

Fig. 2-48 Variable root types often adjust comfortably even in competition. *Photograph credit: Joseph Hudak.*

for humans, and some can stain and disfigure painted surfaces or porous construction materials.

A wiser approach under any circumstance is to seek out and use only plant materials with minimum attraction for either pests or diseases. These resistant selections should then be kept in vigorous health by regular fertilizing, deep watering in drought, adequate air circulation, and pruning sanitation. Neglected plants are more susceptible to problems than well-maintained ones.

SPACING AND GROWTH HABITS

Proper spacing for plants is based on many variables: ultimate size, known rate of annual growth locally, length of the growing season, purchase size, site exposure, moisture and humus content of the soil, expected maintenance, and the planned timetable for the finished growth effect. Budget adjustments reducing plant sizes should still take into account the unchanging expansion rate of the plant and have the spacing reflect this; gaps between plants can always be filled temporarily by annuals or low groundcovers.

Trees are the tallest but slowest plant type to develop into maturity, but when established, they continue upward and outward longer than other plants. Their root competition for available water and nutrients always remains keen, and dominant older trees (Figure 2-47) on a site seldom allow the successful introduction of any other planting into their root domain unless the new plants are totally undemanding and tolerant of these unusual growing conditions. A list of such cooperative plant choices is often minuscule.

Shrubs are often more cooperative with lesser plants introduced near them, but again, established planting will always have first claim on moisture and nourishment, and these interactions have to be understood and managed well to achieve low maintenance and ongoing results. Vigorous groundcovers tend to suffocate interplanted bulbs and herbaceous perennials after a short time, while grass turf close to trees and shrubs will absorb rainfall greedily—to the possible detriment of the other root systems. Intelligently mixing a variety of root types—deep, shallow, and intermediate—encourages most plant collections to exist competitively but favorably together for many years (Figure 2-48).

LANDSCAPE DESIGN GUIDELINES

Landscape design is a visual fine art with a long and distinguished history in human affairs. Design of any sort is a process of problem solving that serves functional needs, creates meaningful forms, and conserves economic means. Where landscape design differs from all other art forms is in its scope, its materials, and in the effect of time on its components. It is the least static in its resolutions, and it is the only profession largely concerned with *living* elements and their skillful placement on the land. All landscape designers must function, however, with only existing plant colors, textures, and shapes. New materials cannot be ordered or created on demand.

Fig. 2-49 Screening from parked cars and nearby traffic is readily arranged with an evergreen hedge. *Photograph credit: Joseph Hudak.*

Fig. 2-50 Privacy and elegance achieved through planting additions. *Photograph credit: Joseph Hudak.*

Fig. 2-51 Dwarfed evergreens consolidate the sculptural arrangement of rocks framing a watercourse. *Photograph credit: Joseph Hudak.*

Fig. 2-52 This hedge-sheltered rose garden is neatly in keeping with an attractive view. *Photograph credit: Joseph Hudak.*

Fig. 2-53 Wind control for pool areas always receives high priority. *Photograph credit: Joseph Hudak.*

Fig. 2-54 Horticultural focus with flowers and foliages of perennials. *Photograph credit: Joseph Hudak.*

Since landscape design is primarily involved with the creation of usable outdoor space, it often incorporates both planting and architectural devices to define and explain the intended use of the design. Landscape planning is also concerned with the effects of light and of third-dimensional volumes. While *horticulture* leads to growing plants well, *planting design* means arranging them well; combining both attractively is the formula for a memorable landscape setting.

Planting is a valuable professional tool for the harmonious and practical resolution of many physical site problems and client requirements because it can offer screening (Figure 2-49), cooling, privacy, enhancement of architectural lines, softening of rigid construction forms, directional emphasis, enframement of views, erosion management, sun and wind control, sound deadening, and horticultural focus and exclusiveness, plus reduced maintenance (Figures 2-50 through 2-54). It further contributes sensory attractions from individual or blended colors, fragrances, moving shadow patterns and foliage, seasonal changes, silhouettes, and textures. Planting has many appeals.

The outlines of plants that are used as specimens can be forcefully dramatic, or they can be submerged and blurred into a common outline when the plants are massed. Foliage and branching textures can provide fine, coarse, and intermediate accents, while each plant's character, the sum of all its inherent growth characteristics, together with the external influences that shape its physical appearance on a site, can be rugged, delicate, flamboyant, somber, wistful, or stately. Plants convey mood and certain symbols to the viewer.

Combinations of the three main plant types—trees, shrubs, and groundcovers—are found everywhere in nature, but the lack of any one of them from the scene, especially in "hand-made" landscapes, can create a genuine sense of omission. This reaction suggests keeping the plant trio together in some form or other. Where necessity and space limitations force a substitution of one of them, arbors with vines might replace sheltering tree branches (Figure 2-55), walls or fences might serve as shrub borders, and pavements might alternate as groundcovers. Extreme use of such construction alternatives, however, can lead to a solely decorative planting layout instead of a relevant planting involvement with the site.

Planting is an elastic design element that is always changing, and it is vital to have a clear design aim before planting is begun. Planning for the intended *use* of the space, the *proportions* of the area to be developed, and the *form* of the design layout have high priorities as basic starting points. As much as possible, normal budget restrictions should be permitted to influence only the selection of materials for the design and not the design itself. Any design concept should be paramount to its details.

Of course, careful site analysis goes hand in hand with the design idea being evolved. One should determine early what surface items will remain—plants, rock outcrops, water features, structures, paving, or grading—and how each will be used to satisfy the final scheme. It is wise, too, to verify the influence of views, neighboring development use, air movement, exposure, soil conditions, and utility lines above and below ground. Entanglement in the fine detailing is to be avoided before the master planning is accomplished. The thrust and durability of interest from any design are

Fig. 2-55 The exuberance of this sweet autumn clematis easily softens the rigid appearance of its fence support. *Photograph credit: Joseph Hudak.*

Fig. 2-56 Simple repetition of plant forms is a well-liked composition. *Photograph credit: Joseph Hudak.*

Fig. 2-57 Ferns, lily-of-the-valley, and a crab-apple arranged in harmonious sequence. *Photograph credit: Joseph Hudak.*

tied to the strength of the basic principles followed and not to decorative additions.

We have design guidelines for reaching the goals we seek. Planting compositions have forms of order: repetition, sequence, and balance (Figure 2-56). Repetition is the most fundamental of these forms and can be acknowledged in the landscape by duplicating color, shape, texture, size, position, or quantity. It must be accompanied, nevertheless, by sequence or balance for visual harmony. *Monotony* comes from the overuse of repetition, and while *variety* is at least a relief from monotony, it is not a principle of order but only the stimulus for a response of the mind—for good or ill—to what is seen. Variety may be the spice of life, but it is not the meal.

Sequence is the arrangement of the diverse materials of a design so that visual attention is easily moved in one direction. It involves a progressive change of at least one plant characteristic—shape, color, or size—in all partners of the series (Figure 2-57). There is a satisfying visual rhythm to sequence when well handled.

Because we are more accustomed to recognizing and accepting objects with equally distributed parts on a vertical axis, we identify this visual satisfaction as balance. When both sides of an axis are mirror images of each other, they are in symmetry, a landscape formula used for generations in so-called formal garden layouts (Figure 2-58). Its opposite is asymmetry (or occult balance) and provides us with the design term "informal" (Figure 2-59). Either can be visually agreeable as long as each is suitable for the total landscape development.

All design elements in a landscape have characteristics of size and relative scale. The human being is the scale by which all things are measured, and the phrase "out of scale" refers to a relationship of items based on our expectations of how they should appear—whether larger or smaller—in a scene, and do not.

Fig. 2-58 Perfect symmetry achieved both architecturally and horticulturally at Taranto in northern Italy. *Photograph credit: Joseph Hudak.*

Fig. 2-59 Oriental designs often favor an asymmetric approach. *Photograph credit: Joseph Hudak.*

Fig. 2-60 An amenable distribution of plant forms and textures is a matter of proportion. *Photograph credit: Joseph Hudak.*

Fig. 2-61 Emphasis through a noticeable contrast of objects needs careful handling. *Photograph credit: Joseph Hudak.*

Distance and perspective change the outline and true appearance of objects. The myriad tiny leaves of a hemlock disappear completely when viewed from far away, and only the conical silhouette helps to identify what the tree is. Planting close at hand reveals all its intricacies.

This relationship of placement provides us with a useful way of enlarging—or diminishing—an outdoor space. Fine-textured planting at a distance will seem optically farther away than it physically is, while nearby, coarse-textured plant material will appear closer. This effect also works with color as "cool" ones recede from us while "hot" ones advance.

Design values are several: *proportion, emphasis, accent,* and *unity* (Figures 2-60 and 2-61). Proportion in outdoor design is the distribution percentage of any element used in the scheme and dictates how many shapes, colors, sizes, textures, and materials comfortably suit the design intent and ought to be included. Emphasis means uniqueness and creates contrast among at least two objects or characteristics of those objects; it should be used sparingly, since we tire easily from constant stimulation.

Fig. 2-62   The simple handling of an accent edging for a path. *Photograph credit: Joseph Hudak.*

Fig. 2-63   Carefully modeled earth forms are essential to a unified landscape. *Photograph credit: Joseph Hudak.*

Accent is a collection of low-keyed, secondary, but noticeable objects into a flowing procession toward a main focus (Figure 2-62). Unity is the harmony of all elements of the total design and clearly illustrates the skill of a designer as a landscape artist.

GROUND FORMS

Land is the base from which all landscape changes evolve. It affects the potential for vision, motion, and a sense of enclosure. Planting can then become a useful transitional element between the ground form and a structure. Plant outlines should also reflect the type of earth modeling used; upright plants are compatible with sharply defined land forms; rounded plant outlines have an affinity for rolling topography. Plants also appear comfortably placed if the ground slopes up toward them (Figure 2-63).

The inclusion of visually satisfying earth forms should contribute a bonus for the total setting—and especially for the plants displayed. Grade changes for surface-water runoff, as well as for structures, roadways, walks, water elements or game areas, however, usually have their own rigid requirements for space and levels; blending each necessary physical element harmoniously while still maintaining an agreeable planting arrangement takes effort and experience. Although treated often as merely icing on the cake, planting design remains an important and useful tool in all landscape developments.

LIGHT AND SHADE

The eye is led by variations of light intensity and will halt when arrested by some noticeable form. We can change the perspective of an area by altering the degree of light provided for it. The amount and location of brightness—or shadowing—inform the eye what the shape, proportion, and intention of a space are. Since natural outdoor light does change with the hour and the season, landscape scenes vary all the time. As third-dimensional spaces meant for movement through them, landscape designs should offer a special opportunity for human enjoyment throughout the year.

Shade is reduced light and every space has some shading if only from the plants themselves. Horticulturally, dense shade usually produces less vigorous growth and lowered flowering effect—not necessarily fewer flowers, but blooms that are less vividly colored and that are produced less often while appearing farther apart on the flower stalks. As light intensity and its heat increase in an area, growth increases, too. The majority of plants are sun-loving.

Shade comes by degrees: full, deep, half, and light. Full shade is year-round dimness caused by tall buildings, heavy-foliaged evergreens, and a northern exposure (Figure 2-64). Plants truly tolerant of all three together are scarce. Deep shading comes from the foliage of deciduous plants, but here some light does reach the ground level in late autumn and winter—times when temperate climate plants are dormantly inactive (Figures 2-65 and 2-66). Half-shade is a proportion of equal shad-

Fig. 2-64 This entry, facing north, is in full shade and limited to a small selection of plants. *Photograph credit: Joseph Hudak.*

Fig. 2-65 Deep shade from oaks and pines is attractively enlivened with plants suited to low light intensities. *Photograph credit: Joseph Hudak.*

Fig. 2-66 Shade for half the day is common in matured landscapes. *Photograph credit: Joseph Hudak.*

Fig. 2-67 Light shading from deciduous trees is generally appreciated and used on many housing developments. *Photograph credit: Joseph Hudak.*

ing and full sun, but the hours when this light penetrates are important, since the heat of the day which promotes growth best extends from 10 A.M. until 2 P.M. Moderate shade is the easiest to utilize because it is usually filtered sunlight for short periods only and allows most of the brightness and heat to reach the plants (Figure 2-67). When trees and shrubs stretch and expand with age, the light intensity beneath them diminishes each season. Landscape planting is always modifying itself and its surroundings.

Plant growth and hardiness are sometimes noticeably affected by increased shade. Such soils remain cooler for a longer period in spring, may dry out more readily in summer because of the vigorous roots of tall plants which create the shade, and are apt to compact more easily because animal life in them is not prolific. Fertilizer boosters take longer to become effective in cold soil and should then be applied only in weak doses.

SEASONAL INTEREST

Because the flowering season with woody plants lasts only a few weeks, having permanent material with a dual seasonal appeal becomes valuable in most planting designs. Summer foliage contrasts in color or texture; attractive and persistent fruiting and autumnal foliage colorings, plus noticeable winter bark or twigs, add welcome interest beyond blooming time. Wintertime settings of bare, deciduous silhouettes against evergreen backdrops can be stimulating, while these same plants, if conspicuous in either flower or fruit (Figure 2-68), can continue their attractiveness later.

Although evergreen plant materials have been rightly called the aristocrats of the landscape, designs filled exclusively with them tend in time to appear gloomy, dull, and with evergreen tree masses, overpowering. Groupings of all deciduous plants, on the other hand, often seem sparse and leggy, with fuzzy outlines during wintertime defoliation. Herbaceous perennial gardens and annual beds either descend into ground-line hibernation or disappear entirely from the scene, leaving sizable blank spaces. An artful combination of all these plant types into a cohesive, year-round picture is the goal, but finding the most attractive resolution of their habits can be elusive.

COLOR

Color in the landscape can make the difference between calmness and chaos, for color is a motivating element for personal response. Take away all color by reducing light to pitch blackness or by adding dazzling, eye-squinting brightness, and the viewer will become disoriented. Color is associated with light, and all objects reflect light to some degree by the structure of their own color pigments. Together, these two types of light identify what colorings we actually see.

In a standard color wheel the primary colors of red, yellow, and blue are evenly separated from one another by the secondary colors of orange, green, and violet. The colors here are arranged in a circle and the point of each color wedge touches the axis; the points directly opposite one another provide a selection of complemen-

Fig. 2-68 Wintertime interest is assured from this mix of evergreen textures and a birch accent. *Photograph credit: Joseph Hudak.*

tary colorings: red and green, yellow and violet, blue and orange. This chromatic arrangement suggests, for example, that yellow will appear to gain a greater intensity when used with a violet-colored complement. The other pairs follow suit.

The color of light reaching an object influences the color of the pigments in that object. The mix of all colors found in light neutralizes each color to create an intensity called "whiteness," a phenomenon particularly evident at high noon in summer on a sunny day at the beach. Mixing all the pigments of color produces black. Tints are colors diluted with white, while shades are colors dulled by black. Hue is the name of the color itself; value is the degree to which the color is lighter or darker than the base coloring; intensity refers to the concentrated strength of a color, where orange, as an example, is of high intensity and apricot is of lower intensity. These color dimensions are interlocked, and changing one of them forces an adjustment in the other. Diluting or tinting any color also reduces the intensity of it.

We can alter the quality of color in natural light in a number of ways: by changing the *intensity* of light as it strikes an object (such as filtering sunlight with foliage); by the type of *surface* used to catch the light (glossy foliage is shiny and reflective while fuzz-covered leaves are dull and light-absorbing); and by a *contrast* of colorings (white flowers enliven nearby, dark-toned blossoms) (Figure 2-69). The time of day also influences color intensity, with the pale light of morning adding a yellowish overtone to the scene, the noontime brilliance often washing out all but the strongest color values, and the sunset hours casting a reddish or violet tone on all objects.

The term "warm" has an affinity with red, orange, and yellow colorings, while blue, green, and violet are considered "cool." The vitality of the warm colors is often emotionally exciting to us, but their overuse, especially in confined spaces, can be mentally exhausting and even irritating. Limpid, cool colors are considered soothing, but here, too, their excessive display can make us dull, dispirited, and even apathetic. Color evidently can control moods.

Green is the dominant color of plant materials—but which green? In spring, both deciduous and evergreen plant foliage is mostly translucent yellow-green, but by summer, these leaves tend to become opaquely darker and blue-green. Aging changes all colors.

Spring flowers usually range naturally from white to yellow in a set of pale tints, while summer blossoming tends to be more intense and brilliant in color. By autumn, most deciduous foliage dominates the landscape with a unique glow throughout the entire plant as age and frost chemically alter leaf pigments. As these leaves drop, fruit and stem colorings emerge. Color variations in plants are available in any season, and with some choices in all of them.

Plants with foliage normally colored other than green are many and add interesting accent if used with discretion. Red-leaved deciduous plants, silvered evergreens, and variegated shrub foliages are eye-catching of themselves, yet most of these color novelties prove jarring if scattered indiscriminately without true regard for the unity of the setting (Figure 2-70). Blending differing groups of them harmoniously, particularly on small sites, is often an impossible task.

The size of leaves or flowers influences the color value returned. Tiny foliage or blossoms of necessity need to be massed for any noticeable effect. Grass lawn is an example of how concentrating fine foliage produces a visually unifying carpet of color and texture. The nearness of similar colorings creates richness in effect. Monochromatic color schemes—including the expected green from foliage—tend to unite diverse areas of a design in a simple but effective way.

Enduring color combinations of landscape materials can be created from a harmony of triads. There should be three related colorings represented either entirely

Fig. 2-69 Bold and bright foliage of the caladium effectively enlivens a shaded corner. *Photograph credit: Joseph Hudak.*

Fig. 2-70 These variegated leaves of *Hosta undulata* are unfailingly eye-catching. *Photograph credit: Joseph Hudak.*

Fig. 2-71 A complete blending of natural growth and human skill with plants and architecture. *Photograph credit: Joseph Hudak.*

by plant materials or by plants combined with construction elements, such as rocks, wood, brick, or even plastic. Selection of the proportion of each should be guided by aesthetic experience, but for the novice a reasonable division is to pair two for emphasis and to add a dash of the third for accent.

Beginning with the primary colors, the designer considers their tones of russet, citrus, and slate; with the secondary colorings, plum, buff, and sage are evaluated as cooperative blendings. One uses tints and tones pleasing to one's own eye while remembering that gray is a helpful foil for enhancing the values of other colors and that white serves to separate intense colorings.

Planting design will always offer a paradox: The designer sees a plant as an individual with all its growth characteristics while learning to subordinate these valuable assets into a larger picture (Figure 2-71). There can be no totally fixed rules for using plants in the landscape, only options for experiments.

CHAPTER THREE
TREES AND PLANTS FOR INTERIOR DESIGN
Everett Lawson Conklin and Susan Korner

INTRODUCTION

People are comfortable with plants. When properly chosen, plants located in a building interior can create design feelings that cannot be achieved in any other way. With the variety of available plant shapes, textures, and patterns, good interior planting can lend its design feelings to any design scheme.

This chapter is written for the design professional and not the horticulturist. It is a distillation of more than 20 years' commercial experience at Everett Conklin Companies, International. It makes no attempt at horticultural completeness and considers only those plants that experience has shown to be readily available in large quantities from commercial growers and that have proved to be adaptable to interior growing conditions with minimum maintenance. Further, the only horticultural details considered here are those that bear on the design possibilities of the plant.

While the maintenance requirements have been simplified, they have been continually emphasized, since unhealthy-looking plants will change any pleasurable design mood to one of depression. Often, unhealthy-looking plants are more the fault of the designer than the maintance staff, since, no matter how carefully they are maintained or how spectacular they looked in the greenhouse, plants will deteriorate and die if they are not provided initially with the proper growing conditions.

Since interior planting is a living design element, the selection of the plants cannot really be separated from the specification of proper growing conditions. Thus, this chapter gives the architect or designer the information needed to specify both the design and the maintenance of interior planting arrangements. Besides giving design hints and design examples that have been highly successful at Everett Conklin, it specifies the necessary maintenance requirements, technical details on how to meet those requirements, and the design feeling associated with each of the listed plants. (Figure 3-1, showing the Ford Foundation Building, is an example of a successful large-scale interior planting design.)

DESIGNING WITH PLANTS

Any successful design uses plants that are compatible not only in an aesthetic design sense, but also in their growing requirements. No matter how beautiful the design, if

Fig. 3-1 Ford Foundation Building and its Interior Garden, New York City. The first large-scale interior garden of its kind. Offices face into the garden on two sides and view a constant green environment all year long. *Photograph credit: Bill Rothschild.*

neighboring plants are not matched to the correct growing conditions, parts of the design will either deteriorate or require elaborate maintenance. The aesthetic design considerations involve choosing the proper variety of plant textures, heights, and spacing to give the desired effect. The growing considerations involve the proper matching of light intensity, soil, and water, as well as proper container size, to the plant environmental requirements.

Of all the growing conditions, the most important is the light intensity. It is easy to underestimate the amount of available light, since the human eye can easily see in 20 footcandles of light, while even the plant needing the lowest light requires 50 to 75 footcandles to remain healthy. If the light intensity is to be below 100 footcandles, even these "low-light" plants must be slowly acclimatized prior to installation.

No matter if the space to be planted is a small office, a large interior garden, or a cafeteria, the first step is to ascertain the actual level of the existing or planned lighting. To allow maximum creativity in the planting design, the light intensity should be considered in the initial planning stages, especially in large areas such as those in shopping malls or corporate interior gardens. Adding the needed lighting fixtures after the initial electrical installation is often expensive or impossible. In smaller-scale situations, such as offices or homes, extra light fixtures should be added or the plants should be chosen according to the available light. If the plants do not have the proper light intensity, they will die. The lower the light intensity below the minimum needed by the species, the faster they will do so.

Since the light source (incandescent, fluorescent, sun, or other) is not important, but the light intensity is, accurate intensity measurements are essential. For these measurements we recommend the General Electric Model 213 or 214 light meter or its equivalent. The measurements must be made at the level of the plant foliage; they must be made several times a day on several days typical of the location if sunlight is used; and they must take curtains, tinted glass, and other light-shielding devices into account. Only light hitting the top of the leaves is effective. While under-lighting with spotlights can create dramatic effects, it does very little to help the plant.

After the light intensity is determined, the plants should be selected from the appropriate light-level group (see Figure 3-2), consistent with the design aims. Plants that will be growing near one another should also have similar water requirements (also given in Figure 3-2). If plants with different watering requirements must be close, they should be kept in their own growing containers so they can be watered separately.

For a given set of design and growing requirements, there will be a number of plants that fit the conditions. The "List of Trees and Plants" section of this chapter describes the textures, shapes, and branching habits (including photographs) so that the designer can pick the plants that are both best for a given design scheme and consistent with the growing conditions. "Growing Requirements," should be used with the following sections in choosing plants for their texture, height, and spacing effects. It is assumed that the light lasts for eight hours each day.

An interior planting designer creates the mood through the interplay of plant texture and plant height, working only with those plants that will live under the prede-termined light intensity. Color cannot really be used as a design element, since the average interior light intensity is seldom more than 100 footcandles and brightly col-ored plants or blooming flowers need up to 1000 footcandles. If flowering plants are used where the lighting conditions are normal, they will generally have to be replaced every few days.

Plant Texture

The good designer will provide for design variety through the clever use of plant texture. The term is used here to describe the general structure, shape, and appear-ance of the plant, regardless of height. It includes the size, shape, edging, and thick-ness of the plant's leaves, as well as its overall shape and the arrangment and num-ber of leaves on the plant. All these factors which determine the texture are given in the plant-list section for each plant, along with photographs of the plant.

When using the plant-description section to select individual plants for plant group-ings, five general rules concerning texture should be kept in mind.

1. Juxtapose fragmented foliage (such as that of a palm) with solid foliage, (say, that of a dracaena).

2. Avoid too much of the same type of foliage (e.g., large flat leaves) in one area, unless a border or hedge effect is desired.

3. An exception to these previous rules on groupings is the palm. Although

Design Type	Plant Name	Watering Requirements
HIGH-LIGHT PLANTS—150 FOOTCANDLES AND UP		
T	Fiddle-leaf fig (*Ficus lyrata*)	W
T	Indian laurel (*Ficus retusa*)	W
T	Rubber plant (*Ficus elastica* cv. 'Decora')	W
T	Weeping fig (*Ficus benjamina*)	W
T	Norfolk Island pine (*Araucaria heterophylla*)	LF
T	Schefflera (*Brassaia actinophylla*)	W
FP	Dwarf date palm (*Phoenix Roebelenii*)	LF
FP	Dwarf schefflera (*Brassaia arboricola*)	W
FP	False aralia (*Dizygotheca elegantissima*)	W
FP	Lady palm (*Rhapis excelsa*)	W
FP	Mock orange (*Pittosporum Tobira*)	W
FP	Ponytail (*Beaucarnea recurvata*)	LF
FP	Southern yew (*Podocarpus macrophyllus* var. Maki)	LF
DTP	Jade plant (*Crassula argentea*)	LF
DTP	Swedish ivy (*Plectranthus australis*)	MF
DTP	Wax plant (*Hoya carnosa*)	MF
MEDIUM-LIGHT PLANTS—100 TO 150 FOOTCANDLES		
T	Indian laurel (*Ficus retusa*)	W
T	Schefflera (*Brassaia actinophylla*)	W
T	Weeping fig (*Ficus benjamina*)	W
FP	Bamboo palm (*Chamaedorea erumpens*)	MF
FP	Corn plant (*Dracaena fragrans* cv. 'Massangeana')	W
FP	Dwarf date palm (*Phoenix Roebelenii*)	LF
FP	Dwarf dragon tree (*Dracaena marginata*)	LF
FP	Dwarf schefflera (*Brassaia arboricola*)	W
FP	Green dracaena (*Dracaena deremensis* cv. 'Janet Craig')	W
FP	Green pleomele (*Dracaena reflexa*)	W
FP	Kentia palm (*Howea Forsterana*)	W
FP	Narrow-leaved pleomele (*Dracaena angustifolia honoraii*)	W
FP	Neantha bella palm (*Chamaedorea elegans*)	W
FP	Reed palm (*Chamaedorea Seifrizii*)	MF
FP	Self-heading philodendron (*Philodendron Selloum*)	LF

Design Type	Plant Name	Watering Requirements
DTP	Boston fern (*Nephrolepis exaltata* cv. 'Bostoniensis')	W
DTP	Chinese evergreen (*Aglaonema commutatum* var. maculatum)	LF
DTP	Common philodendron (*Philodendron scandens oxycardium*)	W
DTP	Dumb cane (*Dieffenbachia maculata* cv. 'Rudolph Roehrs')	LF
DTP	Golden pothos (*Epipremnum aureum*)	LF
DTP	Grape ivy (*Cissus rhombifolia*)	W
DTP	Prayer plant (*Maranta leuconeura*)	W
DTP	Swedish ivy (*Plectranthus australis*)	W
DTP	White flag (*Spathiphyllum* cv. 'Clevelandii')	W
DTP	White-striped dracaena (*Dracaena deremensis* cv. 'Warneckii')	W
LOW-LIGHT PLANTS—50 TO 100 FOOTCANDLES		
FP	Corn plant (*Dracaena fragrans* cv. 'Massangeana')	W
FP	Dwarf dragon tree (*Dracaena marginata*)	LF
FP	Green dracaena (*Dracaena deremensis* cv. 'Janet Craig')	W
FP	Green pleomele (*Dracaena reflexa*)	W
FP	Kentia palm (*Howea Forsterana*)	W
FP	Neantha bella palm (*Chamaedorea elegans*)	W
FP	Reed palm (*Chamaedorea Seifrizii*)	W
FP	Self-heading philodendron (*Philodendron Selloum*)	W
DTP	Chinese evergreen (*Aglaonema commutatum* var. maculatum)	LF
DTP	Common philodendron (*Philodendron scandens oxycardium*)	W
DTP	White Flag (*Spathiphyllum* cv. 'Clevelandii')	W

A Final Word about Lighting Intensity The preceding lighting-intensity recommendations are based on experience and the assumption that these levels will be provided eight hours a day, five days a week, and that the plants have been fully acclimatized. If light can be provided for more hours each day or more days each week, the plant material will look its best for longer periods. On the other hand, often the energy costs of the longer lighting exposure are more than the costs of plant replacement. However, if the plants are not to be maintained by the landscape contractor with a plant replacement guarantee, provision should be made for giving the plants light exposure seven days a week.

Figure 3-2 Growing requirements.

Design type

T = tree; FP = floor plant; DTP = desk or table plant or ground cover

Watering requirements

W = water weekly; MF = water more frequently, as required; LF = water less frequently, as required.

all palms have similar foliage, they vary slightly in color and interest, so that different types of palms may be planted together.

4. To create interest, mix small-leaved with large-leaved plants, and narrow-leaved with broad-leaved plants.

5. When using plants as specimens, especially as interior design elements in offices or homes, pick the plant with the background fabric, carpet, or wallpaper in mind. For example, a "busy" foliage plant will fight with a "busy" fabric.

Plant Height

Plant height not only determines the scale of the design, but it adds variety to the plant groupings. There are six general rules regarding plant height selection to keep in mind.

1. In the plant grouping, build up with the low plants in front. If the grouping can be seen from all sides, the grouping must be well balanced throughout and built up to the center height.

2. If a plant has canes with no lower foliage, try to place the lower plants in front to conceal the absence of foliage of the taller plants in the rear.

3. Uneven sizes throughout a grouping add more interest than consistent levels of foliage.

4. If a single plant is desired to hide a column or some other object, be sure that the plant height, including its container, is about three-fourths the height of the object to be concealed.

5. Keep the scale of the surroundings in mind when choosing the plant height. A 3-foot plant is fine next to a desk, but a plant of at least 6 feet should be selected if it is to be viewed when entering a room.

6. By convention, interior plant heights are measured from the bottom of the root ball or planter, while exterior plant heights are measured from the top of the root ball. The reason is that interior plants are usually placed in a container or raised planter, and the total available height from floor to ceiling is fixed.

Plant Spacing

Under certain conditions, the plants of an interior landscaping design will grow. Therefore, any possible change in the plant size must be considered by the designer. If the lighting intensity is at or below the recommended level, there will be little or no plant growth and the plant size and relationships will change little over time. If the lighting intensity is well above the required level, there will be plant growth, with different plant species growing at different rates.

Unlike outdoor plants, indoor tropical plants seldom grow outward; most of their growth occurs upward. The main exceptions are the *Ficus* family, the schefflera, and the *Philodendron Selloum,* which will spread somewhat outward. If a full plant design is desired, the required number of plants should be placed close together at the time of installation since future growth will seldom fill in the bare spots.

Even if the light intensity is high enough, before the plant can grow significantly, its root system must be able to expand. Thus, the best way to ensure that the size relationships of the plants do not change is to keep them in their original growing containers and not to replant them into a growing medium. If they are kept in the original containers, they will become pot-bound and future growth will be automatically limited.

Plant material is sold on the basis of height or growing-container size, and one must be familiar with the particular species to know what the spread will be. For each plant species considered here, Figure 3-3 lists the height range for each plant in each standard growing-container size and gives a recommended minimum center-to-center plant spacing. This recommended spacing is based on experience with the plant's branching habits and growth patterns and will give a full plant design. If an open or a less full design is called for, the spacing should be increased.

When the plants are to be displayed in individual planters or decorative containers, each plant, still in its growing can, is placed directly into the planter or container, on top of a layer of drainage material of the appropriate depth. However, many standard planters have lips that reduce the interior diameter to less than the overall diameter. This inner diameter should be larger than the growing cans diameter so that the plant can be placed directly into it without being repotted and risking the attendant danger of root damage. To emphasize this requirement, Figure 3-3a, gives the standard planter diameter needed for each standard size of growing container. The size of the lip changes when a nonstandard type is used. If space is limited, this measurement should be carefully checked.

Writing Specifications

The interior landscaping business is very competitive, and a common practice is for the architect or designer to send out the landscaping specifications for bids. Unless the specifications for the job are well-written, however, there are many ways for the contractor to cut corners and still be within the specifications. Consequently, the final installation may not be what the designer had in mind. The lowest bid is not necessarily the best bargain, unless the specifications are very tightly written or unless the architect is dealing with a well-established landscape contractor with a reputation for high-quality work.

The following are some suggested guidelines to use in writing specifications. If they are observed, the bids received will accurately reflect the design requirements of the job.

1. Specify the plant heights within a 6-inch bracket. For example, designate 5 to 5½ feet or 5½ to 6 feet. If the specification were simply "5 to 6 feet," the supplier could use all 5-foot plants, which are considerably less expensive than 6-foot plants.

2. For corn plants, dwarf dragon trees, and the like, specify the number of canes and approximate number of foliage heads, as well as the height. The difference in cost between a two-cane and a three-cane corn plant of the same height is not minor.

3. For reed palms, bamboo palms, and the like, specify the number of stems desired, five to six being medium full.

4. For the green dracaena and white-striped dracaena, list the number of main foliage stems desired. They range from one to three stems.

INDOOR TREES

Species	Height Range	Recommended Center-to-Center Plant Spacing	Growing Can Diameter
Fiddle-leaf fig (*Ficus lyrata*)	3- 4 ft	24–36 in	10 in
	4- 6 ft	30–42 in	14 in
	6–11 ft	42 in & up	17 in
Indian laurel (*Ficus retusa*)	5- 7 ft	42–54 in	14 in
	7- 9 ft	48–60 in	17 in
	9–12 ft	60 in & up	22 in
Rubber plant (*Ficus elastica* cv. 'Decora'), tree standard	4–5 ft	48–60 in	10 in
	5–6 ft	54–66 in	12 in
	6–7 ft	60–72 in	14 in
Rubber plant (*Ficus elastica* cv. 'Decora'), bush type	1½–2 ft	12–18 in	6 in
	2 –2½ ft	12–24 in	8 in
	3 –4 ft	24–36 in	10 in
	4 –5 ft	36–48 in	12 in
	4 –5 ft	48–60 in	14 in
Weeping fig (*Ficus benjamina*)	3- 4 ft	24–36 in	10 in
	4- 5 ft	30–42 in	12 in
	5- 7 ft	36–48 in	14 in
	6- 8 ft	48–60 in	17 in
	9–10 ft	60 in & up	22 in
	9–12 ft	60 in & up	28 in
	10–12 ft	72 in & up	36 in
Norfolk Island pine (*Araucaria heterophylla*)	1½–2 ft	18–30 in	6 in
	2 –3 ft	24–36 in	8 in
	3 –5 ft	30–42 in	10 in
	4 –5 ft	36–48 in	12 in
	4 –6 ft	42–54 in	14 in
	6 –7 ft	54–66 in	17 in
Schefflera (*Brassaia actinophylla*)	3- 4 ft	36–48 in	10 in
	4- 5 ft	36–48 in	10 in
	5- 7 ft	55–66 in	14 in
	7- 8 ft	60–72 in	17 in
	8- 9 ft	60 in & up	22 in
	9–12 ft	72 in & up	Metal tubs

FLOOR PLANTS

Species	Height Range	Recommended Center-to-Center Plant Spacing	Growing Can Diameter
Bamboo palm (*Chamaedorea erumpens*)	3–4 ft	30–42 in	10 in
	4–6 ft	36–48 in	12 in
	5–7 ft	42–54 in	14 in
	7–9 ft	48–60 in	17 in
Corn plant (*Dracaena fragrans* cv. 'Massangeana')	1½–2 ft	24–30 in	6 in
	3½–4 ft	24–36 in	10 in
	4½–6 ft	30–42 in	12 in
	5 –7 ft	36–48 in	14 in
Corn plant bush (*Dracaena fragrans* cv. 'Massangeana')	1 –1½ ft	18–24 in	6 in
	1½–2½ ft	18–30 in	8 in
	3 –4 ft	24–36 in	10 in
	4 –5 ft	30–42 in	14 in
	5 –7 ft	36–48 in	17 in
Dwarf date palm (*Phoenix Roebelenii*)	2–3 ft	30–42 in	10 in
	3–4 ft	36–48 in	12 in
	4–5 ft	42–54 in	14 in
	5–6 ft	48–60 in	17 in
	5–6 ft	54–66 in	22 in

Figure 3-3a   Spacing recommendations

Species	Height Range	Recommended Center-to-Center Plant Spacing	Growing Can Diameter
Dwarf dragon tree (*Dracaena marginata*)	3–4 ft	24–36 in	10 in
	4–5 ft	30–42 in	12 in
	5–7 ft	36–48 in	14 in
	7–9 ft	48 in & up	17 in
Dwarf schefflera (*Brassaia arboricola*)	1 –1½ ft	18–24 in	6 in
	1½–2½ ft	30–42 in	8 in
	3 –4 ft	36–48 in	10 in
	4 –5 ft	42–54 in	14 in
False aralia (*Dizygotheca elegantissima*)	1½–2 ft	18–30 in	6 in
	3 –4 ft	30–42 in	10 in
	5 –7 ft	36–48 in	14 in
	7 –8 ft	42–54 in	17 in
Green dracaena (*Dracaena deremensis* cv. 'Janet Craig')	1 –1½ ft	18–24 in	6 in
	1½–2½ ft	18–30 in	8 in
	3 –4 ft	24–36 in	10 in
	4 –5 ft	30–42 in	14 in
	5 –7 ft	36–48 in	17 in
Green pleomele (*Dracaena reflexa*)	1½–2 ft	12–18 in	6 in
	3 –4 ft	18–30 in	10 in
	4 –5 ft	30–45 in	14 in
	5 –6 ft	36–48 in	17 in
Kentia palm (*Howea Forsterana*)	3–4 ft	36–48 in	10 in
	4–5 ft	42–54 in	12 in
	5–8 ft	48–60 in	14 in
Lady palm (*Rhapis excelsa*)	3–4 ft	36–48 in	10 in
	4–5 ft	42–54 in	12 in
	5–7 ft	48–60 in	14 in
Mock orange (*Pittosporum Tobira*)	1¼–1½ ft	24–36 in	10 in
	1½–2½ ft	30–42 in	12 in
	2 –3 ft	36–48 in	14 in
Narrow-leaved pleomele (*Dracaena angustifolia honoraii*)	3–4 ft	24–36 in	12 in
	5–6 ft	30–42 in	14 in
	6–7 ft	36–48 in	17 in
Neantha bella palm (*Chamaedorea elegans*)	1 –1½ ft	18–30 in	6 in
	1½–2½ ft	24–36 in	8 in
	2½–3½ ft	30–42 in	10 in
	4 –5 ft	36–48 in	14 in
Ponytail (*Beaucarnea recurvata*)	1½–2 ft	24–36 in	10 in
	2 –3 ft	30–42 in	12 in
	3 –4 ft	36–48 in	14 in
	4 –5 ft	42–54 in	17 in
Reed palm (*Chamaedorea Seifrizii*)	4–6 ft	36–48 in	12 in
	6–7 ft	42–54 in	14 in
	7–9 ft	48–60 in	17 in
Self-heading philodendron (*Philodendron Selloum*)	3 ft	30–42 in	10 in
	4 ft	42–54 in	14 in
	5 ft	54–66 in	17 in
Southern yew (*Podocarpus macrophyllus* var. Maki)	4–5 ft	36–48 in	10 in
	5–6 ft	42–54 in	12 in
	5–6 ft	48–60 in	14 in
	6–7 ft	54–66 in	17 in

Figure 3-3a (*Cont.*)

Species	Height Range	Recommended Center-to-Center Plant Spacing	Growing Can Diameter
TABLE OR DESK PLANTS—GROUND COVER			
Boston fern (*Nephrolepis exaltata* cv. 'Bostoniensis')	1 ft	24–30 in	6 in
	1 –1½ ft	30–36 in	8 in
	1½–2 ft	36–42 in	10 in
Common philodendron (*Philodendron scandens oxycardium*)	1 ft	18–24 in	8 in
	1¼–1½ ft	24–30 in	10 in
	1¼–1½ ft	24–36 in	12 in
Chinese evergreen (*Aglaonema commutatum* var. maculatum)	1¼–1½ ft	18–24 in	6 in
	1½–2 ft	24–30 in	8 in
	2 –2½ ft	30–36 in	10 in
Dumb cane (*Dieffenbachia maculata* cv. 'Rudolph Roehrs')	1 ft	18–24 in	6 in
	2 ft	24–30 in	8 in
	3 ft	30–36 in	10 in
	3 –3½ ft	36–42 in	12 in
	3½–4 ft	42–48 in	14 in
Golden pothos (*Epipremnum aureum* or *Scindapsus aureus*)	1 ft	12–18 in	6 in
	1 ft	18–24 in	8 in
	1¼–1½ ft	24–30 in	10 in
	1¼–1½ ft	30–36 in	12 in
Grape ivy (*Cissus rhombifolia*)	1 ft	18–24 in	6 in
	1 –1¼ ft	18–30 in	8 in
	1¼–1½ ft	24–36 in	10 in
	1¼–1½	24–36 in	12 in
Jade plant (*Crassula argentea*)	1 ft	18–24 in	8 in
	2 ft	24–36 in	10 in
	2 –2½ ft	30–42 in	12 in
	2½–3½ ft	36–48 in	14 in
Prayer plant (*Maranta leuconeura*)	1 ft	18–24 in	8 in
	1 ft	24–30 in	10 in
	1–1½ ft	24–30 in	12 in
Swedish ivy (*Plectranthus australis*)	1 ft	18–24 in	6 in
	1 –1¼ ft	18–30 in	8 in
	1¼–1½ ft	24–36 in	10 in
	1¼–1½ ft	24–36 in	12 in
Wax plant (*Hoya carnosa*)	1 ft	12–18 in	6 in
	1 ft	18–24 in	8 in
	1 ft	24–30 in	10 in
White flag (*Spathiphyllum* cv. 'Clevelandii')	1¼–1½ ft	24–36 in	6 in
	2 –3 ft	30–42 in	8 in
	2½–3½ ft	36–48 in	10 in
	3 –4 ft	48–54 in	14 in
White-striped Dracaena (*Dracaena deremensis* cv. 'Warneckii')	1¼–1½ ft	18–24 in	6 in
	2 ft	24–30 in	8 in
	3 –4 ft	24–36 in	10 in
	4 –5 ft	30–42 in	12 in
	4 –7 ft	36–48 in	14 in
Green dracaena (*Dracaena deremensis* cv. 'Janet Craig')	1 –1½ ft	18–24 in	6 in
	1½–2½ ft	24–30 in	8 in
	3 –4 ft	30–42 in	10 in
Neantha bella palm (*Chamaedorea elegans*)	1 –1½ ft	18–30 in	6 in
	1½–2½ ft	24–36 in	8 in
	2½–3½ ft	30–42 in	10 in
Self-heading philodendron (*Philodendron Selloum*)	1 ft	18–24 in	6 in
	2 ft	24–36 in	8 in
	3 ft	30–42 in	10 in

Plant Growing Container Diameter	Recommended Planter Exterior Diameter
4 in	6 in
6 in	8 in
8 in	10 in
10 in	12 in
11 in	14 in
12 in	14 in
13 in	16 in
14 in	16 in
17 in	18–22 in
22 in	24 in

Figure 3-3b Planter selection. These recommendations are based on the fact that most standard planters have either a 1-inch lip or no lip at all. Because the growing cans sometimes have ridges or have become deformed, it is always best to allow for a little extra leeway, even for planters with no lip. Some manufacturers, however, put 2-inch lips on their planters, a possibility that should be checked. If the planter is an automatic watering type, the inside and outside diameters will be quite different, depending on the manufacturer.

5. For ficus trees, it should be specified whether the bush style or standard tree style is desired. In the bush style, the plant has multiple stems (ranging from two to five in number) branching out from the base of the plants. The standard tree or "lollipop" style has one main 5- to 6-foot stem with a sheared, ball-shaped foliage head.

6. Small plants should be specified as to single plants or combinations or several plants. Examples are dumb cane, Chinese evergreen, and white flag.

7. If ivy trailers are desired, their length should be specified. The trailers take up to eight months to grow, depending on the length, so the designer must plan for these up to a year before installation. Examples are grape ivy, swedish ivy, golden pothos, common philodendron, and wax plant.

8. Specifications should call for plant cleaning and spraying before installation.

9. Perlite should be specified as the drainage material for both planters and decorative containers. Styrofoam, which is much cheaper, is often used but has little long-term value.

10. The amount of ingredients in large planters (soil mixture, drainage material, soil separator) should be specified, as should the composition of each of the ingredients.

11. If bark chips, moss cover, or other soil coverings are desired, they should be specified.

12. Special attention should be given to the description of specimen plants, including the number of heads, stems, or canes, and any unusual stem structure that is desired. If canes with character (such as angle and peculiarity of growth), tufts of foliage at various heights, or other unusual features are wanted, they should be specifically mentioned.

13. If the landscape contractor will not maintain the plants after installation, provision should be made for a training program for the maintenance crew. Also, the contractor should provide for two weeks' initial maintenance of the plants and replacement of any that fall below specifications during the period.

14. If the landscape contractor is to maintain the plants after the installation (usually the best all-around solution), such an agreement should be reached before the plants are installed and a maintenance contract should be signed. This contract should include a provision for the replacement of any plant that falls below specifications because of faulty maintenance. This stipulation gives the contractor incentive for professional-quality maintenance.

15. If a large garden is planned and the landscape contractor is given design responsibility for it, the contractor should provide a floor plan of the garden for the designer's approval, before the installation.

16. If the architect or designer provides the landscape contractor with a detailed planting floor plan and the contractor finds it impossible to meet all the specifications (because of unavailability of certain species, etc.), the contractor and the designer or architect should agree in writing on any changes.

USE OF INTERIOR PLANTS AND PROCEDURES

The general rule of interior planting design is to vary the plant heights, shapes, and textures to give the desired design feeling consistent with the available light level and planting space. The best way to learn to apply this rule to specific situations is to study successful designs, such as those shown in the photographs in this chapter. They all show successful planting designs with commentary on the design considerations involved. These particular photographs were selected because they illustrate commonly encountered interior-planting solutions. It is hoped that, with the accompanying commentary, they will give the design professional the tools to solve the unique design problems that will be encountered.

Interior planting designs have usually been found to fall into one of two categories: (1) interior gardens, both large and small, such as those seen in residential and hotel lobbies, corporate headquarters reception areas, and enclosed shopping mall public spaces; and (2) open plan or specimen design, like office landscaping designs and designs that use individual plants as living sculptures. In both categories of design, the main requirements to be considered are the available light intensity, the scale of the design, and the client's wishes and budget. After these basic requirements are determined, however, the design considerations are somewhat different for the two types of design.

Interior Gardens

Interior gardens are planting areas, sometimes contained in built-in planters, that have a variety of plants and that convey their design feeling through plant arrangements rather than through individual plant specimens. Small gardens generally contain only a single grouping of plants, act as a single design element, and have uniform lighting and watering requirements throughout. Large gardens have a variety of plant groupings and varying design feelings among the groupings, and they can encompass areas of different lighting and watering requirements. Since any garden conveys its effects through the juxtaposition of different plants, a single dominant plant cannot be considered a garden from the design point of view, even if it is in a built-in planter with ground-cover plants.

In designing any built-in planter, enough planter depth must be provided to allow the root ball or the planting can to be covered with soil and to rest on 4 to 8 inches of drainage material. Since soil and gravel are expensive, it is best not to overdesign the planter, by making it larger than necessary, and not to buy too much soil to fill in between the plants. (For example, a depth of 1½ to 2 feet is usually enough for most small gardens.) Figure 3-3a in the preceding section lists the size of the growing can for different sizes of plants of each species. Figure 3-15 in this section gives the depth and volume of each of these standard-size growing cans. Thus, the depth of the largest growing can, plus the depth of the drainage material, yields the minimum planter depth for the garden. The volume of the planter minus the total volume of all the growing cans indicates the amount of additional soil and drainage material to be provided.

If the planter is already in place, its depth may limit the size of the plants that may be used. Since soil must reach to the top of the root ball or can, the only way to utilize too shallow a planter is to put the large plant in the center and to build up from the edge inward. The planter must be wide enough to slant the soil gradually so that the slope is not too great.

Small gardens   While a garden may be large enough to have only a single design function, that function can be quite varied, provided that the lighting intensity is appropriate. It can serve as a small glen or a space separator, or it can be simply a large decorative planter. The garden can be airy and open or it can be dense and closed. Planter depth of 1½ to 2 feet is usually sufficient.

Also, some small gardens can be designed to be changed with the seasons. Often, flowering plants, such as chrysanthemums or azaleas, are used, but the plants must then be replaced every two weeks. If the seasonal or flowering plant changes are desired, the plants should be left in their containers so that they may be easily moved. Some care should be given to the planter design so that the growing cans are not obvious and do not detract from the arrangement.

Creative additions of volcanic rocks, small ponds, or fountains can be quite attractive and set off and enhance the plants. However, with the usually limited space in the small garden, these additions can produce a crowded or overdone appearance. Overcrowding will give a jungle effect that is rarely desired.

Just as in other design fields, good proportion and good sense will create a pleasing design that is neither overlooked or overbearing. Examples of this philosophy applied to small gardens are shown in the photographs of the Cleveland State University Student Union (Figure 3-4), the Squibb Corporate Headquarters (Figure 3-5), TWA Headquarters (Figure 3-6), and the Benjamin Moore Company (Figure 3-7).

Large gardens   Large gardens are simply larger versions of small gardens, but their very size opens up more design possibilities, since they may be subdivided into related sections. The shape, height, and texture of the planters may be varied from section to section. The plants may be chosen to reflect varying design moods and functions. The lighting and watering requirements may differ between sections. In fact, variety is often necessary for good large-garden design, since a large mass of similar plants or plant groupings will create the impression of a monotonous forest or field.

Because large indoor gardens usually are in areas of high ceilings, the light level must be very carefully considered. Just the presence of windows or skylights does not guarantee enough light. In addition, if the light sources are distant from the plants, the taller plants may effectively block some of the light from reaching the lower plants and foliage.

Fig. 3-4 University Center at Cleveland State University, Cleveland. The main focal point of the room is a large, square planter containing five 20-foot tall schefflera trees and groundcover of white-striped dracaena. Planters around the eating area contain grape ivy. Natural light for the area comes through the two glass walls of the building. *Photograph credit: Peter Hastings.*

When large areas are to be planted, there is a tendency to use rocks, pools, gravel, or fountains to cut down the plant costs and simplify the maintenance. Care is essential when using these elements to prevent the plant arrangment from looking bare and sterile.

Large gardens are most commonly used in shopping malls. The light level in these areas is usually low to create the proper mood for shopping. The skilled designer will take this illumination into account, as well as design the garden to enhance the shopper's view of the stores.

The designer will always remember that large gardens achieve their *effectiveness* by both the proper variation of plant groupings and the proper variation of plants within the groupings. Examples of *effective* large gardens are shown in the photographs of the Hillside Garden, Crown Center, Kansas City (Figure 3-8), the Ford Foundation Headquarters Interior Garden, New York (Figure 3-9), and the Winter Garden of the Rainbow Center of Niagara Falls (Figure 3-10).

Procedures for planting gardens As pointed out earlier, a successful garden needs proper planting, since improper procedures can inflict severe damage. Correct planting involves not only correct technique and design but also correct organization.

Fig. 3-5 E. R. Squibb and Sons, Worldwide Headquarters, Princeton, N.J. A large cantilevered garden dominated by 40-foot tall schefflera trees. It also contains weeping fig trees, false aralia plants, and hanging vines of grape ivy and common philodendron. The main sources of natural light are a skylight in the ceiling (not shown in the photograph) and side windows. *Photograph credit: Bill Rothschild.*

Fig. 3-6 TWA Administrative Center, Kansas City. A beautiful center-island planter surrounded by water. The main light source is a skylighted ceiling. Offices are around the center atrium. The atmosphere created by the sun and water allows the plants to have very good tropical growing conditions. *Photograph credit: Norman Hoyt.*

Fig. 3-7 Benjamin Moore Corporate Headquarters, Montvale, N.J. This free-form planter creates the effect of a small glen. The soil level is 8 inches above the floor in front and is built up to 2 feet above the floor in the back corner. The planter is made of galvanized metal, which slopes downward toward three drain holes in the center. Although there is a skylight in the center of the room, overhead lights above the planter, lit 12 hours a day, are the main illumination source. The garden also contains a small fiberglass pool with water recirculating through the volcanic rock. *Photograph credit: Bill Rothschild.*

Fig. 3-8 Crown Center Hillside Garden, Kansas City. The rocks in this carefully designed garden were placed in the hillside to create long, cascading waterfalls. Light is obtained from both a skylight and surrounding high-intensity discharge lamps which are turned on during the early morning hours. These lamps produce 4000 footcandles of light intensity at ground level to ensure adequate light for the plants chosen. *Photograph credit: Bill Rothschild.*

Fig. 3-9 Ford Foundation Building and its Interior Garden, New York City. This stairway walkthrough area is lined with both tropical and some temperate zone material. Seasonal flowering plants are scattered throughout the garden. A garden of this size needs maintenance almost daily. *Photograph credit: Bill Rothschild.*

The techniques of proper drainage, spacing, and handling will ensure that the plants remain healthy once they are installed. Experienced supervision of the installation staff will be important in this regard, since a large installation of expensive plants is no place for the on-the-job training of the supervisor.

Proper planning and organization will ensure that the plants remain healthy between unloading and planting. If the plants are left on an unheated loading dock or stored in an unlighted or unheated room until they are installed, irreversible damage may occur.

The following sections on planting procedures are not intended to make the reader into an overnight horticultural expert. If these procedures are followed carefully, healthy gardens will result. However, if a quick installation of a large garden is necessary, professional supervision of the planting staff is often worthwhile.

Drainage Overwatering of plants leads to root rot and is often more harmful than underwatering. To minimize this danger, the planter or container should be installed with proper drainage. The simplest technique is to provide a porous reservoir below the planting soil; any excess water will then drain into it from the root ball and be slowly fed back to the soil as the soil dries out.

To prepare the planter or decorative container, the drainage material is poured into the bottom and leveled. The plant growing can is placed on top of the drainage layer and surrounded with more of the drainage material. For the smaller plants (in pots 6 inches or less in diameter), a 1-inch depth of drainage material is usually enough. For the larger plants, a layer of 3 to 4 inches is suggested. For very large gardens, about one-third of the planter depth should be the drainage layer, provided it leaves enough room for the root ball or planting can.

The drainage material can be perlite (a readily available synthetic material) alone or mixed with small pebbles or gravel. The perlite is suggested since it is porous enough to feed back the excess water to the soil as the soil dries out. If only gravel or pebbles are used, the excess water will sit and stagnate in the reservoir and will not be fed back to the plants.

Fig. 3-10 Winter Garden at Rainbow Center, Niagara Falls. Because this building, designed for community activities, is completely glass, an extensive variety of plants could be used, even in the low-light region of Niagara Falls. Since the plants closest to the ground receive the least light, they were chosen from low-light varieties. *Photograph credit: Bill Rothschild.*

Even with the proper drainage layer, overwatering is possible if so much excess water is used that it fills up the reservoir. The water level in a small container can be determined by tapping the container at various intervals and listening for the change in sound. In large planted areas, it is wise to provide for "dipstick" readings of the water level. To take such a reading, rigid hollow plastic tubes, with a cloth over their lower ends, are "planted" at intervals along with the plants. The hollow tubes reach from the top of the container to just above the drainage layer and the cloth on the bottom prevents soil or drainage material from entering the tube. A dipstick is lowered into the tube until it touches the cloth. If the stick, upon removal, shows more than ½ inch of water, there is too much water in the bottom of the planter.

If gravel is used as part of the drainage material, it should be ⅜ inch to ½ inch in diameter. Under no circumstances should limestone be used, since it is alkaline and will raise the pH of the water to a level that is too high for most tropical plants.

Soil separator   If the plants are removed from their growing cans and replanted in growing soil, it is usually best to use a soil-separator between the drainage layer and the planting soil. The separator is a semiporous sheet, often composed of fiberglass wool, which serves to keep the soil from falling into the drainage material. If the separator is not used, soil will clog the drainage material. Fiberglass wool of building material grade should not be used, as it contains chemicals that will damage the plant (Figure 3-11).

Planting medium   Because the root systems of tropical plants are much finer than those of outdoor plants, pure topsoil is too heavy and too easily compacted to be used as a planting medium. It will constrict the plant roots and will retain too much water.

For the common tropical plants discussed here, we recommend the use of the foliage plant mix developed by Cornell University. Because it is easiest to calculate the quantity of needed soil in terms of the volume of the planter to be filled, the

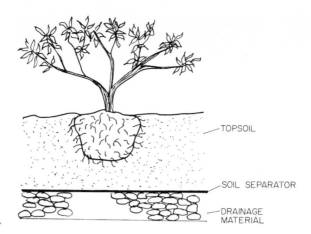

Fig. 3-11 Soil separation.

formula given here is for 1 cubic yard of soil. For conversion purposes, 1 cubic yard equals 21.7 bushels, 765 liters, or 27 cubic feet.

Sphagnum peat moss:	½ cu yd = 383 lit
Vermiculite #2:	¼ cu yd = 191 lit
Perlite, medium fine:	¼ cu yd = 191 lit
Ground limestone, dolomitic:	0.85 gal = 13.5 cup = 3.2 lit
Superphosphate 20 percent solution:	0.21 gal = 3.4 cup = 0.79 lit
10-10-10 fertilizer:	0.32 gal = 5.1 cup = 1.2 lit
Iron sulphate:	0.11 gal = 1.7 cup = 0.41 lit
Potassium nitrate:	0.11 gal = 1.7 cup = 0.41 lit

While this Cornell foliage plant mix gives the best all-round results, a simpler mix that gives good results in most cases is as follows:

⅓ by volume sterilized commercial mix of peat moss and vermiculite

⅓ by volume sterilized topsoil

⅓ by volume perlite

This mix is particularly effective for container planting. If it is to be used in a larger garden planting, such as a shopping mall garden, more perlite should be added for improved drainage.

The peat and topsoil mix is considerably heavier than the Cornell mix and both are heavier wet than dry. If the garden is not situated at grade level, this weight can be an important consideration. Figure 3-12 gives guidelines to be used in estimating the weight of the planting medium.

Planting organization   The basic ingredients for a large planting installation are drainage material, planting medium, soil separator, plant material, material-handling equipment, light, water, and labor. Organization of all these ingredients is important since every one must be ready and available for a successful installation. Arrangements for all these factors should be made ahead of time, and they should be ready and waiting when the plants are delivered.

The amount of interior volume in the planters and containers determines the amount of needed drainage material, soil separator, and planting medium. If detailed blueprints are not available, actually measuring the planters is generally a good way to obtain this volume. The relationship between planting medium, drainage material, and soil separator can be determined using the guidelines of the previous subsection. If the plants are to be left in their cans (as generally recommended), the space between the plants is filled with drainage material. If they are removed from their cans, the space between plants is filled with planting medium. In either case, the amount of volume displaced by the plants is simply the sum of the volume contained in the growing cans. Information for each standard size of growing container is given in Figure 3-13.

The installation should not be started unless all lights and water connections are operating, as the plants will need both light and water during the installation—especially the light. If the plants are delivered dry, they should be watered in their cans unless they are to be planted at once and watered immediately after planting. If the plants are removed from their cans and placed into dry planting medium, they and the planting medium should be thoroughly watered immediately afterward.

Fewer design mistakes will be made if the plants are installed one section at a time, under the direction of a supervisor familiar with the design of the section. If the installation is in an office building, it may be necessary to arrange for a workroom and a freight elevator with access both to the loading dock and the workroom.

Planting Bed Material	Dry Weight	Wet Weight
Cornell foliage mix	12-18 lb/cu ft	25-35 lb/cu ft
Peat/topsoil mix	38-42 lb/cu ft	70-90 lb/cu ft
Topsoil (loam)	80-100 lb/cu ft	100-120 lb/cu ft
Gravel	120-135 lb/cu ft	120-135 lb/cu ft
Sand	95-110 lb/cu ft	120-130 lb/cu ft

Note: For conversion to metric system: 1 lb = 0.454 kg; 1 cu ft = 0.028 cu m.

Figure 3-12 Planting material weight. These figures are the normal weight for each of the materials in both the dry and the wet state. The exact weight depends on the degree of compaction of the material.

Pot Size	Soil Volume	Pot Diameter x Height
6 in	1 gal	6½ in x 6 in
8 in	2 gal	8 in x 7 in
10 in	3 gal	10 in x 9½ in
12 in	4 gal	11 in x 10½ in
14 in	7 gal	13½ in x 12 in
17 in	10 gal	17 in x 16 in
22 in	20 gal	21 in x 17 in
30 in	35 gal	29 in x 17 in
32 in	65 gal	32 in x 22 in
36 in	95 gal	36 in x 24 in

Note: For conversion to different units, use the following factors. 1 gal = .00495 cu yd = .0038 cu m = .134 cu ft = 3.79 lit; 1 in = 2.54 cm.

Figure 3-13 Pot-size and volume proportions.

Depending on the exact arrangements, a crew of four to six workers per supervisor is generally optimum.

It is recommended that each section be planted in the following order. First, left-over building material and other debris are removed from the planting areas. Second, drainage material is added to the proper depth and leveled. Third, the plants, either in or out of their growing containers, are placed on top of the drainage material and the soil separator if present, and arranged according to the design. The spaces between the plants are then filled in with drainage material or planting medium, depending on whether the plants are in or out of their growing containers. If planting medium is used, it should be lightly compacted to prevent its settling later. (If the light intensity is below specifications and periodic replacement of the plants is expected, the plants should be left in their cans.)

After the spaces between the large plants have been filled in, the groundcover, if any, is planted. The use of decorative bark or marble chips on top of the soil is not recommended as they easily mix with the soil and are hard to remove if the plants are replaced.

After all the spaces have been filled, the plants should be thoroughly watered and the maintenance schedule begun. If dry planting medium is used, it should be watered thoroughly several times during the first week to ensure that it is completely wet.

Removing plants from cans or burlap   A healthy root system is necessary for the maintenance of a healthy plant. It is the new, very fine, feathery roots that are the most important and also the most easily damaged. This damage is very likely if the soil between the fine roots is dislodged in the course of repotting. Whether the tropical plants are delivered in growing cans or with their roots wrapped in burlap, the root system must be handled with care.

The best procedure for removing a plant from its container is to lean the pot on its side, tap on the container sides and bottom, and carefully slide out the plant. In large container-grown plants (in 17-inch or larger cans), the root system may be held very tightly in the can. In this case, a can cutter, which works on either metal or rubber cans, may be the most gentle way of removing the can. Once the can is removed, the root ball of soil and roots should be scored by making ¼-inch-deep vertical cuts at 3-inch intervals around the root ball from top to bottom. If the can removal and ball scoring are done near the planting site, the exposed root system is subjected to minimum handling.

Very large plants and trees are frequently field-grown rather than container-grown. The root balls of such plants will come wrapped in burlap. When planting them, only the upper half of the burlap should be removed. The lower portion will disintegrate in the soil after the plant is installed.

Rock formations and decorative pools   Natural elements, such as rock formations, decorative pools, water fountains, and waterfalls, can add an artistic touch and turn an unimaginative large planting arrangement into a full garden. Unfortunately the overuse of such design elements is tempting, since they are usually inexpensive compared with the cost of filling the same area with plants. Provided they are not overused, they can serve as natural sculpture or as the answer for areas with too little light to support plants or where conditions limit the variety of plants that can be used.

In rock formations, volcanic rock is the most commonly used type because it is much lighter than ordinary rock. This weight factor can be of considerable impor-

Fig. 3-14 TAP Portuguese Airlines, New York City. Specimen schefflera plants act as attractive living sculpture in this office, designed in the high style. Lights are placed above both for accent light and for extra intensity. *Photograph credit: Bill Rothschild.*

tance when the weight of the garden must be limited. This type of rock is also easy to shape with a hammer and chisel.

Although a large decorative pool or fountain must be custom-designed, there are small fiberglass pools that can be purchased in a variety of sizes and are available in kidney, free-form, or rectangular shapes. They are usually no longer than 6 feet, but they are of a standard 16-inch depth, which is deep enough to accommodate any water plants, recirculating pump, and a filter tray with mat and gravel. Their high-capacity, low-pressure pumps are usually adequate for small fountains and waterfalls.

If decorative pools are used, some thought might be given to using water plants in them. These plants are very attractive and can be easily grown indoors. As with all plants, different species have different growing and flowering habits. A reputable dealer should be consulted for information.

The use of fish in pools should be carefully studied in light of the plant maintenance requirements. Fertilizer, plant chemicals, and limestone runoff from the planting area may enter the circulating water system and kill the fish. Fish can be an attractive design element, but their maintenance requirements must be considered along with the maintenance requirements of the plants.

Open Plan and Specimen Design

Modern offices are sometimes sterile places in which to work. The introduction of live plants into such an environment is one way of making the space seem less austere and more comfortable without disrupting the integrity of the original design. For windowless offices, plants provide an attractive natural setting appreciated by the occupants (Figure 3-14). For offices and other windowed areas, the plants provide a

Fig. 3-15 Eastern Airlines, Logan Airport, Boston. Freestanding plants separate the seating area from the traffic flow and help create a feeling of privacy. Lights above allow the use of medium-light plants, such as the weeping fig, to be used in the middle of the room away from the windows. *Photograph credit: Bill Rothschild.*

transition which makes indoors and outdoors seem to flow together (Figure 3-15).

In all locations, however, the light intensity must be at the proper level before the plants are introduced. The intensity cannot be taken for granted, since artificial lighting designed for office vision is seldom enough for any but the lowest-light plant species. Even a large window will not provide enough light if it has an overhang or a northern exposure. If the light intensity cannot be directly measured or calculated from detailed ceiling plans, one must assume the worst and use only low-light material. There is sometimes a tendency to use plants to fill in otherwise forgotten spots, such as corners, stairwells, and hallways. Such areas are often poorly lit and no plant will survive there unless additional lighting is installed.

In large areas with barely enough light, the usual design problem is how to arrange the limited number of low-light species so that different areas stand out from one another. Design interest can be accomplished by using different types of foliage (for example, fragmented and solid) in the different areas, varying the plant sizes among the areas or using specimen plants selectively.

Specimen plants usually have fuller foliage or an unusual stem structure and hence appear to be different from other plants of that species. The true specimen plants are more expensive than ordinary plants of the same species, but can solve many a design problem. However, a plant with fuller foliage than most will also require more light than most to maintain the foliage.

If the office has floor-to-ceiling walls, the best design procedure is to select specimen plants that act as living sculptures. Since these plants are used for visual emphasis, the plant height and container size should conform to the scale of the rest of the interior design. The plant texture and container finish should blend with each other and with the wall and floor treatments. The particular plant specimen chosen should have an inherently interesting shape and texture (Figure 3-16).

If the office area is very large or is designed along an "office landscaping" plan with movable partitions, the plants can become an integral part of the design. They can be used with the partitions as space dividers and are excellent for indicating the importance of the space. They also may be effective in relating widely separated areas with one another. They break the monotony of the partitions with both color and texture. They act as sound absorbers. Also, specimen plants can be used in the office landscaping scheme for visual emphasis.

Planting into individual planters   Individual decorative containers are used for individual plants or small plant groupings. The plants are left in their growing containers and placed directly into the decorative planter on top of 4 to 6 inches of perlite as the drainage material. The decorative planter or container must be tall enough to accommodate the growing can and the perlite, and wide enough to accommodate the width of the growing can. The space between the growing can and the inner wall of the planter can be filled with additional perlite. (See Figure 3-3*b* for size-selection guidance.) As a decorative finishing, bark chips or sheet moss may be placed on the surface of the soil in the growing can. This decorative cover can be easily removed if the plant is replaced and it does not mix with the soil, as sometimes happens in large gardens.

Removing the plant from the growing can and repotting it directly into the planter is not generally recommended. Replacing the plant, if necessary, is a messy job unless drainage material and soil separator are added to the bottom of the container. Also, once removed from its growing container, the plant may take up to four weeks to adjust fully to its new environment.

Fig. 3-16 CPC International, Inc. Englewood Cliffs, N.J. **This fiddle-leaf fig serves both as a single specimen to be viewed as a piece of sculpture and as a means of softening the effect of the column behind it. This is a high light-level plant and the window light is necessary to maintain its health.** *Photograph credit: Bill Rothschild.*

LIST OF TREES AND PLANTS SUITABLE FOR INTERIOR USE

Indoor trees   There are only six practical common tropical plants that look like typical northern trees. While some plants in the other categories can grow as tall as these, the following six have the same characteristic tree shape.

Fiddle-leaf fig *(Ficus lyrata)* (Figures 3-17 and 3-18)

LIGHT: High light, 150 footcandles and up, throughout the entire foliage. Very strong direct light may turn or burn the leaves.

SIZE RANGE: 2 to 10 feet. Stakes may be necessary to support the stems in larger sizes.

BRANCHING HABIT: Two to three stems from the base of plant.

TEXTURE: Large, flat fiddle-shaped leaves. Large veins cause ridges in leaves, giving a quilted look.

WATERING: Water thoroughly once a week.

INSECTS: Mealy bug, scale, and thrips.

Fig. 3-17 Fiddle-leaf fig *(Ficus lyrata)* bush type. *Photograph credit: Raymond Kostyn.*

Fig. 3-18 Fiddle-leaf fig *(Ficus lyrata)* tree standard. *Photograph credit: Raymond Kostyn.*

Indian laurel *(Ficus retusa)* (Figure 3-19)

LIGHT: Medium to high light, 125 footcandles and up.

SIZE RANGE: 4 to 30 feet.

BRANCHING HABIT: Either standard type with one main stem, or bush type with several stems branching from a main stem.

TEXTURE: Foliage head is dense, with small, thick leaves.

WATERING: Water thoroughly once a week. If atmosphere is dry, water every five days. Dry soil causes leaves to drop.

INSECTS: Mealy bug, scale, thrips.

Fig. 3-19 Indian laurel *(Ficus retusa)* tree standard. *Photograph credit: Raymond Kostyn.*

Rubber plant (*Ficus elastica cv.* 'Decora') (Figures 3-20 and 3-21)

LIGHT: High light, 150 footcandles and up throughout the entire foliage of the plant. Excessive light may burn leaves. Rotate plant occasionally.

SIZE RANGE: 2 to 20 feet in standard tree shape; 4 to 12 feet in branching shape.

BRANCHING HABIT: Either standard tree shape with one main stem, or bush shape with two to three individual stems from base of plant. These stems may need stakes for support.

Fig. 3-20 Rubber plant (*Ficus elastica* cv. 'Decora') bush type. *Photograph credit: Raymond Kostyn.*

Fig. 3-21 Rubber plant (*Ficus elastica* cv. 'Decora) tree standard. *Photograph credit: Raymond Kostyn.*

TEXTURE: Large, flat elliptical leaves with main center-midrib vein.

WATERING: Water thoroughly once a week.

INSECTS: Mealy bug, scale, thrips.

Weeping fig *(Ficus benjamina)* (Figures 3-22 and 3-23)

LIGHT: Medium to high light, 125 footcandles and up.

SIZE RANGE: 4 to 25 feet.

BRANCHING HABIT: Either standard tree shape with one main stem, or bush type with several stems branching from a main stem.

TEXTURE: Foliage head somewhat open and "weeping," with small, wavy leaves.

WATERING: Water thoroughly once a week. If atmosphere is dry, water every five days. Dry soil will cause leaves to drop.

INSECTS: Mealy bug, scale, thrips.

Fig. 3-22 Weeping fig *(Ficus benjamina)* bush type. *Photograph credit: Raymond Kostyn.*

Fig. 3-23 Weeping fig *(Ficus benjamina)* tree standard. *Photograph credit: Raymond Kostyn.*

Norfolk Island pine *(Araucaria heterophylla)* (Figure 3-24)

LIGHT: High light, 200 footcandles and up throughout the entire foliage. Rotate plant weekly so that all sides receive equal lighting.

SIZE RANGE: 1 to 10 feet.

BRANCHING HABIT: Appearance resembles that of an evergreen. Long, wavy branches with up to ½-inch-long needles symmetrically whorled on a main stem.

TEXTURE: Graceful, evergreen-appearing plant with soft, wavy branches and needles.

WATERING: Water thoroughly once a week. In cooler temperatures, water every ten days.

INSECTS: Mealy bug, scale.

Fig. 3-24 **Norfolk Island pine** *(Araucaria heter-*
ophylla). *Photograph credit: Raymond Kostyn.*

Schefflera *(Brassaia actinophylla)* (Figure 3-25)

LIGHT: Medium to high light, 125 footcandles and up.

SIZE RANGE: 3 to 35 feet.

BRANCHING HABIT: Plants to 8 feet have several stems but are bushy with foliage throughout. Above this size the lower part of the stem loses its lower foliage, giving the plant an umbrella shape with foliage at the top. In the largest sizes, the stems appear woody and grow at a slant.

TEXTURE: The leaves grow in a circular fashion from one small stem. They are oblong, smooth, and shiny. When a plant larger than 10 feet is replanted in a new environment, most of the old foliage will drop and new foliage will appear in several months. This characteristic should be taken into account if the appearance immediately after planting is important.

WATERING: Water thoroughly once a week.

INSECTS: Red spider, scale.

Fig. 3-25 Schefflera *(Brassaia actinophylla).*
Photograph credit: Raymond Kostyn.

Floor plants   Floor plants are any interior plants that have enough design interest to stand alone or in small groupings. They are usually displayed in individual containers on the floor, but they may equally well be included in gardens. While indoor trees are also obviously floor plants, they are discussed in a separate section because of their unique design feeling, which sets them apart from the following floor plants.

Bamboo palm (*Chamaedorea erumpens*) (Figure 3-26)

LIGHT: Medium light, 125 footcandles and up. Leaves may burn if exposed to intense direct sunlight.

SIZE RANGE: 3 to 12 feet.

BRANCHING HABIT: Multiple stems grow in clusters from base of plant.

TEXTURE: Thin, slightly curled leaflets grow along the entire stem of the fronds. Plant has a bushy appearance.

WATERING: Water thoroughly once a week. Do not allow the soil to become very dry between waterings. If atmosphere is dry, water every five days.

INSECTS: Red spider.

Fig. 3-26 Bamboo Palm (*Chamaedorea erumpens*). *Photograph credit: Raymond Kostyn.*

Corn plant (*Dracaena fragrans* cv. 'Massangeana') (Figure 3-27)

LIGHT: Low to medium light, 75 to 150 footcandles.

SIZE RANGE: 2 to 20 feet. Plants below 8 feet generally consist of a single stem with the appearance of bark and many long, pointed leaves growing from the top. Above 8 feet, the plant may have several stems growing from the same base and appearing to be several plants growing side by side.

BRANCHING HABIT: Single thick stem with one or two heads of foliage. With the smaller plants, below 8 feet, it is recommended that several plants of differing heights and, together, having at least three stems, should be potted together to give foliage at varying heights.

Fig. 3-27 Corn plant (*Dracaena fragrans* cv. 'Massangeana'). *Photograph credit: Raymond Kostyn.*

TEXTURE: Thick, sword-shaped leaves in a rosette pattern.

WATERING: Water thoroughly once a week. If the soil is allowed to become too dry, the leaf tips will turn brown.

INSECTS: Mealy bug.

Corn plant bush (*Dracaena fragrans* cv. 'Massangeana') (Figure 3-28)

LIGHT: Medium light, 100 to 150 footcandles.

SIZE RANGE: 1 to 3 feet. This plant is a small corn plant that has not developed a cane stem and hence has a bushy appearance.

BRANCHING HABIT: Usually one stem along which branch sword-shaped leaves.

TEXTURE: Full bush form created by thick sword-shaped leaves.

WATERING: Water thoroughly once a week.

INSECTS: Mealy bug.

Fig. 3-28 Corn plant Bush (*Dracaena fragrans* cv. 'Massangeana'). *Photograph credit: Raymond Kostyn.*

Dwarf date palm (Phoenix Roebelenii) (Figures 3-29 and 3-30)

LIGHT: High light preferred, 150 footcandles and up. Plant can survive in medium light of 125 footcandles.

SIZE RANGE: 1 to 12 feet.

BRANCHING HABIT: Small sizes have arching fronds growing from a rough trunk giving a spherical appearance. Sizes of 5 feet, and larger give a canopy effect, with the trunk bare and the fronds forming a crown.

TEXTURE: Airy and delicate. The fronds have narrow leaves and the trunk has thorns.

WATERING: Water thoroughly once a week. In cooler temperatures, every ten days.

INSECTS: Mealy bug, red spider.

Fig. 3-29 Dwarf date palm (Phoenix Roebelenii). *Photograph credit: Raymond Kostyn.*

Fig. 3-30 Dwarf date palm (Phoenix Roebelenii). *Photograph credit: Raymond Kostyn.*

Dwarf dragon tree (Dracaena marginata) (Figure 3-31)

LIGHT: Low to medium light, 75 to 150 footcandles.

SIZE RANGE: 3 to 8 feet.

BRANCHING HABIT: Airy and oriental in appearance. Thin stems twist and turn at different angles. The end of each stem has a rosette of foliage.

TEXTURE: Narrow, stiff, pointed leaves.

WATERING: Water thoroughly every seven to ten days depending on the atmosphere. A regular watering schedule is necessary to prevent brown tips, but take care not to overwater.

INSECTS: Red spider, mealy bug. Clean and apply insecticide once a month.

**Fig. 3-31 Dwarf dragon tree (Dracaena margin-
ata).** *Photograph credit: Raymond Kostyn.*

Dwarf schefflera (Brassaia arboricola) (Figure 3-32)

LIGHT: Medium to high light, 125 footcandles and up.

SIZE RANGE: 2 to 6 feet.

BRANCHING HABIT: Several slender, vertical stems with small stems branching upward
from them. Leaves also point upward from the stems, giving the plant a full, vertical
appearance.

TEXTURE: Small leaves grow in a circular fashion from one small stem. The leaves
are oblong, smooth, and shiny. A bushy, slender plant.

WATERING: Water thoroughly once a week.

INSECTS: Red spider, scale.

**Fig. 3-32 Dwarf schefflera (Brassaia arbori-
cola).** *Photograph credit: Raymond Kostyn.*

False aralia (Dizygotheca elegantissima) (Figure 3-33)

LIGHT: High light, 150 footcandles and up.

SIZE RANGE: 1 to 12 feet.

BRANCHING HABIT: Thin main stem with very delicate branching stems ending in a circle of slender, jagged leaflets.

TEXTURE: Delicate and airy in appearance. Because of metallic blue-green color, plant needs a light background to be noticed.

WATERING: Water thoroughly once a week.

INSECTS: Red spider, mealy bug, scale. Needs to be cleaned and insecticide applied often, up to once a month.

Fig. 3-33 False aralia (Dizygotheca elegantissima). *Photograph credit: Raymond Kostyn.*

Green dracaena (*Dracaena deremensis* cv. 'Janet Craig') (Figures 3-34 and 3-35)

LIGHT: Low to medium light, 75 to 100 footcandles.

SIZE RANGE: 1 to 5 feet.

BRANCHING HABIT: One or two stems along which branch sword-shaped leaves that are more slender than those of the corn plant bush.

Fig. 3-34 Green dracaena (Dracaena deremensis cv. 'Janet Craig'). *Photograph credit: Raymond Kostyn.*

TEXTURE: Bush form, but the sword-shaped leaves are softer in appearance than those of the corn plant bush.

WATERING: Water thoroughly once a week.

INSECTS: Mealy bug.

Green pleomele *(Dracaena reflexa)* (Figures 3-36 and 3-37)

LIGHT: Medium to low light, 75 to 100 footcandles.

SIZE RANGE: 2 to 6 feet.

Fig. 3-36 Green pleomele (Dracaena reflexa). *Photograph credit: Raymond Kostyn.*

Fig. 3-37 Green pleomele (Dracaena reflexa) specimen plant. *Photograph credit: Raymond Kostyn.*

BRANCHING HABIT: Bushlike appearance with branches twisting in different directions.

TEXTURE: Narrow, small leaves circle around stem. Like an evergreen in feeling.

WATERING: Water thoroughly once a week.

INSECTS: Red spider, mealy bug.

Kentia palm *(Howea Forsterana)* (Figure 3-38)

LIGHT: Low to medium light, 75 to 150 footcandles.

SIZE RANGE: 2½ to 7 feet.

BRANCHING HABIT: Stems grow close together. They end in fronds that hang down slightly.

TEXTURE: Leaflets on the fronds are broader than on most palms. Appearance is that of a tall, narrow, heavily foliaged palm.

WATERING: Plant in small pot and water once a week.

INSECTS: Red spider.

Fig. 3-38 Kentia palm *(Howea Forsterana). Photograph credit: Raymond Kostyn.*

Lady palm *(Rhapis excelsa)* (Figure 3-39)

LIGHT: High light, 150 footcandles and up.

SIZE RANGE: 4 to 7 feet

BRANCHING HABIT: Several "hairy" main stems branch out into slender stems that have fan-shaped fronds somewhat like a human hand in form.

TEXTURE: Leaflets are leathery with rough, naturally brown edges. Palm is interesting but not so delicate in design feeling as other palms.

WATERING: Water thoroughly once a week.

INSECTS: Red spider.

Fig. 3-39 Lady palm *(Rhapis excelsa).* *Photograph credit: Raymond Kostyn.*

Mock orange *(Pittosporum Tobira)* (Figure 3-40)

LIGHT: High light, 150 footcandles and up.

SIZE RANGE: 1 to 3 feet.

BRANCHING HABIT: Bushlike appearance with branching from one main stem. Can be pruned.

TEXTURE: Thick, fleshy, elliptical leaves are arranged in a cluster.

WATERING: Water thoroughly once a week.

INSECTS: Mealy bug, red spider.

Fig. 3-40 Mock orange *(Pittosporum Tobira).* *Photograph credit: Raymond Kostyn.*

Narrow-leaved pleomele *(Dracaena angustifolia honoraii)* (Figure 3-41)

LIGHT: Medium light, 125 to 175 footcandles.

SIZE RANGE: 2 to 6 feet.

BRANCHING HABIT: Several flexible stems grow upward, with smaller stems branching off with a cluster of long, narrow, leathery leaves.

TEXTURE: Both the leaves and stems are bending. Plant does not have stiff appearance of other pleomeles.

WATERING: Water thoroughly once a week.

INSECTS: Red spider, mealy bug.

Fig. 3-41 Narrow-leaved pleomele (Dracaena angustifolia honorii). *Photograph credit: Raymond Kostyn.*

Neantha bella palm *(Chamaedorea elegans)* (Figure 3-42)

LIGHT: Low to medium light, 50 to 150 footcandles.

SIZE RANGE: 1 to 3 feet.

BRANCHING HABIT: Single main stem branches out into stems with fronds at the ends. To create full effect, several plants must often be potted together.

Fig. 3-42 Neantha bella palm (Chamaedorea elegans). *Photograph credit: Raymond Kostyn.*

TEXTURE: This is the smallest of the palms, but several plants together create a busy effect.

WATERING: Water thoroughly once a week.

INSECTS: Very susceptible to red spider. Should be cleaned and insecticide applied once a month.

Ponytail *(Beaucarnea recurvata)* (Figure 3-43)

LIGHT: High light, 150 footcandles and up.

SIZE RANGE: 1 to 12 feet.

BRANCHING HABIT: One or two stems branch from a bulbous trunk. The top of each stem has a rosette of long, dangling leaves resembling a ponytail.

TEXTURE: Foliage is airy, trunk is wrinkled. The trunk and stems create a sculptured effect.

WATERING: Water once a week, or when the soil becomes dry on the surface. Do not overwater.

INSECTS: Red spider.

Fig. 3-43 Ponytail *(Beaucarnea recurvata)*. Photograph credit: Raymond Kostyn.

Reed palm *(Chamaedorea Seifrizii)* (Figure 3-44)

LIGHT: Low to medium light, 100 to 150 footcandles. Considered more durable than the bamboo palm.

SIZE RANGE: 3 to 12 feet.

BRANCHING HABIT: Multiple delicate stems grow from the base. Plant resembles the real bamboo plant more closely than does the bamboo palm.

TEXTURE: Narrow leaflets grow on the fronds and the overall plant appears open and delicate.

WATERING: Water thoroughly once a week. If atmosphere is dry, water every five days.

INSECTS: Red spider.

Fig. 3-44 Reed palm *(Charaedorea Seifrizii).*
Photograph credit: Raymond Kostyn.

Self-heading philodendron *(Philodendron Selloum)* (Figures 3-45 and 3-46)

LIGHT: Low to medium light, 50 footcandles and up.

SIZE RANGE: 1 to 5 feet.

BRANCHING HABIT: Thin stems, with rosettes of large leaves, branch from a main stem. The main stem becomes a thick trunk as the plant matures and will gradually bend. Leaves on a new plant stand upright, but leaves that develop after the plant is moved indoors will spread and may need to be supported by stakes.

TEXTURE: Leaves are large, smooth, and deeply lobed, giving the plant an appearance of bush foliage.

WATERING: Water thoroughly once a week if plant is growing in medium light. If light is low, water thoroughly only when top of soil feels dry. Do not overwater as plant is subject to root rot.

INSECTS: Mealy bug, red spider.

Fig. 3-45 Self-heading philodendron *(Philodendron Selloum). Photograph credit: Raymond Kostyn.*

Fig. 3-46 Self-heading philodendron *(Philoden-dron Selloum)* specimen plant. *Photograph credit: Raymond Kostyn.*

Southern yew (*Podocarpus macrophyllus* var. Maki) (Figures 3-47 and 3-48)

LIGHT: High light, 150 footcandles and up. Can stand cool temperatures and drafts, but must have high light.

SIZE RANGE: 4 to 15 feet.

BRANCHING HABIT: Main stem and branches grow upward, but plant can be pruned to create a bush or hedge effect. Appearance is that of an evergreen shrub.

TEXTURE: Numerous needles create a dense, compact foliage.

Fig. 3-47 Southern yew *(Podocarpus macrophyllus* var. Maki). *Photograph credit: Raymond Kostyn.*

Fig. 3-48 Southern yew *(Podocarpus macrophyllus* var. Maki) specimen plant. *Photograph credit: Raymond Kostyn.*

WATERING: Water thoroughly once a week, in cooler temperatures, every ten days.

INSECTS: Mealy bug, scale.

Table or desk plants—ground cover   These are plants that are small enough to be grown in small pots (from 6 to 10 inches in diameter), and they can fit on a desk or table without dominating it. Because they are generally low-growing, they may also be used as ground cover in a garden to fill in between the larger plants. When used on a desk or table, they should be placed under or near a light to ensure adequate illumination.

Boston fern (*Nephrolepis exaltata* cv. 'Bostoniensis') (Figure 3-49)

LIGHT: Medium light, 100 to 150 footcandles, but not direct sun.

SIZE RANGE: 1 to 3 feet wide.

BRANCHING HABIT: A rosette of arching fronds.

TEXTURE: Compact, graceful foliage of small leaflets.

WATERING: Water approximately every week, keeping the soil barely moist.

INSECTS: Scale, mealy bug, white fly.

Fig. 3-49   Boston fern *(Nephrolepsis exaltata* cv. 'Bostoniensis'). *Photograph credit: Raymond Kostyn.*

Common philodendron (*Philodendron scandens oxycardium*) (Figure 3-50)

LIGHT: Low to medium light, 25 to 125 footcandles.

SIZE RANGE: A spreading plant, 1 foot high. Available in pots 6 to 12 inches in diameter. Trailers can be grown.

BRANCHING HABIT: A vinelike plant that is very good as a ground cover. Will hang over the pot, but can be trained to grow upward on a pole.

TEXTURE: Heart-shaped, glossy, leathery leaves.

WATERING: Water thoroughly once a week.

INSECTS: Red spider, mealy bug.

Fig. 3-50   Common philodendron (Philodendron scandens oxycardium). *Photograph credit: Raymond Kostyn.*

Chinese evergreen (*Aglaonema commutatum* var. maculatum) (Figure 3-51)

LIGHT: Low to medium light, 50 to 150 footcandles.

SIZE RANGE: 1 to 2 feet.

BRANCHING HABIT: From one main stem, many smaller stems branch off and end in lance-shaped leaves. Similar in design and feeling to dieffenbachia, but smaller.

Fig. 3-51   Chinese evergreen (Aglaonema commutatum var. maculatum). *Photograph credit: Raymond Kostyn.*

TEXTURE: A full-leaved plant. Effective both as a single plant and in combination with others. May develop a leggy appearance.

WATERING: Water thoroughly once a week. Can survive under wet conditions and can even be grown in water with no soil.

INSECTS: Mealy bug.

Dumb cane (*Dieffenbachia maculata* cv. 'Rudolph Roehrs') (Figure 3-52)

LIGHT: Medium light, 100 to 150 footcandles.

SIZE RANGE: 1 to 3 feet.

BRANCHING HABIT: One main stem branching into several slender stems that end in large, elliptical leaves.

TEXTURE: Heavy foliage. As the plant matures, the foliage drops from the bottom, producing a leggy appearance. Several plants growing together will give a fuller look.

WATERING: Water thoroughly once a week. Allow top of soil to dry between waterings.

INSECTS: Red spider, mealy bug.

Fig. 3-52 Dumb cane (*Dieffenbachia maculata* cv. 'Rudolph Roehrs'). *Photograph credit: Raymond Kostyn.*

Golden pothos (*Epipremnum aureum* or *Scindapsus aureus*) (Figure 3-53)

LIGHT: Medium light, 100 to 150 footcandles.

SIZE RANGE: 1 foot high; trailers can be grown. Available in 6- to 10-inch pots.

BRANCHING HABIT: A vinelike plant with thick foliage. Sturdy branches may cascade over pot edges and trail along the ground, or they may be trained to climb bark poles.

TEXTURE: Waxy, thick, heart-shaped leaves.

WATERING: Water thoroughly once a week. Allow surface soil to dry before watering.

INSECTS: Red spider, mealy bug.

Fig. 3-53 Golden pothos *(Epipremnum aureum or Scindapsus aureus). Photograph credit: Raymond Kostyn.*

Grape ivy *(Cissus rhombifolia)* (Figure 3-54)

LIGHT: Medium light, 100 to 150 footcandles.

SIZE RANGE: 1 foot high; spreads to fill the pot. Trailers can be grown. Comes in 6- to 12-inch pots.

BRANCHING HABIT: Vinelike plant with outreaching branches.

TEXTURE: Bushy ivy. Small plants have quilted surface.

WATERING: Water thoroughly once a week.

INSECTS: Red spider, mealy bug.

Fig. 3-54 Grape ivy. *(Cissus rhombifolia). Photograph credit: Raymond Kostyn.*

Jade plant *(Crassula argentea)* (Figure 3-55)

LIGHT: High light, 150 footcandles and up.

SIZE RANGE: 1 to 3 feet.

BRANCHING HABIT: A miniature tree shape with a stout, short trunk branching into thick stems that end in short, elliptical leaves.

TEXTURE: A full foliage plant. Head of tree, with thick, fleshy, elliptical leaves appears round.

WATERING: Water every two weeks, but in dry atmosphere, water every week.

INSECTS: Red spider, mealy bug.

Fig. 3-55   Jade plant *(Crassula argentea).* *Photograph credit: Raymond Kostyn.*

Prayer plant *(Maranta leuconeura)* (Figure 3-56)

LIGHT: Medium light, 125 to 175 footcandles.

SIZE: 1 foot high. Available in pots 6 to 10 inches in diameter.

BRANCHING HABIT: Leaves branch horizontally on long stems in bright light and rise to a vertical "praying" position under low levels of illumination. Particularly interesting under a table lamp.

Fig. 3-56   Prayer plant *(Maranta leuconeura).* *Photograph credit: Raymond Kostyn.*

TEXTURE: Velvety finish with leaf veins radiating from center rib in fishbone pattern.

WATERING: Water thoroughly once a week. Between March and October, do not allow soil to dry out.

INSECTS: Red spider, mealy bug.

Swedish ivy *(Plectranthus australis)* (Figure 3-57)

LIGHT: Medium to high light, 125 to 150 footcandles.

SIZE RANGE: 1 foot high; trailers can be grown. Available in pots 6 to 10 inches in diameter.

BRANCHING HABIT: A branching ivy on succulent stems that easily break. Fast-growing and can quickly develop long runners. A good hanging plant.

TEXTURE: A full ivy plant. Leaves are round and wrinkled with scalloped edges.

WATERING: Water thoroughly once a week.

INSECTS: Mealy bug, white flies.

Fig. 3-57 Swedish ivy *(Plectranthus australis)*.
Photograph credit: Raymond Kostyn.

Wax plant *(Hoya carnosa)* (Figure 3-58)

LIGHT: High light, 150 footcandles and up.

SIZE RANGE: 1 foot high, a spreading plant. Trailers can be grown. Available in 6- to 10-inch pots.

BRANCHING HABIT: A vine plant with stiff leaves. The leaves on individual plants are not numerous; several plants potted together give the appearance of sufficient foliage.

TEXTURE: Waxy, leathery leaves spaced out on a stem. Foliage has airy appearance.

WATERING: Water thoroughly once a week.

INSECTS: Mealy bug.

Fig. 3-58 Wax plant *(Hoya carnosa) Photograph
credit: Raymond Kostyn.*

White flag (*Spathiphyllum* cv. 'Clevelandii') (Figure 3-59)

LIGHT: Low to medium light, 75 to 150 footcandles.

SIZE RANGE: 1 to 3 feet.

BRANCHING HABIT: Large, full, sword-shaped leaves that branch upward on thin
stems. White flowers are often produced.

TEXTURE: A cluster of thin stems ending in glossy, thick leaves. Several plants potted
together give fullness.

WATERING: Water thoroughly once a week.

INSECTS: Mealy bug.

**Fig. 3-59 White flag (*Spathiphyllum* cv. 'Cleve-
landii').** *Photograph credit: Raymond Kostyn.*

White-striped dracaena (*Dracaena deremensis* cv. 'Warneckii') (Figures 3-60 and 3-61)

LIGHT: Low to medium light, 50 to 150 footcandles.

SIZE RANGE: 1 to 3 feet.

BRANCHING HABIT: Small plants have a rosette of foliage close to the ground. Taller plants have foliage whorled around the stem.

TEXTURE: Small plants give a full, round effect of narrow, sword-shaped leaves. Taller plants look fuller, especially when several are planted together.

WATERING: Water thoroughly once a week. Can survive under wet conditions and can even be grown in water with no soil.

INSECTS: Red spider, mealy bug.

Fig. 3-60 (*Above*) White-striped dracaena (*Dracaena deremensis* cv. 'Warneckii'). *Photograph credit: Raymond Kostyn.*

Fig. 3-61 (*Right*) White-striped dracaena (*Dracaena deremensis* cv. 'Warneckii'). *Photograph credit: Raymond Kostyn.*

Plants listed in the subsection "Floor plants" that can be used on a table or desk if small enough:

Green dracaena (*Dracaena deremensis* cv. 'Janet Craig')

Neanthe bella palm (*Chamaedorea elegans*)

Self-heading philodendron (*Philodendron Selloum*)

ENVIRONMENTAL REQUIREMENTS

The very process of moving tropical plants from outdoor to indoor conditions will often severely shock them. Only healthy plants that have been properly prepared for the transition will survive without losing much of their beauty.

The environmental requirements that must be met to ease the transition are completely out of the architect's or designer's control. Even though these requirements add to the cost of the plant material, they are essential to ensure a healthy design. All well-established, reputable interior landscape contractors and a few nurseries follow these procedures and will not sell plants unless they have met these requirements. Nevertheless, the architect or designer should be aware of the factors involved and should specify that the plants supplied for installation have met all the following environmental requirements.

Field Grown Plants: The Root Ball Treatment

The larger plants of a species are usually grown outdoors in tree nurseries under natural conditions and are called field-grown plants. Because their growth has not been constrained, their root systems are usually widely spread out. Before such plants can be transplanted indoors, their root systems must be artificially forced to grow into dense, compact balls with enough fine, feathery roots to support the entire plant.

The desired change in root-system structure is accomplished by root pruning; for large, field-grown plants, it must be begun at least one year before installation. If the design calls for large plant material that is likely to be field-grown, a contract for it should be drawn up well before installation. In fact, it is wise to have the specific plant specimens selected and tagged at the nursery up to a year before the transplanting. Such decisions cannot be made at the last minute.

The root-pruning process is begun by digging an 8-inch-wide circular trench away from the plant trunk, the outside diameter of the trench being equal to the size of the root ball desired for replanting to the interior environment. An inward-slanting circular trench is preferred, as it results in a tapered root ball at the time of transplanting. All the soil is removed from the trench, the roots in the trench are cut and removed, and the trench is refilled with a peat moss, sand, and soil mixture (Figure 3-62). At the same time, the top of the tree should be cut back judiciously, with consideration being given to the desired shape and general appearance of the adjusted plant.

When the tree or plant is ready to be moved, it is dug just past the outside diam-

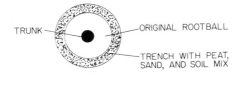

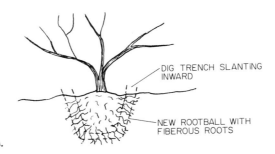

Fig. 3-62   Root pruning process.

eter of the trench and the root ball is tightly and professionally laced (Figure 3-63). This results in an outer 8-inch root ball surface of new fibrous roots, which can best stand the shock of moving. The final lacing step is important, as the chance of the plant's survival is not great if the root ball cracks during the moving. For large, expensive trees, it is often worth the extra cost to have the landscape architect or contractor supervise both the initial trench cutting and final root ball digging and burlapping to make sure they are done properly.

The larger the plant, the larger the root ball and the greater the chance of damaging the root system during the moving. The root ball size is determined in the root-pruning step, and it cannot be further cut or trimmed without harm to the plant. The architect or designer must work closely with the plant supplier to assure that the actual root balls will fit through all doors and into the designed planting space.

The availability of very large plants cannot be taken for granted. If very large specimens or unusual species are to be used, it is wise to locate the exact plants early so that the root pruning can be begun a year ahead of time.

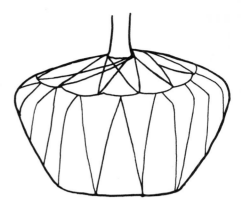

Fig. 3-63 Proper rootball lacing.

Container-Grown Plants: The Best Growing Method

The best way to grow plants in containers is to start them from seedlings in a small container. As they grow, the young plants are transferred to larger growing cans until they are well-established plants of the desired size. This procedure assures that the plant's root system is acclimatized to the small volume of the growing container. As will be seen in the next section, the plant must still be acclimatized to light.

Just because a plant is received in a container, however, does not mean that it was grown there. Some southern nurseries field-grow their plants and then put them into containers for shipping. While this procedure is satisfactory for outdoor material, it is a sure way to kill a plant that is to be transplanted indoors. Even though the plant may have been acclimatized to the light level (and few such plants handled in this way have been), the root system will not be able to adjust to the indoor conditions. The architect or designer should therefore specify that any plants received in containers have been container-grown from seedlings.

Acclimatization to Indoor Light Levels

Many tropical plants are nursery-grown under natural light intensities of many thousand footcandles. A move from such conditions directly indoors would be such a severe shock that the plants would be likely to die. To be certain that the plants will survive under indoor lighting intensities, they must be slowly adjusted to the lower light conditions through a process known as acclimatization.

During this process, which can take up to six months, a plant will adjust its foliage to the lower light intensity. The arrangement of foliage on a plant adjusted to low light will be different from that of an outdoor-adjusted plant, and this change in appearance should be kept in mind when picking specific field-grown specimens. (The photographs shown earlier in the "List of Trees and Plants" section are of fully acclimatized plants.)

Acclimatization should be done at the growing nursery, and it should be done in a light level of less than 800 footcandles. (This step is especially important for larger trees.) Large plants are acclimatized by shading them with fine net shade cloth, held by poles and cables, which excludes about 80 percent of the natural sunlight. Small

113

Plant Type	Acclimatization Period
Bamboo palm	2 months
Dracaena family	3 months
Dwarf date palm	6 months
False aralia	4 months
Ficus family	Not less than 4 months
Lady palm	3 months
Mock orange	6 months
Neanthe bella palm	2 months
Norfolk Island pine	6 months
Reed palm	2 months
Ponytail	Difficult to fully acclimatize
Schefflera	6 months
Self-heading philodendron	3 months
Southern yew	Difficult to fully acclimatize

SHADE-GROWN PLANTS THAT NEED RECEIVE NO FURTHER ACCLIMATIZATION

Boston fern	Prayer plant
Chinese evergreen	Swedish ivy
Common philodendron	Wax plant
Dumb cane	White flag
Golden pothos	White-striped dracaena
Grape ivy	
Jade plant	
Kentia palm	

Figure 3-64   Plant acclimatization periods

plants are grown in wood-lath sheds, shade-cloth houses, or highly shaded green-houses. Figure 3-64 gives the approximate length of time necessary to acclimatize various species of plants under these conditions.

Sun leaf and shade leaf   The best way to check whether a plant was acclimatized is to examine the leaves, since they will look somewhat different, depending on whether they were formed in the sun or the shade. A shade leaf, indicating an acclimatized plant, will be a darker green and it will be thinner and more elongated than the sun leaf, indicating an unacclimatized plant. A plant should not be accepted for installation if there is any doubt that it was acclimatized in the shade. The only exception to this rule is when the plant contractor is operating under a plant-replacement guarantee.

Shipping Methods and Treatments

The safest method of transporting plants is in a closed trailer which is operated by a plant transportation specialist and with the trailer temperature thermostatically controlled to 70°F (21°C). The trailers are unlighted, however, and the plants should not be allowed to go more than three days without light. To prevent damage due to lack of light, the plants should be unwrapped, unboxed, and exposed to light as soon as they have been delivered.

If the carrier is picking up less than a full load, the plants are usually boxed. Since the boxing adds to the cost of the plants, it is usually more economical to have the entire truckload of plants delivered to one spot. If the full truckload has the same destination, the plants are simply protected in brown paper. However, very large plants are always wrapped in paper, and very small plants, such as ivy, are always boxed for protection.

Once plants have been acclimatized, they will be severely damaged if exposed to the direct sun. For this reason, plants should not be allowed to sit unprotected in the direct sun during the unloading process. Likewise, plants are very susceptible to cold and drafts. The unloading, if done in the winter, should be into an enclosed, heated loading dock. If this is not possible, a tunnel of plastic sheeting should be constructed from the truck to the entrance to prevent the plants from being exposed to cold and drafts. (Foliage will totally freeze in five minutes at 15°F and will be seriously damaged in less time.)

VERY LARGE GARDEN CONSTRUCTION

Very large indoor gardens are best viewed as interior landscaping since they are of a scale usually associated with exterior gardens. They have at least 1000 square feet of planting area and are often arranged on several levels to give a feeling of spaciousness in the vertical, as well as the horizontal, direction. Gardens of this scale are able to combine the natural, free feeling of the outdoors with the structured, controlled feeling of interior spaces. The Ford Foundation Building in New York and the Crown Center Hillside Garden in Kansas City are two well-known pioneering examples of this concept (Figures 3-65 and 3-66).

Although the same planting considerations outlined in the previous section apply to all gardens, the very size of the large ones introduces additional complications and makes careful planning even more essential. Most of these complications are architectural in nature and must be considered in the very earliest planning stages. However, care should be taken not to allow the large-scale architectural considerations to overwhelm the equally important small-scale horticultural ones. Proper installation of sufficient drainage material, soil separator, and planting medium is as necessary in very large gardens as in small ones. In fact, proper maintenance, lighting, and plant acclimatization become even more vital in the very largest gardens, since the size of the investment increases the cost of the mistakes.

The first large-scale design problem is to plan for the enormous weight of a very large garden. The weight of the rock, soil, water, and concrete support structure all usually demand that such gardens be placed at ground level and on a sturdy foundation. In addition, the foundation must support the heavy equipment involved in the construction. It is often advisable therefore, to prepare the planting bed of the garden before all the building walls are completed. As outlined previously, the drainage material is added to the appropriate depth, the soil separator is added, and finally the planting medium is added to the depth required by the plant root balls. Since the planting medium will become compacted over time, it is essential that the soil be loosened and broken up before the plant installation.

The planting medium should be made up according to one of the previously given formulas, but with two additional stipulations: (1) Only sterilized loam or top soil

Fig. 3-65 The Ford Foundation Building and its Interior Garden, New York City. The 42d Street view of the garden and its water-lily pond. *Photograph credit: Bill Rothschild.*

should be used in the medium, since unsterilized material may carry weed seed, insects, or diseases that can be spread throughout the entire large garden. (2) Because of slightly different drainage behavior when the medium is in a very large mass, half the perlite or vermiculite in the formula should be replaced with sand.

If the weight of the garden must be minimized, the following planting medium formula, which may be used with good results, is approximately one-half the weight of the loam mix; one-third large-particle peat moss, one-third small-size bark chips, and one-third perlite or vermiculite, using the fertilizer and mineral amounts given previously.

If the design involves tiered gardens with slopes steeper than 30 degrees, some measure must be taken to prevent slippage. As an example, the Hillside Garden at Crown Center used 2x12 redwood planks, spaced horizontally on edge 3 feet apart under the soil and held together by steel rods to create a ladder effect. Two inches of soil covered the planks, and the groundcover was planted into the soil. The root system of the groundcover grew into the ladder and held the soil to the ladder to prevent slippage.

Another weight problem may be caused by the excess water collection in the

Fig. 3-66 Crown Center Hillside Garden, Kansas City. The large rocks in this garden are supported by concrete bases. Clay is mixed with the planting medium to prevent soil erosion. Plant roots are growing over and into a ladder made from redwood planks and steel rods built under the soil to prevent slippage. *Photograph credit: Bill Rothschild.*

drainage material under the large areas of the garden. This great quantity of water can cause severe weight and pressure problems unless arrangements are made to carry it away. Installation of drainage pipe laid in a field pattern and connected to the sewers should precede the installation of the drainage material. The pipe can be tile pipe of the special Orangeburg type or heavy plastic pipe with holes for drainage. In either case, the manufacturer's installation instructions should be carefully followed.

If decorative rocks (for example weathered or volcanic rock) are to be used, they should be placed on the soil separator before the planting medium is added. With steep slopes, the rocks should be supported by a concrete base. Any planting medium used on the steep slopes should contain a reasonable amount of clay to prevent soil erosion. See Figure 3-66, the Crown Center Hillside Garden, for an example of the design possibilities of decorative rock.

Waterfalls may be created by constructing a concrete flume for the general outline of the water flow, with rocks added for the waterfall effect. A pool is built at the lowest elevation to act as a reservoir for the water, which is recirculated by a quiet pump from this low pool to another pool at the highest level. If nearby plants are likely to be sprayed by the waterfall, plant varieties that can stand the wet conditions should be chosen and the drainage arranged so that no soil washes into the circulating water supply.

Water outlets should be located in sufficient number so that the maintenance crew can conveniently obtain the necessary flow for proper watering. Access should be planned so that the crew can work on the rear and middle plants without unduly disturbing the other plants. For very large gardens, an irrigation system should be considered.

Most of these large-scale design problems are also encountered in outdoor landscape architecture. However, a problem unique to interior landscape architecture is one of adequate lighting. This problem is even more important in very large gardens for the following reasons: (1) The very high ceilings, building shadows, and large, dense plants mean that the light intensity reaching the ground is only a small fraction of the light coming from the source, be it skylight or artificial light. (2) Most designs require large areas of groundcover, many varieties of which need strong, even light. (3) Large gardens with large budgets often contain unusual plant species that may require strong light. And (4) plants that are not totally healthy are more obvious when grouped in the large arrangements than when placed in small gardens.

The best solution to the lighting problem is to overdesign. Use HID (high intensity discharge) lamps and design for 600 footcandles or more at ground level. (Any areas likely to be shaded by obstacles or other plants should be planted with low-light material.) If the high light level will be objectionable to human occupants, plans should be made for some variation of the procedure used at Crown Center. In this case, there are many HID lamps in the ceiling, and they are automatically turned on by a timer to supply the necessary lighting intensity during the period from midnight to 7 A.M., when there are few people in the vicinity.

This brief section should make it clear that a very large garden should be planned together with the rest of the building from the very beginning—never as an afterthought. Cost cutting of the environmental requirements will lead only to continual, costly plant replacement. If designed carefully, however, a very large interior garden will repay the careful planning with the pleasure of a design feeling that cannot be created in any other way.

CONTAINERS

Decorative Containers: Different Types

A plant container should be more than decorative. Its proper selection is the first element of proper maintenance, since the container must provide the plant roots with sufficient growing room and with adequate drainage.

All small to medium-size plants are received from the grower in growing containers, usually metal cans or rubber tubs. Large plants are either in large growing containers or their root balls are wrapped in burlap. As a rule, these growing cans provide the proper volume of soil for the size of the plant and have a hole in the bottom for drainage. There is seldom any need to remove the plant from its growing container, especially since rough handling of the root system can shock the plant. Only the smaller plants, such as ivy, can be repotted without much disturbance of the root system. If it is absolutely necessary to repot a larger plant, it should be done carefully as outlined earlier, and it should be always into a larger volume of soil, never into a smaller volume.

Figure 3-16 lists the size of the growing container for different sizes of plants. The decorative container should be chosen so that its inside dimensions are large enough that the plant-growing container can be dropped directly into it. In addition, it should be deep enough for the growing container to rest on at least 2 inches of perlite or other drainage material, and leave about 1 inch between the top of the growing can and the top of the decorative container. Some care must be taken in the choice since the interior dimensions of the decorative container are often not uniformly related to the exterior dimensions. For example, some fiberglass containers have a large lip which limits the size of the growing can that can be dropped directly into them. Also, some containers have a large false bottom, which makes the interior depth much less than the outside height.

With these simple size-selection rules in mind, the proper decorative container can be selected using Figure 3-67 as a guide. This figure lists the decorative pros and cons of the most common types of containers.

Excess Water in Container

As will be discussed in the next section, overwatering of plants is more harmful than underwatering. This problem is most likely to occur when the plants are in individual decorative containers that do not allow the excess water to flow off. To minimize this danger, we have recommended that a plant in a decorative container be double-potted. In the bottom of the decorative container, below the plant growing can, there should be at least 2 inches of perlite or other drainage material to act as a reservoir for excess water. Nevertheless, if the plant is continually overwatered, this reservoir will fill up and lead to root rot because the roots are in a pool of water.

If the plant soil is continually wet to the touch, or if the symptoms discussed later under "Maintenance" appear, excess water may be the problem. The water level in the container may be determined by tapping the sides of the container or using the dipstick method outlined in the subsection "Procedures for Planting Gardens." If the water level indicates excess water, the container is tilted on its side, the plant gently pulled from the container, and the excess water drained from the perlite. If the perlite is completely saturated or appears old, it must be discarded and replaced with new drainage material. If the plant has been sitting in a pool of water for some time, the root ball should be allowed to dry before repotting.

If a very large container or garden has been overwatered and there is no way to drain out the excess water, not really much can be done short of using a small electric pump. One must simply avoid watering the plant or garden at all until the soil has begun to dry out and feels dry to the touch.

Automatic Watering Devices

In areas where regular maintenance would be difficult, the use of automatic watering devices can be of considerable help. Even when they are used, however, the plant must be checked periodically to see that the device is working properly, that its water reservoir is full, and that no other maintenance problems have developed.

Automatic watering devices are either external to the container or are built into the planter. The external devices tend to work well only with small plants, and also, they are likely to detract from the design. For these reasons, the built-in type of device is preferred. The planters with this type come in both cylindrical and rectangular shapes and in several colors. The planter has a hollow space within its double-

Figure 3-67   Comparison of container types

Container Type	Pros	Cons
Fiberglass (Figure 3-68)	Large selection of sizes, shapes, and colors. Light weight, easy to move. Some types have casters. Reasonable prices. Many manufacturers.	Easily scratched. Some types have large lips.
Ceramic	Large selection of sizes, shapes, colors, and textures. Rich appearance. Can be put on casters.	Expensive. Easily broken in shipping and handling.
Metal (Figure 3-69)	Large selection of sizes and styles. Rich appearance. Polished or brushed finish.	Expensive.
Baskets, traditional	Good range of styles and textures. Combines well with all furniture styles. Reasonable prices.	Limited sizes. Tend to sag. Need saucer under plant can to prevent water spillage.
Baskets woven around metal (Figure 3-70)	Good texture range. Reasonable prices. Do not sag. Need no saucers. Combine well with all furniture styles.	Sizes limited.
Plastic (Figures 3-68 and 3-71)	Least expensive. Good for table plants. Versatile.	Available mostly in green or white. Sizes largely limited to standard pot sizes. Need saucers underneath. Cheap appearance.
Hanging planters (Heavy; must be used with a rotating hook which can support the weight and allow for easy plant access.) (Figure 3-71)	Available in ceramic, fiberglass, plastic, and metal. Ceramic in various shapes and textures, metal in various finishes. Plastic and fiberglass are inexpensive. All are versatile.	Makes plants susceptible to drafts from heating and air conditioning. Difficult to water without spilling on floor. Metal very expensive. All need inner pot to allow for drainage. Ceramic is porous and presents condensation problem.

Fig. 3-68   Fiberglass and plastic containers. *Photograph credit: Raymond Kostyn.*

Fig. 3-69   Metal containers. *Photograph credit: Raymond Kostyn.*

Fig. 3-70   Basket containers woven around metal. *Photograph credit: Raymond Kostyn.*

Fig. 3-71   Plastic, ceramic, metal and fiberglass containers, small sizes. *Photograph credit: Raymond Kostyn.*

wall sides which serves to hold a three- to four-week water supply, feeding the water to the plant soil by a wick mechanism, sensor, or capillary action. Most types have a float to indicate the amount of water remaining in the reservoir.

Since the soil must be in contact with the wick or capillary tubes for the device to work, the plant must be removed from its original growing can and repotted directly in the planter. As the soil never drys out, the plant must be watched for symptoms of overwatering. Because different plants use water at different rates under different humidity and temperature conditions, a timetable should be kept for each container so the maintenance staff will know when to refill each reservoir.

The use of automatic watering devices will not eliminate maintenance personnel, but it will reduce the number of workers needed. One person can handle many more plants, devoting more time to cleaning and trimming, since the reservoir has to be refilled only every month or so. Occasionally, however, one will find a client who will resist the use of the automatic devices because he or she likes the assurance of seeing a person with a watering can once a week.

The use of the automatic watering devices is expected to increase in the future as more architects and designers become aware of them and convince their clients of their usefulness, and as the manufacturers produce more colors and styles and improve the efficiency of the devices.

MAINTENANCE

Maintenance requirements must be considered as an integral part of the design process. A well-designed planting arrangement will continue to project the desired effect only when the plants receive proper care. It is important to realize that although proper maintenance need not be complicated, it must be applied at regular intervals and it must be applied correctly. Mistakes in the maintenance, if not remedied in time, will lead to irreversible damage that will require expensive plant replacement.

The plants discussed in this chapter were selected because they are relatively easy to maintain as well as readily available if replacement becomes necessary. In those cases where more than one maintenance procedure will give good results, the simplest one was chosen. Thus, before specifying a species not on the plant list given earlier, some research should be done to ensure that the species does not have some exotic maintenance requirement and that it will not be difficult to replace.

This section discusses the basic elements of proper plant maintenance: watering, fertilizing, spraying, cleaning, and supervising the maintenance staff. If these basic instructions are followed, any planting design will remain healthy with minimum plant replacement. Since few indoor settings have exterior lighting levels, some plant replacement will be necessary eventually.

One of the few complications connected with maintenance is that a given symptom of improper care, such as brown leaf tips, may have several causes. For this reason, this section contains a list of the common symptoms and their possible causes. Using this list, the maintenance crew supervisor should be able to decide on the proper remedial action, based on the particular conditions.

Unfortunately, the architect or designer is often under pressure to skimp on the initial costs of an installation by not providing the correct growing or light-intensity conditions, by specifying plants other than those that will correctly match the conditions, or by not designing fixtures for ease of maintenance. Any of these cost-cutting procedures is false economy, since it is likely to produce a sickly-looking design. In addition, the eventual plant replacement and associated labor costs can quickly deplete a maintenance budget. In the long run, proper maintenance and proper growing conditions pay both aesthetic and economic dividends.

Watering

While everyone is aware of the consequences of underwatering, it is not generally known that overwatering of plants can be just as harmful, a point emphasized earlier but well worth repeating. Indoors, more plants probably die from overwatering than from underwatering. Underwatering will "burn" the plant roots, but overwatering will deprive them of needed air and cause them to rot, with dire results for the plant. A general rule is that the plant should not be watered until the top soil is dry to the touch.

Watering the individual plants on the job is usually done once a week, regardless of whether the plants are located in individual containers or in a large garden. The water is poured directly around the root base in a quantity sufficient for the soil to become soaked. Proper drainage, also very important, must assure that any excess water will drain away and not be allowed to collect in the bottom of the container in contact with the roots. If the container sizes and soil mixtures specified in this chapter are used, the soil will absorb the correct amount of water, so the next watering will not be necessary until one week later, under normal conditions. However, the soil should be felt periodically to ensure that the weekly watering is in fact neither too frequent nor too seldom. For specific watering instructions on specific plant species, refer to the previous "List of Trees and Plants Suitable for Interior Use."

Fertilizing

Experience has shown that it is usually sufficient to fertilize three times a year, skipping the period between November and February when the plants are technically "resting" and do not need fertilizer. Best results are obtained with general-purpose fertilizers containing nitrogen (in the form of ammonia complexes, urea, or nitrates), phosphorus (usually in the form of phosphoric acid), soluble potash, and trace elements such as copper, iron, manganese, and zinc. Many of the less expensive fertilizers do not contain these trace elements, although they are in fact necessary for proper plant growth.

It is best to use fertilizers that come as powders, tablets, or liquids that can be combined with water and applied at the same time the plants are watered. By this "watering in" the fertilizer, proper dispersion of the fertilizer is assured and the danger of too concentrated a fertilizer treatment is avoided.

Time-release fertilizers should be used with care. Many plants come from the growers with a time-release fertilizer already in the soil, and it is difficult to tell when that is exhausted. The best and safest method is to underfertilize a bit and watch for signs of the plant's needing more nourishment. Since each species of plant has its own fertilzer requirements, keeping a log of fertilization is suggested. This is difficult to do with time-release fertilizers in a commercial situation.

Some horticultural books call for a soil mixture very rich in peat moss, with the needed nourishment provided through proper fertilization. While this may seem economically attractive (since peat moss is cheaper than top soil), it greatly complicates the maintenance procedure.

Spraying

Most commercial insecticides were developed for outdoor application and are unsuitable for use in an enclosed space because of the very toxic fumes. The environmental movement, increasingly stringent governmental regulations, and the possibility of lawsuits make the indoor use of strong insecticides a risky proposition. The best approach to insect infestation is one of prevention.

The major nurseries in Florida and California inspect their plants periodically and spray with proper insecticides on a regular basis to ensure that a minimum number of insects are delivered with the plants. As further protection, all reputable plant suppliers give the plants an additional spraying before sending them out for installation. The smart plant customer will insist that this be done before accepting plants at the client's location.

In addition, we suggest that it be specified that no systemic type of insecticide be used in this final step. Systemic chemicals give off highly dangerous fumes for about 48 hours after application and make the soil dangerous to touch for even longer periods. (In many states it is unlawful to use them in a building interior.) While systemic insecticides may be necessary for the growth of plants in warm climates, it is dangerous, unnecessary, and often illegal to use them when a plant is ready to be installed.

Even with the most careful pretreatments, however, plants will sometimes develop insects after installation. The safest and most efficient procedure in this case is first to physically remove the insects with a careful cleaning (see the next subsection) and follow the cleaning with the application of a nontoxic insecticide. As nontoxic insecticides are not very strong, they must be applied frequently until the insects are brought under control. For example, the use of a mild cleaning solution, which contains a nontoxic insecticide, on the plants once a month as part of the routine preventive maintenance is effective.

If a severe insect problem develops, it is usually best to bring in professional horticultural help for the cleaning and insecticide application. Even here, it is sometimes necessary to specify that the outside contractor does not take the easy way out by spraying with strong chemicals.

Cleaning

Since plants take in carbon dioxide and release oxygen through their leaves, it is important that the natural dust and dirt accumulations be removed from the leaves frequently. If the plants are in a large garden arrangement, spraying the leaves with water and letting them drip dry is usually sufficient to remove the dust. However, if the plants are infested with insects or if they are in individual containers, the leaves will have to be cleaned by hand.

The cleaning is best done with sponges, with care taken not to cut or break the leaves or stems. If it is done regularly, clear water is usually sufficient. If the plants have become very dirty, a commercial plant cleaning solution may be used or a very weak soap solution made for this purpose. When a soap or detergent solution is used, the leaves should be rinsed afterward with clear water. If there are insects on the leaves, the sponges should be rinsed frequently and the solution changed often to prevent spreading the insects. A nontoxic insecticide may be added to the cleaning solution for added protection against the insects.

Although it is natural for some leaves to die and be replaced by new ones, the dead leaves and leaves with brown or yellow tips or spots will detract from the plant's appearance. During the cleaning procedure, the dead leaves can be removed entirely and the brown leaf tips trimmed off with scissors without harm to the plant. These cosmetic touches can be easily done with little additional work during the cleaning and will ensure that the plants look their best.

Supervision of the Maintenance Staff

A plant maintenance staff is usually trained by the installing interior landscape contractor. The site management should designate one person to check the performance of the maintenance crew.

The best procedure is to contract out the maintenance to a reputable horticultural maintenance professional. As with all services, the price will depend on the frequency, amount, and quality of the service required. Many reputable contractors will effectively guarantee their work by replacing any plant that falls below specifications because of faulty maintenance. In this case, the key to customer satisfaction is that as many maintenance details as possible, including replacement criteria, be specified in the service contract. The maintenance principles previously discussed in this chapter should serve as a guide to what should be included in such a contract.

Because of the importance of maintenance regularity, it is recommended that a maintenance schedule be set and implemented fairly regularly. The watering should be weekly for green plants and twice weekly for whatever flowering plants are used. The other schedules, such as cleaning, trimming, dead-leaf pruning, and nontoxic insecticide application, can be less frequent, although they should still be regular.

To maintain the schedule, log books that record what was done, when it was done, and notation of any unusual conditions will be very helpful. If symptoms of improper care develop, these log books can be valuable in quickly determining the cause of the problem.

In all cases, someone with knowledge of proper maintenance should check the plants at least twice a month to ensure that the maintenance schedules are correct and are being followed. For example, if it is determined that the plants are not receiving the proper quantity of water, either the frequency of watering or the amount of water applied can be adjusted before any damage is done.

None of these supervisory procedures is difficult or time-consuming, once the initial schedules have been established. Experience has taught that systematic professional supervision leads to systematic maintenance, with lowered labor and replacement costs.

Common Plant Problems and Their Symptoms

The person in charge of maintenance should carefully watch for any changes in the appearance of the plants. Figure 3-72 lists the common symptoms of the most common plant problems and their possible causes. Since a given symptom may have more than one cause, it is up to the professional maintenance supervisor to determine the exact reasons in a given situation. The watering level may be determined by feeling the soil; the light intensity can be measured with a light meter; the fertilization frequency can be checked in the log books; the type of insect problem can be ascertained from the descriptions in Figure 3-72. With these techniques, the supervisor should be able to decide on the appropriate remedial action.

Symptom	Possible Causes
Yellow or brown leaves	a. Not enough water b. Not watered thoroughly c. Too low a temperature d. Insects e. Too much light
Brown leaf tips or edges	a. Insufficient water b. Irregular watering c. Air too dry d. Insects e. Not enough fertilizer
Brown to yellow spots on leaves	a. Overwatering or poor drainage b. Insects c. Leaves bruised from contact d. Too much light
Wilted leaves	a. Insufficient water b. Not watered thoroughly c. Poor drainage d. Insects e. Too much heat
Pale green or yellow leaves	a. Fertilizer, probably nitrogen, needed b. Too little light c. Too much heat or too much light
Leaves curling and falling	a. Drafts b. Too much fertilizer
Small new leaves Foliage leaning toward light	a. Insufficient light. b. Plant needs repotting. c. Fertilizer, probably phosphorus, needed. d. Insects.
Plant's suddenly dying	a. Drafts. b. Soil saturated with water c. Alcohol or other foreign substance poured onto soil
Plant roots on top of soil or coming out of hole in bottom of pot	a. Plant has outgrown pot and needs repotting into next larger size.

Common Plant Insects	Description
Mealy bug	White oval insect, visible to the eye. White cottonlike clusters under leaves and in crevices on leaf tops.
Red spider mites	Red microscopic insects that can be seen by the naked eye only when they cluster together. Advanced infestation will cause visible cobwebs. Initially, the leaves have tiny yellow or brown specks where the mites suck the leaves.
Scale	Hard-shelled, oval, brown or gray insects, congregated on the leaf undersides or on stems.
Aphids	Lice, which may be red, pink, yellow black or brown. They secrete a sticky "honeydew" and congregate on buds and new growth.
White fly	White, tiny insects with wedge-shaped wings. Most visible when they cluster together, but they will flutter off the leaf if the plant is disturbed.
Ants	Black, brown, or red. Visible to the eye. Attracted by the honeydew secreted by aphids, mealy bugs, or scale.
Thrips	Black, brown, whitish, or yellow. Very small and difficult to see. Adults fly or leap when the plant is disturbed.

Fig. 3-72 Common symptoms and problems of plants.

FINANCIAL ARRANGEMENTS

Regardless of the exact method of payment for the plants, the best way to ensure the investment is to deal only with a reputable, well-established interior landscape contractor. The entire process of providing plants, from transporting to installing them, is a very labor-intensive one, and very few ways exist to cut costs greatly without sacrificing the ability of the plants to survive. Since the field is very competitive, a seemingly low price quotation will usually represent low-quality plant material or lack of adequate preparation. In either case, the total cost may be actually higher in the long run because of frequent plant replacement.

Once a contractor has been selected, the possible financial arrangements fall into only three categories. These are outright sale with maintenance and plant replacement guarantee, outright sale with no maintenance guarantee, and plant rental. In each of these methods, a detailed contract should be written with the contractor, specifically stating the obligations of both the client and the contractor. This helps ensure client satisfaction and prevents most common misunderstandings.

Outright Sale with Maintenance Guarantee

Most reputable interior landscape contractors will guarantee their maintenance performance by replacing any plant that falls below specifications. Only in the case of fire, vandalism, theft, or heating or lighting failure does the client incur any additional plant-related expense. Although the monthly maintenance fee may seen expensive, it is usually best for the client for these reasons: (1) The maintenance contractor has a financial incentive to provide high-quality material and good maintenance, since plant replacement is expensive for the contractor; (2) the client has peace of mind and no maintenance responsibilities; (3) the maintenance fee can be written off by the client as an operating expense, while plant-replacement purchase is a capital expense; and (4) when all overhead factors are taken into account, the cost is usually no higher for professional maintenance than for client maintenance.

A well-written maintenance contract is essential in this case for client satisfaction. Figure 3-73 shows a sample Everett Conklin contract that can be used as a guide in writing such contracts. It specifies the maintenance to be provided, lists the conditions under which plants will be replaced, provides a plant inventory on which the monthly fee is based, and details the obligations of both the client and the maintenance firm. Depending on the situation, any of these sections can be written to include more or less detail.

Outright Sale with No Maintenance Guarantee

Although this method of obtaining the plants has the lowest initial cost, it is also the most dangerous, since faulty maintenance provided by the client can destroy the investment and the carefully planned design. It is the recommended course of action in only two circumstances; if there are relatively few plants with simple maintenance requirements; or if the client is willing to invest the large amount of time necessary to train her or his own maintenance staff (which is likely to be ultimately unsatisfactory).

If the option of a no-maintenance contract is chosen, it is worth the small additional amount of money to pay the installing contractor to maintain the plants for a one-month period. This initial period can be used to break in the new staff, and it is usually sufficient for any unhealthy plants to become evident. The contract with the installing contractor should specify that any obviously unhealthy plants can be refused by the client either before the installation or after the month's trial period, and that the contractor will replace the refused plants.

Plant Rental

When the client wants as much of the cost as possible to be operating expense and to minimize the capital expenditure, plant rental may be the answer. Because of the difficulty in reusing planters, however, most plant suppliers will rent only the plants

EVERETT CONKLIN
AND COMPANY INC.

Seven Brook Avenue
Montvale, N. J. 07645
(201) 391-7300

INTERNATIONAL INTERIOR LANDSCAPE CONTRACTORS

The EVERETT CONKLIN Companies

INTERNATIONAL

MONTVALE
NEW JERSEY ● EAST IRVINE
CALIFORNIA ● MONTREAL, P.Q.
CANADA

Contract N° 3298

Date...

MAINTENANCE OF LIVE PLANT INVENTORY AND PLANT REPLACEMENT GUARANTEE

THE FOLLOWING PROPOSAL, WHEN SIGNED BY BOTH PARTIES, CONSTITUTES A CONTRACT:

Everett Conklin and Co., Inc. proposes to maintain and to guarantee for the duration of this Maintenance Contract all plants installed by Everett Conklin and Co., Inc. at:

Name...

Address...

....

As per the following specifications:

DURATION OF CONTRACT   This contract covers the period from...to...

LIVE PLANT INVENTORY   See pages.............................for details.

MAINTENANCE: Includes professional watering, cleaning of foliage, feeding, spraying for insect and disease control and all other items necessary for the health and appearance of Plant Inventory at regular intervals as necessary during the normal working day from 8:00 A.M. to 5:00 P.M.

GUARANTEE: In the event of deterioration of any part of the Plant Inventory during the life of this contract, such plants are to be replaced within a reasonable time with healthy plants of the same variety, size and quantity provided all conditions listed under GENERAL SPECIFICATIONS are met, at NO EXTRA CHARGE TO CUSTOMER for plants or for labor involved in the installation of replacement plants or removal of plants to be replaced.

GENERAL SPECIFICATIONS: 1.   The Live Plant Inventory on pages.............................is and shall remain the property of:

....

2.   This contract is to run for a period of one year and will automatically renew unless notified by either party of any changes at least sixty (60) days prior to expiration of current year contract. This contract may be cancelled by either party on sixty (60) days written notice providing the account is paid in full up to the date of cancellation.

3.   In the event of restrictions on use of local water for plantings, necessary water from outside sources is to be supplied by customer at no charge to Everett Conklin and Co., Inc. or to be supplied by Everett Conklin and Co., Inc. at extra cost to customer.

4.   Customer is to provide convenient water outlets, and hereby permits Everett Conklin and Co., Inc. to draw such amounts of water necessary to maintain Plant Inventory, at no cost to Everett Conklin and Co., Inc. Customer is to provide a minimum temperature at all times of 55°F. in all areas where the plants are located.

5.   Everett Conklin and Co., Inc. is not responsible for damage due to vandalism, fire, theft, acts of God, or failure of customer to provide minimum temperature, normal lighting or water, or failure of utilities such as temperature, light, water, etc., no matter what the cause.

6.   Everett Conklin and Co., Inc. is not responsible for damage due to strikes or other interruptions which restrict its access to Plant Inventory.

7.   Prices quoted do not include sales taxes at any government level.

We agree to maintain and to guarantee the Live Plant Inventory limited to initialed pages attached hereto and made a part hereof as per

the afore listed specifications for the sum of...per month, payable monthly.

EVERETT CONKLIN
AND COMPANY INC.

By...

Title...

Accepted:

By...

Title...

S/D-203

Fig. 3-73 Sample maintenance and guarantee form.

and insist on an outright sale of the planters. Often, the rental contract will give the client the option to buy at a later date, with a portion of the rental fee applied to the purchase price.

When the plants are rented, their maintenance is usually included in the rental fee. Very few firms will rent plants without such a guarantee of their proper maintenance. Nevertheless, even in this case, a detailed maintenance contract is important for client satisfaction.

BIBLIOGRAPHY

Adams, T., Ed., "Landscape Designer and Estimator's Guide," National Landscape Association, 833 Southern Bldg., Washington, D.C., 1971

American Association of Nurserymen, "American Standard for Nursery Stock," American Association of Nurserymen, Inc., 230 Southern Bldg., Washington, D.C., 1973

Boodley, James W., and **Raymond Sheldrake,** "Cornell Peat-Lite Mixes for Commercial Plant Growing," Information Bulletin No. 43, New York State College of Agriculture, Extension Service, Ithaca, N.Y., 1973

Coleman, M. Jane, *Foliage Plants for Modern Living,* Merchant's Publishing Co., Kalamazoo, Mich., 1974

Crockett, James Underwood, *Foliage House Plants,* Time-Life Books, New York, 1972

Graf, Alfred Byrd, *Exotic Plant Manual,* 1st ed. Roehrs Company, East Rutherford, N.J., 1970

Liberty Hyde Bailey Hortorium, Staff, at Cornell University, *Hortus Third,* The Macmillan Company, New York, 1976

Mott, Russell C., *The Total Book of House Plants,* Delacorte Press, New York, 1977

Nelson, William R., Jr., "Landscaping Your Home," Circular No. 858, University of Illinois College of Agriculture Cooperative Extension Service, Urbana, 1963

Pesch, Barbara, Ed., *How to Grow House Plants,* A Sunset Book, Lane Books, Menlo Park, Calif., 1970

Sunset Magazine, Editors, *Gardening in Containers,* Lane Books, Menlo Park, Calif., 1967

CHAPTER FOUR
SCULPTURE
Louis G. Redstone

This chapter is directed primarily toward architects who may wish to consider including sculpture or sculptural elements as part of a building or as part of the total environment contiguous to a building.

It would be worthwhile for the architect to become familiar with the latest trends and directions which are emanating from the federal, state, and local governments as well as from the private sector.

Contemporary art expresses itself in every phase of our living, and people in every walk of life are attuned to, and seek out, the joy and excitement which art can bring them. The contemporary forms of art are applicable to all the various elements that create a good living environment.

The favorable acceptance by the public over the past decade has spurred governmental agencies not only to continue but to broaden the policy of providing art for the people. The General Services Administration (GSA) program is expanding the range of public art by introducing new forms to include earth and lightworks and building crafts such as ornamental grills, woodwork, and decorative brickwork. The program will accelerate efforts to start art projects at an earlier point in building design. Initial building concepts will include provisions for works of art—bringing art and architecture together at the very beginning. The program will now include both existing buildings and historic landmarks.

As of July 1977, the GSA reported works of art commissioned for 56 completed federal building projects and 88 planned in varying stages of execution. The works are located throughout all the states, in large and small cities, and the allotments for the commissions range from a $750 tapestry to a $250,000 monumental painted steel sculpture. It can well be anticipated that the GSA art program will continue to expand, given a continued favorable direction by the federal government.

An added impetus for the integration of the arts was provided by Congress in September 1965 when it established the National Endowment for the Arts (NEA). The NEA allocations were to be used as matching funds for outdoor and indoor art, placed in public places, in all sections of the country that initiate requests for funds to finance their art projects.

These projects involve artists of national, regional, and local reputation as well as temporary experimental exhibitions testing the viability of public art in various situations. As beneficial and stimulating as this federal art endowment program is, it can satisfy only a very limited demand, even though many opportunities to benefit from it still remain unexplored and unused by both large and small cities. Here is where the architect's role in initiating and stimulating the use of art in the environment becomes of utmost importance.

Whether art is sponsored by the federal, state, or city agencies or by private donors, the variety of the art forms and acceptable sites is virtually unlimited. Art forms include sculpture, either freestanding or as bas-relief on interior or exterior walls of buildings; mural paintings; mosaic and brick murals; tapestries; fountains; earthworks; special landscape design; exterior lighting and street furnishings; and graphics and signage. This chapter focuses on sculpture in its many-faceted forms.

In considering the use of sculptural elements, both the owner and the architect must have a common understanding of the necessity of incorporating art as part of the entire building concept, and of budgeting an adequate amount of money for it.

There are several ways to secure an artist's services. The architect who feels sufficiently knowledgeable in the art field may commission an artist who evidently can successfully handle the assignment. Presumably, this artist has performed well in the past and is dependable. Architect and artist should meet at the very inception of the project to discuss location, size, material, scale, and cost of the commission. It is necessary that the artist submit a scale model or drawing for approval by both the architect and the owner. At this point, the conflicts of art expression and concepts are apt to come to the fore. It is here that the architect should guide the owner in reaching an understanding and acceptance of the model. Should the preliminary model be unacceptable, however, the artist may have to submit revised concepts until complete agreement is reached.

Another procedure for commissioning an artist is to invite three or four artists to submit their concepts in the form of models or sketches. In this instance, each artist is paid an agreed amount for this preliminary work. Often, there is a clear understanding that the successful competitor will credit the preliminary remuneration to the total cost of the commission. Here again, the final choice is made jointly by the architect and the owner.

Another method is to set up an art committee consisting of the architect, the owner or his or her representative, and several recognized art authorities, such as the director of a museum, the head of a university fine arts department, the dean of an architectural school, and other persons in this field who are acceptable to the architect and the owner. The procedure thereafter is similar to that already described.

I suspect that one of the reasons why architects and owners shy away from considering art for their buildings is that they generally know only a few outstanding artists whose fees are higher than their budgets allow. The fact is, however, that there are many young and talented artists in every geographical region who can be sought out to execute commissions. My own experience has shown that these young artists, once given a chance, can show competence and responsibility. In many cases, such a commission has been the first big step toward a successful art career. I am certain that this experience has been repeated in many parts of this country and elsewhere throughout the world.

Whether a new or an experienced artist is being engaged, there must always be a businesslike approach in working arrangements. The following factors need to be considered:

- Preparation of detailed specifications for the artwork, similar to specifications for the building trades.

- Guarantees by the artist of the permanency of materials used and of functional operation (as in the case of fountains).

- Definite arrangements for the installation of the artwork on the premises. (The owner or contractor must be consulted as to union requirements.)

- The time limit for completion of the project.

- Periodic visits by the architect to the artist's studio to check progress and to solve unforeseen problems.

- Provision for liability insurance by contractor and artist.

A detailed set of specifications is a very important document for a clear understanding of the proper materials to be used, of the required finishes, and of all component parts, whether mechanical, electrical, or other. Detailed and comprehensive specifications make it possible to avoid misunderstanding and friction between the parties. (A recommended contract form is included as part of this chapter.)

To protect the owner's interest, the artist should provide a written guarantee for a two-year period. The intent of this guarantee is to stimulate the artist to study the permanency of materials and, if necessary, to consult specialists in the field. This is particularly important when art work is exposed to the weather, regardless of climate. In one case for example, the adhesive for an exterior mosaic mural did not stand up in the cold of winter. A more thorough investigation of the properties of the adhesive as claimed by the manufacturer could have avoided this failure. A similar case of much greater proportions occurred in Mexico City. There, thousands of square feet of mosaic tesserae had to be completely replaced because of faulty adhesive. The problem of permanency applies to many other materials, such as marble, welded steel, aluminum, paint finishes, and plastics.

As for the installation of the art work, the artist should be responsible for the delivery of the work in good condition to the premises, but the installation itself should be handled by the general contractor's staff. Because the artist has limited contact with the various trades involved in the installation and because the general contractor has authority over all the subtrades, this procedure makes for a mutually satisfactory arrangement. Another advantage of this arrangement is that the general contractor carries liability insurance, a very important protection for the artist.

The time limit for completion of the artwork is also a very significant factor. The completion of a building project is a big event in every owner's experience. The artwork, which the owner has come to accept as a "luxury item" in the overall building costs, serves as an additional highlight in the opening festivities of the new building. Obviously, the failure to complete the work on time causes a severe letdown for owner and architect alike.

It is important for the architect to keep in touch with the artist during the entire period, but especially in the beginning, when the general character of the composition begins to take shape. At times, the artist may decide to change the concept during the development stage. Even though he or she should have freedom to develop the theme, the concept needs to be kept within the total architectural composition and scale. The architect should visit the artist's studio periodically in order to discuss the problems and, if required, to assist the artist with technical know-how.

There are two main categories of sculpture: (1) freestanding pieces, not connected with the structure and placed either inside or outside of buildings as a part of the landscape and environmental planning; this placement would include interior or public areas, such as lobbies, open or enclosed courts, public squares and gardens. And (2) sculpture in the form of bas-reliefs on interior or exterior walls of buildings, or detached two-dimensional compositions of various materials fastened to the walls.

Materials	Exterior Use	Interior Use	Permanence		Maintenance		Vandalism		Installation Cost	Material Cost	Factors to Consider
			Ext.	Int.	Ext.	Int.	Ext.	Int.			
Free standing granite	1	1	1	1	1	1	1	1	*	High	Weight: 163–177/cub. ft.
Marble	3	1	2	1	3	1	3	2	*	Medium	Weight: 131–177/cub. ft.
Alabaster	4	3	4	3	4	3	4	3	*	Medium	Weight: 131–170/cub. ft.
Limestone	2	1	3	2	3	2	3	2	*	Low	Weight: 131–170/cub. ft.
Mankato	3	2	3	2	3	2	3	2	*	Medium	Weight: 131–170/cub. ft.
Precast concrete	2	2	1	1	3	2	2	2	*	Low	Weight; 140–150/cub. ft. See illustration page 133
Concrete gunite	3	2	3	2	3	2	4	2	High	Low	
Cast bronze	1	1	1	1	2	2	3	1	High	High	Kind of patina finish See illustration page 151
Cast Aluminum	3	2	2	2	3	2	4	2	Medium	Medium	
Stainless steel	1	1	1	1	2	2	2	1	High	High	
Cast plastics	3	2	3	2	2	2	4	2	Low	Medium	
Welded steel	2	2	1	1	3	3	3	2	Low	Low	
Corten welded	1	5	1	1	2	5	2	5	Low	Low	Does not oxidize in interiors
Wood: Walnut	5	2	5	2	5	2	5	2	Medium	Medium	
Oak	5	2	5	2	5	2	5	2	Medium	Medium	
African Hardwood	5	2	3	1	3	1	4	1	High	High	
Ceramic	4	2	5	3	5	1	5	5	Medium	Medium	
Bas-reliefs: Brick	1	1	1	1	1	1	2	1	Low	Low	See illustration page 140
Stone	2	1	1	1	2	2	3	2	Medium	Medium	
Wood: Ebony	5	2	5	2	5	2	5	3	Low	High	
Mahogany	5	2	5	2	5	2	5	3	Low	Medium	
Walnut	5	2	5	2	5	2	5	3	Low	Medium	
Metal-copper enameled	3	2	3	2	3	2	4	2	High	Medium	See illustration page 144
Concrete	2	1	2	1	2	1	2	1	Low	Medium	See illustration page 143
Ceramic	5	2	5	2	5	2	5	3	Medium	High	
Sculptured tapestry	5	2	5	2	5	2	5	2	High	High	

*Varies with size & soil conditions.

Ratings: 1-Excellent;   2-Good;   3-Fair;   4-Poor;   5-Not recommended

One cannot overemphasize the importance of the adaptability of the art to the site and the building. Unless careful consideration is given to the scaled relationship of art and the site and to its placement as viewed by the pedestrian as well as from an automobile, the greatest artwork may lose the effectiveness of its "message."

Another important element in terms of achieving the most effective impact is the type of lighting used. Thorough studies should be made at the time the final model is submitted. Some of the considerations are placement of the light source, type of fixture, light spread, and light color.

In order to familiarize the architect with the extensive range of materials available for art programming, a reference table (Figure 4-1) has been compiled showing my personal evaluations of the preferred use of materials for exteriors and interiors. Also, the factors of permanence, maintenance, and vandalism are rated. It is well to mention that the last decade has brought with it new art forms that have required new techniques of executing these concepts. Materials, such as carbon steel, stainless steel, aluminum, cast fiberglass, and combinations of many of these with other metals and woods, have heretofore not been used on such a large scale. In many instances, because few artists have the fabricating facilities and skills to produce the final assembly, it may be necessary for a specialized shop to enlarge the model according to the artist's specifications. It goes without saying that the present-day artist must be competent and knowledgeable concerning the materials used and the technical requirements for assemblage. Two of the most often used art forms are detailed here in connection with their integration with architecture.

Precast Concrete Bas-Relief Panels

In order to avoid warping, these 10- to 15-ton panels have to be structurally sound as independent units. In addition, they must be designed to be lifted by crane and transported to the site for installation. Installation details must be shown on architectural drawings. It is important that only stainless steel bolts and supporting angles be used for fastening the panels into place (Figures 4-2, 4-3, and 4-4).

Fig. 4-2 Concrete bas-relief panel. *Photograph credit: J. W. Goodspeed.*

Fig. 4-3 Concrete bas-relief panel being erected. *Photograph credit: Photo Service Corporation.*

Fig. 4-4 Concrete bas-relief panel in place. *Photograph credit: Oakland Color Prints.*

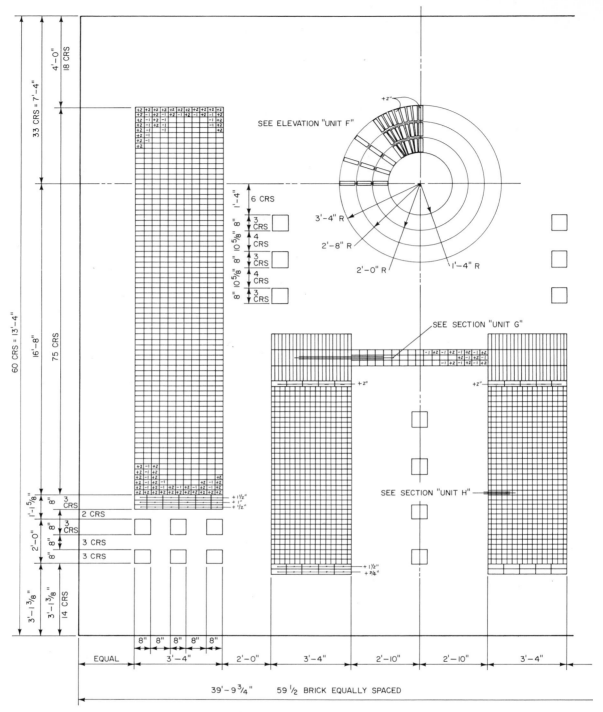

Fig. 4-5 Working drawing for brick mural.

Brick Murals

The simplest form of a brick mural is achieved by using standard-size brick. The sculptor is given the size of the wall area with a scaled drawing of the brick courses. He or she then prepares preliminary sketches of the design, based either on a given theme or an original concept. Once the design is approved, the sculptor has to fit the design within the brick coursing. Brick can be easily sawed to fit any shape required.

134

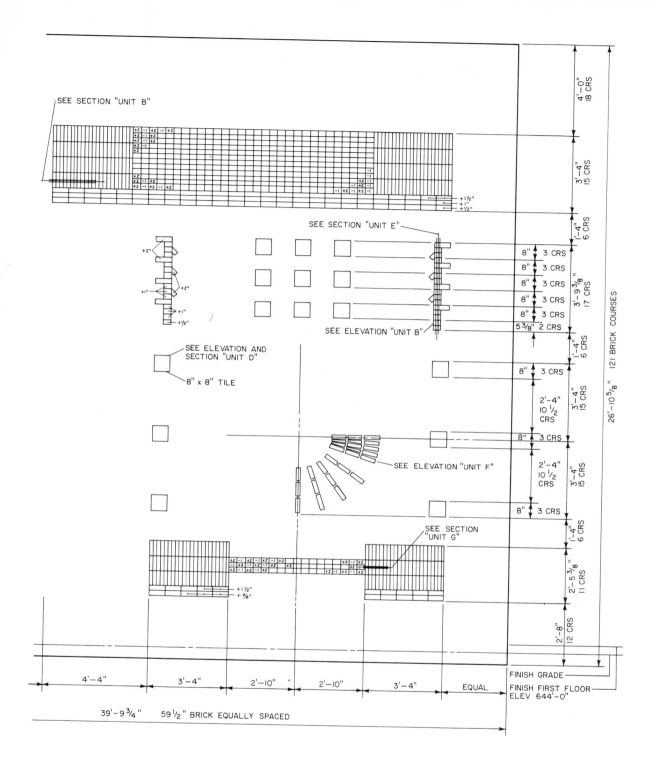

SEE SECTION "UNIT B"

SEE SECTION "UNIT E"

SEE ELEVATION "UNIT B"

SEE ELEVATION AND
SECTION "UNIT D"

8" x 8" TILE

SEE ELEVATION "UNIT F"

SEE SECTION
"UNIT G"

4'-0"
18 CRS

3'-4"
15 CRS

1'-4"
6 CRS

8" 3 CRS
8" 3 CRS
8" 3 CRS
8" 3 CRS
8" 3 CRS
5 3/8" 2 CRS

3'-9 3/8"
17 CRS

1'-4"
6 CRS

8" 3 CRS

2'-4"
10 1/2 CRS

3'-4"
15 CRS

8" 3 CRS

2'-4"
10 1/2 CRS

3'-4"
15 CRS

8" 3 CRS

1'-4"
6 CRS

2'-5 3/8"
11 CRS

2'-8"
12 CRS

26'-10 5/8"   121 BRICK COURSES

FINISH GRADE
FINISH FIRST FLOOR
ELEV 644'-0"

4'-4"   3'-4"   2'-10"   2'-10"   3'-4"   EQUAL

39'-9 3/4"   59 1/2" BRICK EQUALLY SPACED

The design must indicate the projected and the indented bricks with dimensions. These detailed designs become a part of the architectural working drawings (Figures 4-5 and 4-6). Given the capability, the architect can design the mural without other help.

A more complex brick mural design is achieved by preshaping the brick before firing. The advantage of this process is that the sculptor has more freedom to create bas-reliefs of any complex shapes. In this case, the sculptor, with the approval of the

135

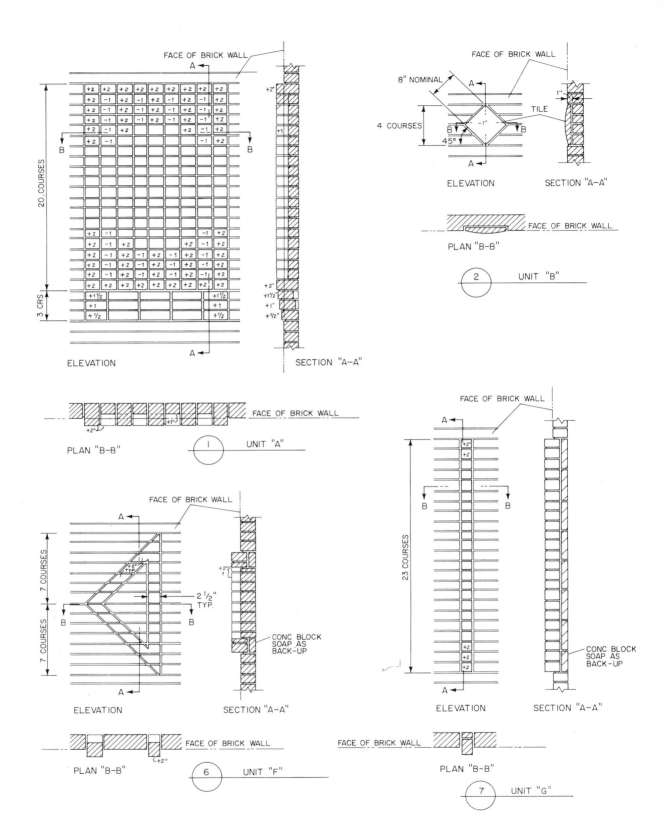

Fig. 4-6 Working drawing for brick mural.

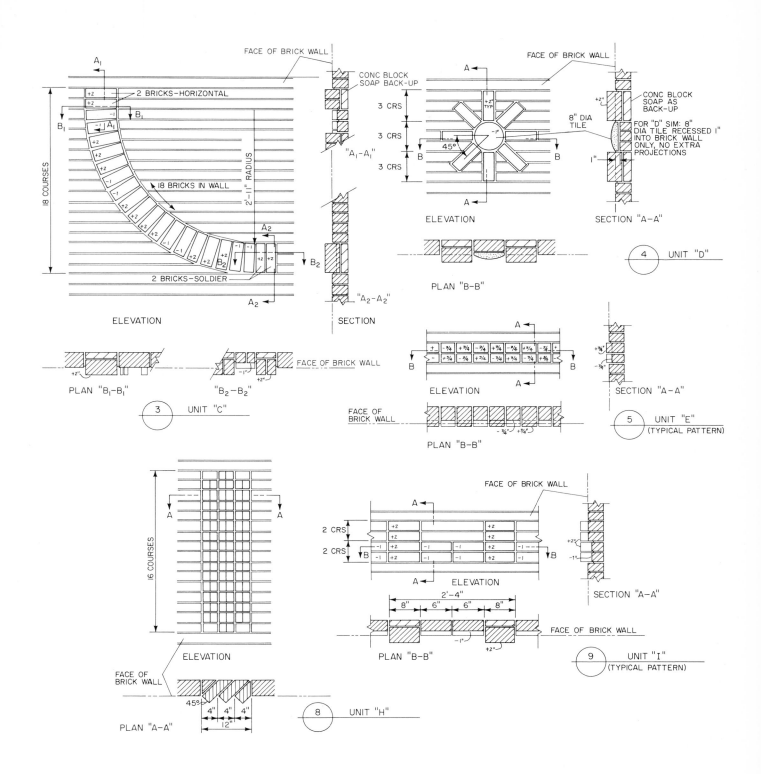

FACE OF BRICK WALL

2 BRICKS—HORIZONTAL

18 COURSES

18 BRICKS IN WALL

2'-11" RADIUS

2 BRICKS—SOLDIER

ELEVATION

PLAN "B₁-B₁"   "B₂-B₂"

③   UNIT "C"

CONC BLOCK
SOAP BACK-UP

3 CRS

3 CRS

3 CRS

"A₁-A₁"

"A₂-A₂"

SECTION

FACE OF BRICK WALL

FACE OF BRICK WALL

8" DIA TILE

45°

ELEVATION

CONC BLOCK
SOAP AS BACK-UP

FOR "D" SIM: 8"
DIA TILE RECESSED 1"
INTO BRICK WALL
ONLY, NO EXTRA
PROJECTIONS

SECTION "A-A"

PLAN "B-B"

④   UNIT "D"

ELEVATION

PLAN "B-B"

FACE OF
BRICK WALL

SECTION "A-A"

⑤   UNIT "E"
(TYPICAL PATTERN)

16 COURSES

ELEVATION

FACE OF
BRICK WALL

45°   4" 4" 4"

12"

PLAN "A-A"

⑧   UNIT "H"

FACE OF BRICK WALL

2 CRS

2 CRS

ELEVATION

2'-4"

8"   6"   6"   8"

PLAN "B-B"

SECTION "A-A"

FACE OF BRICK WALL

⑨   UNIT "I"
(TYPICAL PATTERN)

137

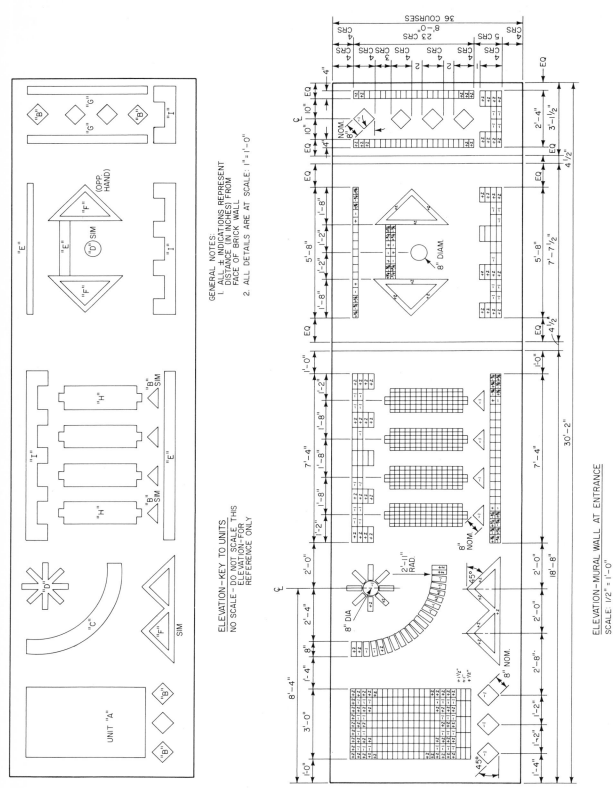

ELEVATION—KEY TO UNITS
NO SCALE—DO NOT SCALE THIS
ELEVATION—FOR
REFERENCE ONLY

GENERAL NOTES:
1. ALL ± INDICATIONS REPRESENT
   DISTANCE (IN INCHES) FROM
   FACE OF BRICK WALL.
2. ALL DETAILS ARE AT SCALE: 1" = 1'-0"

ELEVATION—MURAL WALL AT ENTRANCE
SCALE: 1/2" = 1'-0"

Fig. 4-6 (cont.)

owner and the architect, would have to shape the desired brick in the plant and be able to estimate accurately the shrinkage factor of the clay to fit into the brick coursing.

Another effective method to create brick murals is through the use of various colored glazed bricks. Here too, the bricks can be sawed in any shape, however small the shape may be.

The use of brick as a sculptural element is one of the less expensive ways to incorporate art in a building. It is also easier to include the extra expense of the brickwork in the regular budget (Figures 4-7, 4-8, and 4-9).

The following suggested contract between owner and sculptor is suitable, with adjustments, for a variety of individual conditions. In all cases, it is well to have competent legal advice before executing such an agreement.

AGREEMENT BETWEEN OWNER AND SCULPTOR

Dear _____:

This letter will serve as your authorization to proceed with the design, creation, and fabrication of an _____ titled _____, similar in design to the model submitted by you to _____. This authorization is granted upon the following express understandings:

1. The sculpture will be approximately _____ in width and _____ feet in height, proportioned according to the model and will be made of _____.

2. The sculpture will be completed about _____ and delivered and installed by you at _____ as directed upon ____ days' prior notice after _____.

3. We agree to pay you the sum of _____ ($ _____) for all the work to be performed by you hereunder. Payments to be made as follows:

Fig. 4-7 Brick mural with inlaid ceramic forms 1976. *Artist: Louis G. Redstone, Photograph credit: Balthazar Korab.*

Figs. 4-8 and 4-9 Seminario Eudista de León, Spain. Brick mural relief, 30 feet in height, 1964. *Artist: Efrem García Fernandez with José Perez Paramio. Photograph credit: Courtesy of Efrem García Fernandez.*

One-third (⅓) of the above total sum upon your execution and our receipt of a copy of this letter agreement.

One-third (⅓) of the above total sum upon final completion of the sculpture at your studio, as certified and approved by our architect.

One-third (⅓) of the above total sum will be paid thirty (30) days after installation of the sculpture at _____ as certified and approved by our architect.

4. You guarantee the sculpture against structural defects and defects in the surface finish for a period of _____ (   ) years from date of installation. All expenses and costs necessary to accomplish the repair of such defects will be paid by you.

5. This shall be deemed a personal contract, and shall not be assigned or subcontracted (other than portions of the work normally and usually performed by others) without our prior written consent. In the event of your physical incapacity or death prior to the completion of the work to be done by you hereunder, all payments then made shall be retained by you and all work performed by you to the date of your incapacity or death shall become our sole property.

6. The sculpture shall be signed, fabricated, stored, and delivered at your sole risk or loss or damage from any cause. Upon date of final payment by us, all property rights in the sculpture shall pass absolutely to us.

If this is in accord with your understanding and is acceptable to you, please execute the second copy of this letter agreement in the place indicated and return it to me for my files.

Very truly yours,

_____

(signature)_____

Agreed and Accepted:

_____ /s/

Date:_____

cc: Architect

Here are further examples (Figures 4-10 to 4-60) of the use of sculpture integrated with architecture.

Fig. 4-10 Interior court, Glazer Elementary School, Detroit. "Festival," glazed brick mural, 20 feet by 12 feet, 1966. *Artist: Narendra Patel. Photograph credit: Daniel Bartush.*

Fig. 4-11 Wonderland Center, Livonia, Michigan. Precast concrete mural wall, 120 feet by 11 feet, 1959. *Artist: Marjorie Kreilick. Photograph credit: Louis G. Redstone.*

Fig. 4-12 Sport Center, Deportivo Bahía, Mexico City. Mural of mother-of-pearl, abalone, and oyster shells, 300 feet by 15 feet, 1963. *Artist: Manuel Felguerez. Photograph credit: Manuel Felguerez.*

Figs. 4-13 and 4-14 Federal Office Building, Kansas City. Concrete mural, 1966. *Artist: Costantino Nivola. Photograph credit: Courtesy of Costantino Nivola.*

Fig. 4-15 Interior court, Wilder Branch, Detroit Public Library. Mural of fused metals on copper, 1966. *Artist: Narendra Patel. Photograph credit: Daniel Bartush.*

Fig. 4-16 Federal Building, St. Louis. "The Rivers," hammered and welded sheet-bronze fountain, 1963. *Artist: Robert Cronbach. Photograph credit: Robert Cronbach.*

Fig. 4-17 Federal Building, Grand Rapids, Michigan. "Motu," unpainted steel sculpture, 35 feet in height, 1977. *Artist: Mark DiSuvero. Photograph credit: Louis G. Redstone.*

Fig. 4-18 Grand River, Grand Rapids, Michigan. Fish-ladder sculpture, concrete, 1974. *Artist: Joe Kinnebrew. Photograph credit: Louis G. Redstone.*

Fig. 4-19 Performing Arts Theatre of Quebec, Quebec, Canada. Cement plaster wall, 1970. *Artist: Jordi Bonet. Photograph credit: Louis G. Redstone.*

**Fig. 4-20 Performing Arts Theatre of Quebec,
Quebec, Canada. Cement plaster wall, 1970.** *Artist: Jordi Bonet. Photograph credit: Louis G. Redstone.*

**Fig. 4-21 Oakland Mall Shopping Center, Troy,
Michigan. "Hippopotamus," cast terrazzo play
sculpture, 1971.** *Artist: Samuel Cashwan. Photograph
credit: Louis G. Redstone.*

**Fig. 4-22 Bendix Corporation Headquarters,
Southfield, Michigan. Black painted weathering
steel and aluminum, 1979.** *Artist: Louise Nevelson.
Photograph credit: Louis G. Redstone.*

Fig. 4-23 Bendix Corporation Headquarters, Southfield, Michigan. Black painted weathering steel and aluminum, 1979. *Artist: Louise Nevelson. Photograph credit: Louis G. Redstone.*

Fig. 4-24 Capralos residence, Aegina island, Greece. Stone sculpture grouping. *Artist: Christo Capralos. Photograph credit: Louis G. Redstone.*

Fig. 4-25 Kibbutz En Shemer, Israel. "Memorial to Two Kibbutz Members, Amnon and Hanan, Fallen 1967 War," welded steel sculpture, 1971. *Artist: Roda Reillinger. Photograph credit: Louis G. Redstone.*

Fig. 4-26 Kibbutz En Shemer, Israel. "Memorial to Two Kibbutz Members, Amnon and Hanan, Fallen 1967 War," welded steel sculpture, 1971. *Artist: Roda Reillinger. Photograph credit: Louis G. Redstone.*

Fig. 4-27 Sculpture Garden, Artists' Quarters, Safed, Israel. Large stone and concrete sculptures. *Artist: Moshe Safir. Photograph credit: Louis G. Redstone.*

Fig. 4-28 Civic Center Plaza, Grand Rapids, Michigan. "La Grande Vitesse," red painted steel stabile. *Artist: Alexander Calder. Photograph credit: Louis G. Redstone.*

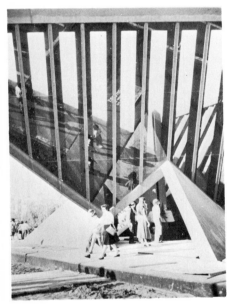

Figs. 4-29 and 4-30 City Hall Plaza, Tel Aviv, Israel. "Monument for the Holocaust," steel, glass, and concrete, 1975. *Artist: Igael Tumarkin. Photograph credit: Louis G. Redstone.*

Fig. 4-31 Zeist Insurance Company, Amsterdam. Concrete, ceramic, and pebble relief panel. *Artist: Josju Smit. Photograph credit: C. Stauthamer.*

Fig. 4-32 (*Above*) Federal Building and Courthouse, Lobby, Philadelphia. "Bicentennial Dawn," painted white wood, 1976. *Artist: Louise Nevelson. Photograph credit: Courtesy of General Services Administration.*

Fig. 4-33 Civic Center, New Orleans. "Aquamobile," cast metal, 1971. *Artist: Lin Emery. Photograph credit: Stuart Lynn.*

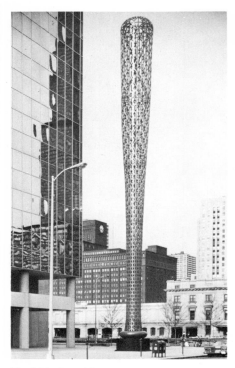

Fig. 4-34 Social Security Administration Building, Chicago. "Batcolumn," welded steel, 100 feet in height, 1977. *Artist: Claes Oldenburg. Photograph credit: Courtesy of General Services Administration.*

Fig. 4-35 Downtown public square, Wilkes-Barre, Pennsylvania. "People Seats," painted **bent steel, 1976.** *Artists: Annie Bohlin, Peter Bohlin, and William Gladish. Photograph credit: Lisa Oliner.*

Fig. 4-36 Oregon State Building, Salem. "Drapery of Memory," laminated pine wood, 7 feet in height, 1977. *Artist: Jan Zach. Photograph credit: Michael Besh.*

Fig. 4-37 Young Men's and Young Women's Hebrew Association, Toronto, Canada. "Jacob Wrestling with the Angel," bronze, 14 feet in height, 1978. *Artist: Nathan Rappoport. Photograph credit: Nir Bareket.*

Fig. 4-38 Queen's University, Kingston, Canada. "Time," aluminum and concrete, 21 feet by 125 feet, 1973. *Artist: Kosso Eloul. Photograph credit: Courtesy of Kosso Eloul.*

Fig. 4-39 Hamilton Art Museum, Hamilton, Canada. "Canadac," weathering steel, 24 feet in height, 1977. *Artist: Kosso Eloul. Photograph credit: Kosso Eloul.*

151

Figs. 4-40 and 4-41 Bateman Hall, San Francisco College, San Francisco. "Socio Sculpture Garden," concrete with inlaid mosaic, 80 feet by 30 feet, 1979. *Artist: Jacques Overhoff. Photograph credit: Jacques Overhoff.*

Fig. 4-42 Cranbrook Academy of Art, Bloomfield Hills, Michigan. "Cranbrook Dance," wooden framed passageway, 180 feet in length. *Artist: Robert Stackhouse. Photograph credit: Courtesy of Cranbrook Academy of Art.*

Fig. 4-43 Theatre for the Performing Arts, Las Vegas, Nevada. "Sorcerer's Apprentice," stainless steel and neon, 52 feet in height, 1976. *Artist: Don Snyder. Photograph credit: Don Snyder.*

Fig. 4-44 Lincoln Mall, Chicago. "Lincoln Tower," laminated wood, 40 feet in height, 1973. *Artist: Jan de Swart. Photograph credit: Jan de Swart.*

Fig. 4-45 Lakeforest Shopping Center, Gaithersburg, Maryland. Untitled, painted black steel and mirror, 1978. *Artist: Buky Schwartz. Photograph credit: Daniel Bartush.*

Fig. 4-46 Fairlane Town Center, Dearborn, Michigan. Untitled, stainless steel and brass, 1976. *Artist: Richard Lippold. Photograph credit: Daniel Bartush.*

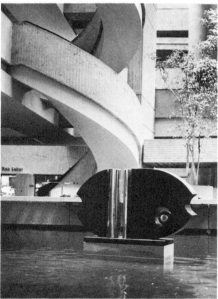

Fig. 4-47 Plaza Hotel, Renaissance Center, Detroit. "Source II," bronze, 8 feet in length, 1977. *Artist: Hanna Steibel. Photograph credit: Kermit Johnson.*

Fig. 4-48 Martin Luther King Memorial Station, Metropolitan Atlanta Rapid Transit Authority, Atlanta. "Aspirations," bronze, 46 feet in height, 1979. *Artists: William Severson and Saunders Schultz. Photograph credit: Gabriel Benzur.*

Fig. 4-49 Blue Cross Blue Shield, Chapel Hill, North Carolina. "Computer Connectors," epoxied metal, 46 feet in height, 1973. *Artists: Saunders Schultz and William Severson. Photograph credit: Gordon Schenck, Jr.*

Fig. 4-50 Bruckner Concert Hall, Linz, Austria. "Organ Fountain," 17 stainless steel columns, 1977. *Artist: Herbert Bayer. Photograph credit: Courtesy of Herbert Bayer.*

155

Fig. 4-51 President Medici Square, Rio de Janeiro. "Monument to Youth, Culture, and Sport," concrete, 60 feet in height, 1974. *Artist: Haroldo Barroso. Photograph credit: Sydney Waissman.*

Fig. 4-52 Collège d'Enseignement Secondaire, Bordeaux-Bègles, France. "Porte-Gille," stainless steel, 20 feet in length, 1972. *Artist: Dietrich Mohr. Photograph credit: Dietrich Mohr.*

Fig. 4-53 (*Opposite*) Roche S.A. Headquarters, Neuilly, France. Untitled, bronze, 5 feet in height. *Artist: Alicia Penalba. Photograph credit: Pierre Joly and Vera Cardot.*

Fig. 4-54 City of Evry, France. "La Dame du Lac," concrete, 51 feet in height, 1974. *Artist: Pierre Szekely. Photograph credit: D. Planquette.*

Fig. 4-55 Graduate School of Commerce, Lyon, France. Untitled stainless steel, 1972. *Artist: Claude Viseux. Photograph credit: Jean Biavegeaud.*

Fig. 4-56 The President's House, Jerusalem, Israel. Painted steel gates, 1971. *Artist: Bezalel Schatz. Photograph credit: Paul Gross.*

Fig. 4-57 Main town square, Redondo, Portugal. Mosaic pavement, 1971. *Artist: Eduardo Nery. Photograph credit: Eduardo Nery.*

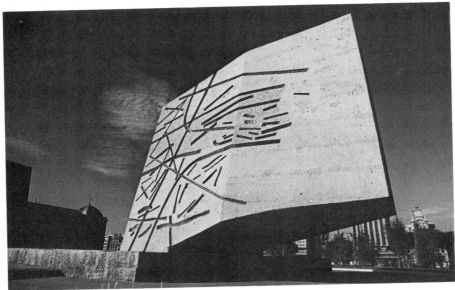

Figs. 4-58 and 4-59 Plaza de Colón, Madrid. "Monument to the Discovery of America," concrete, 1977. *Artist: Vaquero Turcios. Photograph credit: Courtesy of Vaquero Turcios.*

Fig. 4-60 Cemetery, Bottmingen, Switzerland. "Tree-stump figure," bronze, 11 feet in length, 1976. *Artist: Erwin Rehmann. Photograph credit: F. Engesser.*

CHAPTER FIVE
INTERIOR ART
Judith Selkowitz

INTRODUCTION

Until relatively recently, the use of art—paintings, prints, photographs, posters, sculpture, tapestries—has been widely neglected in the realm of commerce. Latter-day Medicis have always collected avidly for their personal use, but thought was seldom given to the logical transference to the working environment of those qualities that make art an enriching addition to residential settings.

This attitude has changed dramatically, and the impact on the art world has been significant. Indeed, the most dynamic force to enter the fine art market in recent years has been the large multinational corporation.

Time was, a decade or two ago, when companies that had selected the finest sources for professional services—a McKinsey for management consulting, an Ogilvy & Mather for advertising, or a Coopers & Lybrand for accounting—would rely on the company purchasing agent or the wife of the president to acquire artwork for corporate offices. The result was usually a predictable collection of portraits of company founders along with reproductions of well-known landscape paintings, highlighted occasionally by show cases of bowling trophies and medals from the local chamber of commerce.

Happily, those days appear to have passed. Following the lead of progressive companies such as Citibank and IBM, the alert company of today has acknowledged the need for a systematic program of art acquisition. In the 1980s, corporate art programs, even among small companies, can be quite comprehensive and can extend well beyond the corporate headquarters to regional offices and even to manufacturing and service facilities.

WHY USE ART?

But why even consider using art in the first place? What justification can there be for furnishing interior spaces with works of art? With so many aspects of business clamoring for corporate funds, why bother?

Fig. 5-1 Roy Lichtenstein, three silk-screen prints. *Photograph credit: Gil Amiaga.*

The most obvious reason is to decorate the spaces in which a company transacts its business. Art is enjoyable, and its presence makes being in a space a much more pleasant experience. And art lends warmth and a secure feeling to what can sometimes be a cold, impersonal, and even forbidding and intimidating world.

But beyond that, an art collection makes a statement that a company has arrived—that it has achieved a status permitting it to go beyond the limits of its commercial endeavors to consider the more timeless aspects of human needs and strivings.

Equally important, as hard-headed business people, corporate executives have discovered that a truly fine art collection is an asset whose value is likely to appreciate over time.

When art is added to the building program, the role of the interior architect is extended beyond the traditional area of creating space and is expanded to encompass the broader psychological territory that results from the use of fine-quality art in a carefully planned environment. This is an adventurous added dimension for the interior planner, one that offers the pertinence and scope to match the opportunities that the building architects have been employing and enjoying for years.

For many years there has been a strong relationship between modern architecture and fine art, but until recently it was almost exclusively the domain of exterior planning. A creative communication between artist and architect is already firmly established, with many leading architects working with artists to make specially commissioned works—principally sculpture—a part of the overall architectural design. (See Chapter 4, *Sculpture,* in this book, as well as *Public Art: New Directions* by Louis G. Redstone, McGraw-Hill, 1980.)

That communication has now been extended to include those who design the interiors of buildings. This long-overdue exchange has resulted in a new and stimulating relationship that has earned the support of government, which spends millions of dollars on art for use in federal, state, and municipal structures. This spending, together with that of corporations both large and small, has yielded a patronage of fine art on an unprecedentedly large scale. With this development, art has found a new audience—not the small, select groups of the past, but a mass audience com-

Fig. 5-2 Kenzo Okada, painting, oil on canvas.
Photograph credit: Gil Amiaga.

posed of the people who are using the work environments where the art is being placed.

Many theories have been advanced to explain this phenomenon, but theories are not the business of art: vitality is. And it is this vitality that the architect is experiencing by maximizing the full potential of commercial space planning. From the Bauhaus onward, the view has been widely held that no integration of architecture and people is complete if the equation does not include the human mind, and art is the tangible expression of this mind. The ability to select and place works of art that best demonstrate this expressive perspective is part of the architect's task.

Largely as a result of the increasing impact of exterior art, architects and corporate management have discovered the importance of the proper display of a collection of interior art. Priority is now being given to this consideration, as in the case of the Chesebrough-Ponds collection in Greenwich (Figure 5-1) and that of Combustion Engineering in Stamford (Figure 5-2), both in Connecticut.

"To the world at large, the architect may seem closer to a plumber than a poet," says Ada Louise Huxtable, architecture critic for *The New York Times*. "He deals with the business of getting things built, which is a bottom-line reality." As a means of bridging the gap between the nuts-and-bolts aspects of architecture's functionalism and the philosophical poetry of the architect's design intent, the placement of artwork within the completed space combines the two poles of intent. The art lends warmth to the interior and humanizes it without intruding on the functioning of the space or altering the "bottom-line reality" of the architecture.

From the client's point of view, the most important reason for considering artwork is a personalization of the space. By the very nature of the commercial or industrial space, an austere atmosphere usually prevails. Studies have shown that by diminishing the impact of this atmosphere, morale and productivity can be improved. Art, after all, is enjoyable. It makes the place where people spend many working hours attractive and pleasant.

The John Deere Corporation in Moline, Illinois (Figure 5-3), found that an art collection in its facility not only increased its employees' satisfaction, but made them so enthusiastic about their environment that they invited relatives and friends to view

Fig. 5-3 Henry Moore, bronze sculpture "Hill Arches," 1974. *Photograph credit: Courtesy John Deere Corporation.*

the collection. This positive public image has been a very important reason why a planned collection has been so appealing to so many companies. By giving consideration to the enhancement of the working environment, the status of the company in turn is greatly enhanced.

The most effective time to include art acquisition in the interior plan is at the initial conceptualizing and budgeting stages. Since art is not merely an extra decoration, and since its intelligent use can be the catalyst that brings all the elements of a project into harmony, the evaluation of its cost should be an essential ingredient of even the most preliminary of budget estimates. The monetary contribution to the budget of the artwork component can range from very little to a very substantial sum, depending on the client's sophistication and commitment. Regardless of the size of the investment in art, its inclusion in the initial planning means that the overall design concept can be well coordinated, ensuring the achievement of the desired pervasive atmosphere.

The sorry fact was, and still is, however, that many companies that have a fairly accurate projection of their expenditures for paper clips in 1987 do not have the vaguest idea of the value of the art they own in 1981. Most people are unfamiliar with art prices, whether they be for posters, original prints, or paintings and other major works. One of the reasons business executives put nothing on their company's walls is that they don't know what to use, where to get it, and how much the actual artwork should cost. Too often, otherwise progressive companies that give careful thought to most aspects of their corporate image are content to pepper their offices with haphazard prints in lieu of taking a thoughtful approach to the acquisition and development of a corporate collection.

But the tide is turning, and is turning fast. With the Chase Manhattans, the Citibanks, the Xeroxes and IBMs, a new policy of art acquisition has been initiated. Today, these multibillion-dollar giants are being joined by many other large-, medium-, and even small-sized companies that are committed to planned programs to incorporate art within their facilities. What may have started as a decorative touch for the president's office has evolved into an aesthetic and financial bonanza for all concerned with the company's well-being.

The development of significant corporate collections began with the steps taken by Chase Manhattan Bank, under the aegis of its chairman, David Rockefeller, in 1959. Continually enlarged since then, the Chase collection now includes work from many countries and several centuries, although it is largely contemporary American art, and is one of the finest corporate collections in existence today. Successful not only from an investment point of view, the artwork has had an enormous effect on the morale of the employees at Chase, who now work in an aesthetically attuned environment (Figures 5-4 and 5-5).

Many other progressive companies are following this lead, acknowledging the need for a systematic art program. The programs developed by these firms vary widely in size, but common to all is a carefully drawn plan for integrating interior art with interior architecture to achieve a mutually complementary and aesthetically pleasing atmosphere.

WHAT IS ART?

A definition of art means one thing to a customs inspector seeking to determine whether import duty must be paid on an object, and something entirely different to

Fig. 5-4 One Chase Manhattan Plaza, Reception area; Adolph Gottlieb, oil on canvas, "Turbulence," 1964; Deborah de Moulpied, plastic, "Form No. 6," 1960 (on coffee table). *Photograph credit: Jan Jachniewicz, courtesy Chase Manhattan Bank.*

Fig. 5-5 One Chase Manhattan Plaza, 17th floor office; Gary Stephan, oil and casein on linen, "Alkahest A," 1973; Salvatore Romano, aluminum, "Empire," 1973. *Photograph credit: Raymond Juschkus, courtesy Chase Manhattan Bank.*

Fig. 5-6   Robert Goodnough, acrylic on canvas.

Fig. 5-7   Thomas Doughty, oil on canvas. *Courtesy of Hirschl & Adler Galleries.*

Fig. 5-8   Fernando Maza, oil on canvas.

a scholar preparing a doctoral dissertation. But for our purposes we will seek to define the types of art that are suitable for interior spaces and that are likely to be considered by those responsible for their selection.

Paintings

Paintings are generally characterized in two ways—by time and by subject. Contemporary or twentieth century and pre-1900 are the two primary groups of chronometric division. The two main subject types are representational and abstract. Naturally, there are almost limitless subdivisions of these groupings, and almost all of them can be considered for inclusion in a corporate art collection.

Oil on canvas is the most widely used medium for paintings, although acrylic paint on canvas is also common, especially among contemporary works. Other grounds may be encountered, such as wood, masonite, plastic, metal, or treated cardboard (Figures 5-6, 5-7, and 5-8).

Works on Paper

The largest number of works of art likely to become part of a corporate art collection are those produced on paper. They include watercolors, drawings, posters, and prints. The first two are represented by unique examples, while the categories of posters and prints are almost always multiples.

Watercolors are usually moderate in size, as are drawings, seldom exceeding 4 feet in any direction. There are exceptions, as with any human endeavor, but watercolors and drawings are, more likely than not, representational in form (Figures 5-9 and 5-10).

Posters tend to be larger than prints and are usually produced by processes that are conducive to mechanization. They are most often printed by offset, lithographic, or silk-screen methods and are produced in very large press runs. While special limited poster editions are sometimes made, and while these may even be hand-signed by the artist, they are usually created in connection with an unsigned and unlimited production run.

A print may be a mechanical reproduction of another work of art (a type of print with which we are not concerned), or it may be an "original print." The artist's intention to create an original print is the key to the "originality" of the finished work. For example, if a painter first creates a watercolor and then has it copied by woodcut, the result is not an original but merely a reproduction. However, if the artist has created the master image in or upon the plate, stone, woodblock, or other material for the express purpose of creating the print, the work satisfies an essential part of the definition of an original print.

Once the artist has created the master image, the prints must be made from that master by the artist or in accordance with his or her instructions. The finished prints must then be approved by the artist. The total number of prints made from the original master is called an edition. The number may appear on the print with the individual print number in the form of a fraction, such as ⁵⁄₂₅, meaning that the edition consisted of 25 examples of which this is number 5. Prints need not be numbered to be "original" nor need they be individually signed by the artist. If intended for use with a written text, they are not likely to be numbered or signed, and may be produced in very large editions.

There are four major techniques for making original prints: relief processes, incised processes, lithography, and stencil processes (Figures 5-11 through 5-14).

Relief processes In a relief process, portions of a flat plate are cut away, and the image or design is printed with the parts of the plate that remain. One of the most common forms of the relief process results in a woodcut. Here, the plate is made by cutting into the broad face of a plank of wood, usually with a knife. A wood engraving is similar, but the block is made up of pieces of end-grain, extremely hard wood. This kind of block is hard and dense, enabling the artist to engrave (rather than cut) a much finer line than is possible on the softer plank surface used for woodcuts. Other materials, such as linoleum, lucite, or plaster, can be used (Figure 5-15). Relief-process plates can also be made in reverse by building up the areas that are to provide the printing surface. This is most often done with cardboard or paper cuts.

Incised processes The principle of incised or intaglio printing is exactly the opposite of relief printing. While in relief printing it is the remaining surface of the plate that prints, in the intaglio process the surface is wiped clean and the part of the plate that has been incised carries the ink and forms the image (Figure 5-16). These incisions are grooves, furrows, or indentations lower than the surface of the plate. Intaglio plates are most often made of copper, although steel, zinc, aluminum, and lucite are also used. These are several distinct types of the intaglio process.

Engraving The design is cut into the plate by pushing a sharp tool, called a burin, across the plate, causing sharp-edged furrows to be formed. The burin cuts a thin ribbon of material away from the plate, which is removed as the work progresses.

Drypoint The sunken lines are produced by pulling diamond-hard tools directly across the plate. The depth of the line is controlled by the artist's muscle and experience. This method of cutting produces a ridge along the incisions, called a burr. It gives the drypoint line the characteristically soft, velvety appearance absent in the clean-edged lines of an engraving.

Etching A metal plate is first coated with an acid-resistant material called a ground. The artist draws the design on the ground with a sharp-pointed instrument. The instrument removes the ground, exposing the metal plate. The plate is then put into an acid bath and the parts of the plate unprotected by the ground are etched away, leaving the sunken line that is to receive the ink. Before the plate is printed, the ground is chemically cleaned off. Then the plate is inked. The ink settles into the sunken areas and the surface of the plate is wiped clean. The plate, in contact with

Fig. 5-9 Tony Palladino, watercolor, "Olive Oil."

Fig. 5-10 Thomas Anschutz, pastel, "Portrait of Helen Thurlow." *Courtesy of Hirschl & Adler Galleries.*

Fig. 5-11 Woodcut: T. Davies, "New York Stock Exchange."

Fig. 5-12 Etching: Leonard Baskin, "Thistle."

Fig. 5-13 Lithograph: Jacob Landau, "Love What?" 1970.

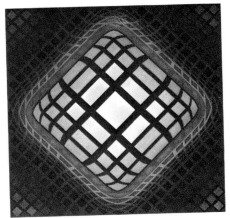

Fig. 5-14 Silk-screen: Victor Vasarely.

Fig. 5-15 Diagram of a relief-process printing plate. *Courtesy Chartcom, Inc.*

Fig. 5-16 Diagram of an incised-process printing plate. *Courtesy Chartcom, Inc.*

a sheet of dampened paper, is passed through a roller press and the paper is forced into the sunken areas to receive the ink. The design that was originally cut into the ground with the sharp instrument now appears as a printed design on the paper.

Aquatint A copper plate is protected by a porous ground that is semi–acid-resistant. The areas that are to remain unprinted (such as a white background) are then coated with a second ground that is completely acid-resisting. The plate is then put repeatedly into acid baths where it is etched to differing depths. The final effect is an image on a finely pebbled background (imparted by the porous ground). Aquatint is usually used in conjunction with line etching.

Lithography The image that the artist wants to print is drawn with a grease crayon or a specially formulated greaselike ink on a flat stone or a specially prepared metal plate. The stone or plate is then moistened. The water adheres to the clean surface in an even film, but it runs off the greased surface. During the printing process, the ink clings to the greased areas but not to the moistened ones. After the image has been printed, the greased area remains on the stone, and the process of moistening, inking, and printing can be repeated.

Stencil processes The stencil process has been used for a wide variety of applications. The basic principle calls for a stencil of thin material to have cutout portions creating the design. When ink is spread over the top surface of the stencil, only the cutout areas permit the ink to pass, and thus the design is transferred to the paper beneath the stencil. The most modern form of the stencil process produces a serigraph, or a silk-screen print. In this process, the artist prepares a tightly stretched screen, usually of silk, and blocks out areas not to be printed by filling in the mesh of the screen with a varnishlike substance. Paper is placed beneath the screen and ink forced through those areas of the mesh that have not been blocked out.

Sculpture

Sculpture, when used in interior spaces, may be purely decorative, or it may be used to define and shape space. It may range in size from small table-top pieces to very large projects that may be considered to be integral with the interior architecture. Virtually any medium used by a sculptor can be suitable for interior sculpture as long as the building structure is capable of carrying the load. If the sculpture is especially large, an access route to the place of final installation must be considered. Since sculpture is usually three-dimensional, it consumes more space than other forms of interior art. Its use should therefore be considered early in the planning so that it can be appropriately integrated with the other space-consuming elements of the project (Figures 5-17, 5-18, and 5-19).

Photography

Owing in large part to the pioneering efforts of the Museum of Modern Art in New York City, photography is now considered a fine art. Photographs are produced in limited editions, numbered and signed, and are sold at appropriate prices. The use of such an art form should receive consideration in planning an interior art program. Limited edition photographs of this sort are usually not larger than 16 by 20 inches (Figures 5-20, 5-21, and 5-22). Larger images can be made, however, and photo-murals, covering an entire wall or even a complete room, are not only possible but are being used with increasing frequency (Figures 5-23 and 5-24). Detailed informa-

Fig. 5-17   Joseph McDonnell, sheet brass, "Bandiere IV."

Fig. 5-18 Nineteenth-century weathervanes.
Photograph credit: Gil Amiaga, courtesy of Combustion Engineering.

Fig. 5-19 Roy Gusso, stainless steel, "Two Forms," 1976. *Photograph credit: Gil Amiaga, courtesy of Combustion Engineering.*

Fig. 5-20 "Woman on Rock," original photograph. *Photograph credit: Alexandre Georges.*

Fig. 5-21 "Brooklyn Bridge," original photograph. *Photograph credit: Gil Amiaga.*

Fig. 5-22 Berkey K&L Photographic Gallery.

Fig. 5-23 Custom photomural for Pizza Inn, Austin, Texas. *Courtesy Meisel Photographic Design Division.*

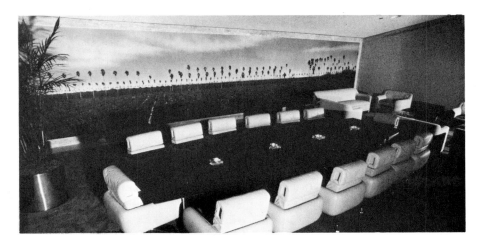

Fig. 5-24 Custom photomural for McAllen State Bank, McAllen, Texas. *Photograph credit: Ruffin Cooper, Jr.*

**Fig. 5-25   Isamu Noguchi, "Study for an Absent
Sculpture," Aubusson tapestry, 6 feet by 8 feet.**
*Credit: Courtesy of Modern Master Tapestries, photo-
graph by Al Mozell.*

tion concerning photomurals and other forms of photographic reproduction may be
obtained from:

> Modernage Custom Darkrooms
> 319 East 44th Street
> New York 10017

> Meisel Photographic Design Division
> Post Office Box 222002
> Dallas, Texas 75222

> Berkey K&L Custom Services
> 222 East 44th Street
> New York 10017

Tapestries

Tapestries may be said to bridge the distance between prints or paintings and sculpture since they offer strongly tactile qualities in addition to their visual ones.

They are basically of two types. The first is two-dimensional, with texture. Examples of this type are the woven tapestries done in the Aubusson method, and the
tufted pile tapestries that are made much like rugs and carpets (Figures 5-25 and 5-
26). The other types comprise a wide variety of fiber works that may be woven,
tufted, tied, or otherwise constructed (Figures 5-27 and 5-28).

Tapestries lend a special warmth and an added dimension to interior spaces, but
their maintenance and cleaning require special care. Each work should be individually considered and appropriate maintenance methods developed.

Diversity

In developing and coordinating a corporate art collection, it is desirable to use works
created in different media in order to foster diversity and to ensure that the collection

will be pleasing to people of various tastes and sensibilities. By using different types of art—paintings, prints, photographs, sculpture, tapestries, posters, murals (Figures 5-29, 5-30, and 5-31)—the experience of enjoying the collection will be a constantly refreshing one

WHERE TO BUY ART

Understanding the diversity of art suitable for a corporate art program or for a modest collection of art for a small project is important, but an equally practical need is a knowledge of where to buy art and how to acquire it. Several options are available.

Auctions

Purchasing art at auction is becoming much more widely practiced since the major auction houses have increased their advertising and public relations efforts and have

Fig. 5-26 Michele Lester, tapestry. *Courtesy of Cameron Iron Works, Houston, Texas.*

Fig. 5-27 Wioska, wall hanging. *Photograph credit: Bevan Davies, courtesy of the Dime Savings Bank, New York City.*

Fig. 5-28 Navajo rug. *Photograph credit: Gil Amiaga, courtesy of Combustion Engineering.*

Fig. 5-29 John Loring, mural painted in place.
Photograph credit: Tom Crane, courtesy of Prudential Insurance Company.

Fig. 5-30 Neil Welliver, oil on canvas. *Courtesy of Cameron Iron Works, Houston, Texas.*

Fig. 5-31 Early French advertising poster.

gone to great pains to tell the public that they sell far more modestly priced items than might be indicated by the media reports of the spectacular sales. Theoretically, the price an item fetches at auction is supposed to be its fair market value, and is generally said to be midway between so-called wholesale and retail. As a practical matter, this is not always the case, since many factors and pressures combine to produce the bid that successfully buys the item.

The rule of caveat emptor prevails at an auction, requiring a would-be bidder to be very careful before signaling the auctioneer. A knowledgeable evaluation must be

174

made of each potential purchase, and a maximum bid limit must be set. With advance preparation and a measure of luck, an advantageous purchase can be made.

Assembling an art collection at auction, however, can be a very time-consuming process. One must wait until suitable works present themselves and the items must then be inspected and evaluated prior to the sale. It is not necessary to be present at an auction in order to bid, but settlement must be made very shortly after the close of the auction. Niceties of billing procedures are seldom encountered, and there is little recourse if a work proves unsatisfactory. Using auctions is not the easiest route to travel in acquiring art, but for a knowledgeable buyer, auctions can be a useful source of supply (Figure 5-32).

Galleries

A gallery is a store in which a variety of items are offered for sale. Comparisons can be made and prices can often be negotiated. Special purchase arrangements and billing procedures can be set up, framing services can usually be obtained, and return or repurchase privileges are not uncommon. However, galleries are run by professionals who are alert to values and aware of prices. This expertise can be a two-edged sword, so, as when purchasing at auction, acquisition of knowledge about the art to be bought is important if one is to buy with intelligence and prudence.

There are two kinds of gallery—cooperative and commercial. Cooperative galleries are run for the benefit of the artists whose work is carried. Some of them are small-scale, informal joint ventures of several artists who set them up as salesrooms for their work. Others are highly sophisticated, large-scale businesses, but, large or small, cooperative galleries return all profits solely to the artists. While this factor may be appealing, the inherent limitations of most cooperative galleries are obvious. The number of artists they represent is likely to be small, and they can be expected to handle most of the output of those artists, whether it be good or bad. Unless the gallery is large and quite successful, the likelihood is slight that the staff will be especially well-trained or experienced in the business of art. Cooperative galleries, however, provide access to young or unproven artists whose work might otherwise be very difficult to obtain. Prices may be expected to be somewhat less than at commerical galleries, and they are more likely to be subject to negotiation.

A commercial gallery is run for the primary consideration of realizing a profit for the gallery owner, who quite logically will use his or her knowledge of art, artists, and the market to increase and enhance that profit. Consequently, a commercial gallery most probably carries items that have a good chance of being sold. While this predilection may preclude finding especially unusual things, it also gives some measure of assurance that a gross mistake is not apt to be made. While some galleries will offer whatever they can obtain, others are specialists, carrying the works of only a specified list of artists. And some galleries are the exclusive agents for the work of certain artists. These situations have their pros and cons: When a gallery specializes, it is more likely to be particularly knowledgeable about the work of the artists it has chosen to carry. It also facilitates the location of particular desired items. On the other hand, a gallery that is an exclusive agent is in a position to set the market for its own artists, a factor that may result in higher prices than the quality of the work justifies.

Galleries, whether cooperative or commercial, are in the business of selling art. As with any other business, to be successful, a gallery must know its market, must

Fig. 5-32 Christie's auction rooms, New York.
Photograph credit: Helaine Messer.

Fig. 5-33   Leo Castelli Gallery, SoHo, New York.
Photograph credit: Bevan Davies.

Fig. 5-34   Hirschl & Adler Galleries, New York.
Courtesy of Hirschl & Adler Galleries.

provide fair value, and must offer the necessary ancillary services, such as arranging suitable financial terms, appropriate insurance and shipping, and installation when required. Galleries, since they are reflections of their owners, often have strong personalities as well as specialties. Some offer established artists and secure value, while others present lesser-known talents and a greater financial risk. Although some gallery directors foster an atmosphere of friendly openness and a willingness to educate prospective customers, others carefully cultivate an aura of elitism, apparently shunning those outside the pale. For a relationship with an art gallery to be a successful one, the needs and personality of the purchaser should be matched with those of the gallery; anything less will be detrimental to both sides (Figures 5-33 and 5-34.)

Artists

Buying directly from the artist can be an efficient, generally less expensive, method of securing art. An artist whose work is admired may not have a piece of the right color or size, and a piece to exact specifications can be commissioned. However, in commissioning works to order, it is important to know in advance about the artist's work habits so as to ensure that the work will be finished when promised, and that it will be in compliance with the original request. Sometimes dealing directly with the artist can be difficult, since by nature the artist is a creator rather than a business person. But knowing in advance that the niceties of packing, shipping, insurance, and framing are very often not to be part of the deal, a satisfactory arrangement can be made. Perhaps the most difficult thing about purchasing art in this manner is locating a suitable artist from whom to buy. Such people are not usually listed in the yellow pages. It is generally only through word of mouth that visits can be arranged and purchases made. The more successful artists are more apt to have working arrangements with established galleries, so direct purchases are usually made only from relatively unknown creators. For this reason, it is essential to have an educated eye and a good knowledge of the art market if one is to avoid buying inappropriate creations (Figure 5-35).

Other Sources

Museums with lending services provide a useful source of art, especially since the works can be rented with an option to purchase if they prove satisfactory. Insurance, shipping, and framing are usually included, and installation service is sometimes provided.

Private dealers may also be helpful, but they are at least as difficult to locate as suitable artists for direct purchase. A private dealer is one who does not maintain a regular gallery open to the public, but, rather, handles specific assignments or sells from his or her own personal and limited stock. A knowledgeable private dealer can be an invaluable source for specific works, since such a person often has the necessary contacts to locate and obtain art that would otherwise be unknown.

Purchasing artworks from private collections can yield fine items at near wholesale prices, *if* one can locate the collection that includes the sort of work one is looking for, *if* one can persuade the owner to sell, *if* one is aware of market values and is a good negotiator, and *if* one is willing to assume all risks. A private collection can be a source of good value, but the work involved in securing that value may be overwhelming.

Works of art may also be obtained from or through a professional art consultant. Art consultants range from young students with a basic knowledge of the field, who, for a fee, will guide clients through the art galleries and help them select items, to highly trained individuals with extensive experience in assembling art collections. Such consultants frequently represent full-service organizations providing all the elements necessary to the creation of a corporate art program, and often buy and resell art for their own accounts.

USING A CONSULTANT

The methods of operation of consultants vary, but most act as a combination adviser, dealer, gallery, framer, and installer—coordinating all the elements as needed. A consultant provides a liaison with other sources of supply to locate specific works of art, and can supply guidance for commissioning major pieces. An area in which consultants may prove to be most valuable is in the actual purchase of the art, since

Fig. 5-35 Robert Dash at Sagaponack, New York, in 1979.

they will know the intricacies of the art market and will be alert to the reality that value is reflected in *both* quality and price. There is a strong probability, when one uses an experienced consultant, that the works selected will be of enduring financial and aesthetic value.

Since good consultants do not promote particular artists, they can concentrate on finding the most appropriate art possible, working as needed with artists, dealers, galleries, museums, auction houses, and publishers. Most consultants maintain communication with their counterparts in other cities and are prepared to work with them in locating desired artworks in distant locations. This kind of contact is especially important for programs that may stress a wide-ranging approach to art in order to parallel the broad geographic base of the corporate client.

The professional consultant provides the client with a qualified art background to assure the acquisition of works of quality, with a knowledge of the market and a range of connections with sources of supply that enable purchases to be made at competitive prices, and with an organization that can provide all the peripheral services needed, whether for a single office space, an entire building, or a multistructure complex.

While an experienced art consultant is unlikely to impose his or her personal taste on a client, the relationship is such a close one that the respective personalities of consultant and client should be reasonably harmonious if the collaboration is to be successful. A prospective consultant should be selected with care, since he or she will be required to develop a full understanding of the client and the client's company and to work with sensitivity regarding the company's history, operations, and general personality. The consultant will make repeated visits to the company's facilities, will interview many of its pivotal people, and will often engage in extensive research to develop a rapport and empathy with the feelings and aspirations of the company and the people who guide it. If the consultant and the company are not on the same wavelength, these efforts will be largely wasted.

Consideration not only of the consultant's personality, but also of his or her ability to perform at a professional level, is essential. Since the profession is still relatively

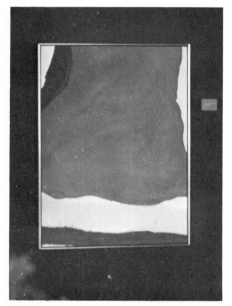

Fig. 5-36 Helen Frankenthaler, acrylic on canvas, 1965. *Photograph credit: Gil Amiaga.*

Fig. 5-37 Ben Shahn, etching. *Photograph credit: Gil Amiaga.*

Fig. 5-38 Photographs by Brassaï and Berenice Abbott. *Photograph credit: Gil Amiaga.*

new, standards vary widely, and no trade organization exists to offer recommendations. However, if requirements and standards are first established, and prospective consultants are interviewed and their past projects compared, it is not difficult to find a consultant who is creative, competent, and attuned to the needs and personality of the interviewing client. By talking with architects, interior designers, and, most important, with companies that have assembled well-coordinated art programs, recommendations for a reputable consultant may be obtained.

CASE STUDY

A good example of a typical consulting service in operation may be found in a brief report of the approach taken by Judith Selkowitz, Fine Art, Inc., with a major art program for Chesebrough-Ponds.

Fig. 5-39 Guatemalan embroidery.

We approached the company in 1975 and suggested they examine the feasibility of an art program for their headquarters building. They were responsive to the idea and commissioned us to conduct a preliminary study in which we inventoried and examined all of their spaces—executive offices, lower level working areas, reception rooms, meeting rooms, corridors, service spaces, malls, and approaches. We studied all of the occupied floors and recorded the usage patterns of the spaces. To augment our notes, we took appropriate photographs of the areas under study, both empty and as normally occupied. We interviewed the company's management to get a thorough grounding in the image of the company, its philosophy and personality. We established criteria and direction for the proposed collection as well as a budget and a set of priorities for the various spaces.

From this basic research we were able to develop a plan which called for the initial use of major works of art only in the three reception areas, the cafeteria, and the executive suite. The remainder of the building was to be provided with suitable, but less important, art. We presented a range of budget alternatives, differentiated primarily by the significance and reputations of the specific artists. For example, one of our first recommendations called for a major Helen Frankenthaler painting and an important Ben Shahn print for the executive floor (Figures 5-36 and 5-37). A variety of media was suggested, and for a less pivotal space in the executive area we proposed photographs by Brassaï and Berenice Abbott (Figure 5-38.)

To reinforce the increasingly international image of the company, we felt it was important to employ art from around the world. To this end we suggested three brightly colored embroideries from Guatemala for the third floor reception space while a Kenzo Okada painting was recommended for an open area on the executive floor (Figures 5-39 and 5-40).

As part of the process of developing the collection, the client, in this case the Chief Executive Officer, was presented with a range of alternative directions the program might take, and was given a series of introductions to the more prominent galleries in New York City. In the process of acquiring a Barbara Hepworth sculpture (Figure 5-41) the client also visited a number of sculptors at work in their studios to observe their techniques in action.

The next step was to "test drive" the recommendations—that is, to place the art in the space for a trial period to determine suitability and acceptance. Artworks were positioned in various places for several weeks at a time, and employee and visitor reaction was elicited. From this sort of testing, the best space for permanent installation could be determined and it could be evaluated to see if it would "wear" well.

For the main entrance lobby a major tapestry was commissioned from Helena Hernmark in Sweden. This important work took a full year to complete and required

Fig. 5-40 Kenzo Okada, oil on canvas. *Photograph credit: Gil Amiaga.*

Fig. 5-41 Barbara Hepworth, sculpture. *Photograph credit: Gil Amiaga.*

considerable contact among the artist, the client, and the consultant. The result was an impressive work that is much admired by both employees and visitors to the building (Figure 5-42).

Following the installation of art in the major spaces of the Chesebrough-Ponds offices, works were placed in the subsidiary spaces, and the collection has now been extended to the research and development facility and to the other operating divisions (Figures 5-43, 5-44, and 5-45).

DEVELOPING A PROGRAM

Attitude and Approach

The most essential part of developing an art program is the determination at the outset of what goals the client wants to achieve and how he or she would like to reach them. It is usually essential to know right from the beginning whether the client wants to purchase works created only by established, well-known names or is more adventuresome and willing to take risks. Whether the program should establish the client as a significant patron of the arts or should merely serve to enhance the working environment of the client's place of business will certainly have an effect on the nature of the specific works purchased.

Fig. 5-42 Helena Hernmark, tapestry. *Photograph credit: Gil Amiaga.*

Assessing the Client

Equally important is the personal taste of the client, since his or her approval will be needed for each work that is to be purchased. A good program will have a variety of media and styles represented, but no one particular approach to art should be forced on a client who feels uncomfortable with it. A corporate art program is not a museum nor is it a laboratory for learning, although it can, and often does, serve both those functions. If selected with care, it can be instructive; it can be a repository of fine things; it can create or reinforce a desired image of the client for which it was created; and most of all, it can give pleasure to those who experience it.

Analyzing the Space

An art program cannot be created in a vacuum; it must relate very closely to the space in which it is to exist. The artworks selected should be appropriate to the functions of the spaces, to their size, their lighting (both natural and artificial) their furnishings, their finish materials and colors, their circulation patterns, and the nature of their occupants.

The most important spaces—reception area, primary conference room, chief executive office—should receive significant selections to reinforce their importance. The image created by these works should be extended, using less expensive selections, to the rest of the company. Notwithstanding the difference in price, the pieces selected should be of an equivalent level of quality. That the president has an original painting, a manager has a limited edition graphic, and a clerical area has an unsigned poster, is irrelevant to the need for care in selecting works for all these people that maintain a consistent quality image.

The mechanics of developing a program are not difficult if a methodical approach

Fig. 5-43 Fairfield Porter, oil on canvas. *Photograph credit: Gil Amiaga.*

Fig. 5-44 **Roy McEwen, tulip prints.** *Photograph credit: Gil Amiaga.*

Fig. 5-45 **Navaho rug and oil on canvas.** *Photograph credit: Gil Amiaga.*

is taken. A list should be made of all spaces that will be provided with artwork. Each should be categorized and assigned a level number to indicate its relative importance. For example, the primary reception area, the boardroom, and the president's office might be level 1, the other executives and the conference rooms might be level 2, the offices of the middle managers and the lunchrooms might be level 3, and the clerical and service areas might be level 4. The general nature of the works assigned to each category might then be selected. It is here that the desirability for a varied and eclectic look should be carefully considered. Since variety of visual stimuli is important and refreshing, the works might include a mix of old lithographs, Japanese woodcuts, Eskimo prints, and primitive weavings, as well as the more conventional and readily recognized types of art.

Budget

With the analysis of the space completed and the area list compiled, it is a simple matter to develop a preliminary budget for the program. Relating the various assigned levels to the current market price for similar items is merely a question of selecting a budget figure that is realistic for purchasing such works. The quantities of works required are taken from the space list and simple arithmetic will yield a bottom-line total. This total can be adjusted up or down within moderately flexible limits, but it should not be shaved so thin that the available dollars try to do too much and so do not achieve the desired results.

It is not at all unusual for the total cost of an art program to be more than the client may wish to spend initially. In that case, the prices budgeted for the individual items can be reassessed, but they should not be reduced to a point where they will no longer be sufficient to buy works of quality. Rather than do that, the quantity of items to be purchased should be reduced. To do so, the total complement of spaces should be reconsidered and an order of priorities set up. The art should be placed first where it will have the greatest impact on the largest number of people. This priority would require that the art for the cafeteria be purchased before the art for the office of the president, although it might be difficult to convince the president of this sequence. If the available funds require that the art program be completed in stages, the scope of the total program should be established at the beginning, nonetheless. Specific works need not be selected until the time comes to purchase them, but the level and general type of work should be indicated on the master schedule so that, when completed, the program will have the appropriate level of diversity so essential to the generation of broad and sustained interest in its components.

SELECTING ART

Within any corporate structure, the number of people who might be appropriate for participation in the art-selection process is likely to be legion. Since it is virtually impossible to please everyone, and it is generally acknowledged that the larger the selection committee the greater the tendency to dissension and inaction, the decision makers should be few in number, and they should be identified at the outset of the project.

Ideally, the final selection and approval should lie in the hands of a client representative who has had experience with the art world and who has a keen appreciation of its creations as well as a willingness to be strongly involved with the program development process. This person's time schedule should allow for the lengthy commitment such an involvement entails. More important, there must be a genuine interest in the assembly of an art program and a capability to accept the disagreements of others without the need to defend the selections that have been made.

The best corporate collections have been assembled because of an intense interest on the part of a top executive who has devoted time and energy in the selection, purchase, and placement of each work of art. Strong chief executives who realize that their corporate art program should reflect their corporate image make the best clients.

One of the most practical ways of handling the selection process is to annotate a floor plan of the organization's entire premises to indicate which spaces are to receive art, coding the indications to show the level or type of art required for each area. When making the actual selections, the plan will provide information on the size of the space within which the art will be viewed and the distance from which it is likely to be seen. The floor plan will also reveal the progression in which a sequence of spaces will be seen, which can be used to advantage in placing works in series or related to one another.

During the selection of the art, two factors must be continuously monitored: the maintenance of variety and consistent quality, and the budget. The budget was developed using estimated unit prices, but of course actual items will vary in price. This is not a problem as long as variations on the up side are compensated for as the selection proceeds. Maintaining the variety and quality level of the collection is not so easy; prices can be kept track of on a sheet of paper, but visual impact is not so easily compared. If works are being purchased from several sources and at different times, it may be convenient to take Polaroid snapshots of each work as it is being selected for later comparison with those chosen earlier. But, regardless of how the comparisons are made, it is extremely important at this stage to exercise discretion and care to assure a balanced collection.

Whether the selections are made by a single representative of the client, by a committee, or by an independent professional art consultant, individual tastes, although not to be ignored, should be a lesser factor guiding the choices. High standards of quality should be maintained throughout the collection and questions of quality should take precedence over personal likes and dislikes. Although the selection should not be guided exclusively by the style of furnishings within the space, the major statement about a company is made by the furnishings it has chosen. It is fairly safe to assume that when traditional or conservative furnishings are used throughout the interiors, the artwork should be complementary. This does not mean that modern art should not be used; however, great care must be exercised to ensure that the forceful colors and forms of much contemporary work do not clash with the ambience created by the furnishings. Similarly, nineteenth-century art or other representational works should be used with caution in a space furnished in a hard-edged, dramatically modern manner.

The most important rule to remember is that the art should be well suited to the space and its furnishings; the one should not fight with the other. The art should also be appropriate to the image of the company. An avant-garde company producing advanced systems technology might want to use art by modern abstract expressionists, while a conservative partnership of corporate lawyers or a large public accounting firm might mirror its own image of itself (and the one it wants to project to visitors) by using more representational art—landscapes, seascapes, and other recognizable subjects. If the works selected are appropriate to the company's image and to the spaces in which they will be placed, if they are of consistently high quality while still maintaining a lively variety, and if they are within the approved budget, then the art program is most likely to be a successful one regardless of the period or style of the individual works.

FRAMING

Tapestries and sculpture usually do not need to be framed, although certain particularly delicate weavings should be protected within some sort of frame. Most other works of art require framing before they can be hung. Sometimes they can be bought already framed, but it is more customary to buy art unframed. The job of framing can be handled by the consultant, if one is used, or by the gallery from which the art is purchased, or it may be handled as a separate transaction. But, in all cases, it is important to have the pieces custom-framed, since ready-made frames are seldom of adequate quality or appropriate design, and they are rarely exactly the right size.

If the responsibility for framing is to be assumed by the client, the establishment of a good relationship with an experienced and skillful framer will be extremely useful—especially if a major art program is contemplated. Since the quality of work can vary widely, and since expensive artwork can be irreparably damaged by improper framing procedures, it is essential that the credentials of the framer be determined before responsibility for the project is assigned.

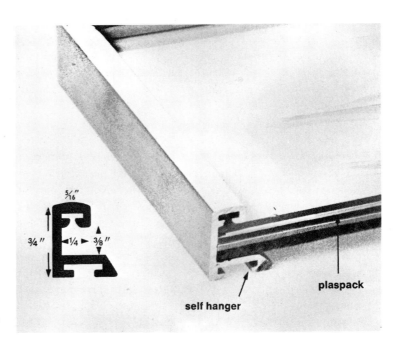

Fig. 5-46 Metal sectional frame. *Credit: Barbara Kulicke.*

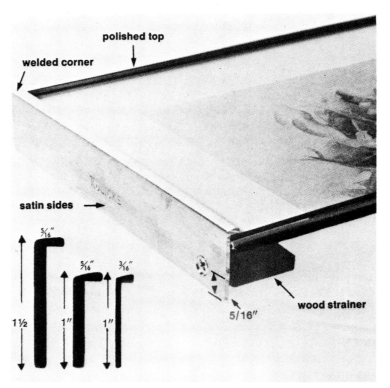

Fig. 5-47 Welded metal frame. *Credit: Barbara Kulicke.*

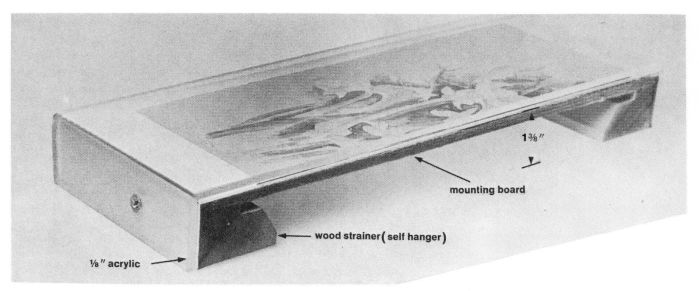

1⅜″

mounting board

wood strainer (self hanger)

⅛″ acrylic

Fig. 5-48 Plexibox frame. *Credit: Barbara Kulicke.*

The framer selected for the work should be more than a mere mechanic. Too many decisions require sensitivity to different types of art and their requirements for the framing specifications to be left to chance, or worse, to the inappropriate selections of an unqualified worker.

Works on paper should be framed behind a hard, transparent, protective sheet. This sheet may be conventional or nonglare glass, or acrylic plastic. Care is needed to see that the artwork does not actually touch the glass or plastic. Oil or acrylic paintings seldom need to be behind glass, since they are usually protected with varnish or by the inherent properties of the paint itself.

Whether or not a mat is to be used between the art and the frame is a matter of taste and appropriateness, and the selection of the material from which it is made is similarly subjective, as long as acid-free materials are used. The addition of fillets within the opening of the mat and liners within the opening of the frame are subtleties that can enhance a work of art when suitably used.

The design of mats and the selection of glass or plastic are almost as important as frame selection itself.

Generally speaking, there are three basic types of frame: metal, wood, and plexiboxes. Metal sectional frames are made from extruded aluminum sections that are available in a variety of premade colors and finishes. They are constructed with assembly angles and clips at the corners, and the miter joint at the corner can always be seen. The unobtrusiveness of the joint to the eye is a mark of the quality of the frame (Figure 5-46). More elegant (and expensive) metal frames are made of similar sections of aluminum or brass that are welded at the corners. The joints are then ground down and polished for a continuous solid effect with no joint line (Figure 5-47).

Plexiboxes are custom-made from flat sheets of Plexiglas (or Perspex, as the English call it) that are folded up to form the sides of the frame. The corners are mitered and glued, and the result is a very neat, clear plastic box. An inner box of wood and board is built and the artwork sandwiched between the two pieces. Plexiboxes are often used for modern art on paper that does not require a mat (Figure 5-48). Cheaper versions of plexiboxes are made in standard sizes by special mass-production methods. These frames are serviceable and may be used in certain situations if the required size happens to coincide with the ones available.

185

Wood frames come in an almost limitless variety of shapes and sizes from the simplest to the most wildly ornate (Figures 5-49 and 5-50). Because of wood's inherent receptivity to a variety of finishing processes, wood frames can be stained, painted, gilded, treated with special applied finishes, chemicals, or mechanical devices, or scorched to alter their appearance. These frames can be constructed and finished to almost any specification and, because of their versatility, may be used to complement almost any type of art. Since the more elaborate wood frames are very labor-intensive, their cost can be extremely high. Simpler wood frames, however, can be competitive with mass-produced metal section frames and plexiboxes.

INSTALLATION

Placement of artwork is almost an art in itself, since the effect of an item depends on where it hangs and how it is seen. Proper placement may be determined in several ways. First, major areas can be identified from floor plans showing furniture locations. Traffic patterns should be considered, of course. Artwork should not interfere with personnel circulation, so the placement of art in narrow hallways should be avoided. Focal points at the ends of corridors, however, are logical places for art when visibility can be assured.

Ideally, the placement and installation of the works of art should be done by someone who understands picture-hanging procedures and the theories of placement. Since there are few hard-and-fast rules other than maintaining a sense of balance with the space and with the other artworks in the surrounding area, extensive experience with picture hanging and wide exposure to museums and galleries where pictures are well hung are the best qualifications for the person entrusted with the hanging assignment.

Frame art is usually hung from picture hooks nailed directly into the wall. The number and size of the hooks needed vary with the size and weight of the item being hung. Tapestries can sometimes be attached to rigid bars or rods, and those in turn attached to the wall or hung from the ceiling. Another method is to use Velcro tape fasteners. These fasteners consist of two mating strips. The hook or male section is covered with stiff little hooks. The loop or female section is covered with tiny soft loops. When pressed together the hooks and loops engage, creating an adjustable, versatile, and secure closure. The number of square inches of Velcro required depends on the weight of the tapestry. Generally, 1 square inch of hook-and-loop fastener will support 10 pounds if it is properly attached to both the wall and the tapestry.

LIGHTING

The means for lighting works of art are many and varied, but almost all require advance planning. Naturally, the ambient light in a room may light the walls sufficiently to permit the artworks hung there to be seen. If the items are to be most effectively lighted, however, special lighting must be provided.

There are two basic approaches to the lighting of art: one is to light the wall on which the art is hung, and the other is to light the art itself. To light the wall, fixtures called wall-washers are used. These can be either fully recessed in the ceiling or surface-mounted. They can use fluorescent tubes with the light directed by means of an angled plastic eggcrate diffuser, or they can use conventional incandescent light

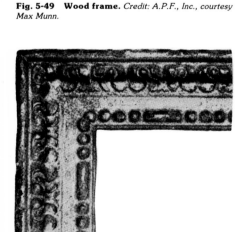

Fig. 5-49 Wood frame. *Credit: A.P.F., Inc., courtesy Max Munn.*

Fig. 5-50 Wood frame. *Photograph Credit: A.P.F., Inc., courtesy Max Munn.*

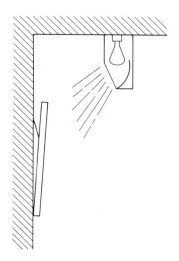

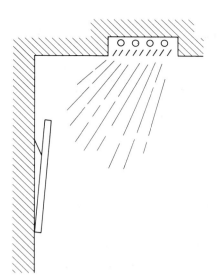

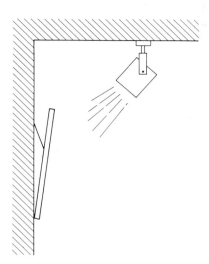

Fig. 5-51 A surface-mounted incandescent wall-washer light fixture.

Fig. 5-52 A recessed fluorescent wall-washer light fixture.

Fig. 5-53 A surface-mounted adjustable spot-light fixture.

bulbs and glass or metal devices to direct the light (Figures 5-51 and 5-52).

Fixed or adjustable spotlights can be aimed directly at the art to provide direct illumination (Figure 5-53). Picture lights, mounted directly above or below the art, can cast their light on the art from only a few inches away, but this method results in uneven lighting and often produces hot spots and glare (Figure 5-54). A special form of highly sophisticated spot lighting can be provided by the Wendelighting Company, 9068 Culver Boulevard, Culver City, California 90230. Wendelights, as the devices are called, may be either surface-mounted or completely concealed in the ceiling showing only a tiny hole through which the light is beamed. The light comes from lighting projectors that concentrate the light with condensing lenses and then define its limits with specially made masks. In this manner, an object can be precisely illuminated with no light spill on the surrounding wall. The cost of these lighting projectors is not insignificant, and their installation can be costly, but the result is dramatic and extremely effective (Figures 5-55, 5-56, and 5-57).

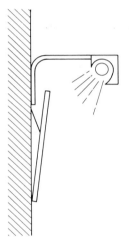

Fig. 5-54 A wall-mounted picture light.

PROTECTING THE COLLECTION

Insurance

It is axiomatic that an art collection should be protected from fire and theft by conventional precautions. But, beyond those, its intrinsic value should be protected by insurance. Many blanket policies carried to insure a company's chattels are not sufficient for a collection of artworks. A specific fine arts policy is frequently needed that includes a schedule listing each work individually and setting forth an exact dollar amount for which each work is insured. Such a policy is a flexible instrument that can be readily augmented as works are acquired. To be effective, however, it should also be periodically reevaluated to reflect current values of the works it covers. A good plan is for an up-to-date inventory of the collection to be maintained, and, at intervals of no more than five years, for an independent appraisal to be made of its appreciated worth by a qualified and generally recognized expert.

While a fine arts policy or rider specifically insures each individual artwork, the

187

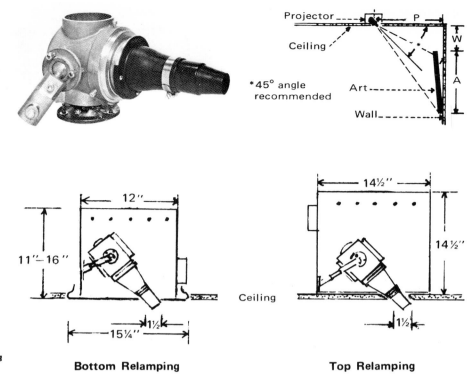

Bottom Relamping

Top Relamping

Fig. 5-55 Concealed Wendelight illuminating projector. *Credit: Peter Jens Jackson.*

need for such coverage may be reduced if one of the many "package" policies that provide "all risk" insurance is carried. As long as recent appraisals are available to furnish proof of value, the provisions of the all-risk package policy should protect fine art items just as well as they protect furniture and fixtures. It must be borne in mind, however, that the same deductible clause that applies to the loss of general equipment will also be applicable to the artworks. Such a general policy protects property only when located at the specific premises mentioned in the contract. There is no coverage during transit; for "all locations" coverage the special fine arts schedule policy is needed.

Art is most vulnerable when it is being handled prior to its permanent installation. For this reason, questions of insurance should be raised before a firm agreement to purchase is reached. The insurance coverage of the seller should be investigated, and it should be dovetailed with that of the buyer so that at no point is the art left unprotected. The point at which title passes should be identified so that the responsibility for insurance can be clarified, and the policies should be scrutinized to ensure that all risks are covered.

Alarm Systems and Security

Insurance is important—just in case—but far better is never having to make use of it. To provide security for an art collection, the nature of the risks must be identified. The most obvious, of course, are fire and theft, but there are others too. There is accidental damage, such as might occur from being hit by an office mail cart if a large painting is hanging low on a wall that adjoins a heavily trafficked circulation path. A tapestry hung facing a large expanse of exterior window may gradually fade from the effects of the sun. An analysis of possible dangers should be made and appropriate steps taken to minimize or eliminate them. Extra fire-detection devices, including smoke detectors and ionization indicators, should be considered, and security devices and procedures against unwanted intrusions and thefts should be instituted.

An alarm system such as might be used in a museum is not usually practical, both from reasons of cost and from the fact that a modern office may be occupied at almost any time of the day or night, including weekends and holidays. Specific artworks can be made secure, however. Special theftproof mounting hardware can be used, and if necessary by virtue of the value of the work, an alarm can be installed that will activate if an attempt is made to remove the work from its installed position.

Maintenance

Maintenance of an art collection is largely a matter of preventive medicine and a watchful eye. Much maintenance is cosmetic, such as periodically cleaning the glass

Fig. 5-56 Painting by Bellini, illuminated with a Wendelight, flanked by two paintings illuminated by conventional picture lights. *Credit: Detroit Institute of Art, courtesy Arlen Kuklin.*

Fig. 5-57 André's Restaurant, Beverly Hills, California, showing five Wendelights that illuminate the paintings and certificates. *Credit: Courtesy Arlen Kuklin.*

of framed works—taking care, of course, not to permit moisture to find its way behind the glass. But, during this sort of work, the picture can be inspected for possible deterioration. The hooks on the wall should be checked to see that they are still secure. The wire used for hanging should likewise be tested for strength and secure mounting. The tape or protective paper at the back of the frame should be checked to see that it is still doing its job of sealing the art within the frame against the incursions of dirt and moisture. The frame itself should be checked for damage or loosening of joints.

Paintings and tapestries should be inspected closely, but any cleaning or repair work should be entrusted only to a qualified conservator.

Most important to the maintenance of a collection in addition to a regular inspection procedure, is a realization that the detection of small problems, if made in time, can prevent the danger of permanent harm to the works of art.

PUBLIC RELATIONS

The creation of a corporate art collection presents an excellent opportunity for a public relations program relating to it. Such a program can exist on several levels. For immediate identification of the artwork, small labels can be placed adjacent to each piece, identifying the artist, the work, the date of creation, and the medium. If desired, additional information may be included, possibly keying the work into a more detailed catalog of the collection. Such a catalog can be an important educational tool for the company employees who will be enjoying the art on a long-term basis. The catalog, especially if it is illustrated, can also serve to educate and please visitors to the company's facilities. Part of the catalog might describe the philosophy behind the development of the collection and explain the process by which the works were assembled.

Pasternak has said that art is "full of things that everyone knows about, of generally acknowledged truths." If everyone is given pertinent information about the art itself, those universal truths are much more likely to become evident, and with that evidence, the pleasure that art can provide will become manifest.

CHAPTER SIX
ADULT OUTDOOR RECREATION FACILITIES
John M. Roberts

ADULT RECREATIONAL EXPERIENCES

The special concern of this chapter is with the design of adult recreation facilities. For the most part, this concern will focus on facilities that provide structured activity and require a specifically designed and constructed environment. Inherent within a recreational design context is provision of a suitable physical and emotional place within which recreation can become an enjoyable experience.

For many adults, recreation is an extension in time of previous children's games and the competitive esprit de corps associated with sports programs during periods of higher education. Sports activities become adult recreation and competition becomes a social involvement with, perhaps, a lessening emphasis upon winning. However, one has only to observe so-called passive recreation among adults, such as lawn bowling and shuffleboard, to note an obvious competitive spirit.

A designer is often faced with the interpretation of the design of a physical recreation facility. Factors must be considered in respect to surfacing, spatial organization, budgets, longevity, and maintenance of facilities. Knowledge of the competitive nature of each game may often help in placing each factor in perspective.

ACCURACY OF DIMENSION AND CONSTRUCTION

The highest order of dimensional accuracy and construction will extend to those activities that are competitive and nationally or internationally scored. These recreational activities are truly sports. They may be professional, semiprofessional, or recreational in nature, but they are, essentially, played on standardized facilities. Wins and losses, numerical scores, and a player's skills must be comparable and interchangeable among facilities in various locations. Any discontinuity in dimension or material through design or construction oversight may reduce the facility's usefulness for regional competition. A designer is bound to those physical facility dimensions set forth within a respective activity's rules and regulations.

A second order of competition extends to sports that are directly dimensionally dependent. Golf, for example, allows a degree of latitude in the facility's dimension

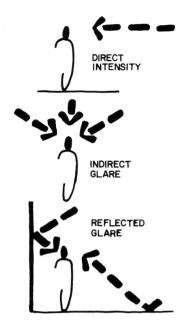

Fig. 6-1 Typical sources of light and glare. (From John M. Roberts, "Sports Facilities," in Jot Carpenter (ed.), *Handbook of Landscape Architectural Construction*, **American Society of Landscape Architects, 1973**).

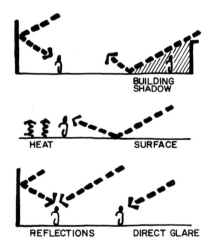

Fig. 6-2 Sources of reflected glare.

and form but is scored on a regionally comparative basis. A good deal of physical difference may exist between regional facilities, but the scoring system allows comparisons between players' scores or between the win/loss statistic.

To the second order of competition might be added those activities which are distinguished by a subdivision of material or equipment. Some games are characterized by the surface upon which they are played. Tennis, baseball, lawn bowling, and handball are examples of activities that change in speed and character because the facility's surface somewhat controls the bounce, roll, direction, and speed of rebound. A change in the character of a club, racket, paddle, ball, or other piece of equipment may also subdivide an activity or scoring system.

A third order of competition may be regarded as "recreational." As recreation, the activity may be socially competitive. A designer may exercise reasonable latitude in the dimensional accuracy and component quality of the layout, if necessary. Competitors play the same game on the same facility. A player's skills must be sufficiently challenged and the facility made fair to all, but exactness need not be an issue. However, a course of action that leads to the construction of less than the regulation facility should be taken reluctantly. A win or loss on a nonregulation facility seems always less than a fair experience.

SOLAR ORIENTATION

A major concern of outdoor recreation facilities will be the relationship of sunlight and glare to the enjoyment of an activity. The adage "If you can't see it you can't hit it" is often too true. If your opponent's skill means that you can't hit the game object, that is one thing. If you can't see it because the sun is in your eyes, that is quite another condition. Total prevention of sunlight and glare in a player's eyes is probably impossible under exterior conditions, but proper orientation will help.

Sunlight and Glare

Direct-Intensity Sunlight Such light is received by persons when they must look directly into the sun. In addition to being unable to see an object near the sun, a player will retain an image of the sun's corona for several seconds after looking away. Extreme hazard will exist to the human eye when repeatedly forced to look into direct sunlight. As people age, their eyes are physically unable to readjust quickly to a normal light level after experiencing direct-intensity sunlight (Figure 6-1).

Indirect Glare Atmospheric conditions, such as cloudy, smoggy, or humid air, may reduce direct intensity while increasing the indirect glare as diffuse radiation from the sky. Under extreme conditions, there may be as much glare received from the northern portion of the sky as from the southern sector. However, indirect glare is most often prevalent in the southern portion of the sky. Very clear air and a clear sky may produce little indirect glare (Figure 6-1).

Reflected Glare This condition is associated with walls or paved surfaces that reflect a good portion of direct sunlight into people's eyes. Generally, the angle of reflectance will match the angle of sunlight striking a reflective surface (Figure 6-2).

The Nature of a Game Major glare-reducing design considerations are often controlled by the game itself. Many games have a direction of player concentration. For example, tennis is an eye-level game in which an occasional lob and the service require a player to look upward. It is often the background behind the opposing player, as well as indirect and reflected glare, that produces problems. Upward-looking games are extremely dependent upon avoidance of direct and indirect glare. For example, a defensive volleyball player must often judge speed and direction of a ball coming out of background sky. Other games, such as shuffleboard, depend upon downward-looking vision as the game is played. Reflection of sunlight from the opposite end of the court's surface must be avoided. Figure 6-2 shows potential glare conditions in a recreation area.

Surface Conditions   Some game playing is often affected by reception of direct sunlight. Both artificial and organic materials respond negatively to variations in direct sunlight. Turf and porous materials will dry unevenly if sunlight falls unevenly on their surfaces. Water will not evaporate as quickly from the portions of a surface exposed to shadow from adjacent buildings, enclosures, trees, or other objects as from those areas in full sun. In the instance of turf, an uneven growth, blade texture, moisture, mowing schedule, and color may make uniform play impossible. Many porous surfaces depend upon even moisture evaporation for uniform surface conditions. Exposed areas will dry quickly and produce dust while, simultaneously, shaded portions may be too moist.

   Nonporous surfaces with uniform surface drainage will not be adversely affected by sun and shade variations. However, court surfaces will often vary in color value from sun to shade, producing discontinuity to vision.

Nonuniform Reflectance   Game play objects, such as balls, may produce varying reflectance when an object is hit or thrown through a sun-and-shade atmosphere. Game skills are often negated, particularly in older people, because the human eye cannot adjust quickly enough to pick up the exact flight path of an object seen in both sun and shade.

Geographical Latitude and Orientation

Each degree of latitude is about 70 miles from another. Each 5 degrees of latitude extend over approximately 350 miles of distance. In general, those latitudes above

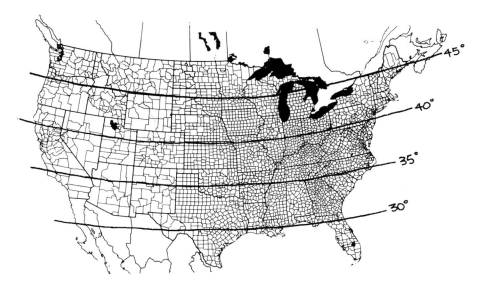

Fig. 6-3   Latitudes of the United States.

40°N latitude have long summer days and short winter daylight. Areas south of 40°N experience a degree of balance between the length of night and day until equality is reached at the equator. Figure 6-3 indicates approximate locations of every fifth north latitude over the United States.

It is the geographical latitude which controls the angle (azimuth) and altitude of the sun in respect to recreation activity. Essentially, the problem is to position a player within a facility so that glare does not become a detriment to game play.

Very often it becomes a matter of determining which player is most vulnerable to glare during certain periods of game play. If a game is played during specific seasons or times of day, orientation may be quite exact. When a game is played during several seasons and at every period of daylight, orientation must be based on average conditions.

Seasonal recreation Figure 6-4 diagrammatically demonstrates sunrise and sunset conditions occurring during seasonal variations in northern latitudes. During summer midday, the sun's angle to earth is at an extreme elevation. Players may often look south at midday without direct glare. But they encounter such glare during morning and afternoon hours in the northeast and northwest directions respectively.

The winter season (Figure 6-4) produces a condition opposite to that of summer. Sunrise and sunset occur south of east and west. The sun's midday angle of altitude is low in the sky. Players are subject to direct sun glare when forced to look south during midday. Intense direct glare will be experienced when looking southeast during morning hours and southwest during afternoon hours.

In the United States, many games are oriented along a direct north–south or east–west axis because of the tendency of property lines to follow these bearings. Recreation facilities are thus "square" with their surroundings. During the spring and fall seasons, an equinox condition occurs when the sun rises and sets due east and due west (Figure 6-4). The sun's angle of altitude is midway between summer and winter. Recreation facilities often present glare problems during these seasons because an average condition exists with players experiencing glare conditions similar to those of both summer and winter.

Seasonal conditions become increasingly critical to site planning from the equator toward the northern latitudes. Latitudes south of 35°N generally experience a comparably small change in seasonal variation of azimuth or solar altitude. Geographical zones generally north of 35°N display a perceptible variation in azimuth and solar altitude between the various seasons and face the most critical orientation problems.

Weather of course controls many outdoor recreation games and therefore will limit certain activities to specific seasons. Although northern latitudes have extremes in solar altitudes, outdoor activities may be physically oriented toward specific and limited seasonal play.

Solar diagrams Figures 6-5 through 6-10 have been adapted from meteorological tables (List, pages 498–502) in an effort to simplify a complex condition. A small-scale plan of a recreation facility may be located in the exact center of a diagram and rotated to visually test various orientation angles. Each diagram generally represents a season and specific latitude across the United States.

Broad, dark arrows have been superimposed upon each meteorological table to indicate relative intensity of direct glare falling upon a player's eyes. The player is assumed to be located at the center of each diagram. Each arrow's relative length indicates the potential magnitude of incoming direct glare encountered while the eyes are level and oriented in the direction of each arrow. The magnitude of direct glare

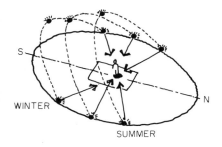

Fig. 6-4 Diagrammatic seasonal variation in solar azimuth and elevation. (From John M. Roberts "Sports Facilities," in Jot Carpenter (ed.), *Handbook of Landscape Architectural Construction,* **American Society of Landscape Architects, 1973).**

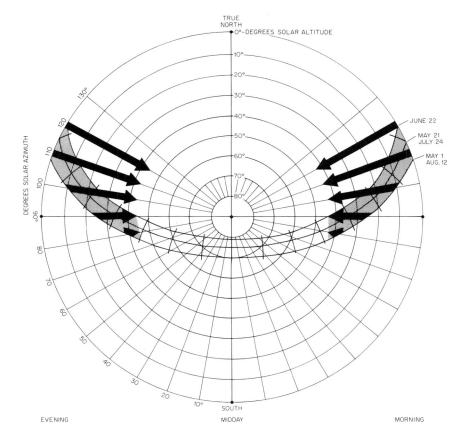

Fig. 6-5 Solar diagram, summer season, 35°N. (From John M. Roberts, "Sports Facilities," in Jot Carpenter (ed.), *Handbook of Landscape Architectural Construction,* **American Society of Landscape Architects, 1973.)**

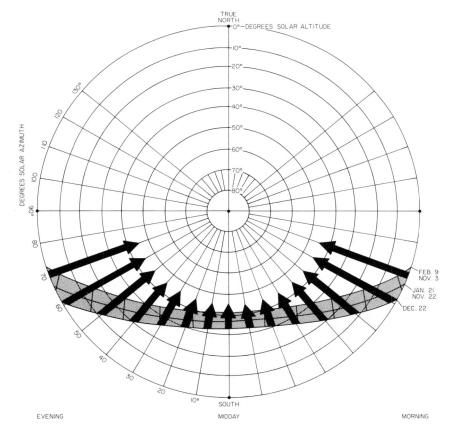

Fig. 6-6 Solar diagram, winter season, 35°N. (From John M. Roberts, "Sports Facilities," in Jot Carpenter (ed.), *Handbook of Landscape Architectural Construction,* **American Society of Landscape Architects, 1973).**

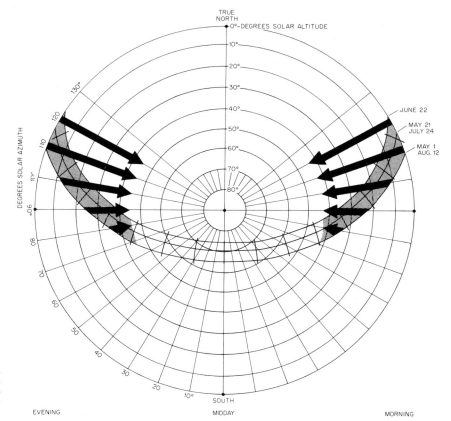

**Fig. 6-7 Solar diagram, summer season, 40°N.
(From John M. Roberts, "Sports Facilities," in
Jot Carpenter (ed.),** *Handbook of Landscape Architectural Construction,* **American Society of Landscape Architects, 1973).**

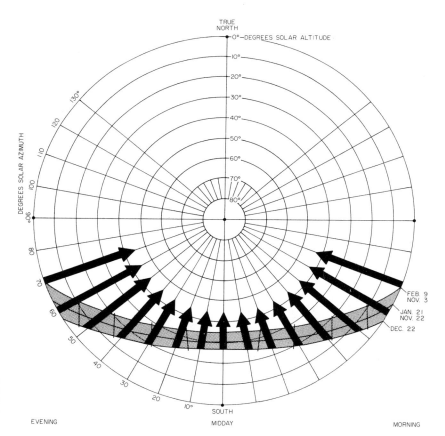

**Fig. 6-8 Solar diagram, winter season, 40°N.
(From John M. Roberts, "Sports Facilities," in
Jot Carpenter (ed.),** *Handbook of Landscape Architectural Construction,* **American Society of Landscape Architects, 1973).**

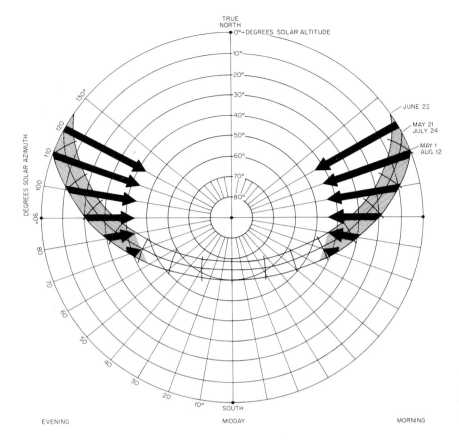

Fig. 6-9 Solar diagram, summer season, 45°N. (From John M. Roberts, "Sports Facilities," in Jot Carpenter (ed.), *Handbook of Landscape Architectural Construction*, **American Society of Landscape Architects, 1973**).

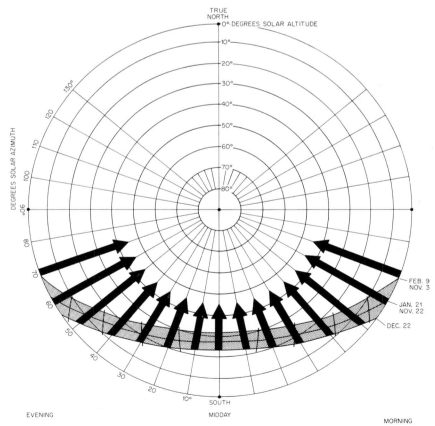

Fig. 6-10 Solar diagram, winter season, 45°N. (From John M. Roberts, "Sports Facilities," in Jot Carpenter (ed.), *Handbook of Landscape Architectural Construction*, **American Society of Landscape Architects, 1973**).

represented by each arrow is intended to present not a metered quantity, but only a subjective degree of difficulty to recreational play activity. Atmospheric conditions, such as smog, fog, or dust, will reduce the intensity of glare at sunrise and sunset. Topography, buildings, and vegetation may exist or be planned to intercept low-angled direct glare.

If the sun's angle of altitude exceeds 45°, direct glare received by the player is not considered detrimental to normal eye-level play. Each diagram in Figures 6-5 through 6-10 delineates only direct glare received from a solar altitude less than 45°. Figure 6-11 indicates the component terminology of these six figures.

The Sun's Altitude   The intersection of a declination line with a solar degree angle and the degree of solar altitude circular line indicates the sun's altitude. For example, at 40°N latitude (Figure 6-8, Winter), a person looking 30° west of south on December 22 would experience the sun at about 20° above the horizon. A person in the same viewing position would experience the sun about 30° above the horizon on February 9 and, similarly, on November 3. During an eye-level game, on December 22, the sun's glare would be about twice as detrimental as on February 9 or November 3 (analysis of the relative length of the arrow on those dates) to a player looking 30° west of south.

Each small line laid perpendicular across the declination line represents one hour of daylight. In the example just given, direct glare would occur about two hours after solar noon, December 22, when looking 30° west of south. On December 22 (Figure 6-8), the most intense and direct glare experienced by a player will occur in the afternoon looking 40° to 55° west of south, about three to four hours after solar noon, when the sun's altitude has dropped below 15° above a clear horizon.

Reflected glare will begin to occur from a shuffleboard court, for example, on December 22, about two hours after solar noon, if the court were oriented about 30° west of south (Figures 6-8 and 6-12). The sun would be about 20° above the horizon and direct glare would also be present. However, reflected glare from the surface would prevent a player from observing play or reading a score during that period, even with limited direct glare.

Figure 6-12 indicates several possible conditions which may occur during the day with regard to solar altitude.

COURT AND FIELD SURFACING

The selection of surfacing materials for recreational events often becomes a dilemma. Usually two extreme views exist, a choice must be made between very expensive materials for a quality play experience and less expensive materials with less than desirable play characteristics.

A choice of materials will usually involve an analysis of play competition, as formerly mentioned, game characteristics, and the budget. In addition, a designer must examine the local weather conditions relative to the conditions of use, provisions for continued maintenance, desired longevity of materials, weathering characteristics, installation conditions, color, reflectivity, and striping.

Hard Surfaces—Nonporous

Concrete   This material is composed of cement, aggregate, and water to form an extremely hard and durable surfacing for court play. Its initial plasticity allows great

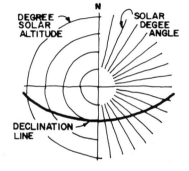

Fig. 6-11 Graphic features of solar diagrams.

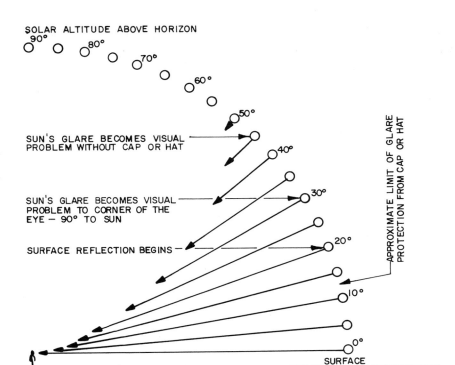

SOLAR ALTITUDE ABOVE HORIZON

SUN'S GLARE BECOMES VISUAL PROBLEM WITHOUT CAP OR HAT

SUN'S GLARE BECOMES VISUAL PROBLEM TO CORNER OF THE EYE — 90° TO SUN

SURFACE REFLECTION BEGINS

APPROXIMATE LIMIT OF GLARE PROTECTION FROM CAP OR HAT

SURFACE

Fig. 6-12 Effect of solar altitude upon recreational activities. Length of arrows indicate relative intensity of glare. (From John M. Roberts, "Sports Facilities," in Jot Carpenter (ed.), *Handbook of Landscape Architectural Construction,* **American Society of Landscape Architects, 1973).**

flexibility in the material's surface texture, color, and uniformity. Its positive feature of hardness may be a negative factor in recreational use because legs and arms quickly tire with this very fast surface.

Concrete is suitable for all gradations of court play from professional to beginner. However, the hard surface will produce a very fast court for games that depend upon the bounce of a ball. For example, basketball, tennis, handball, and table tennis become, perhaps, too fast for a novice when played on a concrete surface. "Fast" has become a term applied to a ball's low and quick rebound from a hard surface, such as concrete.

Games that involve sliding objects, such as shuffleboard, are usually played on a concrete surface that can be troweled to a very hard and smooth finish.

A rotary, or float, finish is necessary to ensure player foot traction on concrete surfaces. Care should be exercised to prevent construction of a surface too slippery for running games, such as tennis, basketball, and handball.

Many court surfaces must be free of normal expansion/contraction and construction joints. Air entrainment of 4 to 7 percent may help to alleviate a material change in temperature within large area slabs. Temperature and structural reinforcement should be verified but, in general, a 4-inch-thick slab will require at least number 5 deformed reinforcement rods at 20-inch centers. Generally, a 5-inch slab will require number 4 rods at 16-inch centers. Temperature reinforcement may be obtained by 6x6 woven wire fabric of 10-gauge wire.

Where expansion joints may occur, for example, beneath a net line, the use of a grade beam, key joint, or horizontal rods across the joint is necessary to prevent any vertical displacement.

To Color Concrete   Color may be achieved with mineral oxide pigments as an integral part of the concrete mixture, incorporation of a pigment compound during the surface-finishing process, or the application of acrylic emulsion color to the especially prepared, cured concrete surface.

Dark color values may be obtained by incorporating a maximum of 10 percent pigment during the concrete-mixing process. Pastel shades with color values lighter than the local gray concrete may be obtained only by the use of white cement. It is recommended that an approved mixture design and cured color be developed by sample preparation prior to completing technical specifications. Superior uniformity of color is usually obtained by constructing an uncolored base and then a finish-color topping course about 1 inch deep.

A compound of color pigment may be uniformly dusted atop the concrete's surface after the screeding operation, and troweled or floated into the wet surface. Normal texturing procedures are used for a final finish.

Coloring will cause concrete to lose some strength, and usually requires an increase of about 10 percent in cement volume. Colored concretes will not weather as well as normal concrete. Air entrainment should be used, particularly in cold climates. Dark-colored concrete will be susceptible to efflorescence, and a weak acid wash should be specified as a construction and maintenance procedure.

Cured and old concrete may be colored by various stains, paints, and acrylic emulsions. In all applications, failure of the color to adhere may be prevented by proper surface preparation. In general, concrete surfaces will tend to scale, craze, and dust in time. Each of these problems may be avoided by proper finishing and curing of the concrete. Most emulsion manufacturers require cured concrete surfaces to be sand-blasted or etched with muriatic acid as a condition precedent to use of their products. Each condition should be reviewed by an expert prior to directing the procedures for coloring.

Court Striping   Such striping may be accomplished by 100 percent acrylic paint or specialty concrete paints.

Asphalt concrete   This material is a mixture of aggregate and asphaltic binder. The surface is normally dark and textured. Like concrete, asphalt concrete is initially plastic and may be formed to any desired configuration. Its surface is usually rough to very rough and, to a player, as hard as concrete. The material may serve as a raw surface or as a base for other surfacing materials. To maintain asphalt concrete, occasional water washing and a renewal of surface sealant are generally required.

Two conditions must be considered with asphalt concrete use: the material's tendency to reflect the texture of the largest aggregate used in a mixture, and the material's tendency to conform to subbase imperfections.

In order to achieve the smoothest possible raw material surface, a fine sand aggregate must be specified in the surface course. Coarse aggregate, street-grade mixtures will produce a surface too rough for professional or recreational play unless a special finish is applied after construction.

When a very smooth surface is necessary, several layers of compounded liquid synthetics may be floated over an asphalt base to increase drainage efficiency, provide a color, and cushion the surface. These materials will be discussed later in this chapter.

A Suitable Base   A key limitation to asphalt concrete's success will lie in the base upon which it rests. If the base—gravel, full-depth asphalt concrete, or other substance—remains intact, the surface normally will not crack or depress. However, if, for example, the subbase depresses into the soil, the flexible asphalt surface will mirror the depression. An unstable soil condition invariably leads to depressions that hold water, the water penetrates through the surface to the base, the base then shifts or heaves when frozen, and the depression becomes a cracked, unplayable surface. Possible maintenance correction is outlined in the following discussion of compounded liquid synthetics.

A permanent soil sterilant is advisable beneath asphalt concrete when locally noxious weeds are present and when subsoil drainage will not transfer the sterilant to adjacent ornamental vegetation or subsurface tree roots.

A Structural Base　Granular crushed rock has traditionally been specified as a structural base with a thin, flexible asphalt concrete surface. The granular material's depth and size are dependent upon the underlying soil structure, frost, and anticipated surface loading. However, investigators have questioned the acceptability of crushed rock and, instead, advocate asphalt concrete alone and in greater thickness. Instead of crushed rock's providing frost protection for example, it may be acting as an "air well" by capturing water, with a resultant increase in heaving due to frost penetration and the weakening of support during a thaw.

Recreational Surfaces　Lightly loaded recreational surfaces do not require the distribution or cushioning effect attributed to a crushed rock base. Recreational paving is chiefly concerned with the ongoing integrity of the surface remaining true to line throughout its useful life. Particular concern for integrity of surface is necessary in regions of frost penetration below the paving. Because each native soil reacts differently, it is suggested that asphalt concrete design include an investigation of greater than traditional asphalt concrete depths and a reduction or elimination of a crushed rock base. Asphalt concrete may then be laid directly upon a prepared soil subgrade.

Recreational surfaces should be constructed with one or two "leveling" surface courses in order to achieve a surface as true to line as possible with a minimum pitch for surface drainage.

Weathering and General Surface Decay　This condition occurs over a number of years on raw court surfaces. The reaction is normal for this type of use, which is not sufficiently compressive in nature; that is, foot traffic is not sufficiently compressive for the material. It is suggested that raw court surfaces be sealed during installation to resist weathering and protect against water penetration.

Reflectivity of Sunlight　Such reflectivity is quite low in the material's natural state. Heat, as reradiated from the surface, may produce an uncomfortable condition during summer seasons over large expanses of the material.

Striping　To apply striping, previously sealed asphalt is painted with 100 percent vinyl paint.

Hard Surface—Porous

Asphalt paving　Porous paving may be suitable for general recreational play and in places where level gradients are necessary. Elimination of fine aggregate, however, produces a coarse-textured surface unsuitable for quality play surfaces. This type of paving may be made porous by eliminating all fine aggregate from the mixture. Generally, normal road-mix asphalts are combined with aggregates passing a number 8 mesh screen. The asphalt concrete course is placed over a crushed stone base with 35 to 40 precent voids. The subsoil must possess sufficient percolation characteristics to drain the crushed stone base within a resonable time period. This design will eliminate or decrease the need for structural interception of storm runoff water. Storm water is stored within the void spaces of the designed crushed stone reservoir.

Common brick or pavers Some recreation activity areas require minimum solar reflection, heat reradiation and barefoot comfort. Common brick or pavers meeting ASTM C62, grade SW, are suitable for these areas. However, variations in the units' dimensions and joints generally create an uneven surface, unsuitable for accurate ball bounce or player footing.

Organic Surfacing—Porous

Turf grasses Turf grass surfacing is suitable for almost all court games from sandlot competition to professional. The closely mowed surface, with correctly selected grasses and special care, allows for the true roll of a golf ball or the consistent bounce of a tennis ball. When compared with concrete or asphalt, the nonreflecting, cool surface produces a "fast" court (high rebound speed and low ball bounce). Moreover, it causes less fatigue in a player's legs, reduces abrasive injuries, allows feet to twist over the surface, and is relatively inexpensive to install.

Disadvantages include the grasses' inconsistent reaction to environmental conditions from day to day and the necessity to wait for the surface to dry after rain or irrigation. The grass surfaces are difficult and expensive to maintain properly, tend to wear unevenly, and need to rest periodically for renewal of growth.

Three conditions must be met if a quality and reasonably consistent turf surface is to be obtained. The soil medium must provide nutrients and firm support, and drain quickly. A grass species must be selected to fit the volume of traffic, provide proper surface texture, and suit the regional environment. Professional and consistent maintenance must be provided.

Soil Beneath Play Areas Soil is simultaneously a storehouse of necessary nutrients and structural support beneath court and heavy play areas. Nutrients may be added during the life of the turf. The soil's structure is created, for the most part, at the time of installation. Two conditions are available for controlling a soil's structural and horticultural nature: the presence of organic matter, and the size of soil particles. Both are necessary to porosity of the soil, but only particle size is a long-term and stable condition. It is suggested that a soil for heavy use consist of a high percentage of sand with very little silt or clay particles. The key is to maintain porous conditions. Silts and clays pack tightly, excluding air and water from the turf root zone. They will require an inordinately long time to dry to playable condition.

Heavily used turf court areas should have a least the top 8 to 12 inches of soil as a combination of about zero to 10 percent silt, zero to 10 percent clay and 80 percent sand or zero to 30 percent silt, 15 percent clay and 55 percent sand, with a pH of about 6.5 to 7.5.

Grass Species The selection of a suitable species of grass is difficult because no one grass possesses all the characteristics desirable for a playable surface. Generally, those grasses most often used for play surfaces are species that may reproduce by underground vegetative growth. The vegetative part, the stolon or tiller, can repair damaged sections by horizontal growth. However, a few subtropical grasses can produce excessively heavy stolons, which may catch on shoes and trip players. These types include Bahia grass, centipede grass, and St. Augustine grass, when unkempt. Very fine textured grasses, such as bentgrass and hybrid Bermuda grass, are of golf-green or lawn-bowling quality. Medium-textured grasses for general recreational uses are varieties of Bermuda grass, bluegrass, tall fescue, and perennial ryegrass. Each of these grasses must be selected for its varietal characteristics within the project's local climate, play conditions, and maintenance program.

Games such as lawn bowling, tennis, and croquet depend upon a uniform plane surface for consistency of ball roll. For maximum quality of competitive play, the turf must be constantly mowed to a ¼-inch to ½-inch height. Occasional top dressing of the grass, to maintain a uniform surface, may require that these grasses be able to grow through the top dressing and reestablish growth in a matlike character. Excessive matlike growth, called thatch, is, however, a detriment to play when the mat becomes a deep cushion. Thatch-cutting machinery (verticut) is required to remove thatch and renew the grass's vigor. In order to maintain one such court in playable condition it may be necessary to provide two courts or to continually shift play to different areas of the court. Lawn bowling, for example, often shifts directions of play 90 degrees in order to allow worn areas to repair themselves, and the pattern of croquet wickets may be realigned.

Aerial games, such as volleyball, badminton, and archery, may be played on medium- to coarse-bladed grasses that are capable of matlike growth. Common Bermuda grass and hybrid varieties of Bermuda grass, bluegrass, tall fescue, and perennial ryegrass can be maintained at mown heights between 1½ and 3 inches. A few special varieties of bluegrass can be mowed to ½ inch, but they usually require special care.

Bermuda Grass   This type of grass and its varieties are generally fine-textured, dark green in color, exceptionally resistant to wear, and drought-tolerant. They are reproduced by sprigging (vegetative parts) or sodded, regionally adapted to mild climates, intolerant of shade, prone to thatch, and salt-tolerant (pH 7.1 +). They become dormant during the winter in cool climates, and repair themselves by stolons and rhizomes.

Bluegrass   Bluegrass and its varieties are generally medium-textured, dark green in color, moderately resistant to wear, and moderately drought-tolerant. Normally seeded or sodded, they are regionally adapted to cool to very cold climates and sun- or shade-adapted but with reduced wear tolerance in shade. They have some thatch, are dormant only in extreme cold, and repair themselves by rhizomes and tillers.

Tall Fescue   Varieties of this grass are generally medium- to coarse-textured, medium green in color, exceptionally resistant to wear, and drought-resistant. They are seeded or sodded, regionally adapted to very cold, very hot, humid, or dry conditions, sun or shade. They repair themselves with difficulty, and require a very sharp and strong mower. Because they tend to clump, they must be mowed consistently (2 to 3 inches), and heavily seeded as the only grass species (6 to 12 pounds to 1000 square feet). Tall fescue may require renewal by seed every few years for a tight turf.

Perennial Ryegrass   The characteristics of this grass must be investigated as to local varietal adaptability and qualifications of new varieties. Its characteristics are similar to those of tall fescue.

Mowing Grass mowing is one major maintenance operation controlling play characteristics. In most instances, the very fine textured species, which must be kept very low, are mowed with a special machine suitable for golf greens. Games such as tennis, lawn bowling, and golf require such a mowing machine. Normal lawn-mowing equipment is suitable for medium- to coarse-textured grasses.

Turf Striping Such striping may be achieved by the use of vinyl tapes pegged to the soil with aluminum nails, or the application of dry lime, wet lime, or roughly, grass-killing sprays.

Inorganic Surfacing—Porous

Subsoils Subsoils beneath inorganic material should be treated with soil sterilant before the court surface is applied.

Sands Firm sand may be used for such games as croquet, rougue, badminton, volleyball, basketball, skeet shooting, and trapshooting. The sand should be sound material graded from fine silt to plaster size. Plaster sand may be mixed with about 40 percent local clay and 43 pounds of calcium chloride per 1000 square feet per 2 inches of depth. The installed material should be firm, yet allow raking to smooth the surface true to line and rolling to firm any filled depressions. Curbs contain the material and provide a consistent means of screeding that material true to line. It must be installed and rolled in layers.

Striping A court may be striped by applying pure linseed oil to the general area and, after 24 hours, striping the line with white or yellow traffic paint. Vinyl tape may also be used, with aluminum nails securing the tape to the surface.

Clay Local conditions will give each clay a particular character. Clays are always difficult when used alone for surfacing. The material is normally mixed with sands, decomposed gravels, brick dust, crushed limestones, and other granular materials. As a binder, it deters gravels from moving underfoot and gives general firmness to the surface. Excessive clays, about 50 percent or more in a mix, will produce muddy to dusty conditions and extremely hard surfaces, and they will become difficult to regrade true to line. Raking and rolling of the surface are a continuous maintenance process. A clay court may be constructed with about one-third clays, one-third silt, and one-third sand, all passing a ¼-inch screen. Clays generally fit a 12 to 20 percent plasticity index. The mixture is usually laid 2 to 4 inches deep over porous aggregate base with subsurface drainage and it must be constructed in uniform layers.

Striping The method described above for sands is suitable for striping clay.

Decomposed granites, crushed limestones, slag, and cinders Local availability will control these materials and their uses. Generally, each consists of larger granuals than sand and is used as gravel, i.e., with a clay binder if insufficient fine particles are naturally present. As loose aggregates, they are best contained within curbs or header boards with particular concern to the prevention of stone being kicked into lawn areas.

Soils Native soil must be examined for each project. Generally, soils graded texturally as loamy sand, sandy loam, sandy clay loam, silt loams, and loam will provide sufficient percolation characteristics for adequate drainage. Recreation play will be affected by occasional muddy or dusty conditions. Availability of water for dust palliation is always necessary.

Wood Under exterior conditions, woods tend to splinter and warp with age, weathering, and use. Softwoods are generally suitable, with some qualifications. Level floor planks should always be spaced about ⅛ inch, no larger than 6 inches in width, with a depth at least 2 inches, and with the bark side laid face up. The highest-quality softwood floors will be graded as to vertical grain. Nails should be flared "finish" type and set. Support framing designed to a live load of 50 to 60 pounds per square foot (psf) and minimum deflection will produce "live" rebounding of balls with a reasonable yield to the floor.

If the floor can be sloped for drainage, tongue-and-groove boards may be used for a tight flooring. Tongue-and-groove planks should be laid bark-side upward, at least 2 inches in depth and, preferably, no wider than 6 inches.

Occasionally, wood may be used for wall enclosures or vertical play zones for handball courts, rougue, and tennis practice. Consideration must be given to structural design, which includes provision of a firm surface. Tongue-and-groove boards of 1 inch or more thickness should be used for wall surfacing, with 1½- to 2-inch planks being preferable. One-inch boards will warp, cup, and produce a considerable noise when struck with a ball. Heavy exterior grades of plywood may be used for walls with suitable thickness if the surface is sanded or overlaid.

Solid, vertical walls must be designed to meet local wind-load requirements.

Spectator and Rest Benches Wood is often used for benches because of its resistance to heating when located in the sun. A laminate design will be best because it allows the use of softwood grades placed on edge. To permit free air circulation, 1 inch by 2- or 3-inch material is set on edge and spaced about ½ inch apart. Placement on edge allows flat-grain grades to be used; thus, the seat surface will consist of the vertical edge grain, which assures fewer splinters and reduced warpage as a seating surface. Special woods exist, such as "stadium grade," that can be laid with the flat bark-side grain up without undue splintering or grain-raise as 2-inch-thick plank seating. However, most common flat-grain softwood planks will, in time, splinter and grain-raise as they weather. Oak planks can be used as they resist splintering, but cupping, twisting, and decay at the soil line can be potential problems. All wooden seat edges should be rounded and sanded to reduce splintering and sharp surfaces.

Wood in Certain Environments When wood is in contact with soil or otherwise placed within a decay-producing environment, special yard grades or chemical treatments are necessary for longevity. The heartwood of redwood and cedar is often specified for untreated wood construction in decay-producing environments. Common yard grades of Douglas fir, pine, larch, and cypress may also be chemically treated with creosote, pentachlorophenol, or salt preservatives to resist decay and weathering. Creosote should be used only for the below-ground or unseen portions of a court structure because it cannot be easily painted or stained. It must never be specified with a heavy oil carrier when bare feet or hands may contact the treated surface. Pentachlorophenol can be used where appearance is to be considered because it may be painted or stained, if a solvent or gas is used to carry the material into the wood.

Decay-producing environments are resisted with salt preservatives produced under a variety of trade names. The salts are carried into the wood in water or volatile solvent solutions. The treated material is clean and odorless, and it can be stained or painted as required.

It should be noted that chemically treated wood must always be handled with the least possible contact with a person's skin. Preservatives themselves may not be reactive to skin, but the oils, solvents, and gases that carry the material into the wood are often reactive. Players and construction personnel should be protected from contact with the reactive agents. As weathering of wood begins, some of the preservatives and their carriers will be leached from the wood's surface. Initially, the leachate may kill vegetation beneath a structure. If particularly valuable plants are present, it may be prudent either not to treat the lumber or to consult with the preservative manufacturer as to its leaching characteristics.

"Fast dry"   A special dark greenstone (a type of rock) is crushed, screened, and blended with a gypsum admixture to form an organic, freely draining material. In theory and practice, a consistent moisture condition must be present within a gravel base to provide moisture movement upward to the greenstone's surface through evaporation. Free surface water moves downward through the surface material, and is stored within a gravel base (Figure 6-13).

The "fast dry" material is generally used for professional-quality surfacing of tennis courts, although there is no reason why it cannot be used for a variety of recreational activities if consistent maintenance is provided.

Construction Costs   The cost of this material will range between $7000 and $12,000 per tennis court depending upon locality. Approximately 40 tons of material are required for one tennis court of 60 by 120 feet and 32 tons for each additional court in a battery.

Freezing   The moisture within the surface and base may freeze, rendering the surface unfit for winter use. After thawing, a leveling and rolling procedure will return the surface to playing condition.

As a Tennis Surface   "Fast dry" is said to produce a "slow" surface, a firm yet shock-absorbing footing, a nonreflective dark green color (dependent upon moisture), and a nonstaining condition.

Maintenance   "Fast dry" material is similar to other organic granular materials in that raking, rolling, and the addition of moisture are necessary after play to ensure

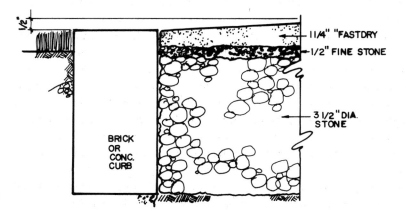

Fig. 6-13 Typical section, porous surfacing with stone base.

a surface true to line. Annual renewal of the surface may be necessary to repair worn areas. Fencing should be designed to allow minimum 4-foot clearance access for power rolling and dressing equipment. Major renewal of the surface may be necessary each five years.

Striping   Reinforced vinyl tapes may be laid on the material's surface and pegged down with aluminum or, if the base is cinder or slag, with copper nails.

Artificial moisture or irrigation   Most organic surfaces will require periodic dust palliation, dressing, or irrigation for optimum play conditions. Water may be applied through inexpensive hose bibb (garden valve) and hose systems or refined automatic sprinkler systems. Hose bibbs should be so located that any portion of an area may be reached with a 50-foot-long hose. Each hose bibb should be designed to supply a minimum of 10 gallons per minute (GPM) at 35 pounds per square inch (psi) for hand sprinkling or 10 GPM at 45 psi for operation of one yard-type sprinkler head.

Manual or Automatic Underground Sprinkler Systems   These systems will vary as to GPM requirements, depending on the number of sprinkler heads in simultaneous operation. Minimal supply volume and pressure, for example, would be about 40 GPM at 50 psi to operate four sprinkler heads with sufficient operational radius to cover a tennis court.

A designer should provide for a sprinkler system to fit the size and surrounding complexity of a court area. Lawn bowling, for example, presents an extremely difficult problem when the court is 120 by 120 feet. Theoretically, one sprinkler head at each corner would provide uniform coverage of water. However, the necessary quarter-circle coverage of over a 90-foot radius and the 60 to 70 psi nozzle-pressure required are unusually high for the average site.

Courts that are similar to or smaller than a tennis court in dimension are irrigated or moistened by sprinkler heads along their edges. The net posts present an obstacle to sprinkler-head throw; therefore four heads are used and water is thrown off the court ends. If water overthrow is unacceptable to the surroundings, a system must be designed that will confine water specifically to the court surface, necessitating an increase in cost. Sprinkler heads cannot be located within the play surface. It is suggested that all sprinkler-head equipment be installed flush with the finish grade to avoid players tripping over equipment. Rotary pop-up sprinkler heads or quick coupling valves are installed flush with the finish grade.

Provision must be made to drain underground pipe for sprinkler systems in regions where the soil freezes, if the pipe is installed above the frost line.

All sprinkler-system designs with fixed sprinkler-head locations should be assessed as to the potential uniformity of water application. Normally, problems develop because sprinkler heads are set too far apart in order to save money. Any discontinuity in uniformity of coverage will invariably produce wet and dry areas in turf or granular surfaces, which in turn affect the quality of play.

Precise Measurement   The uniformity of water application for very critical play surfaces may be accurately measured by computing the Cu (coefficient of uniformity) as a percentage of theoretical uniformity. The following equation, by Christiansen, is often used:

$$Cu = 100\left(1.0 - \frac{\Sigma X}{mn}\right)$$

where Σ = summation

X = deviation of individual catchment observations from the mean

m = mean value (measured depth in catchment container)

n = number of observations (number of catchment containers)

Catchment containers are equally spaced on a grid through the coverage area, from edge to edge, and catchment depths measured. It is important to record weather conditions acceptable at the time of sprinkler operation. A performance-type specification might call for a minimum acceptable Cu of 80 percent under windy conditions and 85 percent under calm conditions with a $\pm$ percent similar to the value of the computed deviation (X).

Water Hoses Around recreational areas, the use of water hoses is very common. Several ways exist for installing the hose bibb. If it is to be installed above finish grade, it must be located out of the foot traffic of players and spectators for safety reasons. The riser should be of metal pipe with a concrete collar or other reinforcement to resist a pull on the water hose. A hose bibb may be located below the finish grade and within a concrete "meter" box with a cast-iron lid. Positive vacuum-breaker protection must be installed with a below-grade hose bibb, and often with above-grade bibbs as well. Each garden valve should be of industrial-quality brass, with a renewable seat and, preferably, a key-operated turn-on, rather than a hand wheel, for vandal protection. Both these hose bibbs must be drained below the frost line during winter or specified as "frostproof" devices. See Figure 6-14 for a typical installation detail.

A second source of hose bibb connection can be obtained with a "quick-coupling" or "snap-valve" unit. The unit is valve-activated by the manual insertion of a hollow, pipelike "key." A water hose is connected to the key. The unit is installed, typically, as in Figure 6-15. When the key is manually removed from the valve, the valve unit remains flush with the finish grade. Various models are manufactured, some with vinyl covers for safety and locking covers to deter vandals. Their small size and vinyl covers allow use in turf and close to the play surface. Vacuum-breaker protection is also ordinarily required for these units.

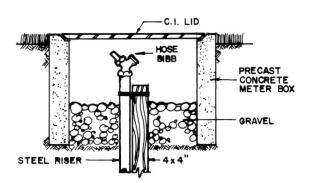

Fig. 6-14 Typical hose bibb installed below grade, ensures positive vacuum-breaker protection of potable water source.

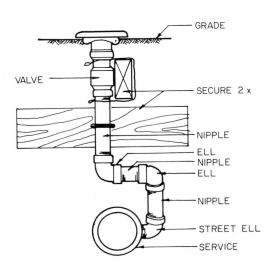

Fig. 6-15 Typical quick-coupling valve installation for use with a hose bibb-type key ensures positive vacuum-breaker protection of potable water source.

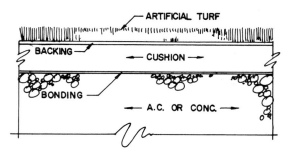

Fig. 6-16 Typical section, artificial turf surfacing with paved base.

Synthetic (Artificial) Surfaces

Artificial turf Although artificial turf has become predominantly a football and baseball surface, its application to general recreation may have merit. The material was developed as a synthetic reproduction of natural turf grasses, i.e., complete with grasslike blades, grasslike texture, and an almost grasslike color. Where a need exists to copy natural turf, artificial turf has everything except the smell of grass clippings.

Monsanto Company, manufacturer of Astroturf®, states its "designed uses" include "football, soccer, lacrosse, field hockey, rugby, softball, baseball, physical exercises, physical education activities, playground surface, marching bands, military drills and other uses with similar surface activities."

Synthetic materials stand up to enormous abrasive pressure from hard usage. Natural grasses simply cannot compete with synthetic turf in this respect. However, the designer should seek expert advice when the difference between the costs of natural and synthetic turf is marginal.

Material Costs For very large areas, such as a football field, artificial turf will cost approximately $4.50 per square foot, excluding the asphalt concrete or concrete base required for support. Most manufacturers insist that installation be handled by a subsidiary company under their own specifications, and that maintenance procedures be carefully controlled. As a petrochemical product, the cost of this material is closely tied to petroleum prices.

Synthetic Material This type of turf generally consists of a nylon or other ruglike material which is bonded to a backing and to a cushion. On-site installation consists of bonding pile and cushion to a firm base, such as concrete or asphalt concrete. Bonding materials must be weather-resistant for outdoor and maintenance use. The pile height is approximately ½ inch with a ⅝-inch shock-absorbing pad (Figure 6-16).

Longevity The life of synthetic materials is controlled to a great extent by maintenance of the surface. Wear is accelerated by heavy traffic on a dirty, gritty surface. High exposures to ultraviolet rays decrease resistance to wear.

At least weekly washing with clear water can remove soil and grit before they become a problem, and a yearly shampoo will provide complete cleaning. Large installations may substitute vacuuming for weekly washings.

Synthetics must be protected against many stains, but most can be cleaned with carpet shampoo. They will burn or melt depending on their particular nature. Large or small repairs can be made by replacement of the damaged area.

Painting Artificial turf may be permanently painted in various patterns or striped with Sherwin-Williams type A-100 white acrylic latex paint (or its equivalent), or materials manufactured by Decratrend Envirocolor paints (or their equal). Temporary patterns may be applied with Sherwin-Williams material B-42WW5 or its equal, by painting, rolling, or spraying. The manufacturer's directions must be closely followed for application procedures and removal of paints from artificial turf.

Synthetic emulsions A family of liquid asphalt or acrylic base materials exists for the surfacing of concrete and road-grade foundations. Great flexibility is possible in the application of various layers of materials that provide bonding, cushioning, smooth texture, color, efficient storm-water drainage, and the filling of cracks and depressions in old or new foundation structures (Figure 6-17).

Bonding Agents These are specialized compounds to be used first over a concrete slab with a waterproof membrane between the slab and the soil. New concrete should be brought to an accuracy of $\pm \frac{1}{8}$ inch in 10 feet by patching if necessary, and aged for 35 to 40 days after finishing. Existing concrete may be patched, brought to $\pm \frac{1}{8}$ inch in 10 feet, and patches aged for 35–50 days. New or old concrete that is soiled or finished by steel trowel will require acid etching or sandblasting prior to bonding agent applications.

New Asphalt This material should be cured for approximately 14 days before the application of filling agents. Construction imperfections in old or new asphalt are usually filled by a bituminous filling material carrying fibrous and fine granular materials. The surface may be brought to $\pm \frac{1}{8}$ inch in 10 feet before finishes are applied.

The Cushion Coat Compounded rubber granules, acrylic polymer with elastomers and resin particles, or natural fibers can be applied as a cushion coat. Various manufacturers will recommend the thickness of this layer to provide the resiliency desired for play. The course may be laid $\frac{1}{4}$ inch in depth or applied as several coats. When multiple coatings are used, four coats provide a minimum effect, seven coats are standard, and a maximum of ten gives "deluxe" resiliency.

Weathering Surfaces Outdoor surfaces will require a weathering surface over the cushion surface or base foundation. Usually, several layers or coatings of surface material are necessary. The final surface may be pure acrylic or asphalt emulsions in a variety of colors. Most finish coatings allow control of the "speed" of, for example, a tennis court by admixtures to the finish coat.

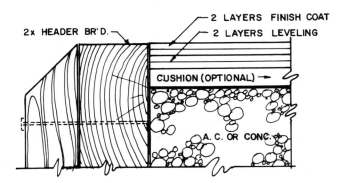

Fig. 6-17 Typical section, synthetic emulsion court surface with paved base.

Striping   Water-base acrylic paint may be applied by hand or machine to create striping.

Special Conditions   In using these materials, several conditions need to be met. First, they are not intended to replace a firm structural foundation of asphalt concrete or concrete. The structural base should meet or exceed local road-construction materials and those of the U.S. Tennis Court and Track Builders Association. Second, the materials cannot be laid during rain or when the temperature falls below 50°F. Last, manufacturers will stand behind their products only to the extent that their directions are followed during the application of specific products.

Synthetic materials, preformed   This is a comparatively new material composed of preformed polyethylene plastic ¾ inch thick, with interlocking edges that may be dismantled and used elsewhere. A structurally sound subbase is required. The material is suitable for all play court uses.

Chlorobutyl Rubber   This material is manufactured in preformed pads, 1 inch thick, with glued interlocking edges. Used normally for padding beneath play equipment, it should not be overlooked as a court surface for players who may fall because of age or physical or mental conditions. Recently the material's uses have been expanded to include the protection of players from contact with steel or wooden poles or posts. A corrugated rubber form is strapped around the vertical pole or post to absorb contact force.

SURFACE DRAINAGE

The need to drain a recreation surface properly generally depends upon a desire to obtain a playable surface as soon as possible after a rain. For the most part, technical needs will consider porosity of the surface, the potential precision of installation, and the competitive nature of play.

Porous Surfaces

These surfaces are controlled as to gradient by the relative porosity of the surface.

Porous Asphalt Concrete   Theoretically, this material may be dead level with storm water having a zero runoff. All water passes through the surface to subterranean storage.

Turf   This material permits a 0.5 to 0.8 percent drainage gradient for competitive play with a porous soil profile, 0.8 to 1.0 percent for recreational play, or medium draining soils on court play. For open recreational areas, 1.5 to 2.0 percent is preferred. Gradients below 1 percent require precision survey work with 15- to 20-foot grid stakes, time for soil to settle, a uniform soil profile depth, several gradient checks during grading operations, and top dressing to fill probable depressions after the turf is semi-established.

Clay   There should be a minimum drainage gradient of 0.5 to a maximum of 0.8 percent on competition-quality courts. General recreation areas require 1.0 to 1.5

percent. Gradient true to line is generally the product of raking and rolling after rain or play but should be initially graded as outlined for turf.

Sands   Sand should be level if used alone with subterranean drainage and should have a gradient 0.5 to 0.8 inch if binder is used (except in rougue or croquet play when dead level is required by the game).

Decomposed Granite and Crushed Limestones   These materials have the same requirements as sand.

Wood   Wooden floors of tongue-and-groove material tend to become watertight when wetted. Slope may be 0.5, depending on the game, and in a direction parallel to the grain. Planks or boards with space between will drain freely at level gradient.

"Fast Dry"   A pitch of 1 inch in 20 feet (0.4 percent) is necessary with "fast dry" materials.

Nonporous Surfaces

Concrete   Concrete, with either steel or float finish should have a drainage gradient of 1 percent with precise control of true-to-line finish work, or 1 to 1.2 percent for recreational quality within courts. For open play as for multiuse with large square footage, 1.2 to 1.5 percent is best.

Asphalt   Without liquid fillers or leveling courses, asphalt with a gradient of 1.2 to 1.5 percent is used for general recreational activities.

Concrete and Asphalt Concrete   When used as a structural base for synthetic surfaces, the concrete is laid in relation to the anticipated final surface gradient.

Artificial Turf   Here, design gradients are somewhat dependent upon the anticipated maintenance program. Usually, the material is installed on nominal slopes, with the anticipated need for hand or mechanized equipment to remove standing water. The gradients on large play areas on asphalt and concrete may be less than 0.5 percent if water is to be so removed. When small recreation courts or walkways are involved, a normal, freely draining gradient of 1 to 1.5 percent is acceptable to avoid depressions and standing water.

Synthetic Emulsions   When these materials are installed as highly competitive and quality surfaces, they can be pitched about 1 inch in 10 feet. The liquid finish material itself is capable of being installed to a precise level, avoiding depressions greater than $\frac{1}{16}$ inch in depth. The finish surface can be pitched less than normal because of the greater precision obtainable true to line. However, precision is very costly and may not always be necessary under average recreational competition and game play.

When synthetics are applied to an asphalt base, the material manufacturer generally requires asphalt concrete to be pitched to one continuous plane.

SURFACE DRAINAGE PATTERNS

Recreation court surfaces should, if possible, slope in one continuous plane with no warpage of the plane. With most court surfaces involving a net or other feature, this will entail an end-to-end, corner-to-corner, side-to-side, or net-to-end pitch. A final selection may depend upon the off-site drainage direction but should always reflect the quality of play.

Net Games   Surfaces that are pitched side to side or corner to corner will produce a variance between a level net and a sloping surface plane. An end-to-end slope places one player higher than the other across the court. Equality of elevation and relation of net to surface are achieved by a net-to-end pitch, with water draining off a full court twice as fast as with an end-to-end pitch.

Level-Surface Games   For shuffleboard, for example, and rougue, the surface must be dead level for true play. For lawn bowling it must be very nearly level.

SUBBASE DRAINAGE

Concrete and porous surfaces are particularly sensitive to subbase drainage, depending on climate and rainfall. In many instances, recreational concrete must be designed with fewer than normal expansion and contraction joints. Any water that enters and freezes below the concrete or that is allowed to weaken the soil support should be avoided. Particular note must be taken to avoid vertical displacement of any concrete joint due to heaving or settling. When concrete or asphalt concrete supports a synthetic surface, particular concern must be given to retaining the structural integrity of the base slab.

Porous materials can perform well when the quantity of rainfall does not exceed the storage capacity or percolation capacity of the subsurface. High rainfall zones will require tile drains or their equal to carry off water that is in excess of a soil's field capacity (Figure 6-18).

The location of any recreation surface in areas of poorly drained and wet soils will eventually result in structural failure of base material or delay of play due to wet conditions.

FACILITY DIMENSIONS AND PLAY

Games with struck objects   Striking an object before or after the object rebounds is critical in such games as badminton, volleyball, tennis, and platform tennis. All these games are essentially aerial in nature; that is, the object is predominantly in the air during play.

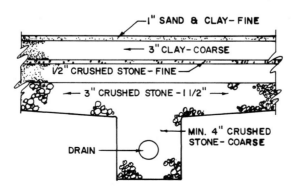

Fig. 6-18 Typical section, sand and clay court surfacing with subsurface drainage.

The nature of the court surface will depend upon the reliability of ball rebound and player footing. Badminton and volleyball are footing- and cushion-dependent because the bird and ball are "dead" upon striking the play surface. Tennis is both rebound- and footing-dependent, since the rebounding of a ball and sure footing are both necessary to play.

Badminton This game requires sure protection from windy conditions because slight air currents will distort a bird's flight. The game should be attempted only in areas devoid of wind.

The court's surface may be any material that provides sure footing, such as concrete, asphalt concrete, wood, closely clipped turf, or clay and sand.

Overhead area is also important. Trees and lighting must be kept clear for a minimum of 24 feet and a maximum of 30 feet for recreation play. National competitions will require more than 30 feet clear overhead space.

See Figure 6-19 for the court plan. Dimensions are to outside of 1½-inch wide lines or on center. Net posts are 5 feet 1 inch in height.

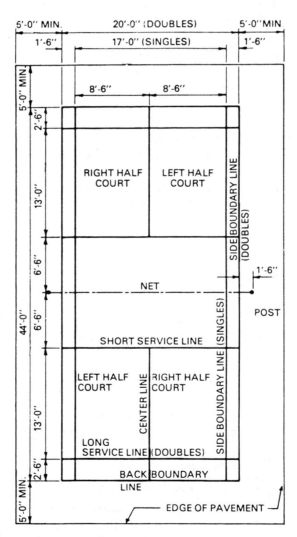

COURT LAYOUT

Fig. 6-19 Typical layout, badminton court. (From U.S. Department of Army, Navy, and Air Force, TM 5-803-10, 1975.)

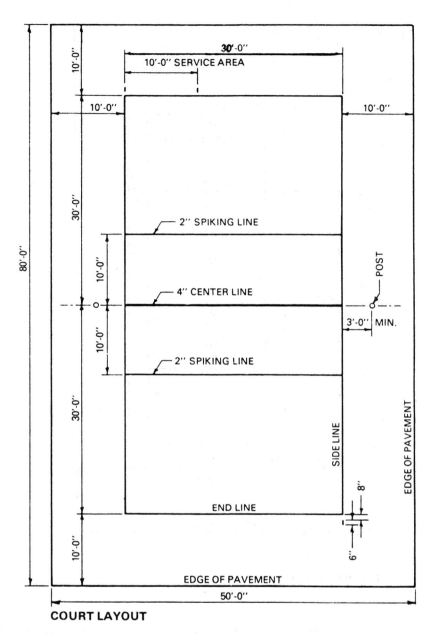

COURT LAYOUT

Fig. 6-20   Typical layout, volleyball court. (From U.S. Department of Army, Navy, and Air Force, TM 5-803-10, 1975.)

Volleyball   Facilities for this game may vary from a small sandlot or beach to professional-quality courts. The game is generally played for outdoor recreation on a turf, concrete, asphalt, or clay and sand surface. However, highly competitive play will require players to touch the play surface during the game, so the surface should have a degree of cushioning, if possible. If the surface is hard, it should be unabrasive to the touch.

Net heights vary from 8 feet for men to 7 feet 4¼ inches for women, at the center. Net posts are a minimum 8 feet 1 inch high. See Figure 6-20 for dimensions, which are to the outside of 2-inch-wide lines except as noted.

Tennis   This game is usually recreationally and competitively played on a court area 60 by 120 feet. Several variations of tennis are played upon smaller court areas, which may be most suitable for older adult play.

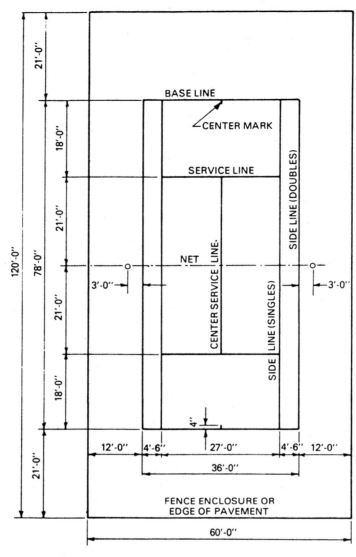

COURT LAYOUT

Fig. 6-21 Typical layout, tennis court. (From U.S. Department of Army, Navy, and Air Force, TM 5-803-10, 1975.)

The game is extremely popular and as full of mystique as golf. Facility design is, perhaps, fraught with potential conflicts between special-user desires and the character of play suitable to everyone.

Several questions should be answered before a surface material is selected. First, the speed of the court should be predetermined. If a "slow" court is desirable for play by amateur or older age groups, a textured or cushion surface will be suitable. For fast and strong play, the very hard surfaces of raw concrete or asphalt may meet the need. Maintenance must be a daily operation of raking and rolling with porous paving, such as "fast dry" or clay. Will continuous maintenance be provided? A budget must be allotted to allow sufficient care during installation. Quality installation of a court's foundation and surfacing is paramount to success and longevity. In general, if the quality of a facility does not match the quality of a game's players, the facility will not be used.

A tennis court should be completely enclosed by a fence at least 10 feet tall and of sufficient quality to contain tennis balls, withstand weathering, and resist vandalism. One gate at each end of the court is preferred. A partial fence, if necessary,

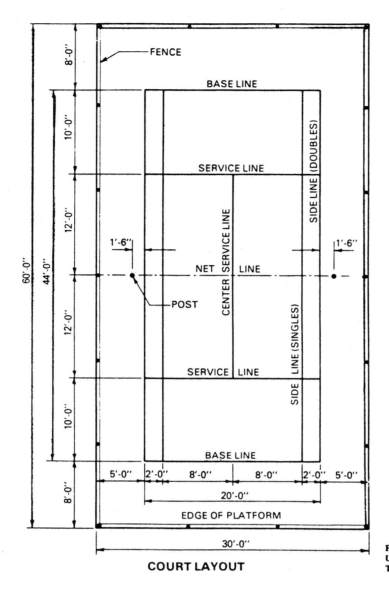

COURT LAYOUT

Fig. 6-22 Typical layout, platform tennis. (From U.S. Department of Army, Navy, and Air Force, TM 5-803-10, 1975.)

may be used at each court end. Amateur courts are often better off with a 12-foot-high enclosure. Wind and visual screening is often attached to the fence material in the form of matte-finish polyethelene or stabilized polypropylene sheets, or cloth canvas. Preference should be given to open-weave patterns that will reduce wind speeds and currents within the court while decreasing the wind load on the fence. When designing the fence, particular care must be given to expected wind loads.

If space is restricted, a minimum court size will be 54 by 100 feet. Such a court will restrict play at the court ends. With multicourt installations, at least 12 feet between court edges should be allowed.

See Figure 6-21 for court dimensions, which are to the outside of 2-inch-wide lines except for those within the court. Net posts are 3 feet 6 inches high with net tension adjustment.

Platform Tennis This game is normally played upon a constructed wooden deck or a prefabricated aluminum structure. Although played similarly to tennis, platform tennis depends upon its fenced enclosure for additional rebounding surface.

The basic platform frees the surface from frost conditions and allows the use of steep slopes or rooftops as sites. In warmer climates, the platform may be placed directly on soil with due consideration for support and decay conditions. These courts will vary between $11,000 and $18,000 each in completed cost.

The basic material is kiln-dried 2x6 Douglas fir with vertical grain for the deck. Exterior plywood may be used with proper spacing of joists. The 12-foot-high enclosure is 16-gauge, flat wire fabric with 1-inch hexagonal mesh. The wire is framed with 2x6 top and bottom rails designed to place tension on the wire for control of ball rebound. Fence posts are 4x4 material solidly anchored to accept their 12-foot cantilever stress. Commercial units are manufactured with steel tube or aluminum framing and floor-heating units. Areas on which snow may fall will require hinged or removable vertical wooden sections, 14 inches in width, directly beneath the fencing, for snow removal. Solid surfacing, such as plywood, will require the deck to slope to drain surface water.

Figure 6-22 shows the court size and dimensions, which are to the outside of 2-inch-wide court striping.

Rolling or sliding play objects   Such objects are a feature of lawn bowling, croquet, rougue, and shuffleboard. All these games are downward-looking types that call for the designer's close attention to reducing reflected surface glare.

Lawn Bowling   This game is most often played on natural turf or where necessary, on sand or clay. Basic court sizes (Figure 6-23) are rectangular or square. A rectangular court allows play in one axis only, with a resultant tendency to wear at each end. Players stand upon mats during play but turf wear does occur. A square court allows play in each of two axial directions and the subsequent resting of previously worn turf. Two rectangular courts will ease the irrigation system design by decreasing the size of sprinkler heads required. Two rectangular grass courts will allow one court to renew itself while the other is in play.

The lawn bowl (ball) is weighted, and it is oval-shaped in one plane, allowing the bowl to curve when rolled. Bowl speed and direction are controlled by the turf's texture and the player's delivery. Basically, the concept is to score points by rolling a bowl as close as possible to a small, stationary white ball (jack ball) at the opposite end of a lane.

A lane (rink) may vary between 14 and 19 feet in width, with a common 120- by 120-foot-square green providing six or eight lanes center to center. A minumum 2-foot-wide area should exist between lanes. The center and each corner of each lane are fixed by visual marker pegs located above the perimeter ditch. If play is to proceed in two cross directions of the green, the markers, to reduce wear, should be removable for repositioning. Corner markers are usually white-topped pins driven flush to the grass slope's surface. Center-line markers may be removable and numbered to identify each lane. Occasionally, international players will stretch green string across the green to mark each side of a lane. A point 81 feet from the end of each lane must be marked with a white peg atop the perimeter ditch.

The green may vary between 120 and 132 feet as a square or measure 132 feet by 99 feet as a rectangle.

Several design approaches may be taken with the perimeter ditch. Figure 6-23 indicates two distinct ditch designs. The traditional turf ditch is necessary for play under English rules. The ditch is a minimum 8 inches to a maximum 15 inches in width, 4 to 8 inches in depth below the green, and has a 35° angle of bank slope. English rules allow the bowl to remain in play if it returns to the green from the ditch. Considerable expense and time must be allowed a contractor to properly grade and

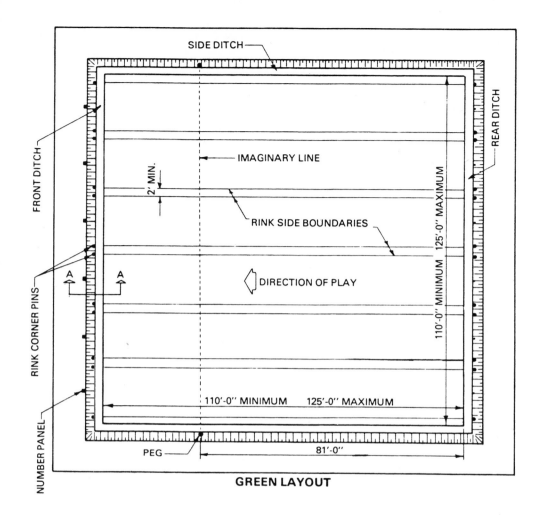

GREEN LAYOUT

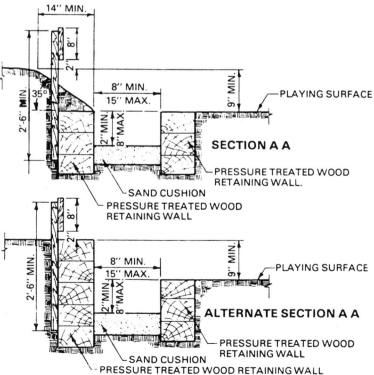

SECTION A A

ALTERNATE SECTION A A

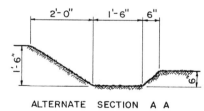

ALTERNATE SECTION A A

Fig. 6-23 Typical layout and edge sections, lawn bowling. (From U.S. Department of Army, Navy, and Air Force, TM 5-803-10, 1975, with author's addition.)

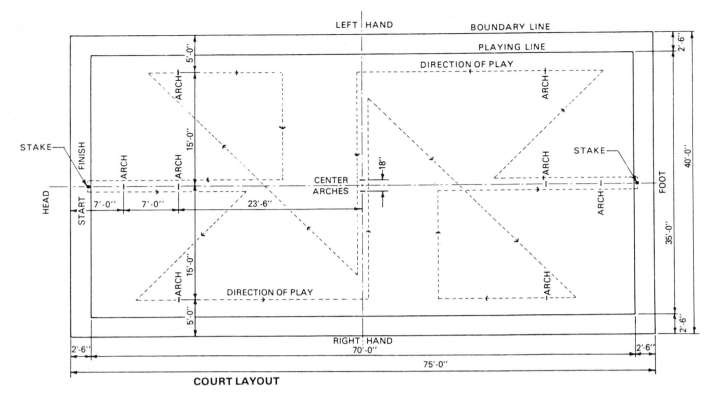

LEFT HAND BOUNDARY LINE

PLAYING LINE

DIRECTION OF PLAY

CENTER ARCHES

DIRECTION OF PLAY

RIGHT HAND
70'-0"

75'-0"

COURT LAYOUT

Fig. 6-24 Typical layout, croquet court. (From U.S. Department of Army, Navy, and Air Force, TM 5-803-10, 1975.)

establish turf in this design. Measurements for scoring are made from the ditch edge, so it must be sharply constructed.

American play may usually follow the ditch design formed by retaining walls of wood. When struck this material will absorb the shock of the heavy bowls. The return of a bowl to the green's surface is nearly impossible with such a design. However, construction and maintenance procedures are more efficient with a retaining wall form.

The entire green is generally set below the adjacent finish grade, with spectators seated on a slightly elevated promenade surrounding the green. The promenade may be surfaced or turf.

In areas of high rainfall, low soil permeability, or both, drain inlets may be located within the ditch below the sand cushion to accept storm water. The green itself is nearly level and may have to be drained by subsurface perforated or tile pipe. It is an old saying that a top-quality bowling surface is but one day away from dying. Proper drainage is not a refinement, but a necessary part of a green's structure.

Croquet Almost every environment that is suitable for turf or crisp sand-court play is suitable for croquet. Competition includes the Sunday afternoon backyard play to very professional and complex international competitions. Wickets (arches) may be temporarily placed at random over a sequential play route or firmly embedded in a precise order, as noted in Figure 6-24. Permanent wickets are steel arches ½-inch in diameter, 3⅜ inches wide, and 9 inches above the finish grade.

When play sequence and wicket layout are random, the terrain may be made a part of the game, somewhat as in golf. Gentle, rolling terrain of any form having a 1 to 3 percent gradient will allow a new game each time a course is reset.

A court play facility should be of fine sand or clay that can be rolled to a smooth and level surface. Wickets are arranged in a set pattern (Figure 6-24) either permanently or (which is best) reinserted into marked locations after regrading and roll-

220

ing of the sand or clay. A turf surface can be used for a court if foot traffic is light. The court play line may be marked by lime or string and the boundary by a wooden or concrete curb.

Rougue This game is very similar to croquet except that it is often a bit rougher and depends considerably upon play off the court's curbed edges. Short-handled mallets are used to give a very high velocity to the heavy ball. Wickets must be of smooth solid steel rod, ½ or ⅝ inch in diameter and set firmly in concrete to withstand the forces produced by the ball striking them. Wickets are arched rods 3⅜ inches wide and 8 inches above the finish grade. Stakes are ¾-inch diameter steel set 2 inches above grade. The court surface is usually of a clay and sand mixture, with clay the chief component. The playing court surface must be level and well drained to the normally lower surrounding grade. See Figure 6-25 for a typical court layout.

Fig. 6-25 Typical layout and curb sections, rougue court. (From U.S. Department of Army, Navy, and Air Force, TM 5-803-10, 1975, with author's addition.)

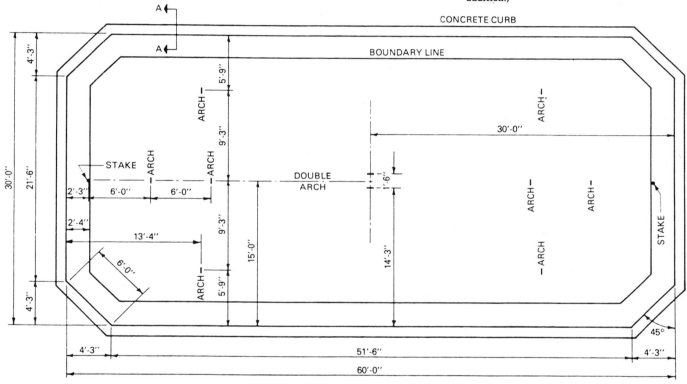

COURT LAYOUT

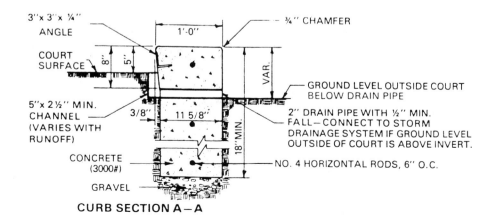

CURB SECTION A-A

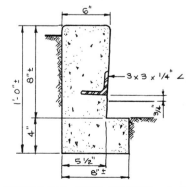

ALTERNATE CURB SECTION A-A

Shuffleboard An old standby for adult recreation, shuffleboard is a game suitable for a Sunday afternoon in the backyard or for high-pressure tournaments with very stiff competition. Basically, scoring is achieved by players at one end of the court pushing a disc into numbered scoring zones at the opposite end. Scores are maintained on a blackboard at one end of the court. Seating is normally provided for the players at both ends. Storage for equipment should be close to the court.

A shuffleboard's surface is an extreme challenge to both the designer and the contractor. Any imperfection within the surface will make it useless for the skilled player. Extreme care must be exercised by the designer to provide a court with very strong structural integrity. Without doubt, the court builder becomes the key to the production of a smooth finish.

Concrete is the chief material for court construction. A very smooth surface can be obtained and later supplemented by a variety of waxes, glass beads, and secret finishes that tune the court to personal satisfaction.

The court must be dead level both ways, evenly and smoothly finished with steel troweling but without loss of surface weathering potential, free of expansion and contraction joints and of any cracking during its life. It must be precisely marked off with painted scoring zones. Imperfections will have to be ground off in the manner of terrazzo construction.

A court's surface may be "tuned" to player preference. If too slow, the surface may be etched with 15 to 25 percent muriatic acid washes until corrected. A degree of surface roughness may be removed by waxing the bare surface with dark-colored, flat, 80 percent carnauba mixed half-and-half with water and applied in two coatings. The bare concrete surface must be cleaned with trisodium phosphate before the wax is applied.

Figure 6-26 shows typical installation details of a competition-type court. Recreation-type courts often use porous drainage or turf between courts and delete the scoreboard, curbing, and wooden bumper at the court's end. Dimensions of ¾-inch line markings are to the centers of the striping. Numerals and letters should be painted in flat black acrylic.

Tossed-object games The tossing of an object to score is common to horseshoes and basketball, but they differ appreciably in their facilities.

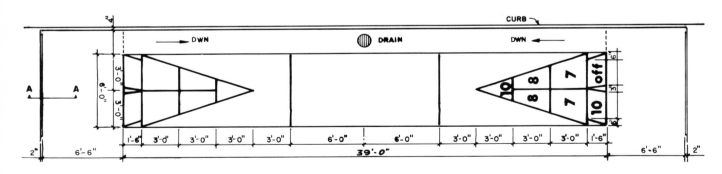

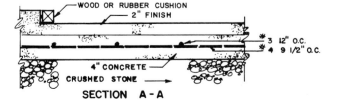

SECTION A - A

Fig. 6-26 Typical layout and paved section, shuffleboard court.

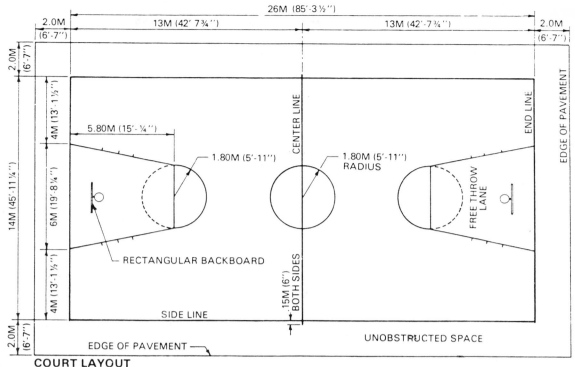

COURT LAYOUT

Fig. 6-27 Typical layout, basketball court, AAU size. (From U.S. Department of Army, Navy, and Air Force, TM 5-803-10, 1975.)

Basketball For adults, this game is probably best played at small full-court or half-court dimensions. Precise court dimensions are not critical as long as sufficient room for movement is allowed. A very firm surface is necessary for rebound efficiency and footing. A firm, binder-supported, sand or soil base is possible for slow games, but footing will become hazardous if wet and unkempt. Asphalt concrete, concrete, or synthetic surfaces are best; however, a common problem is drainage on exterior courts. Particular concern should be given to a stable base beneath asphalt concrete suitable to constant, concentrated pounding of feet from the jumping inherent to the game. Expansion and contraction joints should be placed off court if possible. If joints occur at midcourt, they should be reinforced against vertical displacement.

The choice of backboard and hoop standards will depend on their weathering capabilities and strength to resist vandalism.

Orientation should avoid low sun behind each backboard. See Figure 6-27 for a typical court layout.

Horseshoes Although a somewhat passive game, horseshoes is also a very danger-ous one for spectators as well as players. The horseshoe can become a lethal object while in the air. Normal facilities call for a wooden backstop behind each stake, but the designer should consider this as only minimal protection. Quite often, recreational play is unsupervised, with spectators allowed to wander around the area. The area should be fenced to discourage spectators walking too close to the pitching area. The use of concrete or stones around a stake is discouraged because a horseshoe may rebound in an unpredictable direction for many feet if it strikes a hard surface. The horseshoe pitching area must be located well away from traffic routes and children's play areas.

Clay is the optimal material for use around each stake. However, if the clay can-not be wetted and worked to a soft consistency during play, a sandy or an organic

223

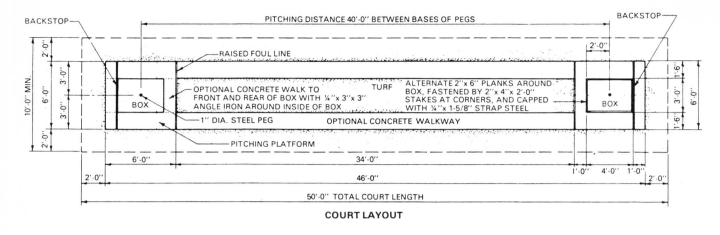

Fig. 6-28 Typical layout and section, horseshoe court. (From U.S. Department of Army, Navy, and Air Force, TM 5-803-10, 1975.)

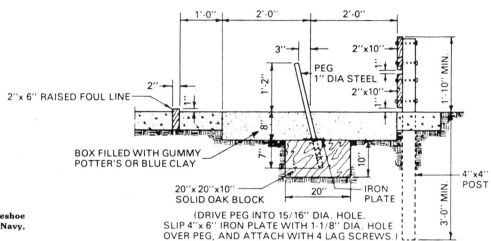

material should be used. Clay is a professional and tournament-quality material. However, if not maintained, it will become too hard and will often rebound, rather than capture the pitched horseshoe. Sand or other friable materials, such as wood barks and sawdust, can be mixed with clay to produce an acceptable substitute for pure clay, but it must be contained within a wooden box.

Water must be available for wetting the areas around each stake, for a drinking fountain, and for dust palliation.

Concrete or asphalt is often used for walkways from one stake to another. For recreation play, the use of either material is to be avoided, since players might hit it with their inaccurate horseshoe tosses. Porous paving is suggested for all surfaces surrounding a horseshoe court to reduce rebounding of errant horseshoes.

Distance between stakes is critical to interchangeable scoring but may be varied to fit the physical abilities of recreationists. See Figure 6-28 for the layout.

Individual and competitive score challenges Such scoring is consistent in such sports as skeet and trapshooting and field and course archery. These activities may be shared by one or more players. Facilities may vary from grassy fields with roughly identified distances to quite elaborate layouts and mechanized targets.

A combination skeet and trap facility is shown in Figure 6-29, which indicates the

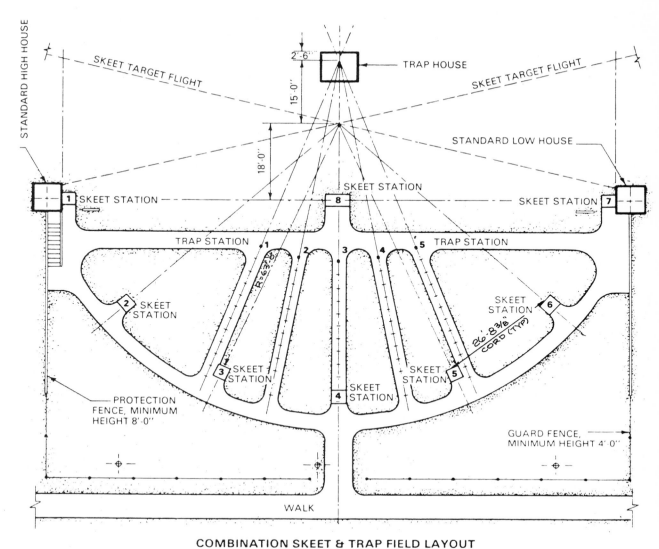

COMBINATION SKEET & TRAP FIELD LAYOUT

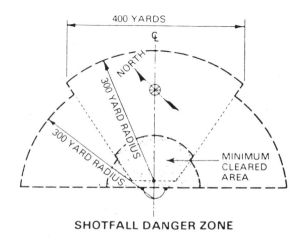

SHOTFALL DANGER ZONE

Fig. 6-29 Typical layout, combination skeet and trap field with shotfall danger zone. (From U.S. Department of Army, Navy, and Air Force, TM 5-803-10, 1975.)

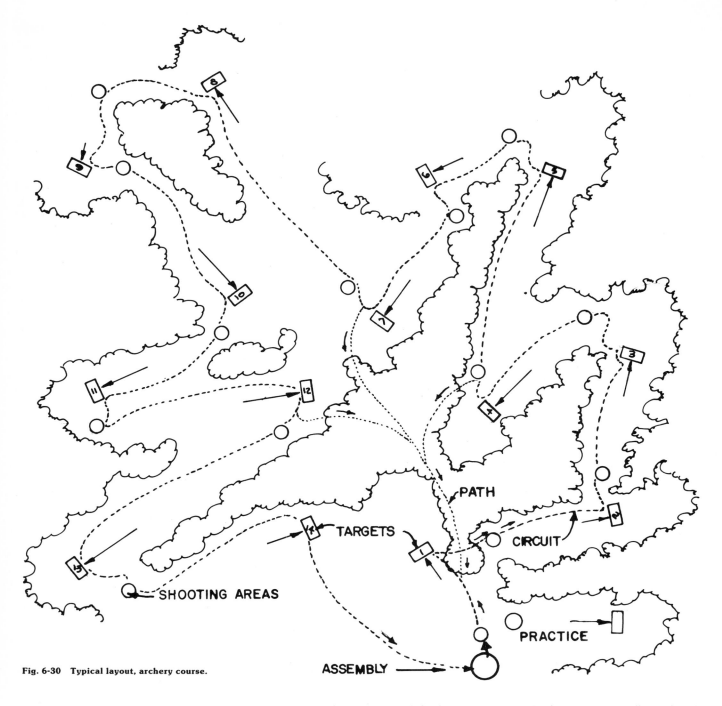

Fig. 6-30 Typical layout, archery course.

approximate dimensions and facilities necessary. Surfacing is normally turf with paved walk areas.

Archery In archery arrows are usually individually or competitively shot from various 10-yard increments up to 100-yard distances. Forty-eight-inch targets are back-stopped with hay bales, bundled round hay, or other manufactured-composition soft material, 10 to 15 feet apart. At least 90 boulder-free feet behind the targets and 30 feet to the target's sides, depending upon the terrain, must be designated as a clear, observable safety zone to contain all arrows that miss the targets. Site planning must recognize a safety zone and the field itself as completely free of pedestrian traffic. In all, 100 level yards, plus a safety zone and a spectator area must be allowed.

Competitive archery must control the competitors' distance from the targets by permanent markings for targets and distance lines. Lines are usually marked with "chalk" line on turf. The sun should always be kept at a player's back.

Course archery   This activity is designed to test particular skills, such as hunting, or to sharpen speed and precision over a variety of targets and distances. A course, such as that shown in Figure 6-30 can be competitive, as numerous persons may be scored over a dimensionally consistent course. For recreation, any number of targets may be designed at distances and in sequences to fit local desires. Safety zones behind the targets are similar to field archery but become more complex and space-consuming because of the quantity and varied direction of shots taken. At least twice the shooting distance should be allowed for a safety zone.

One to five archers progress in roving sequence from target area to target area in a manner similar to golfers proceeding from tee to tee. As the archers enter the shooting area, a target becomes visible. Each shooting area is identified by number and distance to the respective target. After shooting, the archers retrieve their arrows from the target and the scores are totaled.

Fig. 6-31 Typical layout, softball field. (From U.S. Department of Army, Navy, and Air Force, TM 5-803-10, 1975.)

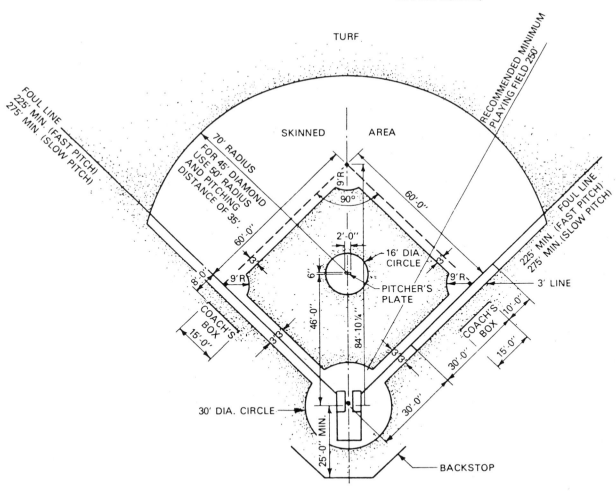

DIAMOND LAYOUT

Generally, about 14 targets are sought. Each target will be one of four diameters—either 6, 12, 18, or 24 inches. The 6-inch target is between 20 and 35 yards from the archer; the 12-inch target, between 15 and 30 yards away; the 18-inch target, between 40 and 50 yards away; and the 24-inch target between 50 and 80 yards distant. The number, size, and distances to be shot will vary with local United States and international rules and the size of the available area.

The site plan should designate a practice area, registration building, tent, etc., and provide for complete control of archers and spectators.

A course may be planned as a maze with terrain or vegetation hiding the targets from sight until the last minute. Mechanized targets may also be set to become visible to the archer as a trigger is tripped.

Softball   This sport involves slow pitches that are often played by adults. Figure 6-31 is indicative of dimensions and tournament-quality facilities.

DRINKING FOUNTAINS

Most games played on exterior courts require that drinking water be accessible to the players. Wind and hot temperatures increase the need to replenish their body water.

Specifications for water fountains should state that they are to be manufactured from durable materials suitable for the local climate. Vitreous china should be avoided because it may be easily broken by vandals. Steel must be of the "stainless" or other rustproof type.

Drainage of excess water is often a problem in areas without storm or sanitary sewer connections. If health codes permit, excess water can be drained into a dry well beneath the fountain, for percolation as a septic tank or cesspool.

When a facility requires connection for both potable drinking fountains and hose bibbs, special concern should be focused on the prevention of cross connections. Local health and plumbing codes should be consulted for approved materials and necessary cross-connection prevention devices. All plumbing should be protected from freezing where regional climate so dictates.

BIBLIOGRAPHY

Bachtle, Edward R., Porous Asphalt Paving, A Newsletter, 1111 Jefferson St., Wilmington, Del. 19801

Brownell, C. L., and and R. B. Moore, *Recreational Sports,* Creative Educational Society, Inc., Mankato, Minn., 1962

Catan, C. Omero, *Secrets of Shuffleboard Strategy,* 2d ed., Omero C. Catan, 901 East Lawn Drive, Teaneck, N.J., 07666, 1973

Christiansen, J. E., "Irrigation by Sprinkling," Bulletin 670, University of California, Berkeley, 1942

Diagram Group, *Rule of the Game,* Paddington Press Ltd., Two Continents Publishing Group, 30 E. 42d St., New York, 10017

Guggenheimer, Elinor C., *Planning for Parks and Recreation Needs in Urban Areas,* New School for Social Research, New York

Hindermann, W. L., "The Swing to Full Depth Asphalt," The Asphalt Institute, Information Series #146 (15-146), June 1968

Keeley, Steve, *The Complete Book of Racquetball,* DBI Book, Inc., Northfield, Ill.

List, J. Robert, "Smithsonian Meteorological Tables," Smithsonian Miscellaneous Collections, Vol. 114, 6th ed., Smithsonian Institution Press, Washington, D.C., 1968

Menke, Frank G., *The Encyclopedia of Sports* Series, A. S. Barnes and Co., New York

National Facilities Conference, *Planning Areas and Facilities for Health, Education and Recreation,* The Athletic Institute, Chicago, 1966

Neal, Charles D., *Build Your Own Tennis Court,* Chilton Book Company, Radnor, Pa., 1977

Official Rules of Sports and Games 1972—73, Kaye & Ward, Ltd., London, 1972

Olgyay, Victor, *Design with Climate,* Princeton University Press, Princeton, N.J., 1967

Pleijel, Gunnar, *The Computation of Natural Radiation in Architecture and Town Planning,* Victor Petterous Bokindustri, Aktiebolag, Stockholm, Sweden, 1954

Reno, Ottie W., "Pitching Championship Horseshoes," 2d ed., A. S. Barnes and Co., New York, 1971

Roberts, John M., "Sports Facilities," in Jot Carpenter (ed.), *Handbook of Landscape Architectural Construction,* American Society of Landscape Architecture, Washington, D.C., 1973

Shivers, Jay S., and **G. Hjelte,** *Planning Recreation Places,* Fairleigh Dickinson University Press, Rutherford, N.J.

Squires, Dick, Ed., *The Complete Book of Platform Tennis,* Houghton Mifflin Co., Boston, 1974

U.S. Departments of the Army, Navy, and Air Force, "Planning and Design of Outdoor Sports Facilities," TM 5-803-10, NAVFAC P-457 and AFR 88-33 Government Printing Office, Washington, D.C., 20402, October 1975

U.S. Department of Housing and Urban Development, Office of Policy Development and Research, and **The American Society of Landscape Architects Foundation,** "Barrier Free Site Design," The Department, Washington, D.C.

U.S. Lawn Tennis Association, *Official Encyclopedia of Tennis,* Harper & Row, Publishers, Incorporated, New York, 1972

Walker, Theodore D., *Site Design and Construction Detailing,* PDA Publishers, Box 3075, West Lafayette, Ind., 47906, 1978

Commercial References

California Products Corp., Cambridge, Mass.
Chevron U.S.A., Inc., Asphalt Division, San Francisco
Cosmicoat, Inc., Wooster, Ohio
Monsanto, St. Louis, Mo.
Robert Lee Company, Charlottesville, Va.

Recreation Associations

Amateur Softball Association of America, 2801 Northeast 50th St., Oklahoma City, Okla. 83111

Amateur Trapshooting Association of America, 601 West National Road, Vandalia, Ohio 45377

American Badminton Association, Inc., 1330 Alexandria Drive, San Diego, Calif. 92107

American Lawn Bowls Association, 10337 Cheryl Drive, Sun City, Ariz. 85351

American Platform Tennis Association, c/o Fox Meadow Tennis Club, Wayside Lane, Scarsdale, N.Y. 10583

American Rougue League, Inc., 4205 Briar Creek Lane, Dallas, Texas 57214

Lawn Tennis Association, 8 West 8th St., New York 10011

National Archery Association of the United States, 1951 Geraldson Drive, Lancaster, Pa. 17601

National Croquet Association, Inc., c/o American Rougue League, Inc., 4205 Briar Creek Lane, Dallas, Texas 75214

National Field Archery Association, Route 2, Box 514, Redlands, Calif. 92373

National Horseshoe Pitchers Association of America, P.O. Box 3150, Eureka, Calif. 95501

National Public Parks Tennis Association, 325 East Central Parkway, Cincinnati, Ohio 45202

National Shuffleboard Association, 10418 Northeast Second Ave., Miami, Fla. 33138

National Skeet Shooting Association, P.O. Box 28188, San Antonio, Texas 78228

U.S. Lawn Tennis Association, 51 East 42d St., New York 10017

U.S. Tennis Court and Track Builders Association, 1201 Waukegan Road, Glenview, Ill. 60025

U.S. Volleyball Association, 557 Fourth St., San Francisco, Calif. 94107

CHAPTER SEVEN
JUVENILE PLAY AREAS
M. Paul Friedberg

INTRODUCTION

The design and construction of juvenile play areas has become more extensive over the past few years—and more sophisticated—but, by its very nature, the discipline does not lend itself to strict mathematical analysis. It is not possible to prescribe specific facilities that will give predictable and quantifiable results. For this reason this chapter will not attempt to describe preengineered play areas that can be reproduced at will. Rather, it will present some guidelines for the exploration of designing children's environments that are capable of promoting rewarding experiences. A book can only guide and suggest; the actual design of play environments is as varied and imaginative as the designer's creativity.

Understanding why we play is vital to an understanding of the design of play environments. Psychologists tell us that all animals play; the higher the animal on the biological ladder, the more complex its play patterns. Since humans are the highest species of animal, their play is the most complex, and it can be assumed that such complex play is an integral part of their childhood development.

This development occurs on three levels: physical, intellectual, and emotional. All of these are geared toward assisting individuals to improve their chances of coping with their environment. The better one adapts to one's environment, the better one's chances for survival. If adaptation is linked to survival, survival to development, and development to play, it is reasonable to assume that play is a process through which we learn to adapt to our environment.

Children in societies we call primitive learn to climb trees, run fast, throw stones, and perform similar skills (Figure 7-1). Although these activities are generally called play, all become meaningful later in life and necessary for the survival of the individual and the group of which he or she forms a part. Since running, jumping, throwing, and climbing help develop physical growth and manual skills and dexterity, this sort of childhood play becomes part of the process by which the child learns the skills necessary for adult life (Figure 7-2). Many primitive societies, however, have generally failed to recognize the importance of play in the development of the child. Indeed, the entire concept of childhood may even be ignored when the child and what the child does is an important economic component of the family life.

Ironically, except in societies capable of supporting economically elite aristocracies, children were not considered as having any special recreational needs until societal development made them no longer essential to the survival of the family or of society. In the United States, it was not until the machines of the industrial revolution became so efficient that they no longer required vast armies of child labor to help operate them (Figure 7-3) that we developed a social conscience and established laws restricting child labor. As a result, we did not see the advent of the playground as a consciously designed environment until the early part of the twentieth century (Figure 7-4).

At that point, the playground was not very different in appearance from the factory. With the exception that one was indoors and the other outdoors, the two had the same general environmental look (Figure 7-5). It made an easy transition for the child to move from a youthful play environment to that of an adult factory.

It was not until the twentieth century was well underway that psychologists discovered the significant connection between the playground and the child's development. Research indicated that children exposed to a rich and varied environment were able more fully to develop their potential, while sterile environments inhibited intellectual growth. Society began to gain a greater respect for play and for the value of the experiences gained in playing. It began to understand that the adaptive process called play readies children for entrance into adult life. Since the prolonged childhood created out of improved production methods provides significant amounts of unstructured time, it is during this time—childhood—that the intellectual and emotional character of the adult is established. And because the child spends a large amount of this unstructured time in one place, rather than wandering aimlessly, much of childhood development depends on what that place has to offer. Before long, that discrete place where the child's unstructured time is spent became known as the child's playground.

The form of the playground as it has developed in the 1900s represents an evolution in society's attitudes and a distinct change in its value structure. The playground's contemporary form is the result of the emergence of play as an important part of leisure time. The old moral code that decreed that work was uplifting and

Fig. 7-1 Children in primitive societies play at activities that are performed seriously later in life. *Photograph credit: M. Paul Friedberg.*

Fig. 7-2 Adult skills are learned as part of childhood play. *Photograph credit: M. Paul Friedberg.*

Fig. 7-3 Children employed as cannery workers preparing beans, about 1910. *Photograph credit: Lewis Hine, courtesy George Eastman House and Eastman Kodak Company.*

Fig. 7-4 Children playing in a tenement alley in Boston, about 1909. *Photograph credit: Lewis Hine, courtesy George Eastman House and Eastman Kodak Company.*

Fig. 7-5 A playground in Boston, about 1909. *Photograph credit: Lewis Hine, courtesy George Eastman House and Eastman Kodak Company.*

good while play was wasteful and bad has all but vanished. Play has come to be correctly viewed as a positive and enriching experience, adapting the child to adult experiences and environments. Consequently, play has received more study, and play environments have been more carefully developed and more creatively designed.

THE PLAY ENVIRONMENT

When we analyze the form of the playground, can we, by improving it, give its users an even better recreational experience? Are there more ways to enjoy a play facility than merely by engaging in activities that produce physical pleasure and emotional elation? Can children themselves grow while engaged in play during leisure time?

Fig. 7-6 A playground convenient to children living in subsidized housing for lower-income residents. *Photograph credit: M. Paul Friedberg.*

Fig. 7-7 A wooden play structure. *Photograph credit: Ron Green, courtesy of TimberForm Division, Columbia Cascade Timber Company.*

The answer to all these questions is a resounding *yes!* It is evident that play can be not only a pleasurable activity, but one that is productive and beneficial to personal development as well.

We place a premium on physical, emotional, and social growth in contemporary American society. The predominant American myth is that the ability to maintain one's own individualism depends on one's being a broader, more creative, and more involved person. Unfortunately, we place an inordinate amount of responsibility for personal and physical development on our educational system. This attitude is carried over to the playground by constantly trying to elicit an educational response in the play area. Fundamentally, there is nothing wrong with this, since part of the function of a playground is to encourage and motivate learning experiences. However, the play environment should not be burdened with the responsibility of educating children at the expense of their need and desire for recreation. If we impose these restrictions, the entire purpose of the facility will be distorted. The real ploy is to involve education as recreation without losing the joy of play.

User Identification

The first step in designing a juvenile play facility is to determine who will use it. Even though we are dealing with children, there is a significant variation in local attitudes and values and therefore in the needs of the children who will be attracted to a particular facility. For example, a child from a lower-income family is likely to be more active physically than one from a middle- or upper-income environment (Figure 7-6). Within a lower-income environment, both parents (or the one with whom the child lives) are likely to be at work all day, so the child is sent out to fend for him- or herself, alone or in the company of a sibling. Such children quickly become more physically precocious and demand greater challenges. It is therefore imperative for the playground designer to have an inventory of the facility's service area population by age, income, and cultural attitudes.

234

Travel Distance

The child, or the supervising adult, must make a decision on whether or not there is sufficient available time to reach the playground. This choice is usually established by a series of subfactors, the most important of which is the nature of the playground itself. A residential playground to which a child will have easy access and can travel to alone is usually within two or three minutes of home and may be nothing more than a neighbor's backyard or a vest-pocket park serving only a single block. The strong feature of a residential playground is that it is immediately available and that it offers the child the opportunity to play for a period from ten minutes to up to a half-hour or an hour (Figure 7-7).

The neighborhood park or community school, in contrast with the residential playground, may be as far away as a ten-minute walk from the child's home—about half a mile (Figure 7-8). Depending on the proximity of the playground to the child's house, a decision will be made about how much free time is available and whether going to the play area is worth the effort.

A large park or playground, on the other hand, is generally more regional in scope and usually requires a planned trip to reach, thereby serving a much larger potential population (Figure 7-9). In preparing an initial planning study for the proposed playground, it is advisable to plot various time-distance relationships to the site location for the play facility, and to consider the area within a five-minute travel time as the catchment area for a neighborhood play environment, and up to ten minutes for a school or community park. A district or regional park will depend for its catchment area on the nature of the transportation available. While the distances mentioned are in terms of travel time, the physical distances depend on the socioeconomic makeup of the area. If the children of the area customarily have bicycles, skateboards, or rollerskates, the time-and-distance equation is different from the one used if the children must walk.

Site Location

Even though the designer often has no say in determining the location of a new playground, whenever possible an attempt should be made to influence the location so that it will be safe, attractive, and visible.

Fig. 7-8 Play plaza at Buchanan Elementary School, Washington, D.C. *Photograph credit: M. Paul Friedberg*

Fig. 7-9 Pool complex at the Harlem River Bronx State Park, New York. *Photograph credit: M. Paul Friedberg.*

Recreation facilities are generally located wherever land happens to be available. Sometimes the site is appropriate and at other times it is not. There are two basic types of site locations for play areas: external and internal. The external location projects the play facility out into the public activity sector. Of these, the corner lot is probably the least desirable, as it requires a barrier to separate it from the adjacent activities—primarily traffic. On the positive side, such a location places the facility where it can be easily observed, making it a generally safer place to play and creating a ready-made audience for the children who use it. A midblock facility is more protected since only one side is exposed to traffic, but nonetheless, it requires a physical barrier to separate it from that traffic and from adjacent competing interests.

An internal playground, on the other hand, may or may not be enclosed, depending on the nature of the site and its users. The younger the children it will attract, the greater the need for control—which usually manifests itself as fencing. An internal playground, intellectually more desirable, should never be entirely cut off from adjacent activities, however, since they provide a stimulus and the complement needed for a successful juvenile facility.

Physical Barriers

It is obvious that difficult topography, traffic, and other physical barriers, either constructed or natural, will diminish the amount of interest a child may have in using a particular play facility. However, there are other factors that establish the level of usage of a playground. One important one is the interest created by the design. For example, a playground with a unique facility, such as a specific type of climbing, jumping, or running opportunity which cannot be duplicated anywhere else, will attract children from distances farther away than might otherwise be expected. A playground's high degree of challenge will attract children who are more aggressive (Figure 7-10). The visibility of a playground will, like convenient shopping, attract children who happen to be going by on an ad hoc basis. On the other hand, competing interests, such as other play facilities or places of greater attraction, may reduce the use of a perfectly adequate facility.

Social concerns and attitudes also are influential factors in determining the area from which the playground users will be drawn and the makeup of those users. For example, if reaching the playground requires travel through potentially hostile or unfamiliar neighborhoods, the child may not make the trip. If socioeconomic conflicts of urban and suburban life are experienced in the playground, or if there is a racial or income conflict, it is likely that the playground will be dominated by one group or another. Such situations keep out a number of children who are actually within the area served by the facility.

Therefore, the boundaries of the service area had best be drawn in a manner that recognizes physical barriers and social ones as well. Determining the limits of the area from which children may be drawn involves the consideration of many variables, including the degree of interest in the opportunities for play the facility provides, the actual travel distance, socioeconomic relationships, physical barriers, and possibly other factors unique to the particular situation. Defining the limits of the service area is an important part of determining who the users of the facility will be. This identification is essential if the needs of those users are to be adequately met.

Orientation and Climate

Just as the location, size, and topography of a play facility are major components in determining the design, so too are orientation and climate. The main factors of these components are sun, wind, rain, and snow.

Sun During the fall, winter, and spring, the sun is instrumental in creating an inviting climate within the play environment. The sunnier the site, the more inviting it is. If areas of the site are in constant shade, the facilities should recognize this and compensate for it. If lack of sunlight is a problem, the designer should manipulate the elements of the playground to create microclimates as compensation. Through a careful use of reflective walls, radiant heat can be reflected into small areas to which the children will gravitate. Facilities located within these microclimate areas are likely to be more heavily used than those outside the sphere of their warmth.

While the sun plays an instrumental role in making the playground environment comfortable during the cooler months, it may be hostile in the summer. Trees can provide a reasonable solution to this problem. Uniquely, they lose their leaves in the wintertime, allowing the sun to penetrate, yet in the summer they provide shade when it is most needed. Certain trees provide greater shade than others. They should be used only when large areas of dense or intermittent shade are needed. For example, if a metal slide is oriented toward the sun, it can become a frying pan during the summer. In such a situation, a carefully located tree will provide the needed shade to permit use of the slide. In other cases, such elements as tunnels, platforms, and other enclosures can provide a reasonable amount of shade in specific locations.

Wind The problem of wind is more difficult to resolve, as the wind is less controllable. But here again the use of strategically placed walls can create areas of refuge that will give a child an opportunity to get out of the wind—if even for a limited time. An effective alternative to walls is screen planting.

Rain and snow Although children are less inclined to go to an outdoor play facility when it is raining, many times they will be playing there when the rain starts. For this

Fig. 7-10 A play structure with a high degree of challenge. *Photograph credit: Ron Green, courtesy of TimberForm Division, Columbia Cascade Timber Company.*

reason, it is generally a good idea to have some type of shelter available (Figure 7-11). It may be a platform (as long as it is elevated sufficiently to provide space underneath), or it may be a fully roofed structure. Snow, on the other hand, extends the playground's range of experiences. Unfortunately, the design of most playgrounds rarely considers the effect of snow, nor does it make accommodation for it. Within reason, topographic changes not only make a playground visually more interesting, but also allow children to integrate natural elements such as snow into their environment (Figure 7-12). Snow, as well as sand (Figure 7-13), probably provides the greatest opportunity for children to change their own environment.

USER NEEDS

The Child

Each child is born with certain latent qualities and potentials. Childhood is a time for the development of those qualities and the discovery of those potentials. It is a time for nurturing the intellect and molding the personality; a time for experience and investigation (Figure 7-14). The more abundant the experiences, the more profound and rewarding the investigations. If you limit the experience, you limit the child; if you limit the child, you limit the adult, and this is no minor consideration. The majority of a child's experience is gained through her or his environment, for it is here that most of every child's time is spent.

To children their play is their work (Figure 7-15). The world is their laboratory and they are the scientists. Children play continuously and everywhere (Figure 7-16); play is their research. Through constant trial and error, they explore themselves in relation to one another and the world. They spend the majority of their time in and around their homes, their neighborhoods, their playgrounds, and their schools. They are affected by who and what are around them.

A child is an immediate and demanding organism that cannot wait for specific times or places to play. For boy and girl alike, play is a continuous process. What

Fig. 7-11 Part of a play environment that can serve as a shelter from the rain. *Photograph credit: M. Paul Friedberg.*

Fig. 7-12 Snow becomes part of the play experience. *Photograph credit: M. Paul Friedberg.*

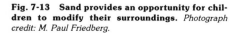

Fig. 7-13 Sand provides an opportunity for children to modify their surroundings. *Photograph credit: M. Paul Friedberg.*

Fig. 7-14 A child investigates the creatures and the world around him. *Photograph credit: M. Paul Friedberg.*

Fig. 7-15 To the child his play is his work. *Photograph credit: M. Paul Friedberg.*

Fig. 7-16 Wherever a child plays is a playground. *Photograph credit: M. Paul Friedberg.*

we see a child doing in play is very much like an iceberg—the cap above the waterline is what is visible. The real substance, which is nine-tenths of the child's play activity, is inside his or her mind and thus invisible to the observer. That substance is a series of thoughts which interweave with every activity in a linear and interconnected manner, the purpose of which is to replace instincts and dependency with choice and logic.

Although it is difficult to attempt to characterize an activity where actions, results, and impacts all occur simultaneously, for purposes of expediency, play has been divided into three major categories: physical play, which is the development of motor skills; social play, which is the interaction between and among children; and cognitive play, which is the development of the child's intellect, or the problemsolving process.

Physical play   Children are constantly testing their physical powers, discovering their strengths, limitations, and physical promise (Figure 7-17). Physical motion is an integral part of bone, muscle, and nerve development. In the play environment, children are provided with opportunities and equipment to find out just how high, far, or fast they can go (Figure 7-18). In the acts of balancing, swinging, jumping, sliding, climbing, and so forth, they are exposed to different challenges. In judging distances, heights, and inclines, they begin to understand how their bodies work and what capabilities they each have (Figure 7-19). Their physical play can extend beyond their own bodies, however, as when a child plays at building with blocks or throws a ball, since these activities teach aspects of spatial measurement.

Social play   Children extend themselves and their world beyond the limits of their immediate reality through role playing. They can fantasize about being a doctor, a builder, a cowboy, or an Indian. They find and test personality situations with which they are most comfortable and at the same time attain the ability to work and play

239

Fig. 7-17 **Play can be a challenge to a child's physical powers.** *Photograph credit: M. Paul Friedberg.*

Fig. 7-18 **Play structures can help children test the limits of their abilities.** *Photograph credit: M. Paul Friedberg.*

Fig. 7-19 **Climbing gives children the chance to discover some of the capabilities of their bodies.** *Photograph credit: M. Paul Friedberg.*

with others. They learn cooperation and interaction (Figure 7-20). In play they create an informal stage and stimulate their imaginations. They discover their talents and personality in relationship to others through cooperative use of play materials and spaces. They learn how to make things, a tire swing for example (Figure 7-21), by working with one another to a common end.

By being together, children also learn by watching others. They can see older children doing things that are beyond their own physical abilities. Instead of learning by doing, children are instructed visually, so that when their bodies have grown sufficiently, their minds will already have acquired the knowledge to enable them to make use of their new physical prowess.

Cognitive play A playground offers a child many opportunities for making decisions and learning their consequences. Problem solving is closely related to a person's ability to choose and decide; in the play environment the child is given the opportunity to make selections and decisions without the burdens of the adult world.

When children are provided with sufficient accessories and materials to make basic changes in the plan of their playground, they will invariably manipulate their environment through the creative activity of deciding how to place lumber (Figure 7-22), create enclosures, study the incline of slides, and so on. With movable materials they are given the choice of going over or under (Figure 7-23), around or through, of jumping or putting a bridge across. The more challenging the problems the child is faced with, the more innovative are his or her solutions. By fitting things together and later pulling them apart again, children can learn about the environment and the objects around them. They can learn sequential relationships by grouping and collecting things and by manipulating them. In short, physical activities can be very important to a child's intellectual development.

Interactive Relationships

One of the more dynamic aspects of good playground design is the degree of user interaction or interrelationship that it inspires. Although all users tend to interact while engaged in activities within the same environment, certain age groups have a special affinity for one another. These interrelationships are important to the understanding of the playground's function.

While progressing from infancy to maturity, a child evolves through various stages of dependency, starting with the parent (Figure 7-24), to the older sibling or relative (Figure 7-25), to the play leader, and sometimes to peers. Since the child's dependency is so varied, the playground must be programmed to respond to a wide range of users' needs.

Fig. 7-20 Play promotes cooperation and interaction. *Photograph credit: M. Paul Friedberg.*

Fig. 7-21 Working together, children can create their own play equipment. *Photograph credit: M. Paul Friedberg.*

Fig. 7-22 A child will use available lumber to modify an existing play environment. *Photograph credit: M. Paul Friedberg.*

Fig. 7-23 Movable play elements give a child more choices. *Photograph credit: M. Paul Friedberg.*

Fig. 7-24 Initially, the child depends on the parent. *Photograph credit: M. Paul Friedberg.*

Fig. 7-25 Later, an older relative provides guidance and help. *Photograph credit: Marco Martelli,* courtesy of TimberForm Division, Columbia Cascade Timber Company.

Fig. 7-26 Parents as protectors are an important part of the playground. *Photograph credit: M. Paul Friedberg.*

Fig. 7-27 The play area must be within sight of those supervising it. *Photograph credit: M. Paul Friedberg.*

Parent–child and parent–parent   The parent–child relationship is important in the playground environment, since the parent has the major role in the protection of the child (Figure 7-26). In order to give adequate protection, the parent must be in constant visual contact with the child. However, the parent is not necessarily satisfied only with monitoring the child's movements. The adult may want to seek the companionship of other parents or to share custodial duties. There may be the wish to participate in some physical activity that requires equipment beyond the skills of the child. It becomes clear that the play environment is faced with the dual task of providing not only for the child's needs, but for the adult's as well. Thus the play area must accommodate two different age groups within visual proximity of each other to allow for play and supervision (Figure 7-27).

Teenager–teenager   Teenagers have a close affinity for their peers and enjoy team activities and competition. On the other hand, they also like individual games and invariably want a special territory to be away from the adult world, reflecting their differences in language, dress, and general behavior.

Child–child   Interrelationships among children are generally confined to those in the same age group. It is only when a sibling is given responsibility for a brother or sister that children of different ages are likely to come together. But even in such situations, the older child has little interest in interaction with the younger. Nonetheless, there is opportunity for observation and learning. The older sibling wants a play experience away from the younger one, but if the facilities are close to one another, the younger child can observe the older and be stimulated by the challenges and new ideas so seen. With a cooperative sibling, the child may even be permitted to participate and learn new skills.

Elderly–child   While it may be interesting and beneficial to have parents or young adults engage in physical recreational activities within the playground, a similar opportunity is of little or no value to the elderly. They mainly enjoy experiences vicariously, through observation of others. By maintaining visual contact, they can also provide custodial care for children. By juxtaposing seating and play areas in a way that avoids conflicts, the elderly can be provided with the rewarding experience of being spectators, while the children, in addition to their normal activities, are given the role of performers.

Elderly–teenager The teenagers' relationship with adults is still not that of equals, although they have often attained much of their level of adult physical strength. Active and competitive play is very important to teenagers, and since the elderly are likely to misunderstand such activities, little interaction can be anticipated between the two groups.

Elderly–elderly Interaction among the elderly is mainly through nonphysical activities (Figure 7-28), such as conversation and, occasionally, board games. They usually seek the security of actively populated spaces, yet refrain from participating in the activities, preferring to watch.

PLAY AREA DESIGN

Programming

The program for a play area is the list of what facilities will be provided and what experiences can be accommodated within the playground being designed. The program is an outgrowth of the specific needs of the particular users for whom the playground is intended. As discussed earlier, first the area that can be expected to be serviced by the playground is determined, then a determination is made of the specific users, defined by age, family income, ethnic, and other characteristics. The characteristics and size of the potential building site have a strong effect on the facility's program. The topography, the climate, and the proximity of competitive support facilities all influence the design. There is a clear interaction, not only among the users, but between the facilities and the people to be accommodated: The program attempts to create as broad a range of experiences as the site will permit, to satisfy the individual and collective needs of the users.

Fig. 7-28 Nonphysical interaction is most common among the elderly. *Photograph credit: M. Paul Friedberg.*

Fig. 7-29 An audience turns the playground into a theatre. *Photograph credit: M. Paul Friedberg.*

Fig. 7-30 The trip is as much fun as the destination. *Photograph credit: Marco Martelli, courtesy of* TimberForm Division, Columbia Cascade Timber Company.

Fig. 7-31 Rope is a useful element for active play. *Photograph credit: Ron Green, courtesy of TimberForm Division, Columbia Cascade Timber Company.*

Because of its potential range, programming can draw people who, given their diverse backgrounds and interests, otherwise might use the park or playground only infrequently, and the more people using the area, the greater the possibilities for social interaction. It is at the programming stage of play area design that the potential group of users can be expanded through the imaginative inclusion of flexible and multipurpose facilities.

Interrelationships If the playground facilities and the ways of using them can be designed to create complex and flexible interrelationships, there will be greater user participation and therefore a more successful design.

There are various types of relationships that can be exploited. A synergistic relationship is one in which two or more elements achieve an effect greater than the sum of the individual parts. For example, playground seating creates a dynamic in which the seated people view the playground as a theater (Figure 7-29). While they are engaged in the passive activity of sitting, they are creating another element of interest by being observers and, in fact, an audience for the playing children. Since most children seek high visibility and recognition, the onlookers' presence results in further animating them. Another benefit is a lower degree of conflict or vandalism due to the presence of an audience.

Symbiotic relationships exist when different elements benefit from a close relationship. For example, a network of climbing bars connected to a platform will create not only greater use of the network since its purpose expands to allow platform access, but more children will seek out the platform simply because the experience of *getting* there is as enjoyable as *being* there (Figure 7-30).

In a catalytic relationship, some element precipitates a reaction in another element. In the play environment, materials such as blocks, boards, ropes (Figure 7-31), and chalk (Figure 7-32) all have potential to provide catalytic relationships. These materials stimulate a broader range of interpretations through their use and can enlarge or modify the initial experience.

Linkages The traditional playground is a series of separate items with individual activities, each having its own space with little or no relationship between the others (Figure 7-33). A more dynamic approach, called linkages, provides, for a similar dollar cost, a richer play experience. The premise is that by interconnecting the specific activities of either passive or active play, the child is provided with a broader set of options (Figure 7-34). Through the decision-making process of choosing which pathway is most desirable, children establish a broader interaction between their physical, social, and cognitive experiences. Not only is the individual activity important, but the experience of getting to it becomes just as significant.

For example, a mound or series of stepping columns (Figure 7-35) will provide access from more than one vantage point to the top of a slide. Then, at the base of the slide, a balance beam can lead to a ladder positioned next to a tree house. A child may take either a net to a bridge or a slide pole to any number of other points. Through linkages such as these, the number of choices and the variety of experiences

Fig. 7-32 A simple stick of chalk is an element for play. *Photograph credit: M. Paul Friedberg.*

Fig. 7-33 A traditional sliding pond does not relate to any other play elements. *Photograph credit: M. Paul Friedberg.*

Fig. 7-34 Linkages provide increased choice. *Photograph credit: Ron Green, courtesy of TimberForm Division, Columbia Cascade Timber Company.*

Fig. 7-35 A series of stepping columns provides many vantage points. *Photograph credit: M. Paul Friedberg.*

from the same number of play items expand (Figure 7-36); the child experiences a wider variety of stimuli within the same space.

Juxtaposition A play environment can amplify and reinforce potential activities by the placement of specific elements in relation to one another. For example, a rope is placed on a platform, enabling a child to swing to another platform (Figure 7-37). The rope not only links the two platforms but allows the child access to other places and levels by more than one method. In the same way, inviting a child to run down one hill and up another on the opposite side creates a reciprocal or pendulum action; without the other hill, only half the play value would exist. It is important, then, for the playground designer to review the possible types of activities within the play environment and to interrelate them to the maximum extent possible by positioning and juxtaposing the various play elements so that they will reinforce one another's functions and uses.

Sequence Linkage provides greater options in play environments; juxtaposition of elements enhances their degree of use. *Sequence* should develop a variety of experiences that engage as much of the child's full potential as possible. Sequence affects the way the child plays by balancing active experiences with passive ones. For example, it allows arm- and hand-muscle use in one part of the play sequence to alternate with the use of a child's leg or torso muscles. Thus, physical potential is expanded and the sequence makes the activity more interesting. By attention to sequence, opportunities for individual and collective action can be related and grouped to create a balance of rewarding experiences.

Multiuse and multipurpose The design of facilities for play experiences should not only allow for individual interpretation, but should be of sufficient complexity and interest to allow for multiple uses. A geodesic dome, for example (Figure 7-38), is

Fig. 7-36 Linkages enable play elements to provide expanded opportunites. *Photograph credit: Marco Martelli, courtesy of TimberForm Division, Columbia Cascade Timber Company.*

Fig. 7-37 A swinging rope provides transportation. *Photograph credit: Marco Martelli, courtesy of TimberForm Division, Columbia Cascade Timber Company.*

Fig. 7-38 A geodesic dome can be a multipurpose play structure. *Photograph credit: M. Paul Friedberg.*

Fig. 7-39 The child needs a choice of social settings. *Photograph credit: Ron Green, courtesy of TimberForm Division, Columbia Cascade Timber Company.*

not simply a climbing structure. It also has the potential to support swings or nets. Sand placed below it provides not only safety if the child falls in climbing and swinging, but is itself a play material. The geodesic structure itself can be subdivided into other forms through the use of paper, cloth, plastic, or other materials. The structures that possess a multiplicity of purpose and interpretation are most successful in the play environment.

Social groupings   In a playground, the relationships and sizes of the elements affect the social groupings they can accommodate. For example, a platform 2 feet wide will hold only one child. This limitation may be desirable when the platform is high and more than one child at a time at that elevation might be hazardous. At a different height, it might be advisable to permit larger social groupings; the platforms might be 4 feet wide to accommodate two or three children, or even as large as 10 feet to hold a group. It is important to relate and limit the size of potential groupings in specific locations within the play environment. However, it is equally important to provide a range of opportunities for social gathering so that the child, rather than the designer, has the choice of area (Figure 7-39).

Active/passive playgrounds   Playgrounds should provide a balance of experiences. A play environment that is totally active and has no provision for passive play may limit the opportunities for learning through observation—an important part of cognitive development. On the other hand, a playground that is primarily passive may not challenge or interest the children and will satisfy neither their active nor their passive needs.

Control   External control of the playground is often advisable. Fences, walls, and other such barriers are the traditional ways in which this control is provided (Figure 7-40). However, when these elements are not complementary to the design—when they inhibit the activity of play—they are considered coercive. All too often, fences give the impression of caging a child (Figure 7-41). Control in a permissive design

Fig. 7-40 Fences are traditional playground control elements. *Photograph credit: M. Paul Friedberg.*

247

Fig. 7-41 Fences can appear to cage a child. *Photograph credit: M. Paul Friedberg.*

Fig. 7-42 Barriers can become a part of the play environment. *Photograph credit: M. Paul Friedberg.*

Fig. 7-43 The younger child cannot reach the top of the trellis. *Photograph credit: M. Paul Friedberg.*

rejects the use of tall iron fences and, instead, is effected by the integration of the play environment and such barriers as decorative walls, changes in grade, and plantings (Figure 7-42).

Not only is it necessary to control the child's horizontal movements, but an equal need exists to limit any access to higher elevations when he or she has limited skills. Generally, children are intelligent enough not to overchallenge themselves. But on occasion they may be egged on to an overextension of their abilities. A very successful method of vertical control to help avoid this problem is to scale the access point to an elevation so high that those lacking skills will not be able to reach it (Figure 7-43). For example, by designing the ladder to a high platform so that it presents a barrier to a small child yet is accessible to an older one, the platform presents no potential danger to the smaller child. Similar methods can be used for designing swings and other climbing apparatus.

Design Issues

Supervised versus unsupervised areas Unsupervised playgrounds require greater care in the selection of the size and type of materials and elements, as there will be little or no control over their use. Not only should these playgrounds be built more sturdily and substantially, but they should have fewer moving or fragile parts.

The supervised playground, on the other hand, may have a limited number of fixed elements. This restriction is desirable since it enables the child to exercise imagination in the broadest possible range. Such a playground provides the greatest opportunity for flexibility and therefore interpretation (Figure 7-44). It offers the opportunity to provide not only movable elements attached to the facility, but also totally movable ones, such as blocks, ropes, ladders, lumber, and the like.

Parental involvement If a parent accompanies the child to the play environment, at least at the early end of the age range, we commonly see the parent playing with the child nearby or assisting directly in a play activity. For example, the parent may not only place the child in a swing, but may also remain to push the swing. Alternatively, the adult may play on an apparatus similar to the child's. The first example is not really an interactive situation because of the dependency on the parent created by the apparatus. The child's role is reduced to a passive one. A parent playing alongside the child, on the other hand, may look silly if the environment is out of scale with the adult's size, or the incongruity may embarrass the child and make the parent's role a confused one, since the parent and the child are clearly not peers. For this reason, the facilities of a playground should allow the child to interact or experience without the necessity for the parent's assistance.

Nonetheless, there are times when a parent or another child can assist in expanding and altering the child's experience—in moving elements around or by offering a boost, for example. These are important learning experiences for the child and should be encouraged. Not only do they demonstrate the effects of cooperation, but they allow the child's participation in a mutually beneficial event. To encourage situations where both the parent and the child can enjoy the play experience at the same time, facilities for each should be visually or physically interrelated. For example, a juvenile play facility with an adjacent exercise course may involve the parent at the adult level while the child is involved in the play environment. The first important point is that the facility should encourage situations where all the constituents involved can participate. Purely passive experiences should not be encouraged— they are rarely rewarding. Second, experiences in the play environment should, as closely as possible, replicate or parallel real life experiences of cooperation, participation, and mutual assistance. Third, by staging the activities so that all participants have a challenge commensurate with their own age and skills, diverse age groups within the family or community are encouraged to participate in recreation together. Not only is this socially beneficial, but it also encourages learning through observation and emulation.

Observer, supervisor, or play leader If a juvenile play environment can have an adult in attendance when the facility is in use, an opportunity exists to further expand the participants' level of experience. The designer should first of all investigate the type of adult involvement expected. In rather simplistic terms, an observer is someone who does not get involved with activities, but is mainly concerned that no

Fig. 7-44 A supervised playground can provide expanded opportunities. *Photograph credit: M. Paul Friedberg.*

activity has the potential for conflict or danger. An observer might be a parent, an elderly person, a passer-by, or a paid custodian.

A supervisor, on the other hand, is involved with the activities and gives direction, order, and structure. The term "supervisor" is, in many cases, considered synonymous with discipline. Although the supervisor's role can be beneficial in the degree of structure imposed, there always exists, however, a possibility of limiting the child's imagination and inventiveness.

The play leader provides the protective elements of the observer and the supervisor, but more important, he or she is a guide to the experiences of the play environment. Through being present within the play area, this person can allow the children to explore and invent at the speed and level appropriate to each one. By indicating alternative methods of using materials or facilities or by suggesting a variety of different social arrangements, the play leader can encourage fantasy, dramatic, and cognitive play (Figure 7-45). The creative leader requires the least amount of structure within the play environment and the greatest amount of flexible, movable materials.

Where play facilities are governed merely by observation, they should be complete, self-contained entities, easy to manage and maintain. Where supervision is possible, it offers the potential for greater flexibility and the use of movable facilities, such as wagons, carts, blocks, and planks. With a play leader, a built environment is significantly less structured, offering children, in conjunction with the play leader, the opportunity to create environments of their own. The basic armature is provided by the designer through materials available on the site or introduced periodically into the play environment.

Mixing age groups It is not appropriate to intermix the facilities of two significantly different age groups within the same area. The potential for a variety of separate conflicts exists. Definition of territory and physical accidents are two obvious problems. Nevertheless, it is important to visually interrelate facilities for different age groups because of the possibility for expanded learning experiences. For example, the younger child, in observing older peers as they develop physically and men-

Fig. 7-45 A play leader can encourage fantasy.
Photograph credit: M. Paul Friedberg.

Fig. 7-46 The spectator/performer relationship is important. *Photograph credit: M. Paul Friedberg.*

tally, will emulate their activities in order to master additional skills. An additional benefit of close interrelationships among the play areas for different age groups is that parents can more easily observe the play activities of their children, who may be of different ages. Since older siblings are often required to monitor the play activities of brothers and sisters, this job becomes easier and therefore more dependable when the play areas are visually connected. Play areas containing significantly different levels of challenge should be separated for reasons of safety and territory, but for learning and observation, they need to be close. The optimal balance of separation and closeness is a reflection of the designer's skill.

Visual interaction   Every play activity has within it the potential of a relationship between spectators and performers—those who take part in the activity and those who watch. This may range from the obvious observation of a team game to the more subtle watching done by strollers as they pass activities, seated people, or other strollers. When children are observed, they are also watching. Spectators and performers are relating visually—people enjoy watching other people. The spectator-performer relationship (Figure 7-46) is helpful in generating contact, energy, and interest. Careful thought should be given to it in the design of those parts of the play environment that are intended for the performers and those that are meant for the spectators so that both groups can interact and relate in a comfortable and natural manner.

Representation versus abstraction   In play environments, adults seem to desire a literal expression of objects, e.g., use of airplanes, giraffes, turtles, even a giant button (Figure 7-47). Although this choice may be visually attractive, it severely limits the child's imagination. If a fire engine, for example, is in a neighborhood facility, the problem is accentuated, since the facility is used repeatedly by the same children. Initially, they might be attracted to the form of a fire engine or a truck, but upon continuous exposure to the object, this interest diminishes.

Abstract forms with component elements, such as wheels, steps, seats, and level changes, provide a child with a far broader range of opportunities for interpretation and fantasy. They tap the unique ability of children to transport themselves into different worlds through their individual ways of perceiving objects. When you limit opportunities for interpretation, you are limiting the ability to fantasize. A child who brings a small toy truck (Figure 7-48) to a playground can imagine being within the vehicle and driving around in it without feeling the need of a full-size replica.

On the other hand, playgrounds that are designed as unique experiences and visited infrequently may very well be appropriate for the creation of literal worlds rarely found in the child's daily environment. In such cases, because the experience may be intended to assist in the understanding of some natural phenomenon, such as leverage or electricity, or some common facility, say a fire station, there is obviously greater latitude in designing with representational objects. The basis for the use of representational rather than abstract forms in the creation of a play environment is therefore the frequency of the use of the play facility by the individual children who visit it.

Sculpture versus design   A commonly held myth is that children like to play on sculpture and that, therefore, sculptors should design playgrounds (Figure 7-49). From time to time, a piece of sculpture may have play value, but to think that sculpture and play are synonymous is an exhibition of insensitivity to both the child's needs

Fig. 7-47   A giant button is more a piece of sculpture than a play element. *Photograph credit: M. Paul Friedberg.*

Fig. 7-48   A toy truck can be more imaginatively used by a child than a full-sized one. *Photograph credit: M. Paul Friedberg.*

251

Fig. 7-49 A herd of ossified horses. *Photograph credit: M. Paul Friedberg.*

and the sculptor's intention. The concept of play sculpture originated from a limited understanding of art and the notion that the presence of art in the playground will enhance the cultural development of the child.

The sculptor's forms are created to express an idea, but not necessarily a function. In creating, the sculptor attempts to communicate a very private experience—a particular view of the world. It would be completely inappropriate for the artist to modify these forms and compromise the purpose of the sculpture so that the particular piece will function better as a play facility. Generally, where this has occurred, the result is poor sculpture.

Recognition and familiarity Although a successful play facility places great emphasis on manipulative objects and variations in self-made environments, it is beneficial to have at least one core structure that is familiar and easily understood by the child. Every child needs a certain amount of reassurance provided by known and understandable objects within the environment. Although children wish to be challenged, at the same time they have to fulfill their other psychological and social needs for security and familiarity. They also need time to perch and passively observe—to dig in a sandpile, for example—and for this, a consistent and familiar element is best (Figure 7-50).

Safety The adult world has much potential for danger: crossing the street, climbing stairs, scaling a ladder. Yet, we learn to function in these situations. If the playground is to be a learning experience, the child should have similar opportunities to cope with potentially dangerous situations. The play area is an ideal place for the child to test skills and abilities. This does not mean that dangerous or unexpectedly hazardous situations should be built in. Rather, the design of a safe facility should enable children to encounter and understand potentially dangerous situations and allow them time to deal with them intelligently. The solution in the playground is not the elimination of all dangerous aspects, since most playground accidents are caused by unexpected situations, such as collisions between children, crowding in elevated places, and sudden unexpected drops. Furthermore, the playground, by its very nature, must have a certain degree of challenge to hold the child's interest. If the challenge of the outside world is greater, the child will not use the play area (Figure 7-51).

There are, however, a number of conditions that should be avoided if at all possible (Figure 7-52): Acute angles, called pinch points, can do just that; distances between vertical or horizontal bars should be great enough to permit a child to pull his or her head out from between the bars without getting stuck, or they should be too small for a child's head to be there in the first place. Wherever possible, surfaces should be soft; decks and platforms should be contained if they are elevated; facilities that generate a high degree of activity should not be placed adjacent to one another; and moving elements should have sufficient surrounding space to reduce the chances of collision.

Challenge The concept of what constitutes a challenge is subjective and not at all universal. The variables that determine the level of challenge presented by a play element include age, sex, culture, economic status, and individual intelligence level. For example, a child from a lower-income family is likely to be more physically independent and adventuresome at a younger age because of being forced to be on his or her own earlier, thanks to the impact of limited living space, absence of parents, or a large family size. Middle- and upper-income children are generally kept within the protective custody of a parent, an older sibling, or a hired helper until a later age. Also, until very recently, girls were generally more protected than boys, so they were exposed to fewer challenging situations.

Physical relationships Various interactive relationships occur among age groups as well as among the different social strata of children's society. Each user group has a demonstrated or verbalized need, which should be met through the design of the physical facility. The interrelationships of these facilities within the juvenile play area can reinforce or fragment the users' experiences. It is important, therefore, that the juxtaposition of facilities be carefully considered once the program is set. For example, the designer should try to relate the elderly's seating area with the tot or preteen facility so that there is a visual interaction between the two. The intent is to create more interest for the elderly person visiting the playground, as well as to provide an audience for the children's activities. This is important, since a child is basically an actor who perceives an audience as a significant part of approval and recognition. However, since the elderly may have other interests than watching children, an additional, more sequestered location should be provided for more passive experiences.

Fig. 7-50 Sand provides an opportunity for quiet play. *Photograph credit: M. Paul Friedberg.*

Fig. 7-51 The play area often must compete with nearby attractions. *Photograph credit: M. Paul Friedberg.*

Fig. 7-52 Playground equipment hazards. *Photograph credit: The American City & County.*

ALLOW SUFFICIENT SPACE AROUND EQUIPMENT.

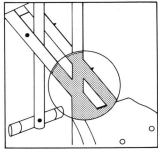

PINCHING OR CRUSHING POTENTIALS SHOULD HAVE PROTECTIVE GUARDS.

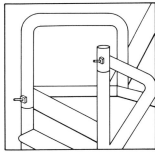

AVOID EXPOSED FASTENERS THAT ARE NOT ROUNDED AND SMOOTH.

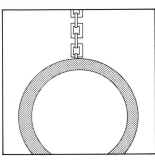

RINGS BETWEEN 5" AND 10" IN DIAMETER CAN TRAP A CHILD'S HEAD.

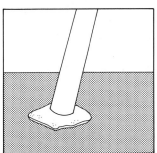

USE SOFT SURFACES BENEATH PLAY EQUIPMENT TO REDUCE INJURIES.

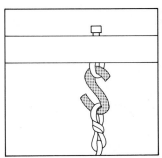

OPEN-ENDED S-HOOK CAN CATCH CLOTHES AND SKIN.

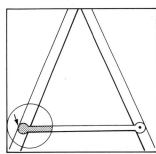

AVOID SHARP EDGES ON ALL PLAY ELEMENTS.

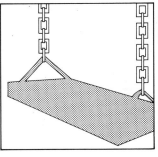

AVOID HARD ELEMENTS THAT CAN SWING AND HURT.

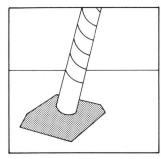

ANCHOR ALL PLAY EQUIPMENT SECURELY.

Reciprocation and manipulation A child needs flexible opportunities that can be provided by manipulative materials and facilities (Figure 7-53), such as sand, wheels, springboards, (Figure 7-54), balancing boards, and nets. Take the simple pendulum action of a swing (Figure 7-55). It is not unusual to see a child pushing an empty swing just because the swing will return. In the same way, a revolving door or an elevator button will intrigue the child. The child manipulates an object and it has an effect on the environment. This so-called playful act is, in reality, an exploration and experimentation with the world. Through the effects of their own actions, children learn how they can control or modify real situations and explore their own ability and power in the environment.

Fixed versus flexible equipment Through various play experiences children broaden their understanding of themselves in relation to the world. Because real-life environments are constantly altered by various factors while still maintaining a cer-

Fig. 7-53 A trampoline is play. *Photograph credit: M. Paul Friedberg.*

Fig. 7-54 A springboard is play. *Photograph credit: Ron Green, courtesy of TimberForm Division, Columbia Cascade Timber Company.*

Fig. 7-55 A swing is play. *Photograph credit: Ron Green, courtesy of TimberForm Division, Columbia Cascade Timber Company.*

Fig. 7-56 Construction materials provide elements for play. *Photograph credit: M. Paul Friedberg.*

Fig. 7-57 Altering the environment is part of play. *Photograph credit: M. Paul Friedberg.*

Fig. 7-58 The forces of gravity and friction can be elements for play. *Photograph credit: M. Paul Friedberg.*

Fig. 7-59 Climbing is an important aspect of play. *Photograph credit: Ron Green, courtesy of TimberForm Division, Columbia Cascade Timber Company.*

tain amount of consistency, the most stimulating play environment should offer the child a similar opportunity to experiment and adapt to both known and unknown situations. Such an environment would be a microcosm of the real world. Fixed playgrounds, even with some movable equipment, have a tendency to provide repetitious experiences, limiting the child's imagination and skills. While there are of course various economic and administrative problems that mandate fixed play environments, it is always more beneficial to have elements available that can alter the playground.

The range of alterable materials is probably as broad as the designer's or the child's imagination—blocks, planks, ladders, and ramps are only the most elementary. Construction materials on a more sophisticated level can also be used (Figure 7-56). Where there is no supervisor or play leader, the design should encourage children to bring their own materials or objects, such as wagons, trucks, pails, and shovels. Physical, cognitive, and social development is enhanced by the child's ability to engage, alter, and participate in the environment (Figure 7-57). Anything from a toy truck or a cardboard box to a piece of styrofoam contributes to this end.

Movable versus static facilities Most children are intrigued by experiences involving a reduction in the effect of gravity, such as swinging, sliding, and jumping (Figure 7-58). This phenomenon is accomplished not only by moving facilities such as seesaws, but also by static elements, like slides, that also decrease the effects of friction. Where possible, equipment, such as nets and ladders, should be totally detached from the fixed play environment, to be brought out, used, and then stored again. However, built-in equipment is advisable where no supervisor or play leader is available. It is for the designer to determine the balance of flexible physical experiences that can be available within a static playground while still making it possible to maintain the facility with relative ease.

Special phenomena The most compelling physical activities found within the play environment are those that allow the child to have experiences not ordinarily found within the everyday environment. Swinging and sliding, for example, bend the laws of gravity, freeing the child to experience exhilarating sensations. By climbing to a new height, children can feel taller (Figure 7-59), thus changing their physical relationship to other children and adults (Figure 7-60). Swinging (Figure 7-61) and jumping are two of the most important components in a play environment because they are physically exciting for the child, easily understood, and fun. While an adult may seek out a rewarding experience in recreation, a child simply seeks fun, excitement, and activities that he or she understands.

Mystery, surprise, discovery The most interesting experiences in the play environment are those that unfold slowly, providing unexpected results. These experiences create interest and excitement, giving the child an opportunity to adapt and cope with the unfamiliar and unexpected. They also provide complexity to ordinary situations. Where the variables are greatest, such as in flexible environments, the opportunities for mystery, surprise, and discovery are also greatest. Within a structured or static playground, the designer, having a stronger challenge to provide such experiences, will rely more heavily on those facilities that can bend natural phenomena, such as swings, seesaws, and slides.

Natural versus synthetic environment Before playgrounds, children had to rely on immediately accessible environments for recreation. A child in the country could use trees, rocks, streams (Figure 7-62), farm tools, machinery, and animals,

Fig. 7-60 Climbing alters normal height relationships. *Photograph credit: M. Paul Friedberg.*

Fig. 7-61 Swinging is easily understood and is fun. *Photograph credit: Ron Green, courtesy of TimberForm Division, Columbia Cascade Timber Company.*

Fig. 7-62 Country play using available opportunities. *Photograph credit: M. Paul Friedberg.*

Fig. 7-63 City play using available opportunities. *Photograph credit: M. Paul Friedberg.*

Fig. 7-64 A natural sliding pond. *Photograph credit: M. Paul Friedberg.*

while the city child played in the street (Figure 7-63). Although the city is probably one of the most exciting environments a child can encounter, it can also be the most conflicting. There are all too few places where a child can engage in play activities without being in conflict with some other interest group. It has therefore become necessary to create a playground—a synthetic environment—where experiences of a natural environment can be replicated. In the natural environment a wide variety of different materials and opportunities can be found, ranging from rocks, wood, and water, to sliding and climbing situations (Figure 7-64). The synthetic play environment, in trying to emulate this, should not try for literal duplication. Rather, it should aim to abstract the natural setting so that the same experiences can be obtained within a more limited amount of space. While the juvenile play environment can use a wide variety of materials ranging from hard to soft, wet to dry, rough to smooth, this variety must be tempered with discretion so as to avoid a chaotic environment that can confuse and frustrate the child.

Materials The materials used within a play environment depend for their selection on the factors of expected use, maintenance requirements, and economics. Perhaps the most overriding factor is the location, since it affects the amount of vandalism to be anticipated. In an area subject to such incursions, the materials must be as vandal-resistant as possible. Although such protection can be accomplished in many ways, probably the most logical is to modify the design to make the elements strong enough to resist attack. While this procedure will of course increase initial costs, it may be foolhardy not to undertake it.

Level Surfaces The most desirable material for level surfaces within a playground is one with a soft, resilient surface to protect against injury and to allow manipulation. Such materials as sand or earth are generally the most attractive and initially the least expensive. However, they generate high maintenance costs since they can migrate, and they have the potential for housing all sorts of undesirable foreign elements, such as debris, animal excrement, and even germs and bacteria. In addition, they dry slowly and so are subject to downtime following a heavy rain.

Manufactured items that soften the impact of falls may be used as alternatives to natural materials. They range from rubber matting to resilient plastics that are applied to existing paved surfaces. Although these so-called safety surfaces are more desirable than the raw concrete or asphalt surface, they are not so effective or so attractive as the natural materials. Where some degree of safety is advisable, they are good alternatives, and while they will not necessarily prevent broken bones from hard falls, they will reduce the likelihood of abrasions and concussions.

At the lowest end of the maintained-cost scale are the commonly used surface materials of concrete and asphalt. Both dry rapidly and are easy to maintain, but asphalt is generally preferable since it is somewhat more resilient than concrete and its installation is less costly.

Inclined Surfaces   Inclined surfaces require hand- or footholds so that children can easily traverse them. The surface materials generally used for level surfaces are not appropriate for this function. Instead, wood, granite, brick, or any other kind of small paving-type block is recommended. The hand- or footholds should be recessed rather than projected from the surface, as this design provides the necessary perches without creating potential danger. The recesses should be rounded if possible, and designed so that water will easily drain out. Granite blocks that have formerly been used for street paving have proven to be extremely successful in the play environment, since they have already been rounded and smoothed by the friction and abrasion of automobile traffic.

Structures   Almost any material can be used for a play structure. Permanent materials such as wood, metal, plastic, or fiberglass can be used, as can more temporary and flexible ones, such as cardboard, canvas, and rope. The selection will depend on the degree of supervision provided, the level of maintenance expected, the need for vandal protection, and of course the budget.

Metals are usually the cheapest of the permanent materials. They are strong and can cover a significant amount of space in relation to the amount of material used. However, they are very good conductors and therefore can be unpleasantly hot in the summer and uncomfortably cold in winter. Their lack of visual warmth, however, is a factor that a skilled designer can overcome. Metal can rust or corrode, and this possibility must be counteracted with some kind of surface treatment. Despite its limitations, steel, because of its durability and economy is the most frequently used metal.

Wood is visually the most interesting material, and after metal, has the potential for the widest variety of shapes and forms. While it has the advantage of not conducting heat or cold very well, it tends to splinter or split. Although this characteristic is a liability, most children are able to adapt to it; in fact, it provides one more step in learning to deal with the materials in their environment. Wood also has the disadvantages of being both flammable and capable of rotting. In using wood, therefore, it is necessary to specify that it be treated with some form of nontoxic preservative to prevent rot. While heavy timbers will not support fire but will merely char, lighter wood members should be fireproofed.

Plastic and fiberglass materials are relatively new. Although they may be very attractive in color and texture, they can pose serious maintenance problems, since they are prone to scratching and discoloration, and sometimes can be flammable or smoke-producing. As the manufacture of fiberglass items requires expensive molds, repetitive elements are likely to be used, which mitigates against the child's modification or interpretation of the form. Plastic and fiberglass are expensive, but their use can be considered for special situations.

Temporary Materials   The most desirable play environments usually consist of materials that are meant for temporary use lasting a day, a month, a year. These tend to be easily manipulated, readily changed, or renewed by children. Because of the low investment needed for such materials, the child can be provided with a wide choice with which to experiment. Ideally, a play environment should offer a combination of permanent and temporary materials. The balance between the two types should be an outgrowth of an analysis of the budget, the maintenance level, the supervision provided, and the type of play program desired.

Graphics and color   The design of the playground should reinforce the concept of playfulness and freedom. Color and graphics can be very helpful in achieving this end (Figure 7-65). The use of these elements tends to be simplistic, reflecting society's general attitudes toward children. But since the play environment provides learning experiences, it is not inconsistent to include complex graphics and subtle color schemes, stimulating the adult's as well as the child's interest and imagination.

Toilet facilities   Although toilet facilities are generally considered to be a management and maintenance liability, they are essential for the child, who is an immediate animal. By the time a child realizes that a toilet is needed, it is usually too late to return home or to travel very far. While such facilities do require some supervision, they are sufficiently important generally to justify the expense of installing and maintaining them.

ADVENTURE PLAYGROUNDS

Much of what has been indicated suggests that the best possible environment for the child is one that is unstructured. With a rich array of materials and opportunities and a creative adult play leader, children can be provided with direction and instruction. They can each discover, explore, experiment, and manipulate this environment in relation to themselves in order to have opportunities for social interaction and emotional and physical development.

The problems of economics and administrative procedures usually inhibit a full expression of these objectives. However, in recent years there has been limited experimentation with adventure playgrounds, which generally embody most of the challenges and opportunities considered so desirable. These special play areas are undesigned environments that have an abundant array of building materials and tools that are usually under the control and supervision of a play leader. The child is provided with the challenge of creating and interpreting a personal play environment. Older children are allowed the use of power tools. As young children develop knowledge and sufficient skill, they too are permitted to use the tools and materials. The playground is never completed; there is constant construction and alteration as each new person or group uses the tools. Materials challenge the imagination; the wide variety of opportunities encourages, and in some cases mandates, cooperation and a significant amount of social interaction. The adventure playground resembles more closely the microcosm of the adult world that do most playgrounds with fixed forms and structures.

One of the difficulties that arises in developing and administering an adventure playground is the disheveled visual appearance of the space, since it is designed by children and always under construction. There is no attempt to develop an aesthetic inherent to a well-designed, conventional playground. Many adults claim that these

Fig. 7-65 Bold decorative forms imply play and freedom. *Photograph credit: M. Paul Friedberg.*

are dangerous facilities because of the loose materials, the use of tools, and the possible introduction of water and fire. Another difficulty is the paramount need for effective supervision. Despite the relatively low capital cost involved, this concept is difficult for many municipalities and agencies to accept, since they are usually geared to spending money to buy things but not to maintain them. While a full adventure playground may not be feasible, elements of the concept can be integrated into an otherwise conventional play facility.

PLAYGROUNDS FOR THE HANDICAPPED

In addition to the physical and intellectual limitations of different age groups, children may have special physical, intellectual, and emotional difficulties that require attention if those children are to be accommodated within the play environment. Although research and information on this subject are limited, there are two fundamental approaches.

In the first, handicapped children are separated from so-called normal children and a specific play environment is created to provide for their special needs. Barrier-free environments are designed for those confined to wheelchairs, and special swings, slides, and climbing facilities are provided for those with limited mobility. The greater the disabilities, the more accommodation is made within the environment to relate to the problem. Some playgrounds for the handicapped, for example, are constructed totally from benign materials such as soft blocks and resilient pads.

A second approach to design for the handicapped is to attempt to integrate the disabled child into the normal playground. Since the same fundamental principles of play apply to all children, the issue is to tailor the design of the facility to a level of activity that can be used by the majority of the children and that also can be mastered by the handicapped child. Through this approach, a slide might accommodate a child who must maneuver backward to get up the steps to the top, while still being suitable for use by other children in a more conventional manner. Horizontal ladders can be placed low enough for a child in a wheelchair to reach them from beneath, while more agile children can still crawl over the top of it.

It is important to determine the amount of accommodation that can feasibly be included. This task will involve determining the likely number of handicapped children within the area served who would be able to use the facility, as well as the types of disabilities they possess. While it is difficult to design a play environment that can be usable by severely handicapped children, research in this field is continuing. In time, we will gain additional knowledge to understand and deal with this problem.

THE OVERALL GOAL

Since we are beginning to incorporate concepts of personal growth and enrichment more and more into daily adult life, does it not follow that these growing experiences for the child should not be confined to the playground? Logic brings us to conceive of the entire environment as becoming the child's playground. In this way, personal growth can advance continuously as children are exposed to experiences and activities all around them, without the overwhelming structure and judgment of the adult world. By expanding their horizons, they can make use of the entire world, and recreation can be integrated into their total living experience. If a child were to carry this integration forward while developing into an adult, the living, playing, and working potential of his or her entire life span would be enhanced, increasing the limits of the human learning capacity—physical, social, and cognitive.

To date, although our attitudes toward the value of play have changed, and although we have improved the quality of experiences found in the play environment, we still have not changed our fundamental attitudes toward designing those environments. We continue to improve separate facilities for recreation rather than to interconnect the natural and the especially made environments into a cohesive, fulfilling recreational experience. When we are able to effect this integration, the playground will then assume the specific role within the total environment of being a place for spending unstructured time enjoyably and for sharing in high-intensity activities away from surrounding conflicting elements.

BIBLIOGRAPHY

Aaron, David, *Child's Play,* Harper & Row, Publishers, Incorporated, New York, 1969
Advisory for Open Education, *Building with Tires*
Allen, Hurtwood, *Planning for Play,* Thames and Hudson, London
Bengtsson, Arvid, *Adventure Playgrounds,* Frederick A. Praeger, Inc., New York, 1972
Cooper, C. C., "Adventure Playgrounds," *Landscape Architecture,* October 1970, pp. 18–29, 88–91
Dattner, Richard, *Design for Play,* Van Nostrand Reinhold Co., New York, 1969
Education Digest, "Adventure Playgrounds," March 1972
Farralones Designs, *Farralones Scrapbook*
Friedberg, M. Paul, *Handcrafted Playgrounds,* Random House, Inc., New York, 1975
————, *Play and Interplay,* The Macmillan Company, New York, 1972
Huizinga, Johan, *Homo Ludens, A Study of the Play Element in Culture,* Beacon Press, Boston, 1970
Lederman, Alfred, and **Alfred Trachsel,** *Creative Playgrounds and Recreation Centers,* Frederick A. Praeger, New York, 1968
Lincoln Savings and Loan, Linda Vista Playground Project Poster, Lincoln Savings and Loan, P.O. Box 600038, Los Angeles
Murphy, L. B., and **S. M. Leeper,** *The Ways Children Learn,* No. 73-1026, U.S. Department of Health, Education, and Welfare, Washington, D.C., 1970
Natural History Magazine, "Special Play," reprint, The American Museum of Natural History, New York
North Carolina State University School of Design, *Planning Outdoor Play (POP),* North Carolina State University, Raleigh, N.C.

Osman, Peter, *Patterns for Designing Children's Centers,* Educational Facilities Laboratory, 850 Third Avenue, New York

Sanoff, Henry, et al., *Learning Environments for Children,* North Carolina School of Design, Raleigh

Schoolworks, Inc., *Schoolworks Primer,* Schoolworks, Inc., 33 Union Square West, New York, N. Y. 10003

Stone, J., and **N. Rudolph,** *Play and Playgrounds,* National Association for the Education of Young Children, 1834 Connecticut Ave., N.W., Washington, D.C., 20008, 1970

CHAPTER EIGHT
DECORATIVE POOLS AND FOUNTAINS
M. Paul Friedberg and Cynthia Rice

INTRODUCTION

Water is a forever-changing feature of the physical environment. It holds our fascination as few other natural elements can. Flowing, spraying, falling from above, or shooting into the air, in turbulence or at rest, it performs at times like a living organism and, as such, has the singular capacity to energize its inanimate surroundings.

Subject to the physical laws of hydraulics and gravity, water is responsive to the designer's manipulations. At the same time, it behaves independently of its physical constraints. Natural phenomena or mechanical devices will change its state from solid to liquid or mist, and water itself can change the color or apparent texture of whatever it touches. It can be enclosed, directed, or pressurized, but whatever its form, even in the serenity of a reflecting pool, water is never static. By employing and directing the continual motion of water, the designer introduces an added dimension, the element of time, into an otherwise stationary environment.

HISTORY

Arid climates required the development of irrigation technology and because of the scarcity and great value of water, desert societies made early use of this technology to incorporate water into their gardens as a decorative feature.

Ancient Persia

Contemporary descriptions of the Mesopotamian and Egyptian water displays illustrate this point by depicting decorative pools and channels that doubled as reservoirs and irrigation canals. These pools tended toward simple geometric shapes, providing the major focus in a garden or courtyard; they often included papyrus, lotus, and other water-associated plants; some were used to raise fish for food.

Within the walled gardens of Persia, water served to cool and humidify the atmosphere and, by its reflection of the sky and trees and with the gentle sound of many small jets, created an oasis of tranquillity in contrast with the relentless desert without. The Persian use of water in garden design maximized its aesthetic properties as well as its capacity to modify the immediate environment.

Islamic religious sanctions against standing water and the representation of living things led to the Persian emphasis on the play of moving water itself, rather than the statuary associated with Western gardens, as a decorative element (Figure 8-1). The Islamis developed their own sophisticated technology for pressurized displays, which was then transported to Spain with the Moslem conquest in the eighth century and from there to Italy and all of Western Europe.

Medieval Europe

The use of water in the gardens of medieval Europe, as in Persia, had utilitarian origins. The *savina,* or cistern, was the central focus for the monastic cloister or palace garden, containing water for medicinal herbs and flowers as well as for drinking and communal bathing (Figure 8-2).

Renaissance Italy

The Italian Renaissance witnessed the liberation of water from pure function and modest displays to a grandiose exhibition of temporal wealth as well as human technological control of natural elements. Originating in the medieval tradition, the Renaissance fountain began as a single basin, often adorned by statuary containing the water source. Such a piece was "Florence Rising from the Waters," depicting a woman wringing out her long wet hair. The grotto, also a popular feature of the Renaissance garden as a cool, shady retreat, often included a small waterfall or, as at the Media Villa of Castello, hidden jets. Called a "water joke," these jets could be secretly turned on to surprise and drench the unsuspecting visitor.

Hilly terrain north of Rome provided the necessary topographical variation to support complex gravity-powered displays, epitomized at the Villa d'Este in Tivoli and the Villa Lante in Bagnoia (Figure 8-3). The water garden of the Villa d'Este was begun in 1550 with the diversion of an entire river to supply jets, cascades, reflecting pools, and the famous water organ with its special effects ranging from the sound of canon shots, to the song of birds, to the appearance of rainbows (Figure 8-4). At the Villa Lante, the water is still the major element in the gardens (Figure 8-5); on a smaller, quieter scale, the water descends the mountainside between twin villas through a variety of cascades, jets, and troughs to rest in a large geometric composition of four reflecting pools.

France

The famous fountains of Versailles represent the French adaptation of the spectacular Italian water displays to more level terrain (Figure 8-6). The grand canal acts as a unifying spine for the gardens, reinforcing their predominant east–west axis, which centers on the château. These canals, as well as the lake at Chantilly, are an extension of the medieval moat, which was originated as a defense and was retained as a

Fig. 8-1 The Court of the Canal at the Generalife Gardens, Granada, Spain. *Photograph credit: Richard Arioli.*

Fig. 8-2 The *savina* as a focus for the social life of the medieval palace garden. *Credit: "Giardino della giovinezza," from the manuscript* **De Sphaera** *in the Biblioteca Estense, Modena, Italy. Photograph by Foto Roncaglia, Modena.*

Fig. 8-3 Villa d'Este, Tivoli, Italy. *Photograph credit: M. Paul Friedberg.*

Fig. 8-4 Terrace of 100 Fountains, Villa d'Este.
Photograph credit: M. Paul Friedberg.

Fig. 8-5 Fish rill at Villa Lante, Bagnoia, Italy, designed by di Vignola in 1566. *Photograph credit: M. Paul Friedberg.*

Fig. 8-6 Fountains at Versailles. *Photograph credit: M. Paul Freidberg.*

Fig. 8-7 André Le Nôtre's design for the gardens at Chantilly expanded the role of the medieval moat to a decorative reflective setting for the château. *Photograph credit: M. Paul Friedberg.*

decorative feature, framing and reflecting the building in the landscape (Figure 8-7). They also provided recreation in the form of boating for the royal courtiers.

A total of 1400 jets at Versailles required the construction of a giant pumping station several miles away at Marly to divert water from the Seine. Despite the apparently unlimited resources of horse, human, and wind power, however, the pumps never completely succeeded in supplying the jets to their fullest capacity, but did lower the water table for miles around.

England

The use of water in the English garden developed, as on the Continent, from a single basin at the center of a courtyard in Elizabethan days. Then came the French-style canal or "Long Garden" at Hampton Court under King Charles in the seventeenth century, followed by an increasingly "natural" style of the large ornamental lakes at Blenheim and Stonehead in the eighteenth century.

China

Water played a major role in the Chinese garden. In fact, the Chinese word for garden is a combination of the words "land" and "water"; together, they symbolized the Taoist opposites: yin and yang. As an idealization of natural forms, the garden was a microcosm of the landscape at large. The water as river, lake, or ocean provided the links in a series of landscape compositions that were intended to be perceived sequentially as though reading a scroll.

A French missionary visiting Peking in the eighteenth century describes the Emperor's garden:

> The sides of the canals or lesser streams are not faced (as they are with us) with smooth stones, and in a straight line; but look rude and rustic, with different pieces of rock, some of which jut out, and others recede inward; and are placed with so much art that you would take it to be the work of Nature.

Japan

Chinese principles of landscape design traveled to Japan with the expansion of Buddhism. The original Japanese word for garden means "island," again revealing the significance of water in the design. The Japanese garden almost invariably included a lake with islands; unlike the Chinese garden, it was designed to be perceived as a single composition. Strict rules of symbolism and composition govern the use of the landscape elements: rocks, water, and plant material. The extent to which this symbolism and convention developed is illustrated by the garden at the Zuihoin Temple, where water has been idealized into nonexistence and replaced by sand meticulously arranged in a pattern of waves and currents (Figure 8-8).

The waterfall, another important feature of the Japanese garden, was codified into ten distinct forms: glide falling, linen falling, thread falling, uneven falling, left and right falling, straight falling, side falling, vis-à-vis falling, detached falling, and repeated falling.

Contemporary Design

The forms of contemporary water displays are drawn from the full range of historic, cultural, and environmental vocabulary. They embody the selection and adoption of various elements in order to satisfy specific functions or create a unique experience. Today's water feature tends to be an abstraction of these basic elements rather than a duplication. For example, the fountain in Peavey Plaza, Minneapolis, does not imitate nature, but it incorporates the freedom, vigor, and capacity for refreshment displayed by a mountain cataract (Figures 8-9 and 8-10).

DESIGN WITH WATER

The water feature in the contemporary environment may perform numerous functions: It may provide an aesthetic experience, create a mood, reinforce or direct circulation paths, and modify the environment.

Fig. 8-8 Garden at the Zuihoin Temple, Japan.
Photograph credit: SK Color Company, Ltd., Tokyo.

Fig. 8-9 **Peavey Plaza, Minneapolis, designed by M. Paul Friedberg.** *Photograph credit: M. Paul Friedberg.*

Fig. 8-10 **Peavey Plaza, Minneapolis, designed by M. Paul Friedberg.** *Photograph credit: M. Paul Friedberg.*

The first step in designing a water feature is to determine its desired functional components, the aesthetic potential of the design, and the inherent limitations of the particular situation. The two major design parameters of *objectives* and *constraints* guide the development of a design that exhibits the appropriate form, scale, and quality of experience for the particular site.

Objectives

Aesthetic satisfaction The passive forms of water in lakes, pools, and slow-moving channels can achieve a number of aesthetic or visual results, many of them simultaneously.

- As a mirror reflecting the landscape, or simply as an uninterrupted surface implying added horizontal dimension to a space (Figure 8-11)

- As a vertical dimension introduced by incorporating the image of the sky into the ground plane as well as by creating the illusion of depth beneath that plane

- As a reactive surface upon which to introduce the constantly changing, moving image of clouds and the patterns of rain or snow

- As a means of intensifying the weather's moods, appearing as a cold gray surface on a gloomy day or sparkling under the brilliance of sunlight

- As a way to introduce serenity into an otherwise congested or densely developed site

- By its tranquillity, as a reinforcement of the dignity of a ceremonial or culturally significant site (Figure 8-12)

- By its kinetic potential, as an invitation to the interaction of dabbled fingers or the toss of a coin and as a reward for that interaction through its familiar splashing sound and expanding ripples

- As the creator of allusions to a different time or place, such as a farm pond, a mountain stream or, as in the Japanese garden, the sea (Figure 8-13)

More active water displays will require changes in elevation, either natural or artificial, or energy to generate pressure. This type of display is useful in a confined area where there is no room for a large pool, or where the image that might be

Fig. 8-11 This water display reflects and animates the garden at Tivoli, Copenhagen, Denmark. *Photograph credit: M. Paul Friedberg.*

Fig. 8-12 Cool dignity in the Abby Aldrich Rockefeller Sculpture Garden at the Museum of Modern Art, New York, designed by Philip Johnson, 1955. *Photograph credit: Soichi Sunami, courtesy of the Museum of Modern Art.*

Fig. 8-13 A tropical waterfall in the Wintergarden, Niagara, New York, designed by M. Paul Friedberg. *Photograph credit: M. Paul Friedberg.*

Fig. 8-14 Fort Lincoln New Town in Town, Washington, D.C. *Photograph credit: M. Paul Friedberg.*

Fig. 8-15 Fort Lincoln New Town in Town, Washington, D.C. A water feature with no water flowing. *Photograph credit: M. Paul Friedberg.*

reflected is not particularly interesting. The performance of the water itself becomes the attraction and different visual effects can be achieved.

1. The form and speed of the flow can simulate a natural rivulet such as a wide, shallow, slow-flowing meadow stream, or, with the introduction of irregularities and obstructions in the channel sides and bottom, a mountain brook (Figure 8-14).

2. The appearance of the structure or container without water must always be a major aspect of the design since winter shutdown, maintenance, and mechanical failure are virtually inevitable despite the skills of the designer and the best efforts of the caretaker (Figure 8-15).

3. The designer can choreograph the motion of the pressurized water by programming changing displays and heights of the jets into the mechanical system (Figure 8-16).

Fig. 8-16 The jets of the fountain in front of the Metropolitan Opera House, Lincoln Center, New York, are capable of many changing combinations and heights, providing dynamic interest. *Photograph credit: Andrew Alpern.*

Fig. 8-17 A retention basin that forms a part of the air-conditioning system for the A. C. Nielsen corporate headquarters, Chicago, is also a significant feature of the site design. Designed by M. Paul Friedberg. *Photograph credit: Mark K. Morrison, courtesy of M. Paul Friedberg.*

Environmental control A fountain can incorporate principles of environmental control along with its aesthetic objectives. To name only four:

An air conditioning retention basin can become a major feature in the landscape (Figure 8-17).

The ability to raise or lower the jets also allows for adaptation to changing environmental conditions. The display can be lowered during cold or windy weather to make it seem less chilly or to avoid splash. It can be raised on a hot, sunny day to maximize evaporation. Finer-textured displays will have the greatest cooling capacity.

The splash of many jets or the cascade of a waterfall can mask undesirable ambient noise (Figures 8-18 and 8-19).

The introduction of oxygen into the water by means of aerating jets or

Fig. 8-18 The steady roar of the waterfall at Paley Park, New York, muffles the din of city traffic. *Photograph credit: M. Paul Friedberg.*

Fig. 8-19 The multiple jets of the fountain at Lincoln Center provide auditory insulation from the sounds of New York City. *Photograph credit: Andrew Alpern.*

Fig. 8-20 Sculpture by Henry Moore reflected in a still pool at Lincoln Center, New York. *Photograph credit: M. Paul Friedberg.*

oxygenating plants such as arrowhead or eelgrass can purify an existing water supply to support fish or help prevent stagnation in a decorative pool.

Programmatic functions A pool or channel can direct or restrict traffic as well as provide opportunities for selected recreational activities. For example: A piece of sculpture in the center of a reflecting pool is not only complemented by its reflected image, the decorative quality of the water's surface, and the play of reflected light on the sculptured form, but it is also isolated from human contact and protected from vandalism (Figure 8-20). Or an island in a courtyard pool can serve as a stage for concerts or dramatic performances. (Figure 8-21).

Furthermore, boating, wading, or ice skating can also be made available as an adjunct to the decorative properties of the display.

Constraints

Constraints of climate, geography, surrounding conditions, size, configuration, and functions of the site, combined with the available construction and maintenance budget, will all help define the final design and, if thoroughly understood at the outset, will ensure that the water display can function to its greatest potential. The following annotated checklist indicates possible solutions for certain situations and will suggest others by association.

Climate

Temperature A warm climate may dictate a fine spray of water with a greater potential for evaporation, since this will increase the water's ability to cool its surrounding area.

A northern climate will tend to require a long period of winter shutdown. Therefore the design of the support structure of the display and its appearance or role in

274

the overall design of its setting when the water is turned off are of equal importance to the performance of the water itself.

Alternatively, when frozen, the display might become a skating rink. In such a case, the system must accommodate the expansion of the water as it freezes, as does a pond with shallow, sloping sides.

Wind   In a windy location, a low, compact bubbler jet is preferable to a tall geyser that would drench the surrounding area. To minimize spray, the diameter of the pool surrounding a jet should usually be at least twice its height.

Winds will introduce a rippling texture to a water surface, limiting the reflective qualities and therefore creating a more dynamic display than a reflecting pool.

Precipitation   In areas that receive infrequent heavy rainfall, the design must accommodate fluctuating water levels. A cantilevered pool edge will conceal the water line and will make the changes in level less obvious. Overflow drains and a "makeup" water line should be standard equipment. Nozzles or other features requiring a precise water level should be avoided.

Sun Angles   Sunlight as it sparkles on the water surface or as its reflection plays on surrounding objects can be part of the display if patterns of light and shade are identified at the outset. Also, a carefully placed jet may allow rainbows to appear.

Intense sunlight will heat the water in a pool, encouraging the growth of algae. A light-colored bottom will help reflect the light and limit algae growth.

Geography   A rural site will permit the use of less expensive, low-maintenance natural materials, such as mud or asphalt pool bottoms in nongeometric configurations. But a more heavily trafficked urban site will require frequent cleaning of a pool and will dictate simpler forms. The creation of pockets or crevices where debris may lodge should be avoided. A raised pool is more protected from the airborne dust and pollution of an urban area.

Existing level changes in a site present opportunities for waterfalls and flumes.

Fig. 8-21 **The courtyard pool at the State Street Bank in Quincy, Massachusetts, can serve as an outdoor theatre.** *Photograph credit: M. Paul Friedberg.*

Abrupt level changes will produce more vigorous displays as a point of emphasis within the site. In a flat terrain, the same effect can be achieved through pressure. Topographical changes will also allow for different views of the display.

Additional Considerations

When planning for the decorative use of water, the following factors should also be considered.

Views to be maximized or screened.

Circulation to and within the site.

Nuisances, including the proximity and effect of such offsite elements as noise and pollution.

Utilities that already exist: water, sewer, electric, gas, steam, telephone, underground transit. The pool or fountain should be located to obtain necessary service as well as to avoid conflicts with new construction.

Use patterns at different times of the day for vehicular traffic and for pedestrians—shoppers, business people, children.

Surrounding structures, in terms of scale and location.

Budget, including first cost as well as the cost of operating and maintaining the facilities.

Zoning restrictions and building lines.

Existing elements, such as structures or vegetation, that may be located within the site.

Size and scale in relation to the space, which may already be defined by existing buildings or other forms of enclosure. If not, the designer must fix the territorial limits of the proposed water feature in order to arrive at an appropriate scale and configuration for it.

Materials and Methods

Still-water pools

Surface A successful reflecting pool requires a smooth surface undisturbed by the turbulence of water and wind currents. To ensure its serenity, a pool should be screened from the wind, to achieve protection from the intrusion of airborne leaves and debris on its surface as well as from excessive wave action. If the water is to be recirculated, the velocity of flow and form of the inlet should be carefully controlled in order not to disturb the reflective quality of the surface (unless this movement is to become part of the display).

Edges Riprap or a rough-surfaced sloping edge will accommodate a fluctuating water level and will not cast a shadow on the water surface (Figure 8-22).

A raised rim provides seating at the water's edge while simultaneously acting as a barrier (Figure 8-23).

The shadow cast by a cantilevered lip will conceal stain caused by fluctuating water levels. This lip will also prevent the water from splashing out onto adjacent surfaces (Figure 8-24).

Fig. 8-22

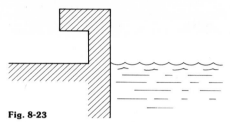

Fig. 8-23

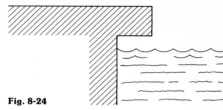

Fig. 8-24

Wood, in the form of pilings or railroad ties, is an informal, inexpensive material that can be useful in a rural site (Figure 8-25).

Lawn is another inexpensive natural material. It is appropriate only for a gradually sloping edge (not more than 4:1) and will not sustain heavy traffic. Precast, perforated concrete slabs may be installed at the water's edge to stabilize the turf. These slabs will quickly be obscured from view as the grass grows around and through them.

Fig. 8-25

Pool Bottoms   A dark-colored pool bottom will not conflict with the reflected image on the pool surface, but in a warm, sunny location, it will absorb more heat and thereby induce the growth of algae in the pool.

A light-colored bottom will emphasize the water's clarity. Decorative two- and three-dimensional designs can be included, using such materials as terrazzo, mosaic tiles, or stones (Figure 8-26).

Less expensive materials for a rural site range from mud or bentonite to asphalt or plastic lining on earth.

Flowing water   The quality of flowing water is influenced by velocity of flow, water depth, surface texture of channel bottom and sides, directional changes, and the introduction of obstacles in the water's path. These can produce effects ranging from an imperceptibly moving glassy surface to a rugged torrent. (Figure 8-27).

A shallow stream in a gently sloping, smooth-sided channel will create a smooth water surface. Increased water depth will not appreciably affect turbulence, but as the slope increases, so does the rate of flow and concomitant turbulence.

Fig. 8-26   Pebbles in the pool bottom at the Honeywell headquarters, Minneapolis. *Photograph credit: M. Paul Friedberg.*

Fig. 8-27   A series of cubes in the channel bottom creates turbulence in this flume at the Honeywell headquarters, Minneapolis. *Photograph credit: M. Paul Friedberg.*

A textured channel bottom will produce a greater turbulence at slower velocities and shallower depths. Roughly textured channel sides will agitate the flow independently of water depth and will have an increasing impact as the velocity of flow increases.

Falling water   The specific form taken by falling water is related directly to the quantity and velocity of flow as well as the texture of the surface or weir over which it cascades (Figure 8-28).

Quantity   To achieve a smooth sheet of water in still air, the flow over the weir crest should be at least ¼ inch deep. Depths greater than ⅜ to ½ inch, however, will begin to produce turbulence, while water depths of less than ¼ inch will fail to sustain a continuous sheet of water (Figure 8-29). The precise control of water depth is essential to the success of any weir-associated display. Valves that regulate the water supply and quantity of the flow through the recirculating pumps should be installed in order to manipulate the display in the field (Figure 8-30). In any case, the crest of the weir must be absolutely level to ensure uniformity of display. In limited applications, the weir height can be made adjustable by installing a slotted plastic or metal strip on the spill lip, to be moved up or down as required.

Texture   Degrees of texture in the weir or other surface may range from the precision of a sharp metal edge through-bush-hammered concrete to roughly cut granite. In combination with different cross sections and profiles, an unlimited variety of water designs can thus be achieved.

A straight, sharp-crested, or knife-edged weir (Figure 8-31) will provide the smoothest sheet of water, the flow of which will move out away from the vertical surface in direct proportion to its approach velocity. At low velocities, the vertical face of the weir must be inclined slightly back from the falling water to break its surface tension and allow the water to drop freely (Figure 8-32). A saw-toothed crest with V-shaped notches at regular intervals (Figure 8-33) and a "Cipolletti" profile composed of trapezoidal depressions (Figure 8-34) are common variations of the weir profile.

Fig. 8-28   The water cascade at Greenacre Park, a mid-block vest-pocket park in midtown New York, designed in 1971 by Sasaki, Dawson, DeMay Associates. *Photograph credit: Andrew Alpern.*

Fig. 8-29   A smooth sheet of water flows over a circular weir at Jeannette Park, New York, designed by M. Paul Friedberg. *Photograph credit: M. Paul Friedberg.*

Fig. 8-30   A shallow depth of flow over the weir causes the falling water to separate into droplets, at Peavey Plaza, Minneapolis. *Photograph credit: M. Paul Friedberg.*

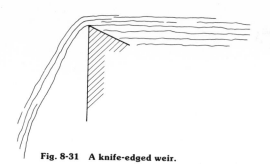

Fig. 8-31   A knife-edged weir.

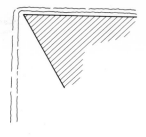

Fig. 8-32   An inclined vertical face allows water to fall freely.

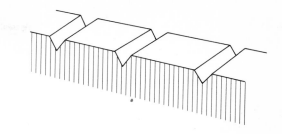

Fig. 8-33   A saw-toothed weir.

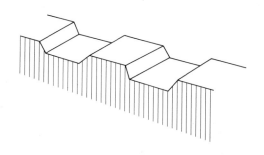

Fig. 8-34   A cipolletti weir.

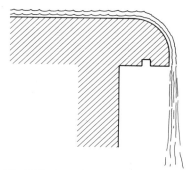

Fig. 8-35   A notch under a cantilevered weir permits the water to fall freely.

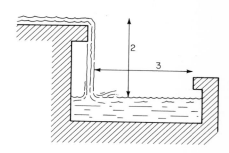

Fig. 8-36   To contain the splash of falling water, the ratio of height of fall to width of pool should be no greater than 2 to 3.

Broad-crested Weirs   Broad-crested weirs require a greater depth of water to produce a continuous sheet as the radius of the crest increases. The increased cross-sectional radius of the tip will also induce the water to fall vertically from the face of the weir and will require greater velocity for the angle of fall to approach the horizontal. If the weir is cantilevered over its vertical surface, a small notch on its underside is necessary to allow the water to fall freely from the lip (Figure 8-35).

The Pool Below   The pool below a weir must contain the total volume of water flowing into it as well as provide sufficient horizontal distance to the pool edge in order to sustain the splash and wave action of the falling water. A comfortable ratio of horizontal distance to depth of fall is 3 to 2, but this proportion will vary according to the volume and velocity of the flow (Figure 8-36).

The lower pool must of course be large enough to contain all the falling water in the system when the pump is turned off, as well as a desirable minimum when the water is in circulation. The upstream pool or source of flowing water will also influence the display and must be free of turbulence when a controlled texture or smooth flow is desired. To control turbulence, the velocity of water feeding the pool is kept slow, and the supply line is located at the bottom of the pool.

Aperture Flow   Water flowing from a spout or orifice represents an extension of the basic principles that control a weir display (Figure 8-37). As the volume and velocity increase, the falling water will approach a horizontal direction and more closely reflect the cross-sectional shape of the opening from which it flows. Size, shape, length, and slope of the spout will all contribute to the performance of the flowing water.

279

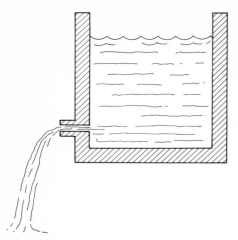

Fig. 8-37 Water flowing through a spout.

Fig. 8-38 A single-geyser fountain at Bowling Green, New York, designed by M. Paul Friedberg. *Photograph credit: M. Paul Friedberg.*

Fig. 8-39 Spray nozzles at Untermeyer Park, Yonkers, New York, designed by M. Paul Friedberg. *Photograph credit: M. Paul Friedberg.*

Fig. 8-40 Geysers produced by a group of aerating nozzles at the Worcester Center Galleria, Worcester, Massachusetts, designed by M. Paul Friedberg. *Photograph credit: M. Paul Friedberg.*

Pressurized displays

Smooth-bore Nozzles A single smooth-bore nozzle will produce the simplest geyser, a high, straight stream of water (Figure 8-38). This nozzle produces the greatest height with the least water, but it is a relatively thin stream, without mass.

Nozzles are often mounted in clusters and thus produce a column of multiple streams. When mounted on a manifold, the pressure at each nozzle may not be uniform, nor will the nozzles themselves be precisely the same. Therefore, a valve at each nozzle will be required to adjust and equalize the displays.

Spray Nozzles A spray nozzle is simply a cluster of very small diameter, smooth-bore nozzles that can produce effects ranging from a fine mist to a powerful and massive spray (Figure 8-39). The same variables of hole diameter, pressure, and quantity of water that influence smooth-bore nozzles control the performance of spray nozzles as well.

Aerating Nozzles   An aerating nozzle produces a foamy turbulent geyser by introducing air into the water as it is discharged (Figure 8-40). Three types of aerating nozzle are available.

1. *The bubbler jet* is mounted below the water surface and produces a low, compact mound of water. This type of jet is often useful in an exposed location where a spray or high jet would be carried by wind currents and would drench the surrounding area. This nozzle produces a relatively massive display with a small amount of water. It is also appropriate for small pools and interior fountains.

2. *The cascade nozzle,* like the bubbler, is mounted below the water surface but produces a higher, conical display of frothy water. The success of this jet depends on a carefully controlled water level in its pool, since the nozzle must remain submerged very close to ½ inch below the water surface. Because these nozzles are submerged, they are concealed, leaving an uninterrupted water surface when the geyser is not operating.

3. *Foam nozzles,* on the other hand, must project a minimum of 1 inch above the water surface. While they are always visible, their advantage is that they do not require such precise water-level control as do the cascade nozzles. They can therefore be installed in a situation where the water level must be allowed to fluctuate. (Figure 8-41).

Special Shapes   "Mushroom" or "morning glory" jets produce a clear sheet of water which falls in a circular pattern (Figure 8-42). "Dandelions," both hemispherical and spherical, achieve their effect through a cluster of very small nozzles, each producing a circular sheet of water (Figure 8-43).

General considerations   When designing any pressurized display, the influences of wind, wave action, splash, and air pollution must be considered. For example, a windy location will call for a lower, more compact display. To avoid splash on adjacent surfaces, the distance between the nozzle and the pool edge should equal or exceed the height of the display. Furthermore, since water, when circulating through the air, will capture airborne particles and chemicals, an efficient filtration system is an inevitable component of an urban fountain or one in a dusty or otherwise polluted environment.

THE MECHANICAL SYSTEM

The basic components of the mechanical system for a recirculating fountain are the pump, with a screen protecting it from debris, a line connecting the pump and the fountain, and another line connecting the pump and the display. A main drain, an overflow drain, and control valves should be added to regulate the operation of the system and facilitate its maintenance (Figure 8-44). The complexity of the system will range from a simple submersible pump in the fountain pool itself to a computerized, multipump, variable mode system requiring a substantial building to contain it. The basic determinants of design for all systems are quantity of water, velocity of flow, and head of pressure.

Quantity of Water

To determine the quantity of water in a pool, the calculation is a simple computation of volume:

Fig. 8-41   A foam nozzle at Bridgeport Plaza, Connecticut, designed by M. Paul Friedberg. *Photograph credit: M. Paul Friedberg.*

Fig. 8-42   The "morning glory" style jet at the Wintergarden, Niagara, New York, designed by M. Paul Friedberg. *Photograph credit: M. Paul Friedberg.*

Fig. 8-43   A "dandelion" nozzle cluster at the Embarcadero, San Francisco. *Photograph credit: M. Paul Friedberg.*

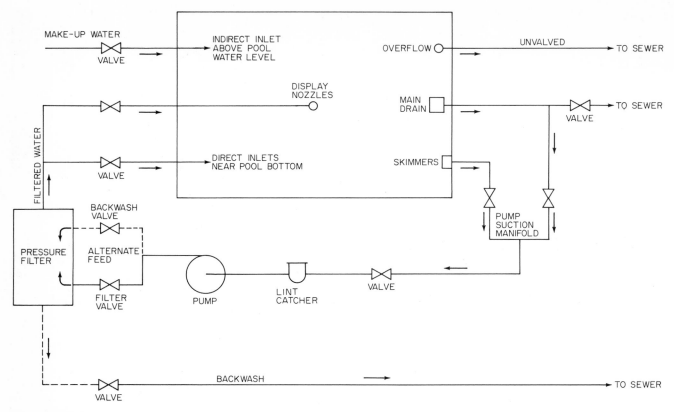

Fig. 8-44 Mechanical system for a pressurized display. *Credit: Gerald Palevsky, P.E.*

$$V = Ad$$

where V = volume of water in cubic feet
A = area of the water surface in square feet
d = average depth of water in feet

To convert this volume in cubic feet to gallons, the number of cubic feet is multiplied by 7.5 gallons. When the recirculating system is submerged in the pool, the displacement of this mechanical equipment must be determined and considered in the calculation. However, the amount of water circulating within the system itself is negligible and can be ignored.

Weirs When water is in motion and flowing over or through a controlled outlet, not only the quantity of water in the pool, but also the amount of water flowing from the outlet at any time, must be determined. This will determine the required performance of the pump and the necessary storage capacity for the total volume of water when the fountain is at rest.

In the case of a sharp-crested weir, the formula for calculating the quantity of water flowing over it is

$$Q = CLH^{3/2}$$

where Q = quantity of water in cubic feet per second (ft^3/s)
C = coefficient of overflow (3.33 is generally used)
L = horizontal length of the crest of the weir (or the circumference, if the weir is circular) in feet
H = desired height of the water surface with respect to the crest of the weir at the point of discharge. H should be measured at a point 7 times H

upstream from the crest of the weir, where the height is not affected by the downward curve of the water at the edge (Figure 8-45).

Pump performance is generally indicated in gallons per minute. The quantity of water calculated in cubic feet per second should therefore be converted to gallons per minute by multiplying it by 448.331 (450 may be used, for practical purposes).

With broad-crested or bull-nosed weirs, the coefficient C will vary according to the radius of the crest, the depth of flow, and the horizontal length. As the radius increases, the contact surface increases and a greater quantity of water is required to create the desired effect. The value of the coefficient will vary from 3.10 to 3.95. For most small fountains, it is practical to use a coefficient of 3.33, the same as for a sharp-crested weir.

In the case of a V-notched weir where the interior angle of the notch is 90° (Figure 8-46), the formula for flow from each notch is

$$Q = 2.5 \times H^{5/2}$$

where Q = quantity of water in cubic feet per second (multiply by 450 to find gallons per minute). (Figure 8-47.)

H = height of water surface in feet above the lowest point of the V-notch measured $7H$ upstream from the actual crest

Similarly, the formula for computing the quantity of water flowing over a Cipolletti weir (Figure 8-48) is

$$Q = 3.367 \times H^{3/2} \times L$$

The side slope of the trapezoidal notch is assumed to be 1 in 4 (Figure 8-49).

Orifices   To calculate the quantity of water flowing through an orifice or spout (Figure 8-50), the formula is

$$Q = CA \sqrt{2gH}$$

where Q = quantity of water in cubic feet per second (ft³/s) (to be multiplied by 450 for gallons per minute)

C = the coefficient (average value is .61)

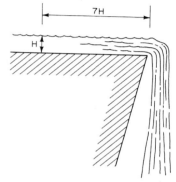

Fig. 8-45   Point at which to measure the desired height (H) of the water that is to flow over a weir.

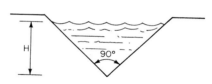

Fig. 8-46   A V-notched weir.

Fig. 8-47   Flow over a 90-degree triangular-notch weir in cubic feet per second. *Credit: Armco, Inc.*

Head in Feet	Head in Inches (Approx.)	Flow in Cubic Feet Per Second
0.1	1³⁄₁₆	.0085
0.2	2⅜	.0473
0.3	3⅝	.129
0.4	4¹³⁄₁₆	.262
0.5	6	.455
0.6	7³⁄₁₆	.714
0.7	8⅜	1.044
0.8	9⅝	1.452
0.9	10¹³⁄₁₆	1.943
1.0	12	2.520
1.1	13³⁄₁₆	3.189
1.2	14⅜	3.954
1.3	15⅝	4.818
1.4	16¹³⁄₁₆	5.785
1.5	18	6.860

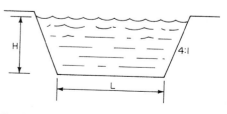

Fig. 8-48   A Cipolletti weir.

Fig. 8-49 Flow over a Cipolletti weir in cubic feet per second. *Credit: Armco, Inc.*

Head in Feet	*Head in Inches (Approx.)*	*Crest Length (Flow in Cubic Feet per Second)* 1.0 ft.	1.5 ft.	2.0 ft.	3.0 ft.	4.0 ft.	*For each add't'l foot of crest in excess of 4 feet (Approx.)*
.1	1 3/16	.107	.16	.21	.32	.43	.107
.2	2 3/8	.301	.45	.60	.90	1.20	.301
.3	3 5/8	.553	.83	1.11	1.66	2.21	.553
.4	4 13/16	.852	1.28	1.70	2.56	3.41	.852
.5	6	1.190	1.79	2.38	3.57	4.76	1.190
.6	7 3/16	1.565	2.35	3.13	4.69	6.26	1.565
.7	8 3/8	1.972	2.96	3.94	5.92	7.89	1.972
.8	9 5/8	2.409	3.61	4.82	7.23	9.64	2.409
.9	10 13/16	2.875	4.31	5.75	8.62	11.50	2.875
1.0	12	3.367	5.05	6.73	10.10	13.47	3.367
1.1	13 3/16	3.884	5.83	7.77	11.65	15.54	3.884
1.2	14 3/8	4.426	6.64	8.85	13.28	17.70	4.426
1.3	15 5/8	4.990	7.48	9.98	14.97	19.96	4.990
1.4	16 13/16	5.577	8.36	11.15	16.73	22.31	5.577
1.5	18	6.185	9.28	12.37	18.56	24.74	6.185
1.6	19 3/16	6.814	10.22	13.63	20.44	27.25	6.814
1.7	20 3/8	7.462	11.19	14.92	22.39	29.85	7.462
1.8	21 5/8	8.130	12.20	16.26	24.39	32.52	8.130
1.9	22 13/16	8.817	13.22	17.63	26.45	35.27	8.817
2.0	24	9.522	14.28	19.04	28.57	38.09	9.522
2.1	25 3/16	10.245	15.37	20.49	30.74	40.98	10.245
2.2	26 3/8	10.986	16.48	21.97	32.96	43.94	10.986
2.3	27 5/8	11.743	17.61	23.49	35.23	46.97	11.743
2.4	28 13/16	12.517	18.78	25.04	37.55	50.07	12.517
2.5	30	13.308	19.96	26.62	39.92	53.23	13.308
2.6	31 3/16	14.114	21.17	28.23	42.34	56.46	14.114
2.7	32 3/8	14.936	22.40	29.87	44.81	59.75	14.936
2.8	33 5/8	15.774	23.66	31.55	47.32	63.10	15.774
2.9	34 13/16	16.626	24.94	33.25	49.88	66.51	16.626
3.0	36	17.494	26.24	34.99	52.48	69.97	17.494

A = cross-sectional area of the orifice in square feet
g = acceleration of gravity (32.2 feet per sec^2)
H = height measured from the centerline of the orifice to the top level of the water reservoir behind. This measurement determines the head or potential energy of the water.

Fig. 8-50 Water flowing from an orifice. *Photograph credit: M. Paul Friedberg.*

Just as the shape and profile of the weir influence the preceding formulas, the shape and means of connection of the orifice will vary the coefficient C in the orifice formula (Figures 8-51 and 8-52).

Pressurized displays While the main determinants of the gravity-associated displays are the quantity and velocity of water flowing through the system, pressurized displays require additional energy, supplied by a pump, to overcome the force of gravity and to enable the display to reach the height desired to produce the design effect. In order to select the proper pump for the particular display, the designer must calculate the quantity, velocity, and pressure head required.

Quantity of discharge from a nozzle The quantity of water discharged by a pressure nozzle is given by the formula

$$Q = KA_2\sqrt{2gh}$$

where Q = quantity in cubic feet per second (ft³/s) (multiply by 450 for gallons per minute)

$$K = \cfrac{Cj}{\sqrt{1 - \left(\cfrac{A_2}{A_1}\right)^2}}$$

Cj = nozzle coefficient (supplied by the nozzle manufacturer and usually ranging between .92 and .96)

A_2 = area of nozzle in square feet

A_1 = cross-sectional area of the pipe feeding the nozzle, in square feet

g = the force of gravity (32 ft per sec²)

h = the pressure at the base of the nozzle, a figure generally recommended by the nozzle manufacturer

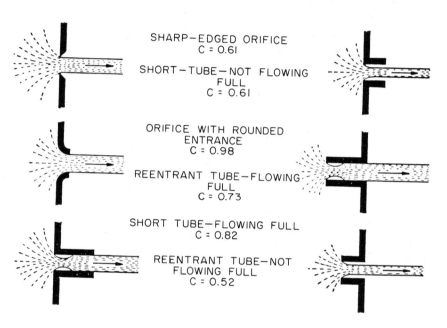

SHARP—EDGED ORIFICE
C = 0.61

SHORT—TUBE—NOT FLOWING FULL
C = 0.61

ORIFICE WITH ROUNDED ENTRANCE
C = 0.98

REENTRANT TUBE—FLOWING FULL
C = 0.73

SHORT TUBE—FLOWING FULL
C = 0.82

REENTRANT TUBE—NOT FLOWING FULL
C = 0.52

Fig. 8-51   Types of orifices.

Head in Feet h	Cross-Sectional Area of Orifice A						
	0.25 sq. ft.	0.333 sq. ft.	0.50 sq. ft.	0.75 sq. ft.	1.00 sq. ft.	1.50 sq. ft.	2.00 sq. ft.
0.10	0.387	0.518	0.773	1.16	1.56	2.32	3.09
0.15	0.474	0.631	0.947	1.42	1.90	2.84	3.79
0.20	0.547	0.729	1.09	1.64	2.19	3.28	4.38
0.25	0.612	0.815	1.22	1.83	2.19	3.28	4.38
0.30	0.670	0.892	1.34	2.01	2.68	4.02	5.36
0.35	0.724	0.963	1.45	2.17	2.89	4.34	5.78
0.40	0.774	1.03	1.55	2.32	3.09	4.64	6.19
0.45	0.820	1.09	1.64	2.46	3.28	4.92	6.56
0.50	0.865	1.15	1.73	2.59	3.46	5.19	6.92
0.55	0.907	1.21	1.81	2.72	3.63	5.44	7.25
0.60	0.947	1.26	1.90	2.84	3.79	5.68	7.58
0.65	0.986	1.31	1.97	2.96	3.94	5.92	7.89
0.70	1.02	1.36	2.05	3.07	4.09	6.14	8.18
0.75	1.06	1.41	2.12	3.18	4.24	6.36	8.48
0.80	1.09	1.46	2.19	3.28	4.38	6.56	8.75

Fig. 8-52   Flow through rectangular submerged orifices in cubic feet per second. *Credit: Armco, Inc.*

Under normal design considerations, the value of K is 0.95. Under special circumstances its value should be calculated.

To compute the quantity of water flowing through the enclosed piping system, the continuity equation can be applied. This formula is

$$Q = AV$$

where Q = quantity in cubic feet per second (ft³/s) (multiply by 450 for gallons per minute)

A = cross-sectional area of the pipe in square feet

V = velocity of the water in feet per second

Sample problem   A long, tapered nozzle with a 2-inch discharge diameter is fed from a 10-inch-diameter pipe having a pressure of 20 pounds per square inch (psi). Assuming a nozzle coefficient $Cj = 0.95$, how high will the water rise in still air?

For 2-inch-diameter nozzle, A_2 = .022 square feet

For 10-inch-diameter pipe, A_1 = .545 square feet

$$K = \frac{Cj}{\sqrt{1 - \left(\dfrac{A_2}{A_1}\right)^2}} = \frac{.95}{\sqrt{1 - \left(\dfrac{.022}{.545}\right)^2}}$$

$$K = \frac{.95}{\sqrt{1 - .0016}} = \frac{.95}{\sqrt{.9984}} = \frac{.95}{.9992} = .951$$

Since $Q = AV$, solve for V first and then obtain Q.

$Vj = K\sqrt{2gh}$ where h is the head due to pressure (in this case, 20 psi)

h = 20 psi × 2.307 feet/psi = 46.14

Vj = .951 $\sqrt{2 \times 32.2 \times 46.14}$ = .951 × 54.51 = 51.84 fps

Q = .022 SF × 51.84 fps × 450 = 513 gpm

Rise = $\dfrac{(Vj)^2}{2g}$ = $\dfrac{51.84^2}{2 \times 32.2}$ = 41.73 feet

Velocity

The velocity of flow in a pipe flowing full under pressure is usually established by means of the following formula, together with a table illustrating the Hazen Williams formula (Figure 8-53).

$$V = CR^{.63}S^{.54}$$

where V = velocity of flow in feet per second

C = a coefficient of friction which varies according to the pipe material:

plastic pipe = 140 to 170

cast-iron pipe = 100

concrete pipe = 100 to 110

R = hydraulic radius, or cross-sectional area of the pipe in square feet divided by the wetted perimeter (the entire circumference for a pipe under pressure)

S = the slope of the energy gradient in a decimal unit representing feet per foot (for example, 1 percent slope = 0.01)

Lower velocities of flow tend to result in a more economical system because they produce less frictional resistance than high velocities in the pipes and require less energy from the pump to overcome that resistance. The optimum velocity in a recirculating system under normal conditions is 5 to 6 feet per second (fps). This velocity will readily transport debris through the system to the filter. High rates, above 8 fps, tend to produce a scouring action inside the pipes and to cause vibration and resonance throughout the system.

Operating costs also dictate a low velocity, since 4 times the energy is required to double the velocity. Using the Hazen Williams formula, the designer will vary the pipe size to maintain an acceptable velocity (Figure 8-53). The piping material and its coefficient of friction will also affect operating costs. Smoother pipes such as PVC (polyvinyl chloride) have higher C values and will therefore produce a greater velocity of flow than the same diameter pipe with a lower C value, such as cast-iron pipe. Consequently, a pipe with a higher C value can carry more water for the same diameter, or carry the same quantity with less energy required.

Head

The nozzle manufacturer will indicate the required quantity of flow (gallons per minute, or GPM) and head of pressure needed for a particular nozzle to produce a desired spray height configuration. Quantity and velocity are determinants of pipe size, but the head required for a selected nozzle, combined with the anticipated head loss in a piping system, will dictate the pump size required.

The total head of a pressure system is measured in feet of equivalent elevation, that is, the amount of energy available if the water were to drop from that elevation. The head is composed of three elements:

- *Static lift,* or the difference in elevation between the free water surface of the source of supply and the level of free discharge

- *Pressure* required by the nozzle, a figure supplied by the nozzle manufacturer

- *Frictional resistance* in the piping

Frictional resistance is an important and often underestimated component of the total head in a pressurized system. Piping, fittings, filters, valves, and other appurtenances in a complex recirculating system can diminish the original head substantially and must be accurately determined in order to anticipate the full amount of energy required of the pump. To this end, the designer normally refers to a standard chart of equivalent pipe loss which converts the friction loss in specific fittings to its equivalent resistance in a straight run of pipe (Figure 8-54).

Sample problem   Given a typical fountain arrangement in which the flow is 50 GPM and all piping is 2-inch diameter, what is the theoretical head requirement of the pump? (Figure 8-55)

The pressure head required at the nozzle is 30 feet and the total length of all piping is 170 feet. There are seven elbows, three tees, and two globe valves, a check valve, and a strainer on the line. The loss through the strainer is assumed to be 3 feet.

From the friction chart, 50 GPM through a 2-inch-diameter line has a velocity of 5.11 fps and a frictional head loss of 9.9 feet per 100 feet. Therefore, for 170 feet of piping, the loss is $1.7 \times 9.9 = 16.83$ feet. The losses due to fittings are found by

Fig. 8-53 Friction losses in pipes and fittings.
Credit: Jacuzzi Brothers.

FRICTION LOSSES in PIPES and FITTINGS—⅛ through 2½ inch

½ inch		Friction Losses in Feet Head per 100 ft. of Pipe		¾ inch		Friction Losses in Feet Head per 100 Ft. of Pipe	
U.S. Gallons/ Minute	Steel C = 100 0.622 id	Copper C = 130 0.625 id	Plastic C = 140 0.622 id	U.S. Gallons/ Minute	Steel C = 100 0.824 id	Copper C = 130 0.822 id	Plastic C = 140 0.824 id
0.5	0.58	0.35	0.31	1.5	1.13	0.70	0.61
1.0	2.10	1.26	1.14	2.0	1.93	1.21	1.04
1.5	4.44	2.67	2.38	2.5	2.91	1.82	1.57
2.0	7.57	4.56	4.10	3.0	4.08	2.56	2.21
2.5	11.4	6.88	6.15	3.5	5.42	3.40	2.93
3.0	16.0	9.66	8.65	4.0	6.94	4.36	3.74
3.5	21.3	12.9	11.5	4.5	8.63	5.40	4.66
4.0	27.3	16.4	14.8	5.0	10.5	6.57	5.66
4.5	33.9	20.4	18.3	6.0	14.7	9.22	7.95
5.0	41.2	24.8	22.2	7.0	19.6	12.2	10.6
6.0	57.8	34.8	31.2	8.0	25.0	15.7	13.5
7.0	76.8	46.1	41.5	9.0	31.1	19.5	16.8
8.0	98.3	59.4	53.0	10	37.8	23.7	20.4
9.0	122	73.5	66.0	15	80.0	49.1	43.3
10	149	89.4	80.5	20	136	83.5	73.5

1 inch		Friction Losses in Feet Head per 100 Ft. of Pipe		1¼ inch		Friction Losses in Feet Head per 100 Ft. of Pipe	
U.S. Gallons/ Minute	Steel C = 100 1.049 id	Copper C = 130 1.062 id	Plastic C = 140 1.049 id	U.S. Gallons/ Minute	Steel C = 100 1.380 id	Copper C = 130 1.368 id	Plastic C = 140 1.380 id
2.0	0.60	0.35	0.32	4.0	0.56	0.36	0.30
3.0	1.26	0.73	0.68	6.0	1.20	0.77	0.65
4.0	2.14	1.24	1.15	8.0	2.04	1.31	1.10
5.0	3.42	1.88	1.75	10	3.08	1.98	1.67
6.0	4.54	2.63	2.45	12	4.31	2.75	2.33
8.0	7.78	4.50	4.16	14	5.73	3.64	3.10
10	11.7	6.77	6.31	16	7.34	4.68	3.96
12	16.4	9.47	8.85	18	9.13	5.81	4.93
14	21.8	12.6	11.8	20	11.1	7.10	6.00
16	27.9	16.2	15.1	25	16.8	10.7	9.06
18	34.7	20.1	18.7	30	23.5	15.0	12.7
20	42.1	24.4	22.8	40	40.0	25.6	21.6
25	63.6	37.1	34.6	50	60.4	38.7	32.6
30	89.2	51.6	48.1	60	84.7	54.1	45.6
40	152	88.0	82.0	80	144	92.4	77.9

1½ inch		Friction Losses in Feet Head per 100 Ft. of Pipe		2 inch		Friction Losses in Feet Head per 100 Ft. of Pipe	
U.S. Gallons/ Minute	Steel C = 100 1.610 id	Copper C = 130 1.600 id	Plastic C = 140 1.610 id	U.S. Gallons/ Minute	Steel C = 100 2.067 id	Copper C = 130 2.062 id	Plastic C = 140 2.067 id
6.0	0.57	0.36	0.31	10	0.48	0.27	0.23
8.0	0.96	0.61	0.52	15	0.92	0.57	0.50
10	1.45	0.92	0.79	20	1.55	0.96	0.84
12	2.04	1.29	1.10	25	2.35	1.45	1.27
15	2.95	1.86	1.59	30	3.29	2.03	1.78
20	5.24	3.31	2.83	40	5.60	3.47	3.03
25	7.90	5.00	4.26	50	8.46	5.24	4.57
30	11.1	7.00	6.00	60	11.9	7.34	6.44
40	18.9	12.0	10.2	70	15.8	9.78	8.53
50	28.5	14.9	15.4	80	20.2	12.5	10.9
60	40.0	25.3	21.6	90	25.1	15.6	13.6
70	53.2	33.8	28.7	100	30.5	18.9	16.5
80	68.1	43.1	36.8	120	42.7	26.6	23.1
90	84.7	53.6	45.7	150	64.7	40.1	35.0
100	103	65.1	56.6	200	110	68.0	59.4

	$2\frac{1}{2}$ inch	*Friction Losses in Feet Head Per 100 Ft. of Pipe*	
U.S. Gallons/ Minute	*Steel C = 100 2.469 id*	*Copper C= 130 2.500 id*	*Plastic C = 140 2.469 id*
20	0.66	0.40	0.35
30	1.39	0.79	0.75
40	2.36	1.35	1.27
50	3.56	2.04	1.92
60	4.99	2.86	2.69
70	6.64	3.82	3.58
80	8.50	4.88	4.59
90	10.6	6.06	5.72
100	12.8	7.37	6.90
115	16.6	9.55	9.00
130	20.9	12.0	11.3
150	27.3	15.6	14.7
200	46.3	26.6	25.0
250	81.7	47.3	44.1
300	98.1	56.8	52.9

FITTINGS—$\frac{1}{2}$ through $2\frac{1}{2}$

Friction Losses as Equivalent Lengths of Pipe—Feet

Type of Fitting and Application	*Material of Pipe and Fitting*	*Nominal Size of Pipe and Fitting*						
		½	¾	1	1-¼	1-½	2	2-½
90°	STEEL	2	3	3	4	4	5	6
STANDARD	COPPER	2	3	3	4	4	5	6
ELBOW	PLASTIC	4	5	6	7	8	9	10
STANDARD TEE	STEEL	1	2	2	3	3	4	5
Flow through	COPPER	1	2	2	3	3	4	5
RUN	PLASTIC	4	4	4	5	6	7	8
STANDARD TEE	STEEL	4	5	6	8	9	11	14
Flow through	COPPER	4	5	6	8	9	11	14
BRANCH	PLASTIC	7	8	9	12	13	17	20
ADAPTER—Copper or	COPPER	1	1	1	1	1	1	1
Plastic to Thread	PLASTIC	3	3	3	3	3	3	3
INSERT-COUPLING	PLASTIC	3	3	3	3	3	3	3
GATE VALVE (Open)	Threaded	0.35	0.45	0.60	0.80	0.95	1.15	1.40
SWING CHECK VALVE	Threaded	4	5	7	9	11	13	16

NOTE: The various weights of PLASTIC pipe have the same inside diameter. Consequently the outside diameter increases with the pressure rating, but the friction losses are not affected.

Note that STANDARD and XS weights of STEEL pipe have the same outside diameter. Consequently XS-weight pipe has a smaller inside diameter than STANDARD-weight, and will create greater friction losses for the same flow. The friction losses through XS-weight pipe can be estimated from those for STANDARD-weight by the approximate method shown in the next column.

The inside diameter of COPPER pipe also varies with wall thickness.

$$\text{Friction losses through XS-weight pipe} = \text{Friction losses through STANDARD weight pipe} \times \left[\frac{\text{Inside diameter of STD-wt. pipe}}{\text{Inside diameter of XS-wt. pipe}} \right]^2$$

EXAMPLE: 25 gpm through 1½″ XS-weight pipe.

$$\text{Friction losses through } 1\frac{1}{2}'' = 7.90 \times \left[\frac{1.610}{1.500} \right]^2 = 7.90 \times 1.073^2$$
$$\text{XS-weight pipe} = 7.90 \times 1.155 = 9.10 \text{ ft. head/100 feet}$$

Fig. 8-53 cont.

FRICTION LOSSES in IRON and STEEL PIPES and FITTINGS—3 through 30 inch

3 inch U.S. Gallons/Minute	Velocity-feet per second	C = 100 3.00 id Head Loss-Feet Head/100 feet		4 inch U.S. Gallons/Minute	Velocity-feet per second	C = 100 4.00 id Head Loss-Feet Head/100 feet		5 inch U.S. Gallons/Minute	Velocity-feet per second	C = 100 5.00 id Head Loss-Feet Head/100 feet
40	1.82	0.91		50	1.28	0.34		75	1.22	0.24
60	2.72	1.94		75	1.92	0.72		100	1.63	0.42
80	3.63	3.30		100	2.55	1.23		125	2.04	0.63
100	4.54	4.98		125	3.19	1.87		150	2.45	0.88
120	5.45	6.98		150	3.83	2.61		175	2.86	1.17
140	6.35	9.28		200	5.11	4.43		200	3.27	1.50
160	7.26	11.9		250	6.38	6.70		250	4.09	2.27
180	8.16	14.8		300	7.66	9.38		300	4.90	3.17
200	9.08	18.0		350	8.93	12.5		400	6.54	5.39
250	11.3	27.1		400	10.2	16.0		500	8.17	8.15
300	13.6	38.0		500	12.8	24.1		600	9.80	11.7
350	15.9	50.5		600	15.3	33.8		700	11.4	15.2
400	18.2	64.7		700	17.9	45.0		800	13.1	19.4
450	20.5	80.5		800	20.4	57.6		1000	16.3	29.4
500	22.7	97.8		900	23.0	71.6		1200	19.6	41.1

6 inch U.S. Gallons/Minute	Velocity-feet per second	C = 100 6.00 id Head Loss-Feet Head/100 feet		8 inch U.S. Gallons/Minute	Velocity-feet per second	C = 100 8.00 id Head Loss-Feet Head/100 feet		10 inch U.S. Gallons/Minute	Velocity-feet per second	C = 100 10.0 id Head Loss-Feet Head/100 feet
100	1.13	0.17		200	1.28	0.15		300	1.22	0.11
150	1.70	0.37		300	1.91	0.32		400	1.63	0.19
200	2.27	0.62		400	2.56	0.55		500	2.04	0.28
250	2.84	0.94		500	3.19	0.83		600	2.45	0.39
300	3.40	1.30		600	3.83	1.16		800	3.26	0.67
400	4.55	2.22		700	4.47	1.54		1000	4.08	1.01
500	5.68	3.36		800	5.11	1.97		1200	4.90	1.41
600	6.81	4.70		1000	6.38	2.98		1400	5.71	1.88
700	7.95	6.25		1200	7.66	4.18		1600	6.53	2.40
800	9.08	8.00		1400	8.95	5.56		1800	7.35	2.99
900	10.2	9.95		1600	10.2	7.12		2000	8.16	3.63
1000	11.4	12.1		1800	11.5	8.85		2500	10.2	5.49
1200	13.6	16.9		2000	12.8	10.8		3000	12.2	7.69
1400	15.9	22.5		2200	14.1	12.8		3500	14.3	10.2
1600	18.2	28.9		2400	15.3	15.1		4000	16.3	13.1

12 inch U.S. Gallons/Minute	Velocity-feet per second	C = 100 12.0 id Head Loss-Feet Head/100 feet		14 inch U.S. Gallons/Minute	Velocity-feet per second	C = 100 14.0 id Head Loss-Feet Head/100 feet		16 inch U.S. Gallons/Minute	Velocity-feet per second	C = 100 16.0 id Head Loss-Feet Head/100 feet
400	1.14	0.08		500	1.04	0.05		750	1.20	0.06
500	1.42	0.12		750	1.57	0.12		1000	1.60	0.10
600	1.70	0.16		1000	2.09	0.20		1250	2.00	0.15
750		0.24		1250	2.61	0.30		1500	2.40	0.22
1000	2.84	0.42		1500	3.13	0.42		2000	3.19	0.37
1250	3.55	0.63		1750	3.65	0.56		2500	3.99	0.56
1500	4.26	0.88		2000	4.17	0.71		3000	4.79	0.78
1750	4.97	1.17		2500	5.22	1.07		3500	5.58	1.06
2200	5.68	1.50		3000	6.26	1.50		4000	6.38	1.33
2500	7.10	2.27		3500	7.30	1.99		4500	7.18	1.65
3000	8.52	3.17		4000	8.34	2.55		5000	7.98	2.01
3500	9.95	4.21		4500	9.40	3.17		6000	9.58	2.82
4000	11.4	5.39		5000	10.4	3.85		7000	11.2	3.75
4500	12.8	6.70		6000	12.5	5.39		8000	12.8	4.79
5000	14.2	8.15		7000	14.6	7.17		10000	16.0	7.25

20 inch U.S. Gallons/Minute	Velocity-feet per second	C = 100 20.0 id Head Loss-Feet Head/100 feet
1000	1.02	0.04
1250	1.28	
1500	1.53	0.08
2000	2.04	0.13
2500	2.55	0.19
3000	3.06	0.26
3500	3.57	0.35
4000	4.08	0.45
5000	5.10	0.68
6000	6.13	0.95
7000	7.15	1.26
8000	8.17	1.62
10000	10.2	2.45
12000	12.3	3.43
14000	14.3	4.56

24 inch U.S. Gallons/Minute	Velocity-feet per second	C = 100 24.0 id Head Loss-Feet Head/100 feet
2000	1.42	0.05
2500	1.78	0.07
3000	2.14	0.11
3500	2.50	0.14
4000	2.85	0.18
5000	3.56	0.28
6000	4.27	0.39
7000	4.99	0.52
8000	5.70	0.66
10000	7.11	1.00
12000	8.55	1.40
14000	9.95	1.86
16000	11.4	2.42
18000	12.8	2.98
20000	14.2	3.61

30 inch U.S. Gallons/Minute	Velocity-feet per second	C = 100 30.0 id Head Loss-Feet Head/100 feet
2500	1.14	0.03
3000	1.37	0.04
3500	1.60	0.05
4000	1.83	0.06
4500	2.06	0.08
5000	2.28	0.09
6000	2.73	0.13
7000	3.18	0.17
8000	3.64	0.22
10000	4.56	0.34
12000	5.47	0.47
14000	6.40	0.63
16000	7.30	0.81
18000	8.20	1.00
20000	9.12	1.22

FITTINGS—3 through 30 inch
Friction Losses as Equivalent Lengths of Pipe—Feet

Type of Fitting and Application	Nominal Size of Pipe and Fitting											
	3	4	5	6	8	10	12	14	16	20	24	30
ELBOWS—												
90° STANDARD—or Run of Tee reduced by ½	7.7	10	13	15	20	25	30	35	40	50	61	76
90° Long Radius—or Run of Standard Tee	5.2	6.8	8.5	10	14	17	20	24	27	34	40	50
45° STANDARD	3.6	4.7	5.9	7.1	9.4	12	14	17	19	24	28	35
STANDARD TEE through Side Outlet	16	20	26	31	40	51	61	71	81	101	121	151
GATE VALVE (fully open)	1.6	2.1	2.7	3.2	4.3	5.3	6.4	7.5	8.5	11	13	16
SWING CHECK VALVE (fully open)	20	26	33	39	52	65	77	90	104	129	155	193
Ordinary Entrance	4.5	6.0	7.3	9.0	12	15	17	20	22	28	35	43

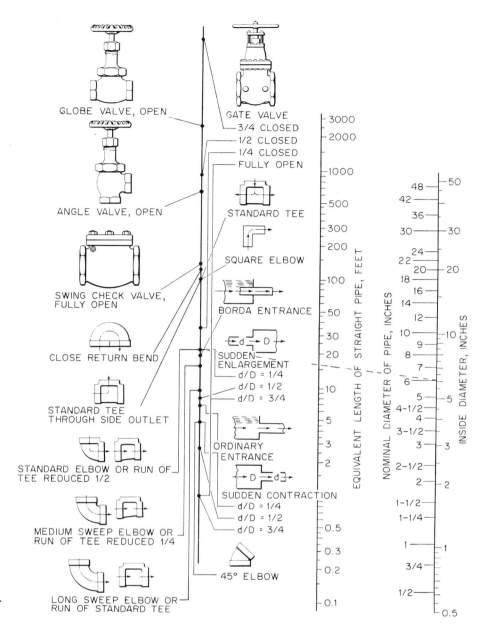

Fig. 8-54 Frictional resistance in pipe fittings.
Credit: Crane Company.

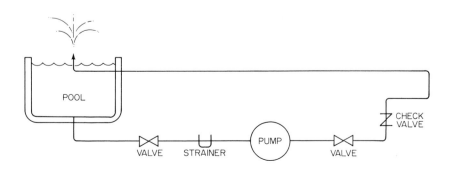

Fig. 8-55 Sample problem.

connecting each fitting with the size pipe and reading the equivalent length of straight pipe from the chart (Figure 8-54).

entry = 3 feet

elbows = 5.5 feet each: 7 × 5.5 = 38.5 feet

tees = 3.5 feet each: 3 × 3.5 = 10.5 feet

globe valve = 52 feet each: 2 × 52 = 104 feet

check valve = 13 feet

strainer = 3 feet

Adding these figures, the total equivalent length of pipe is 172 feet. This represents a pressure head loss of 1.72 × 9.9 = 17.03 feet. Notice that the loss due to the fittings is greater even than the loss due to the actual piping in the system.

The pump must therefore be capable of producing a head sufficient to overcome the losses in the pipe and the losses due to the fittings, and still yield the pressure required by the nozzle. The head requirement of the pump is therefore 16.83 + 17.03 + 30 = 63.86 feet.

The Pump

The pump generally used in a recirculating fountain is a recirculating one that may be either submerged in the pool or installed in a separate pump house. Submersible pumps are normally installed in small fountains or connected directly to single nozzles for an individual display. These pumps require service only infrequently and are therefore generally used for simple installations, or when the problems of draining the fountain and servicing the pump and motor are not difficult or critical. Pumps that are installed outside the pool itself are of two types: flooded suction pumps, which must be installed below the level of the water surface; and self-priming pumps, which can be used where the centerline of the pump is above the water level.

In selecting and installing a self-priming pump, one critical factor is the net positive suction head of the pump, or the amount of resistance the pump can overcome on its suction side to draw water up from the pool. The manufacturer will indicate a pump's capability in this respect (normally, less than 6 feet), or the maximum height above the water surface at which the pump will function.

The size, or pump horsepower, needed in any given pressure system is a function of the total quantity of the flow (GPM) and the total head required by the piping system and nozzles to produce a particular display. The formula for computing the required brake horsepower of a pump is

$$HP = \frac{GPM \times head}{3960 \times pump\ efficiency}$$

where HP = total brake horsepower required of the pump
GPM = gallons per minute required by the system to create a particular display
head = total head in feet including static lift, nozzle requirements, and the frictional loss in the piping system
pump efficiency = a value representing the efficiency of the mechanical device (generally about 75 percent) supplied by the pump manufacturer

A 75 percent rate of efficiency is about average. Greater efficiency is of course preferable, since this will decrease the energy costs of operation, and life-cycle cost efficiency is more important than the initial cost of a piece of equipment.

The ratio of discharge to head can be influenced by the use of two or more pumps, installed either in series or parallel operation. Pumps installed in series are mounted so that one pump discharges into the suction end of another to produce an increase in the head without changing the quantity of flow. Parallel operation produces a sum of the pump discharges while maintaining essentially the same head. However, this arrangement adds to the frictional resistance within the system so that the net increase in GPM will never actually equal the sum of the pumps' independent performance.

Filtration

Even the simplest pump requires a screen or hair and lint catcher on its suction side to strain out debris and to protect the pump. Larger outdoor fountains or water displays exposed to airborne particles, dust, litter, and algae growth call for a filtration system, usually a pressure sand-and-gravel system. In all water displays, larger pieces of debris and heavier particles will sink to the bottom of the pool, and then periodically should be swept out with a stiff bristle brush or removed by a vacuum cleaner. The vacuum cleaner may be a self-contained unit brought in by the maintenance crew, or it may be connected to the filter within the recirculating system.

In outdoor installations, the entire volume of water in a display should circulate through the filtration system at least once in 48 hours to maintain water clarity. The normal filtration rate for a sand-and-gravel filter is 10 to 20 gallons per minute per square foot of surface area of the filter. This rate will rarely match the rate of flow required for the display; therefore, the filter will require a separate piping system. The normal arrangement is to place a skimmer and vacuum system in the pool wall, connected through a small pump to the filter and back again to an inlet in the fountain bottom. The normal rate of flow for a vacuum system is 3 to 4 gallons per minute per inch of vacuum head. The small vacuum heads available today are usually up to 13 inches in head size, requiring at least 35 to 40 gallons per minute to work effectively. To have the skimmer or vacuum system connected to a filter with a flow-through rate of less than 30 to 40 GPM is generally ineffective and uneconomical. Lower filtration rates do not warrant a vacuum system.

Surface debris can be removed by a continuous overflow gutter, which may be tied either to the filter or flow directly to a drain. A gutter is of course incompatible with a weir display but can often be installed in the pool downstream from the weir. A skimmer is a mechanical device that removes surface debris; it functions on the suction side of the pump. There must be a flow of at least 15 GPM for a skimmer to work effectively. Between 15 and 35 GPM, one unit is used; Greater flows will call for a second or even a third one.

Chlorination

Most fountains that are equipped with a sand-and-gravel filter will not require chemicals to disinfect the water or control algae. However, chlorine should be added to the system if the physical design or location of the fountain may tempt people to enter the water; in most cases, chlorine tablets placed at the bottom of the pool will suffice. The automatic distribution of chlorine into the water is appropriate only for very large fountains where the total volume of water is more than 70,000 gallons and the rate of filtration is greater than 50 to 60 gallons per minute. In these cases, diaphragm pumps, called hypochlorinators, are used to inject a solution of hypochloride into the filtered water as it returns to the pool. The solution should enter the pool toward the bottom so that it will circulate throughout the water, as chlorine is rapidly dissipated when exposed to sunlight and aeration.

Valves

Valves serve to control or adjust the display and to isolate parts of the system for maintenance. On the suction side of the pump, a butterfly valve is most often the type used before the hair and lint catcher. Its ease of operation and quick action simplify routine cleaning of the catcher. On the discharge side, a gate valve, ball valve, globe valve, or ratchet-controlled butterfly valve can control the quantity of water delivered to the water display. Gate valves or wafer-type butterfly valves provide less precise control than do globe or ball valves, but they are often quite adequate for throttling purposes and are less expensive than other types. When the mechanical system is below the water level of the fountain, or when more than one pump is employed in parallel, check valves on the discharge lines will prevent water from flowing back into the pumps when they are shut off or being serviced. When check valves over 4 inches in diameter are used for this purpose, they should be manually controlled by means of an outside lever or counterweight so that they can be opened to drain the fountain pool.

When the particular fountain design calls for precise control of the display height, such as several equal jets or geysers on a manifold, each nozzle should have a globe valve at its base for field adjustment of the display.

Additional Equipment

Flow meter   A flow meter to monitor the rate and quantity of flow can be installed on the discharge line. An impact-type meter is normally sufficient and will provide a reading which is accurate within 3 to 5 percent.

Wind sensor   Fine-spray jets and highly aerated nozzles are particularly susceptible to wind currents and may drench the surrounding area. Airborne spray causes slippery pavement and wet pedestrians and, if chlorinated, can be harmful to plant material. To control the spray in a breezy location, a wind sensor, mounted level with the height of the display, can actuate a switch to turn the fountain off or change the mode of display depending on the wind velocity. Alternatively, the sensor can be connected to an electric valve on the discharge side of the pump and can simply reduce the height of the display as needed. The cost of a wind sensor is not insignificant and the need for it may not be absolutely certain during the design phase, but it is often a good idea to lay the conduit and provide for its future installation if necessary.

Water-level control   The displays produced by submerged aerating nozzles and certain weir configurations require the precise maintenance of a predetermined water level despite the unpredictable exigencies of rain and evaporation. In these circumstances, an overflow drain and a makeup water line will be standard equipment. The overflow drain may be a simple standpipe, its top mounted flush with the

Fig. 8-56 Untermeyer Park, Yonkers, New York, at night, designed by M. Paul Friedberg. *Photograph credit: M. Paul Friedberg.*

desired water level and connected to the main drain line downstream of its control valve for free discharge.

A ¾-inch-diameter makeup water line is normally sufficient to replace water lost through evaporation, and it can be activated by a float or pressure release device. More sophisticated, electrically controlled water-level sensors are also available for larger displays.

To compute the theoretical maximum daily rate of evaporation, find the surface area of the pool in square feet, and multiply this by 0.02 feet (¼ inch) to obtain cubic feet. To convert this figure to gallons per minute, multiply by 7.5 (gallons per cubic foot) and then divide by 1440 (minutes in a day). This figure is an approximation of the rate of evaporation in gallons per minute and is used to determine the pipe size required for the makeup water line.

Drains To drain the fountain for winter shutdown and for periodic maintenance, the pool bottom should slope toward a valve-operated main drain connected to a waste line. All low points throughout the piping network must also be provided with drain connections.

Lighting

Creative application of the many types of available lighting can make a fountain an even greater spectacle at night than in daylight (Figure 8-56). Since a geyser of aerated water will act as a lens for light from below and appear as a column of light itself at night, this is one of the most effective modes of fountain lighting. Similarly, lights mounted horizontally below the water surface in the side walls of a pool can cause the entire pool to glow with light. And floodlights and spotlights may be trained on the pool from above as well. This design is cheaper than underwater lighting and does not require low-voltage transformers. It makes the water sparkle, but it cannot make the water glow the way underwater lights can.

Whatever form the lighting may take, it should be adjustable in the field by means of flexible conduit on underwater lights, or universal joints on flood- or spotlights mounted outside the pool. Dimmers on the lighting controls will also increase the

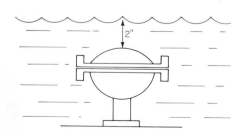

Fig. 8-57 A submerged lighting fixture.

range of possibilities for field adjustment.

Submerged lights require at least 2 inches of water covering the lens to prevent overheating, which will cause the lens to break (Figure 8-57). All exposed lighting must be equipped with vandal-proof fittings, or be secured behind a sturdy metal grill that can be removed for relamping. The most important consideration regarding fountain lighting, and also of all other electrical components of a recirculating fountain system, is that it must be grounded in accordance with the National Electric Code. For this reason, as well as for an accurate projection of all electrical service requirements of the recirculation system and coordination with local utility companies, the consultation services of an electrical engineer are fundamental to the successful design of any but the very simplest of decorative water displays.

CASE STUDY: THE DELACORTE FOUNTAIN, NEW YORK CITY

Introduction

Late in 1977, George Delacorte commissioned M. Paul Friedberg and Partners to design a fountain as a gift to New York City from Mr. Delacorte (Figure 8-58). City Hall Park was selected as the location because of its prominence as the setting for municipal government and as a green oasis for thousands of office workers. A park rich in both civic and national history, it had recently suffered from lack of maintenance and overuse. The design of the fountain, therefore, had to originate within the context of a master development plan for the park itself. If the park was, after all, an appropriate site for a fountain, where should it be built, and what form should it take? The first step was an analysis of the site, its history, existing conditions, and patterns of use.

Site Analysis

History The park has undergone generations of construction, demolition, and reuse which began in the seventeenth century with a windmill built by the Dutch settlers. Two previous fountains had existed on the site. One of them, the Croton Fountain, stood at the southern tip of the park (Figure 8-59). It was described in

Fig. 8-58 The Delacorte Fountain, City Hall Park, New York, designed by M. Paul Friedberg. *Photograph credit: M. Paul Friedberg.*

Fig. 8-59 The Croton Fountain, City Hall Park, New York, erected in 1842, removed in 1867. *Credit: courtesy of Seymour Durst.*

contemporary literature as having jets " . . . which are so arranged as to admit of various combinations, which is far more pleasing than a uniformity of the most beautiful figure." The analysis also revealed certain park renovation plans which included the restoration of this fountain, a project that was abandoned because of lack of money.

Existing conditions and patterns of use Historic precedent established, the study went on to explore the current needs of the site and its users. The park was well used as an area of passive recreation at lunchtime for strolling and sitting, picnicking, and occasionally for sun bathing—so well used, in fact, that every seat was occupied on a pleasant day—benches as well as other perches such as railings and police barricades. Special events are the norm in the park, ranging from impromptu demonstrations to the arrival of visiting dignitaries, but there was no appropriate ceremonial open space to accommodate these functions. They took place among parked cars and in competition with the daily bustle on all sides.

Avenues of approach to the park and circulation paths within it were also studied in order to understand the nature of the spaces formed by these lines and the ways in which the pedestrians approach them, some with definite destinations and some who are merely strolling through.

Visual considerations The piecemeal development of the park over the years failed to create a unified setting for City Hall. Path systems were haphazard and the logical vista from City Hall through the park to the southern tip was interrupted by trees and lacked a clear terminus. The building itself, an elegant neoclassical structure, appeared disoriented within its setting.

Subsurface constraints Any substantial construction project in an urban setting must find its place among the complex infrastructure of underground utilities and transportation arteries. In this case, a preliminary investigation of subway lines, water mains, sewers, gas, electricity, steam, and telephone lines was made, not only to avoid conflict, but also to determine the existence of the electric, water, and sewer services required by a fountain.

Conclusions Analysis complete, the conclusions presented themselves.

1. There was historic justification for a fountain, its location at the southern tip of the park, and its form: a variable display of multiple jets. Earlier plans to restore the fountain reinforced that precedent.

2. A fountain also appeared to make sense in the context of the park today, within its physical layout. The analysis revealed the need for a visual anchor at the southern end of the park to reinforce a link between City Hall and its park setting (Figure 8-60).

3. Patterns of use suggested that the fountain should be placed at the center of a large plaza as a focus for ceremonies, special events, and civic gatherings.

4. The analysis also began to suggest a form. The need for seating in the park prompted the incorporation of steps or seats into the fountain itself.

5. The concern for a visual focus at the southern end of the park, combined with a reluctance to obscure the main façade of City Hall from the south, suggested that the major impact of the fountain should be from the water itself rather than from a solid object.

Fig. 8-60 City Hall Park, New York, before the construction of the Delacorte Fountain. *Photograph credit: M. Paul Friedberg.*

6. The sometimes ceremonial function of the park and the dignified neo-classical style of City Hall prescribed a simple geometry and elegant materials, with a prototype in the Croton Fountain and its variable display.

Future Development

Having demonstrated the historic facts and the contemporary need for a fountain, the report went on to establish guidelines for further restoration of the park. It recommended alternative parking areas for the official vehicles which filled a large area of the park during working hours, proposed the relocation of trees that blocked the view of City Hall, and offered methods of masking the noise and visual distraction of the busy downtown streets surrounding the site. The fountain would represent the first step in this improvement process. As a visual and auditory focus, it would diminish the impact and confusion of the daily bustle outside the park.

Fundamental Design

Alternating between drawings and scale models, the fundamental design of the fountain evolved into a large circular pool with a central island and a rim of granite. Limestone steps surrounding the pool accommodate the need for additional seating and at the same time provide a frame for the fountain—an amphitheater for the performance of the water itself. The program for that performance was selected to include a wide range of moods, activities, and forms. The various modes represent water in a reflecting pool, flowing over a weir, cascading down an irregular surface, surging into the air, gently bubbling, or in a massive, three-dimensional pressurized display of jets similar to the one shown in the contemporary print of the Delacorte Fountain's nineteenth-century antecedent (Figure 8-61).

Design Development

Mechanical design and formal development of the fountain represented only one aspect of the overall design and consultation process. In this case, the original client and the final owner were separate entities. Mr. Delacorte, and the City of New York in the form of municipal agencies and community review boards, all interacted with the designers and other concerned groups in the progression toward a finished project (Figure 8-62). This large number of participants is perhaps extreme, but the development of any large-scale water feature in a major open public space will inevitably involve an assortment of municipal agencies, civic groups, and private utilities, each with specific sets of criteria to bring to bear.

Physical constraints Physical constraints were the first consideration. The Parks Department provided a survey of the park, its topography, boundaries, existing structures, utilities, vegetation, and other materials. The department also performed a series of test borings at the fountain site itself to determine the bearing capacity of the soil below. Often the supervising agency for any development in public open spaces, the Parks Department played a major role in reviewing the design at each stage of completion.

MODE I

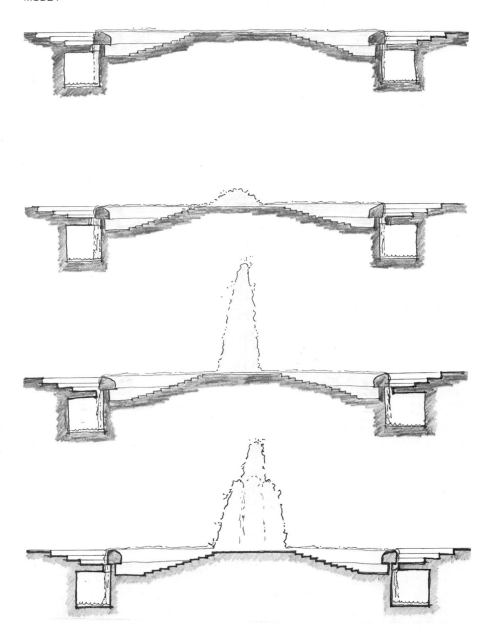

**Fig. 8-61. Various display modes of the Dela-
corte Fountain, City Hall Park, New York.**

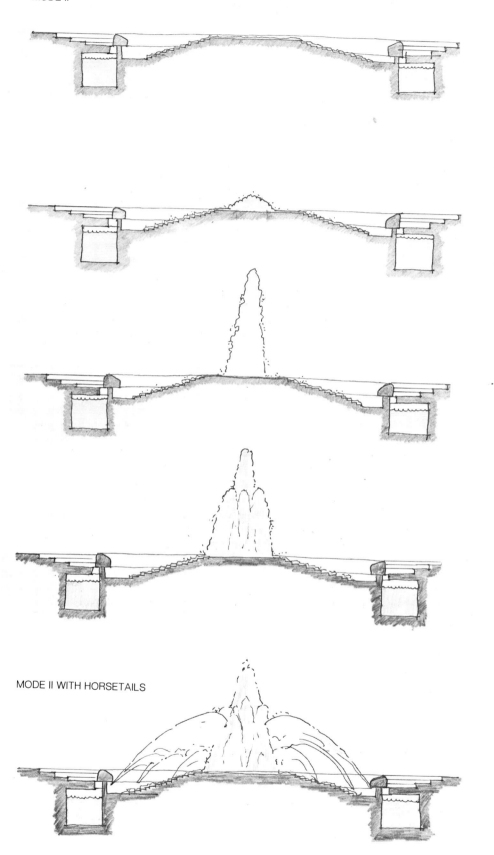

MODE II WITH HORSETAILS

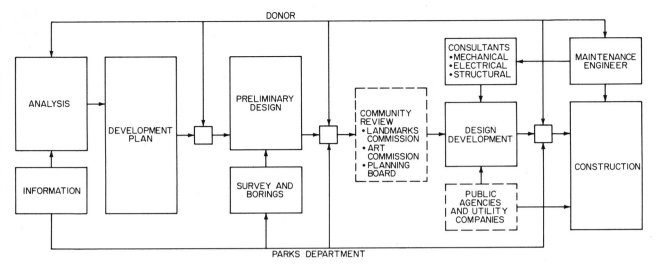

Fig. 8-62 Development process of the Delacorte Fountain, City Hall Park, New York.

Mechanical design   The development of the mechanical design was the next step (Figure 8-63). All the different modes of display had to be compatible. The two major categories of display to be considered were the full pool with water cascading over the weir, and the pressurized display with all nozzles at full performance with the pool empty.

Based on the initial design of a main pool 40 feet in diameter, and with ¼- to ⅜-inch water depth over the weir, the minimum flow out of the central well was determined to be between 1350 and 1400 GPM. The main spray, to suit the desired architectural effect, was to be 15 feet in height at 200 GPM from a nozzle that required a pressure head of 50 to 60 feet. Six manifold aerating nozzles were provided, each capable of a 50 GPM, 10-foot-high display requiring 40 feet of head pressure at the base of each nozzle. Ten horsetail spray nozzles were provided around the perimeter, each requiring a 40-foot head and yielding 30 GPM.

The plans for the architectural design of the fountain required a 12,400-gallon volume of water. The water in motion when the fountain is running was established to be 400 GPM.

In order to shift from display mode I to display mode II, the water within the inner ring must be stored in the outside ring or moat while mode II is in operation. The volumetric storage capacity for this portion of the fountain had to be determined.

Head losses, static lift, required nozzle pressures, and other frictional losses were tabulated to determine the size of the pumps, pump room, and related equipment. The motors were sized for maximum possible load configuration and total 15 horsepower.

Similar calculations were made for the supply lines to each fountain display element and for each other item required for the fountain to function as designed.

Maintenance and Operation

Filtration   Debris, airborne dust particles, and chemical pollutants are an ever-present nuisance for urban fountains. This one was to be particularly vulnerable because of its location in a densely developed area with heavy traffic, both automotive and pedestrian. The design of the fountain aggravated this vulnerability: Geysers and horsetail sprays would trap airborne particles and return them to the pool, and the pool itself, as a depression in the park floor, was bound to collect its share of windblown flotsam. The filters in the pump room would remove the bulk of the smaller particles, but the pool would need to be vacuumed periodically to remove the inevitable falling leaves and candy wrappers. The rate of flow through the filtration system was limited and not fast enough to provide the suction required by an integral vacuum head. Since the client's own staff was to be responsible for maintenance of the installation, it would vacuum the pool periodically. An electric outlet was provided in the pump room for that purpose.

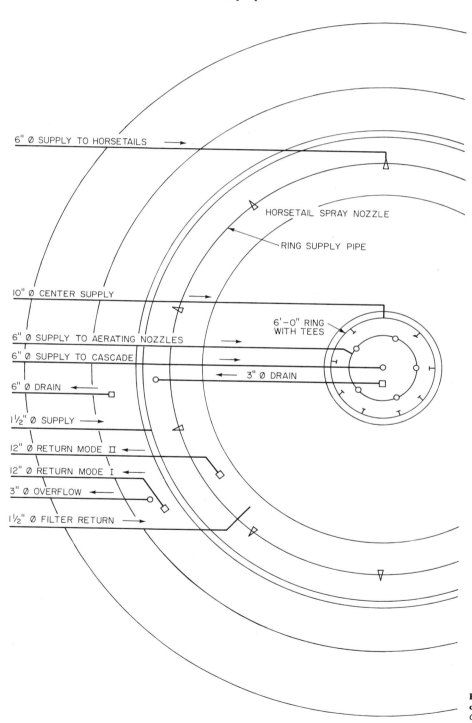

Fig. 8-63 The mechanical system of the Delacorte Fountain, City Hall Park, New York. *Credit: Gerald Palevsky, P.E.*

Chlorination   As an easily accessible central feature of a heavily used space, the fountain was bound to attract an occasional dabbling of feet or more. To control bacteria in anticipation of this human contact and to restrict the growth of algae encouraged by the fountain's sunny location, chlorine was prescribed. Quantity of water and rate of flow did not warrant an automatic chlorination system, so the maintenance program would also include periodic addition of chlorine tablets at the pool bottom.

Winter shutdown   Several possibilities to allow for operation of the fountain during cold weather were explored before winter shutdown was accepted as the inevitable solution.

1. Heating the water to keep it from freezing might dictate a temperature rise to 50°F, requiring 400,000 BTU per hour. Even then, this would allow only for still water display, since the additional "cooling tower" effect of nozzle display would further aggravate the problem. Energy costs made the use of any sort of heaters capable of producing the necessary BTUs an unrealistic solution.

2. The addition of a nontoxic antifreeze such as propylene glycol to the water was also explored. Winter operation of a fountain of this size would demand at least 4400 gallons of antifreeze annually, an unjustifiable extravagance in this case, but worthy of consideration in a smaller installation.

3. Another approach, that of allowing the water to freeze and form an ice sculpture in winter, was not feasible because of the complexity of the recirculating system and the danger of ice dislodging the granite blocks.

Record drawings   One essential step in the construction process not to be underestimated is the need to furnish a complete set of "as-built" drawings. In this case, the final locations of all pieces of equipment and their function were labeled in the pump room, color-coded to an operating chart and a maintenance manual. The procedures for filling and draining the pool and piping system and for changing and regulating the many modes of display were defined, and a manual for the normal operation, routine maintenance, and repair of each piece of equipment was supplied to the maintenance engineer.

CHAPTER NINE
EXTERIOR LIGHTING
Ernest Wotton

INTRODUCTION

The outdoor environment is normally seen in light—the light from the sun. But buildings and the areas around them are also used at times when there is little or no sunlight available. For this reason, the art and science of electric exterior lighting have been developed.

This chapter makes no pretense at being an exhaustive and detailed review of outdoor lighting situations and techniques. Rather, it is intended to provide sufficient information to enable the architect to evaluate situations and identify problems, and to discuss outdoor lighting requirements knowledgeably with a lighting designer.

The scope of the chapter comprises the floodlighting of buildings; the lighting of parking lots, campuses, and parks; and the use of light as a means for making outdoor spaces safe. Information on the selection of luminaires and lamps is also included.

BUILDING FLOODLIGHTING

Floodlighting reveals a building in a way that sunlight never does. A building is usually designed to be illuminated from above; in other words, the building and its surface modeling and ornament are designed to cast shadows downward (Figure 9-1). However, with floodlighting, the flow of light is usually reversed; it comes from below and the shadows are cast upward (Figure 9-2). Since most buildings are designed with little thought given to how they might look with their shadows reversed, it is surprising that building floodlighting succeeds at all—and yet it does, often with great effectiveness (Figures 9-3 through 9-11).

Floodlighting relies for its effect on light reflected from the building surface. If the surface is dark, little light will be reflected; most will be absorbed. For this reason, a dark building will require a much greater quantity of light than will a light-colored one in order to appear equally bright. For example, a conventional red brick building requires about 3 times the light level of one built of limestone. A very dark building,

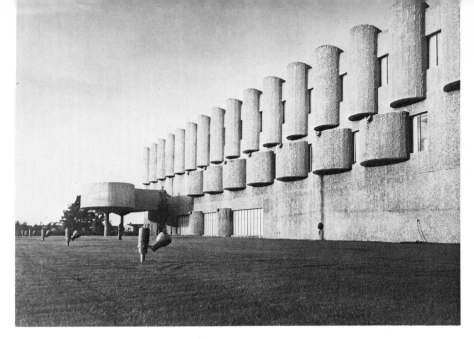

Fig. 9-1 A building façade in sunlight with shadows cast downward. *Photograph credit: Keene Corporation, Lighting Division.*

Fig. 9-2 (*Above*) The same building floodlighted at night with reversed shadows. *Photograph credit: Courtesy Stonco Electric Products, Kenilworth, N.J.*

Fig. 9-3 (*Above right*) A high-rise commercial structure dramatically floodlighted. *Photograph credit: Keene Corporation, Lighting Division.*

Fig. 9-4 An effectively lighted church façade. *Photograph credit: Keene Corporation, Lighting Division.*

Fig. 9-5   A church floodlighted, using a variety of means to accentuate its distinctive architectural features. *Photograph credit: Keene Corporation, Lighting Division.*

Fig. 9-6   The unusual architectural design of the State House in Hawaii required an imaginative approach to its floodlighting design. *Photograph credit: Keene Corporation, Lighting Division.*

Fig. 9-7   Extensive use of building façade lighting in this European city results in a fantasy-like atmosphere. *Photograph credit: Courtesy of Raymond Grenald.*

Fig. 9-8 Night lighting of large monuments can be very similar to facade lighting of buildings. *Photograph credit: Courtesy of Raymond Grenald.*

Fig. 9-9 A floodlighted tower, like that of the Philadelphia City Hall, can provide a nighttime focal point. *Photograph credit: Raymond Grenald.*

Fig. 9-10 The elegant architecture of the American Red Cross building in Washington, D.C., is enhanced at night by floodlighting. *Photograph credit: Courtesy of T. A. Dugard, GTE Sylvania Canada, Ltd.*

Fig. 9-11 A combination of building lighting and the spill from street lighting can have a pleasing effect on a building facade. *Photograph credit: Raymond Grenald.*

Fig. 9-12 This building, designed by Paul Rudolph, has a light-colored and rough-textured surface that responds well to floodlighting. *Photograph credit: Keene Corporation, Lighting Division.*

such as one with a façade clad in black glass, is impossible to floodlight; it will appear dark no matter how much light is poured on it.

Floodlighting is most effective if the surface to be lit is light in color and rough in texture (Figures 9-12, 9-13, and 9-14). It is sometimes assumed that a shiny material, such as aluminum cladding, is ideal for floodlighting, but this assumption is wrong. Such materials will appear either dark, or spotty with image reflections of the floodlights.

In general, when planning the floodlighting of a building, the following points should be borne in mind:

- The effect of the floodlighting must be clear and decisive. If the lighting is vague and the building appears indistinct, then it were better that the lighting be omitted. This is particularly important for buildings that will be seen mainly from afar. When the viewer and the building are separated by a significant distance, the effect of atmospheric absorption must be taken into account or a building that appears bright from close up will lose its identity at a distance.

- If the building is viewed from very close to the floodlights, no shadows will be seen and all modeling will be lost. For the floodlighting to be effective, it is best that the floodlights be located away from the principal angle of view. In that way the shadows cast by the lighting can be perceived, providing the modeling that articulates the building. A motorist's principal angle of view of a building adjacent to the road on which he or she is driving is a glancing or angled one. Straight-on floodlighting will therefore throw shadows and create modeling that can be seen by the motorist (Figure 9-15).

- The best effects will be achieved when the shadows all run the same way. To achieve this goal, the principal lighting must come from one main direction.

- Shadows that are too large and out of scale will result if the light strikes the building very obliquely. It is preferable, therefore, for the light to hit the building at an angle of not less than 30° to the building surface.

Fig. 9-13 This wall was deliberately heavily textured and lighted to accentuate the texture as a decorative and eye-catching device. *Photograph credit: Keene Corporation, Lighting Division.*

Fig. 9-14 The lighting of the building shown in Figure 9-13 was accomplished in this way. *Photograph credit: Keene Corporation, Lighting Division.*

Fig. 9-15 Head-on floodlighting that creates modeling enables the building's architectural features to appear accentuated. *Photograph credit: Keene Corporation, Lighting Division.*

• It is important to carry out lighting trials to ensure that the color and color-rendering properties of the light accord well with the surface of the material being lighted. For example, red brick takes on the color of mud under the light from a mercury lamp. Appropriate preliminary experiments will quickly identify such problem situations.

Level of Illumination

The level of illumination needed to floodlight a building adequately depends on the reflectance capability of the surface material and the general ambient light level of the surrounding area. The illuminance may range from a low of 5 footcandles for a very light building in a dark surrounding to as much as 50 footcandles for a very dark building in a bright surrounding (Figure 9-16).

The demands for energy conservation impose restrictions on building floodlighting. The standards set by the American Society of Heating, Refrigeration, and Air-Conditioning Engineers ASHRAE 90.75 (paragraph 9.4.3) limit the façade lighting of a building to 2 percent of the total interior lighting load of that building. A consequence of this limitation is something of an anomaly. It is that the more carefully the interior lighting is designed to keep down the power loading, the smaller is the power load permitted for the building façade lighting.

Consider the lighting of an office building. Traditionally, the power loading for office interior lighting has been about 3 to 4 watts per square foot of floor area. Carefully designed, energy-conserving lighting, however, will consume only half as much electricity, or about 1½ to 2 watts per square foot. But this is not enough information to determine the power loading for façade lighting permitted by ASHRAE. Further assumptions must be made. The façade area total is directly related to the dimensions of the building perimeter, but the perimeter is not in constant ratio to the floor area. Doubling the floor area does not double the perimeter length. And of

IES RECOMMENDED ILLUMINATION LEVELS FOR FLOODLIGHTING

		Surround	
		Recommended Level (Footcandles)	
Surface Material	Reflectance (Percent)	Bright	Dark
Light marble, white or cream terra cotta, white plaster	70 to 85	15	5
Concrete, tinted stucco, light gray and buff limestone, buff face brick	45 to 70	20	10
Medium gray limestone, common tan brick, sandstone	20 to 45	30	15
Common red brick, brownstone, stained wood shingles, dark gray brick	10 to 20*	50	20

*Buildings or areas of material having a reflectance of less than 20 percent cannot usually be floodlighted economically unless they carry a large amount of high-reflectance trim.

Fig. 9-16

ILLUMINATION LEVELS FOR FAÇADE LIGHTING

Luminaire Using This Lamp	Approximate Average Maintained Illuminance (footcandles) at	
	⅒ W/sq. ft.	⅓ W/sq. ft.
Mercury	1½	5¼
Deluxe white mercury	1¾	5¾
Metal halide	2½	8½
High-pressure sodium	2½	8¼
Low-pressure sodium	5¼	17½

Fig. 9-17

course the floor-to-floor dimension—which affects the façade area—varies from building to building.

Taking all these variables into account, the power loading permitted under ASHRAE 90.75 for lighting an office building is likely to be about ⅒ watt per square foot of façade if all four façades are completely illuminated, or about ⅓ watt per square foot if only one façade is completely lighted.

The level of illumination that can be achieved from this power loading will vary widely, depending on the nature of the light source. At ⅒ watt per square foot, a mercury luminaire will produce an average maintained illuminance of about 1½ footcandles, while a low-pressure sodium one will yield more than 5 footcandles. At ⅓ watt per square foot, the mercury floodlight will produce 5¼ footcandles, while the low-pressure sodium one will yield 17½ footcandles (Figure 9-17).

Comparing Figures 9-17 and 9-16, it will be seen that if all four façades of an office building are to be illuminated, the illuminance will not reach even that recommended for a building with a very light surface material in dark surroundings. Under those circumstances, the nighttime appearance of the building is unlikely to be acceptable. It may be more satisfactory if the electricity consumption permitted under ASHRAE 90.75 is concentrated on a single façade, or on only the most important features of the building. Entire façades do not need to be illuminated for effective lighting of buildings, however. Nighttime use of outline lighting may be sufficient (Figures 9-18 and 9-19).

PARKING AREAS

A well-lighted parking area is important to virtually all projects in which cars are to be accommodated. Whether the building served be a shopping center, an industrial plant, an office building, or a residential complex, good lighting discourages vandalism, is an essential element in an effective security program, and enables motorists to maneuver their vehicles more easily (Figures 9-20 and 9-21).

While it is possible to light a parking area with luminaires whose light sources are below eye level, such an arrangement would not be advisable, since faces would not be easily visible (a security problem), and only a virtual forest of luminaires would be effective. A parking area can be illuminated by luminaires at only 15 feet above the ground. But as high a mounting height as possible within the scale of the surroundings

Fig. 9-18 A row of attractive nineteenth-century buildings. *Photograph credit: Keene Corporation, Lighting Division.*

Fig. 9-19 The buildings shown in Figure 9-18 are made equally attractive at night through the use of outline lighting rather than floodlighting. *Photograph credit: Keene Corporation, Lighting Division.*

is usually desirable, since it prevents the proliferation of poles which the use of a low mounting height entails. Also, it keeps down the initial cost of the lighting installation. A 40-foot pole height is about the maximum that can be conveniently serviced from a standard cherry picker or similar maintenance vehicle. If higher poles are needed, however, it is possible to incorporate a winch device that will enable the luminaires themselves to be lowered for servicing.

The factors that interact upon one another in developing an arrangement of lighting fixtures are:

- the pole height
- the pole spacing
- the nature of the light source

Fig. 9-20 Well-designed lighting for parking will clearly illuminate the pavement markings and increase the safety of the parking lot. *Photograph credit: Raymond Grenald.*

Fig. 9-21 Lighting for parking areas is essential for safety and convenience, and can also serve as an intended visual attraction to a store, for example, or an entertainment facility. *Photograph credit: Raymond Grenald.*

- the distribution of light from the luminaire
- the reflectance of the paving material
- the desired level of illumination

The Illuminating Engineering Society of North America recommends an average maintained illuminance of 1 footcandle for self-parking areas and 2 footcandles for attendant parking areas. Common practice, however, has been to exceed these figures, especially for parking areas that service retail establishments. The argument is given that the brighter the parking area, the more the customers will be attracted to it.

It is important to take into account the material of which the parking surface is constructed, since the reflectance of that surface can have a significant effect on the actual illumination of the area. As an example, a parking area of concrete will be about 5 times as bright as one of conventional black asphalt with the same illuminance.

The light-distribution characteristics of luminaires should be obtained from their manufacturers so that these patterns can be taken into account in making the appropriate selection. The manufacturers' data sheets will also provide the information from which the pole height and pole spacing can be calculated.

The power loading required for illuminating a parking area will vary in relation to both the type of light source used and the desired level of illumination. For four commonly used light sources, the approximate number of watts required to illuminate a 1000-square-foot area to a level of 1 footcandle is as follows:

low-pressure sodium lamps	17 watts
high-pressure sodium lamps	20 watts
metal halide lamps	28 watts
deluxe white mercury lamps	46 watts

The requirements of energy conservation have resulted in mandatory limitations on the connected lighting load for outdoor parking areas. For example, the Commonwealth of Massachusetts sets a limit of 50 watts per 1000 square feet. Although a limit such as this one should provide no hardship to the design of reasonable parking area lighting, it is prudent to verify whether state or local regulations may place restrictions on any of the parameters for lighting design.

In addition to lighting the main parking area, particular attention should be given to providing illumination of an appropriate intensity and type for such auxiliary areas as the entrance and exit driveways, building access points, loading docks, and any other special areas that may require a different design approach from the one used throughout the bulk of the parking area.

Both floodlighting luminaires (Figures 9-22 and 9-23) and roadway luminaires (Fig-

Fig. 9-22 A parking area illuminated by pole-mounted floodlights. *Photograph credit: Keene Corporation, Lighting Division.*

Fig. 9-23 Close-up of a floodlight cluster used for parking lighting. *Photograph credit: Raymond Grenald.*

Fig. 9-24 An ordinary roadway lighting unit can be used to illuminate a parking area. *Photograph credit: Andrew Alpern.*

Fig. 9-25 Even a 100-year-old cast-iron unit can serve to provide lighting for parking. *Photograph credit: Andrew Alpern.*

Fig. 9-26 A lighting fixture of moderate height often used for parking areas. *Photograph credit: Keene Corporation, Lighting Division.*

ures 9-24 and 9-25) can be used for parking area lighting, depending on the effect desired and the design approach taken. If luminaires are used that are designed primarily for roadway lighting, then ones with a non-cutoff distribution appear to be preferred, despite their brightness. Indeed, this added "sparkle" to the lighting may be considered an asset, especially if a secondary usage of the lighting is to attract people. Nonetheless, care should be taken that the light does not impinge upon neighboring property.

Other kinds of lighting units for parking areas are of course available (Figures 9-26 and 9-27).

LIGHTING FOR PEDESTRIANS

It is suggested that good lighting for pedestrians should help to make them want to stroll in the park or visit a shopping mall. Yet all too frequently one sees lighting in parks and malls that does little more than provide sufficient illumination to enable people to hurry from point A to point B by the most direct route. This type of lighting is comparable with lighting in a restaurant that, while aspiring to providing fine dining, encourages its patrons to eat their meals as quickly as possible and then to hurry back home.

Most modern roadway-lighting equipment ignores the needs of pedestrians. These light sources are designed almost exclusively with vehicular traffic in mind; they are generally inadequate for pedestrian comfort and safety, thereby discouraging the use of the walkways paralleling the roads. The fixtures are often of an inappropriate style and scale, and the color of the light is usually unpleasant, rendering skin tones in ghastly shades most appropriate to a horror movie. The bright luminaires direct most of their light onto the roadway pavement. Consequently, if buildings are set well back from the road, and particularly if they are dark in color (of red brick, for example), they will appear dark in contrast with the luminaire and the pavement.

Fig. 9-27 Globe-shaped luminaires that are commonly used both singly and in clusters for general lighting and for parking. *Photograph credit: Keene Corporation, Lighting Division.*

315

The result is that the neighborhood will be given a dark, forbidding atmosphere.

Lighting for pedestrians should not be what is left over from the lighting of roadways, parking areas, or buildings. It should be especially designed with the needs of pedestrians in mind and should

> Be appropriate to its location. (A luminaire suitable for the bustle and sparkle of a world's fair will certainly not be suitable for a quiet park.)
>
> Be designed to a people-oriented scale.
>
> Use lamps that do not distort colors violently. (Both men and women like to look natural under artificial light and want others to do so also.)
>
> Help create a space which is safe at night for pedestrians.

Good lighting for pedestrians does not mean as high an illuminance as possible. And in a shopping mall or on a campus, it does not usually mean uniform illumination, but rather, pools of light toward which people tend to be drawn. In a park, however, where lighting makes a valuable contribution to safety, a fairly even illuminance of about ½ footcandle on the footpath is appropriate.

The use of light for the safety of pedestrians cannot be too strongly stressed. This purpose dates back at least to the time of King William III's reign in England, when an early form of road lighting was introduced into Hyde Park in London, then plagued by an early English variety of muggers. And today, communities are using lighting both as a nonviolent defense against an increasing incidence of violence and as a way to reinspire the sociability of the community.

When a sidewalk or footpath runs alongside a road, it may be desirable to provide lighting designed specifically for people in addition to the roadway lighting scaled for vehicles. As a reasonable compromise solution, the same poles that support the roadway lighting (assuming that they adjoin the footpath) can also be used for mounting people-oriented lighting. Such lighting ought to meet the criteria for color, quality, and intensity that are applicable to all lighting for pedestrians.

Types of Lighting

Lighting for pedestrians can be provided by pole-mounted luminaires—either starkly modern, classically simple, or elaborately ornate (Figures 9-28, 9-29, and 9-30). It can also be supplied by light sources mounted within the branches of nearby trees or on adjacent buildings (Figure 9-31).

Bright luminaires, such as those with exposed refractors—or even exposed lamps—may be acceptable in a shopping mall where the brightness of the lighting fixture fits into the general brightness of the location. But bright light sources should be used with great caution, since in many instances they would be out of place. For example, the luminaire chosen for a park should not appear bright. If it does, the contrast of the bright light with the dark surroundings will make it very difficult to see those surroundings—or see into them. Also, it reduces the effectiveness of illuminated features such as trees, buildings, or fountains, since they will appear to lose some of their brightness by comparison. If there are specially illuminated features near the pedestrian path, the use of pathway luminaires with shielding elements is to be preferred. This cutoff type of luminaire will keep the glare of the light source from washing out the brightness of the specially illuminated features.

Fig. 9-28 A simple fixture designed for pedestrians. *Photograph credit: Raymond Grenald.*

Fig. 9-29 A classic bronze light standard for pedestrians—in this case, Columbia University students. *Photograph credit: Andrew Alpern.*

Fig. 9-30 An exuberant lighting unit that lights the way for visitors to Columbia University's Low Memorial Library, designed by McKim, Mead & White. *Photograph credit: Andrew Alpern.*

Some lighting situations may call for low, closely spaced luminaires, often called bollards. Because of their low height and resultant limited light spread, they should be closely spaced if they are to provide anything even approaching an even wash of light on the path. A single low bollard is not so obvious by day as a single luminaire on a pole. A row of bollards semiconcealed in the underbrush along a winding path will be similarly unobtrusive during the daylight hours, but a sequence of bollards that can be seen as a group by day will be far more obvious than more widely spaced, pole-mounted luminaires. This fact should be taken into consideration when planning lighting for pedestrians (Figure 9-32).

It should also be borne in mind that the light produced by a bollard-type fixture does not illuminate an oncoming person's face. This can be a distinct disadvantage from the standpoint of safety. While appearances can very often be exceedingly deceiving, most pedestrians like to be able to make out the face of someone approaching—and in sufficient time to be able to make a judgment about that person.

LANDSCAPE LIGHTING

Landscape lighting does not usually attempt to duplicate the effect of daylight. Instead, the lighting should capture the nighttime mood; trees retire into mystery; the surface of a pool becomes calm (Figures 9-33 through 9-38).

The lighting designer should consider how the lighting will affect both close-up and distant views of the scene. He or she should decide what landscape features and relationships should be emphasized and which ones should be permitted to fade into the darkness. The topography of the area should be studied, since the relative elevations of the features in view can have a profound effect on their visual importance and may result in their being viewed from above as well as from ground level.

Fig. 9-31 Tree-mounted lighting illuminating pedestrian paths. *Photograph credit: Keene Corporation, Lighting Division.*

317

Fig. 9-32 Low luminaires lighting a pedestrian path with pools of light. A well-floodlighted building is in the background. *Photograph credit: Keene Corporation, Lighting Division.*

Fig. 9-33 In this night-lighted residential landscape, the foreground is appropriately bright, the mid-distance lighted to a lower level, and the background highlighted rather than being evenly illuminated. *Photograph credit: Raymond Grenald.*

Fig. 9-34 Well-designed landscape lighting will highlight special features, such as a statue. *Photograph credit: Raymond Grenald.*

Fig. 9-35 This carefully placed landscape lighting has created a nighttime outdoor "room." *Photograph credit: Raymond Grenald*

Fig. 9-36 The outdoor environment can be made usable at night without the light sources being obvious. *Photograph credit: Raymond Grenald.*

Fig. 9-37 A variety of garden and landscape lighting devices have been used here to create this pleasant setting. *Photograph credit: Keene Corporation, Lighting Division.*

Fig. 9-38 Tree lighting reflected in a placid swimming pool makes a relaxing nighttime environment. *Photograph credit: Keene Corporation, Lighting Division.*

It is good practice for the foreground to be the brightest part of the scene, with the middle ground at a lower key to promote the sense of distance. The background should be neither strongly nor uniformly illuminated; lighting the entire background area will defeat the effect of depth.

It is difficult to put a figure on an illuminance for landscape lighting because of the inherent great diversity in the situations encountered. However, a lighting level of 5 to 10 footcandles is usually appropriate for interesting foreground features such as flower beds and rock gardens, with about 2 footcandles for the background. Regardless of the light level, however, a cardinal rule for landscape lighting is that no light source shall be visible to the user.

A campus presents many interesting problems to the lighting designer. The campus itself sets out to achieve an outdoor environment that will lend itself naturally to the life of the student. It should be designed to an overall scale that permits harmony within itself as well as with its surrounding neighborhood. That harmony must not be disturbed by the lighting. The lighting should be consistent and work well within the campus; and on no account should loud lighting intrude itself, directly or indirectly, onto any neighboring space.

Within any unified outdoor unit such as a campus or a park, there is likely to be a variety of spaces, each with its own scale. These can range from large, public, unenclosed spaces to small and private ones. The lighting should reflect these differ-

Fig. 9-39 Tree lighting. *Photograph credit: Raymond Grenald.*

Fig. 9-40 Tree lighting. *Photograph credit: Raymond Grenald.*

Fig. 9-41 Tree lighting. *Photograph credit: Raymond Grenald.*

Fig. 9-42 Tree lighting. *Photograph credit: Raymond Grenald.*

Fig. 9-43 Tree lighting. *Photograph credit: Raymond Grenald.*

ences in scale as well as the different purposes to which the spaces will be put. The lighting equipment will correspondingly range from large luminaires on tall poles to very small fixtures so well concealed that only the light they throw reveals their existence.

Trees

There are almost as many ways of illuminating trees as there are botanical varieties of them. Individual trees are so variable in shape, even within a single variety, and groups of trees exhibit such an extraordinary variety of form, that each tree-lighting assignment merits being approached afresh, with no preconceived notions of any "ideal" effect or "ideal" lighting solution (Figures 9-39 through 9-43).

A tree with full and branching growth lends itself to illumination from within. A luminaire with a wide light distribution is placed in a crotch of the tree to create an umbrella of light from the illumination of the undersides of the leaves.

When a tree is illuminated from below, the light must come from more than one direction if the three-dimensional character of the tree is to be retained. If one of the light sources is strongly directional in character and is brighter than the others, the sculptural qualities of the tree will be emphasized.

A dappled glade results from shadows cast by trees that are illuminated by luminaires mounted in adjacent trees. As the branches sway, the shadows move, creating a shifting pattern of light and dark that is very pleasant.

Affixing lighting equipment to a tree can present difficulties. One method is to use threaded studs screwed into holes drilled into the tree, with the holes painted with a special wound treatment before the studs are inserted. The use of straps pulled tightly around the trunk or branch is not recommended. As a tree grows older, its parts get fatter, and the strap would either snap under the strain or would cut into the bark. As the tree grows taller, a wire fixed tautly to the growing parts could be stretched to the breaking point. Regular inspection of tree-mounted lighting equipment is essential if problems are to be avoided (Figures 9-44, 9-45, and 9-46).

Flower Beds

Flower beds provide masses of bright color that enliven a landscape during the day. With electric light, it is possible to illuminate them to provide an equal amount of interest and sparkle in the nighttime environment.

A good way of illuminating a flower bed is with the simple mushroom type of luminaire (Figures 9-47 and 9-48). This type of fixture, while low, provides light from above the plants—the natural direction—and it is usually tall enough to remain above all but the most vigorous growth. The light is widely spread around the luminaire, thus enabling the use of fewer units. Although closer spacing will provide a smoother light, satisfactorily even lighting may be obtained by setting the luminaire spacing up to 10 times the distance each luminaire stands above the plants.

If spotlights are used for flower-bed illumination, they are most effective when mounted some distance away from the plants—possibly in a nearby tree (Figure 9-49). If they are too close, a patchy lighting effect will be the result, and the heat from the lamps may damage the plants.

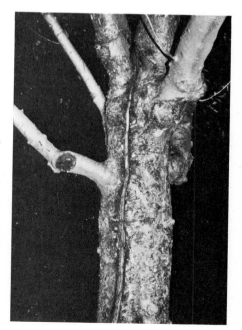

Fig. 9-44 Affixing a luminaire to a tree. *Photograph credit: Keene Corporation, Lighting Division.*

Fig. 9-45 A luminaire fixed to a tree. *Photograph credit: Raymond Grenald.*

Fig. 9-46 An electrical wire attached to a tree that has been partially overgrown by the bark of the tree. *Photograph credit: Raymond Grenald.*

Fig. 9-47 A mushroom-type luminaire for illuminating a flower bed from close to the ground. *Photograph credit: Keene Corporation, Lighting Division.*

Fig. 9-48 A low luminaire designed to provide both strong down-light for illuminating flowers and ground cover, plus a moderate amount of general ambient light. *Photograph credit: Keene Corporation, Lighting Division.*

Fig. 9-49 Bullet-shaped fixtures can cast effective light on flower beds from a greater distance than the mushroom type. The louvers shield the glare of the light from viewers and confine the light to the area for which the lighting is intended. *Photograph credit: Keene Corporation, Lighting Division.*

Water Features

Water has been an important architectural feature for centuries. Water displays were used as important elements in the earliest palaces and stately homes and in public places as well. Despite their inherent need for regular maintenance, decorative pools and fountains are again being used to enhance the outdoor environment.

When water is churned into a spray, it acts as a good diffuse reflector of light, and the effect can be changed by changing the color of the light (Figure 9-50). Still water, however, acts as a mirror. This can be a two-edged sword. While general reflections in still water can add charm to a scene, reflections that show the details of concealed lighting equipment should be considered—and avoided.

The best effects in lighting water features are obtained when the lighting and the feature are designed together. Nonetheless, even when the lighting is added later, the results can be entirely satisfactory when skillfully handled (Figures 9-51, 9-52, and 9-53).

Sprays and jets are generally best illuminated from just under the surface of the water, which will then enhance the sparkle of the display. Luminaires used for underwater lighting should have a narrower beam spread than would be provided for open-air use, since this spread counteracts the diffusing effect of the water.

Earth-leakage protection must be provided with submerged lighting fixtures to prevent the possibility of an electric shock through the water should a fault in the grounding circuit occur. And, of course, submerged fixtures must have integral seals to keep the water out of the luminaire. It is also very useful for the fixture to be adjustable so that its direction can be altered in the field for the most appropriate illumination angle (Figure 9-54).

Augmenting the submerged luminaires and occasionally replacing them, a wide range of lighting fixtures is available that can illuminate water from the air while withstanding the constant spray from the water feature. This sort of lighting will add sparkling highlights to fountain displays, and it can be used where underwater luminaires are not possible.

Water features are generally of low brightness regardless of how they are lighted. This is especially true when colored light is used, as is often done for special effects. As a result, it is easy for the surrounding ambient light to wash out the brightness of an illuminated feature and diminish or destroy its effectiveness. For the best effect, a fountain's immediate environment should have a very low or nonexistent level of ambient light.

Light Sources

Great care should be exercised in selecting light sources; they should emit light that is compatible with the particular color of the landscape being illuminated. For example, the bluish-green light from a mercury lamp will strongly bring out the green of tree leaves during the spring and summer, and will brilliantly render certain types of evergreens. That same light, however, will make the red and gold leaves of autumn look dull brown. In Autumn, incandescent lamps are a better light source for illuminating tree leaves.

Gardens with a mixture of colors will look best under white light. Incandescent lamps or fluorescent lamps with good color-rendering properties are suitable light sources.

Tinted light can be used for emphasis, although it should be done with great care. It should be remembered that the light output from a tinted lamp is less—in most

Fig 9-50 **Effective lighting of the spray of a water feature.** *Photograph credit: Keene Corporation, Lighting Division.*

Fig. 9-51 **A different sort of lighted water spray.** *Photograph credit: Keene Corporation, Lighting Division.*

Fig. 9-52 **An outdoor fountain in a European city, whose lighting, although designed and installed many years after its construction, is very effective.** *Photograph credit: Raymond Grenald.*

Fig. 9-53 **A fountain in a shopping center, the lighting design of which was integral with the fountain design itself.** *Photograph credit: Raymond Grenald.*

cases much less—than the output from a lamp of corresponding wattage emitting white light. The output from a green lamp, for example, is only one-fifth that of the corresponding white lamp. It is also worth remembering that while the light from a tinted lamp will emphasize objects of its own color, it will deaden others. A green lamp will exaggerate green objects, but it will almost totally kill pinks and reds, turning them muddy or black. Used with care, however, tinted spots, particularly for illuminating massed plantings of a single species or color, can be very effective.

LIGHTING FOR SECURITY AND SAFETY

Floodlighting of a façade is often used as a means of identifying a building. But flood-lighting can serve a dual purpose—functional as well as artistic—since it is an excellent method of providing security lighting. A loiterer or potential intruder can be seen, either in silhouette or picked out by the floodlights, by a guard patrolling the area or by a television camera.

One method of security lighting is to locate the luminaires high up on the building and to direct them outward. This method works well in a residential setting or in any other situation where the person protecting the building is inside the building itself, since anyone approaching the entrance is clearly illuminated and can be identified. On the other hand, if the building is patrolled from the outside, this method puts the guard at a disadvantage, since he or she must see through the glare from the luminaire in order to determine what is going on within the area being patrolled. Assuming the loiterer is closer to the building than the guard, it is the guard who is well lighted and the intruder who is capable of being hidden. With façade lighting, the building is a bright background against which an intruder will be silhouetted, making it much easier for the guard to control the property.

A pedestrian likes to recognize someone approaching. Dark alleys may conceal prowlers, yet roadway lighting may not help. Indeed, bright street lighting and bright facade lighting will make shadowed areas appear even darker by comparison. Unlighted shrubbery may be menacing, and dark buildings may conceal those wearing dark clothing.

To provide a safe and secure environment, the necessity for strong lighting can first be minimized by using light-colored materials for building façades and for paths and pavements.

Then, the lighting designer will generally follow these rules:

- Illuminate building façades.

- Illuminate all pathways and the areas immediately adjacent to them.

- Keep the trees and shrubbery well-trimmed and well-lighted to prevent their being usable as hiding places for intruders.

- Locate luminaires to light any places where unwanted people may lurk or hide, or where legitimate visitors may want to go.

- Use light sources of moderate brightness so that any areas in shadow are not excessively dark by comparison.

- Try to simulate the thinking of one who might wrongfully want to gain admittance or one who might be intent on committing a crime, and then counter with appropriate lighting.

LUMINAIRE SELECTION

The choice of luminaires for a particular project is not something done as an after-thought, but rather, is an integral part of the lighting design itself. Luminaires have been designed for a multitude of purposes, and the choice of a particular one will of course depend on what it is expected to do. A familiarity with what is available is essential before any lighting design can begin, while the final choice is likely to be the result of several trial designs, using different luminaires with varying design features.

Fig. 9-54 An adjustable submersible luminaire.
Photograph credit: Keene Corporation, Lighting Division.

324

Luminaire Performance

It is not usual for a lighting designer to have the opportunity to construct a trial lighting situation, so manufacturers' data must be relied upon to provide the necessary performance information. Much of their data is highly technical, arcane, and far beyond the scope of this chapter or the general practice of most designers. Nonetheless, the data can be useful if certain precautions and general points are borne in mind.

The photometric data taken by a reputable laboratory from a test luminaire will be accurate. These are the data that manufacturers will publish and distribute. But, in practice, it will not be possible to use those data in the design of a typical exterior lighting system within an accuracy closer than about ± 15 percent. Conditions contributing to this inherent inaccuracy are these:

- The actual light distribution can be expected to vary from one luminaire to the next.

- The actual light output will likewise vary from one lamp to the next, even within the same batch.

- The supply-line voltage to be found at the site may vary from the theoretical voltage on which the design data are based. During actual operation, too, the voltage may vary, especially during peak load periods. It is not uncommon during such high-usage periods to experience voltage drops of up to 8 percent, usually in increments but otherwise completely without warning. Such drops will of course reduce the actual light output.

- During installation, it will probably be impossible to aim the luminaire with total accuracy, nor will it be possible to ensure that a particular light intensity is directed at a particular point.

Many manufacturers construct luminaires that may appear superficially to be identical, but substitutions should not be made without first consulting the published data sheets, since performance characteristics can be quite different. The difference may be due, for example, to slightly altered lampholder position, or to a slightly different reflector finish.

Modifications to a manufactured luminaire should similarly be made only with great caution, since a comparatively simple change may produce an unexpected reduction in the luminaire's performance. For example, the addition of a wire safety guard to a luminaire may reduce its overall performance by as much as 20 percent.

Safety

When used in the United States, a luminaire (and its ballast) is usually required by the local safety inspection authorities to carry an Underwriters Laboratories (UL) label. In Canada, a Canadian Standards Association (CSA) label is generally obligatory. These labels indicate that representative samples of the luminaire have been tested by UL or CSA and found to meet the mechanical and electrical safety standards of those organizations. The labels do not indicate that the luminaire meets any particular standard of lighting performance.

Certain discharge lamps (such as some types of mercury and metal halide lamps) will continue to give off light even when the outer glass bulb is broken. While at first

LAMP CHARACTERISTICS

	Cool White Fluorescent	Cool White Deluxe Fluorescent	Warm White Fluorescent	Warm White Deluxe Fluorescent
Approx. initial efficacy (Lm/W)	80	55	80	55
Lamp appearance on neutral surface	White	White	Yellowish white	Yellowish white
Colors strengthened	Orange, yellow, blue	All nearly equally	Orange, yellow	Red, orange, yellow, green
Colors grayed	Red	None appreciably	Red, green. blue	Blue
Effect on Caucasian complexion	Pinkish, grayed	Natural	Sallow	Ruddy

Fig. 9-55

LAMP PERFORMANCE

Lamp	Beam Control	Physical Size of Luminaire	Projection Range	Light Patch Shape Perpendicular to Beam	Cold-Weather Operation	Hot-Weather Operation
PAR (d) (e)	Good	Small	Short	Circular or elliptical	Good	Good
General-service incandescent (d) (e)	Good	Small to large	Short to long	Circular or elliptical	Good	Good
Tungsten-halogen (d) (e)	Good	Small to medium	Short to long	Ellipse	Good	Good
Mercury	Fair	Medium to large	Short to long	Circular or elliptical	(a)	Good
Phosphor-coated mercury	Poor	Medium to large	Short	Circular	(a)	Good

Note:
(a) Ballasts usually suitable for starting lamp in an ambient temperature down to − 20°F.
(b) Requires special ballast for low-temperature operation. Also usually requires special lamp; otherwise low-temperature operation will result in loss of lamp light output.
(c) High-temperature operation will result in loss of lamp light output.

Fig. 9-56

Incandescent	Clear Mercury	Deluxe White Mercury	Metal Halide	Phosphorcoated Metal Halide	High-pressure Sodium	Low-pressure Sodium
20	50	55	85	85	120	180
Yellowish white	Greenish-blue white	Greenish white	Greenish white		Yellowish	Strong yellow-orange
Red, orange, yellow	Yellow, blue, green	Red, yellow, blue	Yellow, blue, green		Yellow, orange, green	Yellow-orange
Blue	Red, orange	Green	Red		Blue, red	All except yellow-orange appear brown-black
Ruddy	Greenish, grayed	Ruddy	Grayed		Yellowish	Yellow

Lamp	Beam Control	Physical Size of Luminaire	Projection Range	Light Patch Shape Perpendicular to Beam	Cold-Weather Operation	Hot-Weather Operation
Metal halide	Fair	Medium to large	Short to long	Circular or elliptical	(a)	Good
Phosphor-coated metal halide	Poor	Medium to large	Short	Circular	(a)	Good
High-pressure sodium	Fair to good	Medium to large	Short to long	Circular or elliptical	(a)	Good
Low-pressure sodium (e)	Fair to poor	Medium to large	Short	Elliptical	Good	Good
Tubular fluorescent (d) (e)	Poor	Long	Short	Elliptical	(b)	(c)

(d) These lamps emit their full light output immediately they are switched on. The other lamps take some minutes after being switched on before they emit their full light output.

(e) These lamps will emit their full light output immediately the electrical supply has been restored following a short interruption. The other lamps will take some minutes before they emit their full light output after the electrical supply has been restored following a short interruption.

glance this may appear to be an advantage, in reality the opposite is true, since they will also continue to emit ultraviolet radiation. If such a lamp in an open luminaire is broken, that radiation could be concentrated into the eyes of a viewer. This is very dangerous, since ultraviolet radiation can cause conjunctivitis and similar disorders of the eye.

A luminaire with a glass front is likely to protect passers-by from the effects of a broken discharge lamp, since the glass will prevent the radiation from leaving the confines of the luminaire. On the other hand, most plastics will not bar the passage of ultraviolet rays, so a plastic-front luminaire is of no use in this regard.

Construction

Luminaires used outside become dirty very quickly. Obviously, the outside of a fixture will get soiled, but so will the inside. Most luminaires breathe; air, carrying dirt with it, is drawn into the fixture when the lamp is turned off and the fixture cools. Insects are attracted by the light, and it is not unusual to find a thick layer of dead insects inside the luminaire. Unless one is prepared to clean each luminaire on a regular and frequent basis in order to maintain its light output, the fixture should be very tightly gasketed or, alternatively, completely sealed and fitted with an air-filter breather.

The glass used in luminaires is quite capable of withstanding both the heating caused by turning the lamp on and the slow cooling caused by turning it off. The rapid and uneven cooling caused by rain or snow hitting the glass may call for specially treated glass, however, and this option should be considered.

Plastics, despite the rising cost of petroleum, are increasingly being used in place of glass for refractors and enclosures. While this usage can have significant advantages, such as lightness of weight and resistance to vandals and other causes of breakage, there are disadvantages to be considered. Polystyrene is brittle and can evidence considerable discoloration over relatively short periods of time. Butyrates discolor only slightly, and then only over long periods. Acrylics do not discolor and are most resistant to both heat and ultraviolet radiation from both discharge lamps and from the sun.

While polycarbonate has a slight tendency to discolor, it also has an impact strength many times that of any of the other plastic materials, making it an obvious choice for use where vandalism is a recurrent (or a potential) problem.

All the plastics mentioned are slow-burning except for polycarbonate, which is self-extinguishing. Metal and glass, of course, will not burn at all. These factors should be considered if a possible fire might pose a serious threat to the surrounding area.

While light fixtures are normally thought of as static items, a luminaire, when mounted atop a tall pole, can be subjected to a considerable amount of vibration. This should be considered in the selection of both the luminaire and the lamp it houses. The method of attachment to the pole should be scrutinized closely, and the installation should be checked carefully.

LAMPS

Many different types of lamps are available for exterior lighting applications. While incandescent lamps are the ones most commonly encountered in a residential setting, they are the ones least likely to be used in most outdoor applications because they consume a very large amount of electrical energy to produce a given amount of light. Fluorescent lamps, almost universally used to light office interiors, have limited application to outdoor environments because of the extremely large luminaires required to hold them, the difficulty in controlling their light distribution, and their low light output under extremes of heat or cold.

Figure 9-55 indicates the salient characteristics of lamps used for exterior lighting, while Figure 9-56 tells how they can be expected to perform.

CHAPTER TEN
FLAGPOLES
James E. Coane

INTRODUCTION

Origin of Flags and Flagpoles

We do not know when the first flagpole and flag were raised, but certainly it was many thousands of years ago. Archeology supports this contention through numerous pictures, sculptures, and reliefs that depict flag-like objects dating back to the earliest days of society when civilization had its birth.

In its earliest form, a "flag" was usually nothing more than a symbolic ribbon, cloth, or animal skin attached to a wooden staff and carried forth into battle. As the centuries passed, flags took a more formalized structure, finally evolving into the forms we know today.

At first they were almost exclusively flown at religious and military ceremonies, but they now have many more uses and their display is more common than ever. Americans, more than most other people, have become a flag-conscious nation. "Old Glory" is an everyday object appearing on government installations, commercial, and institutional buildings, parks, playgrounds, and homes. In addition to the national flag, we have created an enormous variety of flags for nearly an infinite number of specialized uses: state flags, municipal, county, town, and advertising flags, those to distinguish military and civilian ranks, those representing clubs, associations, and many others.

But what supports these flags is often taken for granted. And yet the flagpole has been around as long as flags themselves, though certainly not the sophisticated architectural product that it is in this century.

Before companies engaged in the manufacture and sale of flagpoles came into existence, they were generally made by the project carpenter who cut down the nearest straight tree, trimmed it up, and planted it firmly in the ground. It was not particularly attractive, and its aesthetic contribution to the building was not significant. When something more sophisticated was desired, the services of a mast-and-spar maker were employed to produce the flagpole. In the United States, poles were fashioned from northern pine shipped in by schooner from Canada. Expert craftsmen would shape them with draw knives, sand them to a fine finish, and hand-rub them with animal fat. The rubbing operation usually required several days, since total saturation was desired to assure long life. Carefully crafted wooden flagpoles could be expected to last half a century, and indeed today, some that made their debut in the early 1900s have outlasted some steel flagpoles that postdated their existence by some 30 years.

The Development of Today's Flagpoles

The steel flagpole was an outgrowth of the telescopic steel trolley pole innovated by the National Tube Division of United States Steel. By the mid-1930s, this steel flagpole dominated the flagpole market and had forced the wooden flagpole into obsolescence.

However, although wooden flagpoles disappeared, their tapered design did not. As steel became dominant, the architects, wanting the tapered appearance that characterized the wooden pole, began specifying the telescopic steel flagpole.

During the 1930s, the Union Metal Manufacturing Company began making tapered steel shafts for pile-driving components and for ships' cargo booms. The few small flagpole manufacturers in business at the time immediately recognized the application, and the tapered steel flagpole was born. Its popularity skyrocketed overnight, and until the introduction of the tapered aluminum pole in the late forties, the tapered steel flagpole was specified in more than 80 percent of the design orders.

Ironically, as the telescopic steel and the tapered steel flagpoles had been by-products of industry, so, ultimately, was the tapered aluminum flagpole. When the flagpole industry learned of the significant strides made by the manufacturers of aluminum light standards, they jumped into the development and came out with a complete line of tapered aluminum flagpoles. Rapidly, the aluminum pole moved from nonexistence to almost total acceptance by architects and consumers alike. It was a sure success.

Particularly attractive to the architect and the consumer was the non-maintenance aspect. No longer was it necessary to employ the expensive services of an experienced and hard-to-find steeplejack to paint the flagpole periodically. No longer was it necessary to employ expert welders to field-weld the flagpole sections at the job site, nor was it necessary to hire heavy cranes to accomplish installation. Now poles up to 60 feet in height could be installed with a strong back and a simple A-frame. The new poles also offered considerable savings in maintenance. Furthermore, the lighter weight of the aluminum resulted in reduced shipping costs as well.

Now metal flagpoles are made not only of aluminum and steel but also of bronze and stainless steel. And let us not forget the most recent introduction of fiberglass. All these poles are tapered, but the architect does have a choice of two forms. One is the traditional straight-line conical taper, the other a parabolic curved "entasis" taper resembling the classic Greek columns that were designed and constructed 2500 years ago.

The Flagpole Industry

The flagpole industry, while small and specialized, has an impressive history of continuing product improvement and contribution to the architectural and general construction community. It has kept abreast of changing times and continues to make technical advances in its development. While flagpoles are a comparatively simple product, they take on substantial significance in the overall development of a plaza or building site plan. Omit them and they will be sorely missed.

Architects are well aware of this and, unlike other relatively unnoticed features of construction, their many variables must be considered in order to select and specify them properly. Flagpoles do not just happen. As someone has to manufacture them to exacting specifications, someone also must make the appropriate choice for every building and site on which each pole will ultimately be placed. This selection requires knowledge of the product, materials, finishes, methods of mounting, and costs.

It is for the purpose of providing the architectural profession with adequate information about flagpoles and their uses that this chapter has been prepared. It covers the usage of flagpoles, pole types and sizes, materials and finishes, mounting information, construction details, accessories and fittings, detailed guide specifications, and the proper display of the flag.

The information included represents the consensus of recommendations and objective advice of the leading manufacturers of flagpoles. Portions of the data were originally developed by the Flagpole Division of the National Association of Architectural Metal Manufacturers (NAAMM). Special thanks are due that group for granting its permission to use some of those data for this chapter, specifically the guide specifications that have been reproduced verbatim and arranged in the format of the Construction Specifications Institute. Special thanks are also extended to Wayne F. Koppes, technical consultant to NAAMM, who contributed nearly all the sketches and whose close work with me on the NAAMM manual made my job in preparing this chapter much easier than it otherwise would have been.

Early Architectural Flagpoles

During the nineteenth century and the early part of the twentieth, flagpoles were often designed by architects and were treated with much greater attention to detail than they generally are today. A classically designed, bronze-based flagpole was designed in 1929 by John Russell Pope to complement his Theodore Roosevelt Memorial wing of the American Museum of Natural History in New York (Figure 10-1). His flagpole was similar in feeling to one designed 30 years earlier by McKim, Mead & White for Columbia University, but the 1899 version thoughtfully provided an integral bench for weary students as part of its stone base (Figure 10-2). Carrère and Hastings included a pair of exceedingly elaborate flagpoles as part of the forecourt terrace to their 1911 New York Public Library (Figure 10-3). The form of their fantastic horned creatures was mirrored in the 1918 memorial flagpole in New York's Madison Square that commemorates the actions of the United States Armed Forces during World War I (Figure 10-4). Perhaps one of the most grandiose flagpoles ever erected (now only a base without its pole) was built in 1926 in New York's Union Square to honor the 150th birthday of the United States. It is 36 feet in diameter and includes bronze bas-reliefs by Anthony de Francisci that symbolize the forces of good and evil during the Revolutionary War (Figure 10-5). Along with elaborate flagpole bases went very ornamental finials (Figures 10-6 through 10-9).

Usage and Mounting of Flagpoles

Flagpoles can be mounted and used in a variety of ways, each with its particular effect and impact. The simplest and most common is the single groundset flagpole

Fig. 10-1 American Museum of Natural History, New York. *Photograph credit: Andrew Alpern.*

Fig. 10-2 Columbia University, New York. *Photograph credit: Andrew Alpern.*

Fig. 10-3 The New York Public Library. *Photograph credit: Andrew Alpern.*

Fig. 10-4 Madison Square, New York. *Photograph credit: Andrew Alpern.*

Fig. 10-5 Union Square, New York. *Photograph credit: Andrew Alpern.*

334

Fig. 10-6   Columbia University, New York. The crown is symbolic of the university's original name, Kings College, from 1754 to 1776. *Photograph credit: Andrew Alpern.*

Fig. 10-7   Columbia University, New York. *Photograph credit: Andrew Alpern.*

Fig. 10-8   The New York Public Library. *Photograph credit: Andrew Alpern.*

Fig. 10-9   Madison Square, New York. Illuminated star is a World War I memorial. *Photograph credit: Andrew Alpern.*

Fig. 10-10 Single ground-set pole. *Photograph credit: Courtesy Kearney National, American Flagpole Division.*

Fig. 10-11 A cluster of poles. *Photograph credit: Courtesy Kearney National, American Flagpole Division.*

Fig. 10-12 A row of poles. *Photograph credit: Courtesy Kearney National, American Flagpole Division.*

Fig. 10-13 Outrigger flagpoles. *Photograph credit: Ransdell Inc., courtesy of Kearney National, American Flagpole Division.*

Fig. 10-14 Rockefeller Center, Fifth Avenue, New York. *Photograph credit: Andrew Alpern.*

(Figure 10-10). While a single pole's drama depends on its setting, a cluster of poles or a closely spaced row of them has a strong impact regardless of the surrounding environment (Figures 10-11 and 10-12). Outrigger poles can be attached to the side of a building at angles ranging from the nearly horizontal to practically vertical, but the most common position is 45° (Figures 10-13 and 10-14). A perfectly vertical flagpole attached to the side of a building or a wall has a different appearance and impact from an outrigger type (Figure 10-15). And a roof-mounted one is perhaps the most dramatic of all (Figure 10-16).

POLE TYPES

Flagpole Shafts

Homegrown flagpole shafts are sometimes of continuously constant diameter, but commercial ones are either cone-tapered or entasis-tapered. Both are available in aluminum, steel, bronze, stainless steel, and fiberglass. The less costly cone-tapered configuration is the most commonly used, with the entasis taper being reserved for projects of exceptional architectural character.

Cone-tapered   A cone-tapered pole has a lower section of constant diameter with the conical portion generally consisting of from one-third to two-thirds of the exposed height of the pole. The reduction in the diameter of the conical section is usually 1 inch to every 5 to 7½ feet of length, varying with the pole material and the manufacturer's standard practices.

Butt and top diameters will vary depending on the pole material and length. The ratio of top diameter to butt diameter ranges from 50 to 60 percent on cone-tapered poles up to 40 feet in length and then drops off to a low of 25 percent on a 100-foot aluminum flagpole (Figure 10-17).

Entasis-tapered   The entasis taper was developed by architects in ancient Greece as a solution to the optical illusion that makes a cone-tapered pole or column appear skinnier in the middle than it actually is. Virtually all the columns on Greek classical temples were built with an entasis taper.

Fig. 10-15 Vertical wall-mounted pole. *Photograph credit: Courtesy Kearney National, American Flagpole Division.*

Fig. 10-16 A roof-mounted pole. *Photograph credit: Hi-Tone for Chase Federal Savings and Loan Association, Miami Beach, Fla.*

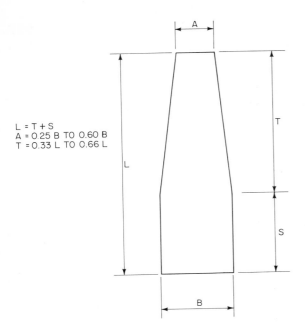

$$L = T + S$$
$$A = 0.25\ B\ TO\ 0.60\ B$$
$$T = 0.33\ L\ TO\ 0.66\ L$$

Fig. 10-17 Cone-tapered shaft configuration.

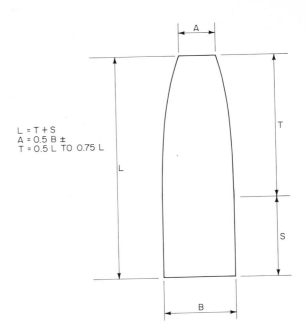

$$L = T + S$$
$$A = 0.5\ B\ \pm$$
$$T = 0.5\ L\ TO\ 0.75\ L$$

Fig. 10-18 Entasis-tapered shaft configuration.

An entasis-tapered pole has a precisely calculated parabolic taper. The length of the taper is generally one-half to three-fourths the exposed height of the pole, and the top diameter runs about one-half the butt diameter. As with the conical shaft, however, the top dimension will grow smaller in proportion to the butt as the tapered section gets longer (Figure 10-18).

POLE MOUNTING

The Ground-Mounted Pole

The ground-mounted free-standing flagpole is by far the most common type. Conventional poles may be made of aluminum, steel, bronze, stainless steel, or fiberglass, and may have internal or external halyards. Normal heights above ground range from 20 to 100 feet, but may be greater. Wood is very rarely used any longer (Figure 10-19). Besides conventional poles, there are three other varieties of ground-set poles: flag-storing, tilting, and nautical.

The flag-storing type Self-storing flagpoles are designed to allow for the storage of the flag within the flagpole shaft. The flag is raised, lowered, and drawn into the pole either manually or electrically. If motorized, the unit may be activated electronically by a photoelectric assembly or a remote manual switch. If manually operated, a simple direct-drive handcrank mechanism, located in the base of the pole, is employed.

Self-storing flagpoles are generally ground-set and made of aluminum, but they may be wall-mounted or roof-set. They can be produced in all the same materials and finishes available for conventional poles.

Standard heights run from 30 to 50 feet but may be taller (Figures 10-20, 10-21, and 10-22).

CONE TAPERED ALUMINUM FLAGPOLE
(GROUND SET)

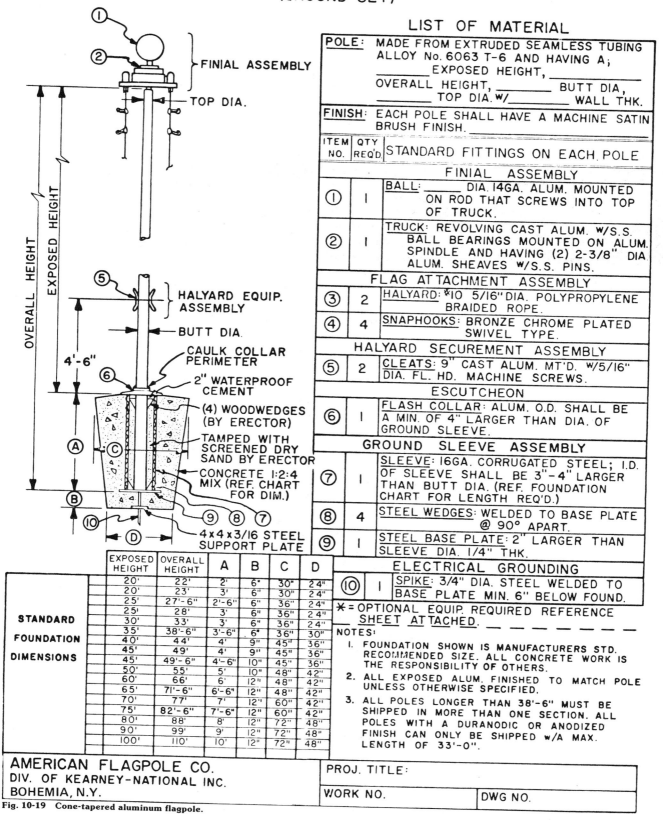

LIST OF MATERIAL

POLE: MADE FROM EXTRUDED SEAMLESS TUBING ALLOY No. 6063 T-6 AND HAVING A; _____ EXPOSED HEIGHT, _____ OVERALL HEIGHT, _____ BUTT DIA, _____ TOP DIA. W/ _____ WALL THK.

FINISH: EACH POLE SHALL HAVE A MACHINE SATIN BRUSH FINISH. _____

ITEM NO.	QTY REQ'D	STANDARD FITTINGS ON EACH POLE
		FINIAL ASSEMBLY
①	1	BALL: ____ DIA. 14GA. ALUM. MOUNTED ON ROD THAT SCREWS INTO TOP OF TRUCK.
②	1	TRUCK: REVOLVING CAST ALUM. W/S.S. BALL BEARINGS MOUNTED ON ALUM. SPINDLE AND HAVING (2) 2-3/8" DIA. ALUM. SHEAVES W/S.S. PINS.
		FLAG ATTACHMENT ASSEMBLY
③	2	HALYARD: *10 5/16"DIA. POLYPROPYLENE BRAIDED ROPE.
④	4	SNAPHOOKS: BRONZE CHROME PLATED SWIVEL TYPE.
		HALYARD SECUREMENT ASSEMBLY
⑤	2	CLEATS: 9" CAST ALUM. MT'D. W/5/16" DIA. FL. HD. MACHINE SCREWS.
		ESCUTCHEON
⑥	1	FLASH COLLAR: ALUM. O.D. SHALL BE A MIN. OF 4" LARGER THAN DIA. OF GROUND SLEEVE.
		GROUND SLEEVE ASSEMBLY
⑦	1	SLEEVE: 16GA. CORRUGATED STEEL; I.D. OF SLEEVE SHALL BE 3"-4" LARGER THAN BUTT DIA. (REF. FOUNDATION CHART FOR LENGTH REQ'D.)
⑧	4	STEEL WEDGES: WELDED TO BASE PLATE @ 90° APART.
⑨	1	STEEL BASE PLATE: 2" LARGER THAN SLEEVE DIA. 1/4" THK.
		ELECTRICAL GROUNDING
⑩	1	SPIKE: 3/4" DIA. STEEL WELDED TO BASE PLATE MIN. 6" BELOW FOUND.

✱ = OPTIONAL EQUIP. REQUIRED REFERENCE SHEET ATTACHED. ____ ____ ____ ____

NOTES:

1. FOUNDATION SHOWN IS MANUFACTURERS STD. RECOMMENDED SIZE. ALL CONCRETE WORK IS THE RESPONSIBILITY OF OTHERS.
2. ALL EXPOSED ALUM. FINISHED TO MATCH POLE UNLESS OTHERWISE SPECIFIED.
3. ALL POLES LONGER THAN 38'-6" MUST BE SHIPPED IN MORE THAN ONE SECTION. ALL POLES WITH A DURANODIC OR ANODIZED FINISH CAN ONLY BE SHIPPED W/A MAX. LENGTH OF 33'-0".

STANDARD FOUNDATION DIMENSIONS

EXPOSED HEIGHT	OVERALL HEIGHT	A	B	C	D
20'	22'	2'	6"	30"	24"
20'	23'	3'	6"	30"	24"
25'	27'-6"	2'-6"	6"	36"	24"
25'	28'	3'	6"	36"	24"
30'	33'	3'	6"	36"	24"
35'	38'-6"	3'-6"	6"	36"	30"
40'	44'	4'	9"	45"	36"
45'	49'	4'	9"	45"	36"
45'	49'-6"	4'-6"	10"	45"	36"
50'	55'	5'	10"	48"	42"
60'	66'	6'	12"	48"	42"
65'	71'-6"	6'-6"	12"	48"	42"
70'	77'	7'	12"	60"	42"
75'	82'-6"	7'-6"	12"	60"	42"
80'	88'	8'	12"	72"	48"
90'	99'	9'	12"	72"	48"
100'	110'	10'	12"	72"	48"

AMERICAN FLAGPOLE CO.
DIV. OF KEARNEY-NATIONAL INC.
BOHEMIA, N.Y.

PROJ. TITLE:

WORK NO.   DWG NO.

Fig. 10-19 Cone-tapered aluminum flagpole.

Fig. 10-20 Flag-storing poles, - A. *Credit: Courtesy Electronic Flag Poles, Inc.*

Fig. 10-21 Flag-storing poles, - B. *Credit: Courtesy Electronic Flag Poles, Inc.*

Fig. 10-22 Flag-storing poles, - C. *Credit: Courtesy Electronic Flag Poles, Inc.*

The tilting type   Tilting flagpoles are counterbalanced to permit easy lowering for periodic maintenance, including painting, halyard replacement, and parts repair. They are accurately balanced, making them easily operable by one person. Tilting poles are available only in aluminum, may be ground-set or roof-set, and generally range in height from 30 to 60 feet. Longer poles are available, but as height is increased, so must be the size of the counterweight unit, making poles over 60 feet appear cumbersome (Figures 10-23a and 10-23b).

The nautical type   Nautical flagpoles may be either single- or double-masted, although the latter is the more traditional design. They are used for displaying more than one flag. The single-masted unit employs a crossarm or yardarm from which code, signal, or state flags may be flown. The United States flag would fly from the top of the main mast (Figure 10-24). With the double-masted pole, a burgee, or private flag, would fly from the peak of the top mast. The gaff would be used exclusively for the American flag, as its peak is the highest point of the main mast construction (Figure 10-25). The yardarm or crossarm is dressed in the same manner as it is on the single-masted pole.

Naval, marine, and coastguard facilities almost always utilize these types of flagpole, and they are also popular at boat and yacht clubs, swimming pools, and lakeside and seaside locations.

A wide range of height is available, as is the choice of material. The typical proportions and dimensions of double-masted poles are:

Exposed height (100 percent): 30 to 75 feet

Lower mast: 60 percent, plus 10 percent for embedment and 10 percent of topmast length for overlap (23 to 56 feet)

Top mast: 40 percent (12 to 30 feet)

Yardarm length: 27 percent (8 to 21 feet)

Gaff length: 18 percent (5½ to 13½ feet)

Fig. 10-23a (Above) **Counterbalanced tilting pole, Robert Moses State Park.** *Photograph courtesy Kearney National, American Flagpole Division.*

Fig. 10-23b *(Right)* **Counterbalanced tilting pole.** *Courtesy Kearney National, American Flagpole Division.*

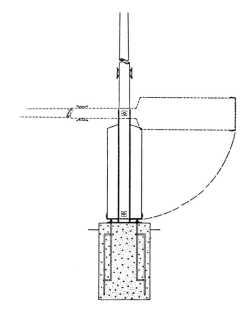

Fig. 10-24 (Above) **Single-masted nautical flagpole.** *Photograph credit: Peter B. Treiber, courtesy of Kearney National, American Flagpole Division.*

Fig. 10-25 *(Right)* **Double-masted nautical flagpole.**

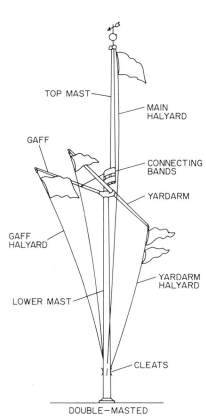

TOP MAST

MAIN HALYARD

GAFF

CONNECTING BANDS

YARDARM

GAFF HALYARD

YARDARM HALYARD

LOWER MAST

CLEATS

DOUBLE-MASTED

341

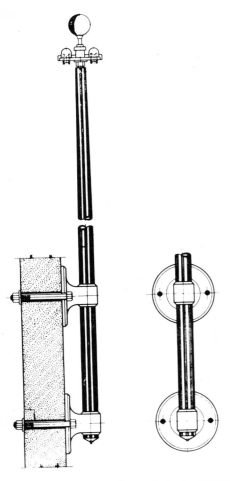

Fig. 10-26 Vertical wall-mounted pole. *Courtesy Kearney National, American Flagpole Division.*

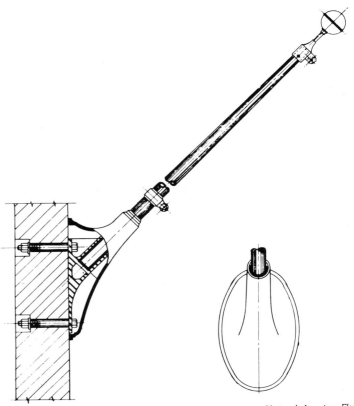

Fig. 10-27 Outrigger wall-mounted pole. *Courtesy Kearney National, American Flagpole Division.*

The Wall-Mounted Type

When site conditions prohibit the use of a freestanding flagpole, either a vertical or an outrigger wall-mounted flagpole can be employed. Representative examples of both types are shown in the "Construction Details" section of this chapter.

Vertical poles Vertical wall-mounted flagpoles are available in all five materials with a variety of bracket designs.

Typically, pole lengths are from 10 to 40 feet, and butt diameters range from 3 to 8 inches. Larger poles are available, but custom brackets must be designed for the specific application (Figure 10-26).

Outrigger Outrigger flagpoles are also available in all five materials. A variety of mounting bases are available, and they are illustrated in the "Construction Details" section of this chapter. The angle of inclination is usually 45°, but a few designs are made 30° and 60°. Not all styles are available in all mounting degrees, so particular attention should be paid to manufacturers' published data when selections are being made.

Typical pole lengths are from 8 to 20 feet in the unsupported styles, and butt diameters range from 3½ to 5 inches.

The bracket unit usually consists of two parts: the ornamental base or cover unit and the inner shoe or mounting sleeve. The inner shoe-and-sleeve assembly is typically bolted to or through the building wall. The base, slipped over this unit, provides a decorative mounting for the pole (Figure 10-27).

The Roof-Mounted Type

Most conventional flagpoles can be roof-mounted and supported in several different ways. The most popular method employs three or four braces of rod, pipe, or structural angle, although in certain instances a mandril or simple flange or shoe base is used (Figure 10-28). The pole length and structural considerations will usually dictate the type of mounting necessary. Whatever the case, the roof structure must be checked out for adequate strength to carry the loads imposed, and firm anchorage must be provided. In all instances, the pole manufacturer should be consulted before a mounting method is selected.

Poles up to 55 feet in length can usually be safely anchored to the roof structure, using the now popular bracing arrangements. Higher poles, however, generally have to be extended through the roof to specially designed anchorage that has been provided in the building construction below.

The "Construction Details" section of the chapter illustrates a number of typical bracing arrangements. For flag storing or tilting poles, the same base figures as are utilized for ground mountings are employed for roof installations.

FLAGPOLE SIZES

The following tables present complete information on typical heights, diameters, lengths of taper, and wall thicknesses of the popular ground-set flagpoles. The data cover all the materials customarily offered to the industry in both the conical- and entasis-tapered configurations (Figures 10-29 through 10-32).

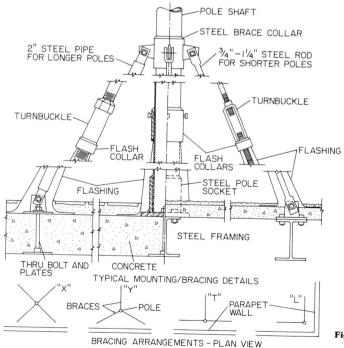

Fig. 10-28   Roof-mounted flagpole.

Exposed Length Ft.	No. Ship'g Sections	Cone-Tapered Diameters OD, inches Butt	Top	Length of Taper ft.-in.	Wall Thickness, inches Taper	Straight	Entasis-Tapered Diameters OD, inches Butt	Top	Length of Taper ft.-in.	Wall Thickness, inches Taper	Str't.
20	1	5 5	3 3¼	11-0 9-8	.188 .188	.188 .188	5	2½	16-0	.188	.188
25	1	5 5 5½	3 3¼ 3½	11-0 11-0	.188 .188 .188	.188 .188 .188	5	2½	16-0	.188	.188
30	1	5 5½ 6 6 7*	3 3½ 3¼ 3½ 4*	11-0 11-0 13-9 13-9 15-0	.188 .188 .188 .188 .188	.188 .188 .188 .188 .188/.376	5⁹⁄₁₆ 6	3 3½	20-0 20-0,24-0	.250 .188	.250 .188
35	1 or 2	6 7 7 7*	3¼ 3¼ 3½ 4*	13-9 20-6 19-3 20-6	.188 .188 .188 .188	.188 .188 .188 .188/.376	5⁹⁄₁₆ 7	3 3½	23-0 24-0,25-0	.250 .188	.250 .188
40	2	6 7 8 8	3¼ 3¼ 3½ 4	13-9 20-6 24-9 22-0	.188 .188 .188 .188	.188 .188 .188 {.188 & .188/.376*	7⅝ 8	3½ 3½	25-0 30-0,31-6	.188 .188	.250 .188
45	2	8 8	3½ 4	24-9 22-0	.188 {.188 & .188/.250*	.188 {.188 & .188/.376*	8	3½	31-6	.188	.188
50	2	8* 8 10	3½* 4 4	22-0 22-0 33-0, 38-0 & 38-8	.188/.250 .188 .188	.250/.438 .188 .188	8⅝ 10	3½ 4	35-0 36-0,40-0	.188 .188	.250 .188
55	2 or 3	10 12	3½ 4	49-6 38-6,43-9,44-0 49-0 & 56-0	.250 .188/.219, .188/.250, .250	.250 .250	12	4	55-0	.188/.250	.250
60	2 or 3	10 12	4 4	44-0 44-0	.188 .188	.188 .250	8⅝	3½	37-0	.188	.312
65	2 or 3	12	4	38-6	.188/.250	.250					
70	2 or 3	12 12	4 5	38-6,44-0, 56-0 & 66-3 49-0	.188/.250 & .250 .250	.250 .250	10¾ 12	4 4	45-0 55-0	.188/.250 .188/.250	.312 .375
75	2 or 3	12	4	38-6 & 56-0	.188/.250	.250/.375	12	4	65-0	.188/.250	.250/.375
80	3	12 12	4 5	38-6,44-0 56-0 & 66-3 66-0	.188/.250 .250 &.375 .188/.250	.250/.375 & .375 .250/.375	12¾	4	50-0	.188/.250	.312
90	3 or 4	14	4	55-0 & 62-6	.250	.375	14	4	65-0	.188/.250	.375
100	3 or 4	16	4	66-0 & 76-6	.250	.375	16	4	65-0	.188/.250	.375

Note: Heavier 30 to 80-ft. cone-tapered poles made from pipe, and 25 to 40-ft. cone-tapered poles with thinner walls and longer taper are also available from some manufacturers.

*Flag-storing poles only.

Fig. 10-29 Flagpole sizes, aluminum.

		Cone-Tapered					Entasis-Tapered				
Exposed Length Ft.	No. Ship'g. Sections	Diameters, OD, inches		Length of Taper	Wall Thickness, inches		Diameters, OD, inches		Length of Taper	Wall Thickness, inches	
		Butt	Top	ft.-in.	Taper	Str't.	Butt	Top	ft.-in.	Taper	Str't.
20	1	4	2⅜	15-0	.188 & .250	.247	4	2	13-0	.226	.226
		5	3¼	12-6	.188 & .250	.247	5⁵⁄₁₆				
		5	3½	15-0	.188 & .250	.247	6	3	13-0	.258	.258
25	1	5	3¼	12-6	.188 & .250	.247	4½	2½	17-0	.237	.237
		5⁵⁄₁₆	3¼	16-6	.188 & .250	.258	6	3	17-0	.250	.250
30	1	5	3¼	12-6	.188 & .250	.247 & .258	5⁵⁄₁₆	3	20-0	.258	.258
		5⁵⁄₁₆	3¼	16-6	.250	.250	6	3½	20-0		
		6	3¼	19-6 & 24-0	.250	.280	6⅝			.280	.280
35	1 or 2	5⁵⁄₁₆	3¼	16-6 & 19-6	.188 & .250	.250 & .258	5⁵⁄₁₆	3	23-0	.258	.258
							6				
		6⅝	3¼	24-0	.188 & .250	.280	6⅝	3½	23-0	.280	.280
40	2	6	3¼	19-6	.188 & .250	.250	6-⅝	3½	25-0	.280	.280
		6⅝	3¼	24-0	.250	.280	8-⅝	4	25-0	.280/.322	.322
		8⅝	4	33-0	.250	.322					
45	2	8⅝	4½	33-0	.250	.322	6⅝	3½	30-0	.280	.280
							8⅝	4	30-0	.280/.322	.322
50	2	6⅝	3¼	24-0	.188 & .250	.280	8⅝	3½	35-0	.280/.322	.322
		8⅝	3¼	38-6	.188 & .250	.322	10¾	4½	35-0	.322/.365	.365
		10¾	5	41-0	.250	.365					
60	2 or 3	10¾	3¼	53-6	.188 & .250	.365	8⅝	3½	40-0	.280/.322	.322
		11¾	5½	44-6	.188 & .250	.375	10¾	4½	40-0	.322/.365	.365
70	2 or 3	8⅝	3¼	38-6	.188 & .250	.322	10¾	4	45-0	.280/.365	.365
		14	5½	60-9	.250	.500	14	5	45-0	.322/.500	.500
75	2 or 3	12¾	4	62-6	.250	.375	12¾	4	50-0	.280/.375	.375
		14	5½	60-9	.250	.500	14	5	50-0	.322/.500	.500
80	3	10¾	3¼	53-6	.250	.365	14	4	55-0	.280/.500	.500
		14	4	71-6	.250	.500	16	5	55-0	.322/.500	.500
		14	6	71-6	.250	.500					
90	3 or 4	14	4	71-6	.250	.500	14	4	60-0	.280/.500	.500.
		14	6½	82-0	.250	.500	18	5	60-0	.322/.500	.500
		16	4	78-6	.250	.500					
100	3 or 4	12¾	3½	66-0	.250	.375	16	4	65-0	.280/.500	.500
		14	4	85-9	.250	.500	20	5	65-0	.322/.500	.500
		16	4	85-9	.250	.500					
		20	6½	96-0	.150	.500					

Fig. 10-30 Flagpole sizes, steel.

| Exposed Length Ft. | No. Ship'g Sections | Diameters, OD, inches | | Length of Taper | Cone-Tapered Wall Thickness, inches | | | |
| | | Butt | Top | ft.-in. | Stainless Steel | | Bronze | |
					Taper	Str't.	Taper	Str't.
20	1	4	2⅞	7-0	.083	.083	.180	.180
		5	3¼	12-6	.188	.247	—	—
25	1	4½	2⅞	12-3	.250	.258	.250	.258
		5	3¼	12-6	.188	.247	—	—
		5⁹⁄₁₆	3¼	16-6	.120&.188	.120&.258	.180	.180
30	1	5	3¼	12-6	.188	.247	—	—
		5⁹⁄₁₆	3¼	16-6	.250	.258	.250	.258
		5⁹⁄₁₆	3½	14-3	.134	.134	.180	.180
		6	3¼	19-6	.188	.250	—	—
35	1 or 2	5⁹⁄₁₆	3¼	16-6	.188/.250	.258	.250	.258
		5⁹⁄₁₆	3½	14-3	.134	.134	.180	.180
		6⅝	3¼	24-0	.188/.250	.280	.250	.280
40	2	6	3¼	24-0	.188	.250	—	—
		6⅝	3¼	24-0	.250	.280	.250	.280
		6⅝	4	19-0	.134	.134	.180	.250
		7⅝	3¼	31-3	.188/.250	.301	.250	.301
50	2	6⅝	3¼	24-0	.188/.250	.280	.250	.280
		8⅝	3¼	38-6	.188/.250	.322	.250	.322
		8⅝	4½	29-0	.148	.148	.180	259
60	2 or 3	7⅝	3¼	31-3,34-9*	.188/.250	.301	.250	.301
		8⅝	4½	29-0	.148	.148	—	—
		10¾	3¼	53-6	.250	.365	.250	.365
		8⅝	3¼	38-6	.188/.250	.322	.250	.322
70	2 or 3	10¾	4½	45-0	.165	.165	.180/.250	.375
		11¾	3¼	60-6	.250	.375	.250	.375
80	3	10¾	3¼	53-6	.250	.365	.250	.365
		12¾	5	55-9	.130	.180	.180/.250	.375
		14	4	71-6	.250	.500	.250	.500
90	3 or 4	11¾	3½	58-9	.250	.375	.250	.375
		14	4	71-6	.250	.500	.250	.500
		14	5	64-6	.188	.188	.180/.250	.375
		15	4	78-6	.250	.500	—	—
100	3 or 4	12¾	3½	66-0	.250	.375	.250	.375
		16	4	85-9	.250	.500	.250	.500
		16	5	88-6	.188	.312	.180/.250	.375

*Stainless steel only

Fig. 10-31 Flagpole sizes, stainless steel and bronze.

Diameters, OD, inches		Length of Taper	Wall Thickness, inches			
			Stainless Steel		Bronze	
Butt	Top	ft.-in.	Taper	Str't.	Taper	Str't.
4	2	13-0	.226	.226	.226	.226
5	2½	16-0	.083	.083	.180	.180
5⁹⁄₁₆	3	13-0	.258	.258	.258	.258
4½	2½	17-0	.237	.237	.237	.237
5	2½	15-0	.120	.120	.180	.180
6	3	17-0	.250	.250	.250	.250
5⁹⁄₁₆	3	20-0	.134 & .258	.134 & .258	.180 & .258	.180 & .258
6⅝	3½	20-0	.280	.280	.280	.280
5⁹⁄₁₆	3	23-0	.134 & .258	.134 & .258	.180 & .258	.180 & .258
6⅝	3½	23-0	.280	.280	.280	.280
6⅝	3½	25-0	.280	.280	.280	.280
7⅝	3½	25-0	.134	.134	.180	.250
8⅝	4	25-0	.280/.322	.322	.280/.322	.322
8⅝	3½	35-0	.280/.322 & .148	.322 & .143	.280/.322 & .180	.322 & .250
10¾	4½	35-0	.322/.365	.365	.322/.365	.365
8⅝	3½	37-0 &40-0	.280/.322 & .148	.322 & .148	.280/.322 & .180	.322 & .250
10¾	4½	40-0	.322/.365	.365	.322/.365	.365
10	4	45-0	.165	.165	.180/.250	.375
10¾	4	45-0	.280/.365	.365	.280/.365	.365
14	5	45-0	.322/.500	.500	.322/.500	.500
12	4	50-0	.180	.180	.180/.250	.375
14	4	55-0	.280/.500	.500	.280/.500	.500
16	5	55-0	.322/500	.500	.322/.500	.500
14	4	60-0	.188 & .280/.500	.188 & .500	.180/.250 & .280/.500	.375 & .500
18	5	60-0	.322/.500	.500	.322/.500	.500
16	4	65-0	.188 & .250/.500	.312 & .500	.180/.250 & .280/.500	.375 & .500
20	5	65-0	.322/.500	.500	.322/.500	.500

Exposed Height, Feet	Overall Height, Feet	Butt Diameter, Inches	Top Diameter, Inches	Wall Thickness, Inches	Ball Size, Inches
20	22	3.8	2.5	.150	4
25	28	6.0	3.25	.180	5
30	33	6.6	3.25	.180	6
35	39	7.0	3.3	.200	6
40	44	7.0	3.3	.200	8
50	55	9.9	4.0	.275	10
60	66	10.5	4.0	.300	10
70	77	11.4	4.1	.325	12
78	85.5	11.8	4.2	.350	12

Fig. 10-32 Flagpole sizes, fiberglass.

The tilting and nautical flagpoles are adaptations of the standard ground-mounted flagpoles and therefore information on their sizes, is not included here. Generally speaking, these poles are manufactured almost exclusively in aluminum, and the manufacturer should be consulted directly for the specific sizes available.

Outrigger flagpoles are customarily furnished in lengths from 10 to 20 feet. Vertical wall-mounted flagpoles are offered as standard up to an overall height of 35 feet. Because these poles are seldom specified, precise data on heights and other physical dimensions are not given in this discussion. Again, the manufacturers should be asked for detailed information on these types of poles.

FLAG SIZES

The size of the flag to be flown on a flagpole is not governed by established standards. Therefore, the size becomes a matter of personal taste. The flagpole industry does, however, make recommendations regarding appropriate flag sizes for respective pole heights. Those recommendations are listed in Figures 10-33 through 10-36. Approximate costs of flags, by size and type of material, are given in Figure 10-37.

It should be noted that due to the lack of good empirical data on flag loads and flag drag under wind loading, the industry designs its poles unflagged and does not make any representations regarding pole designs under flagged conditions.

MATERIALS

Architectural flagpoles are available in five materials: aluminum, carbon steel, copper alloys, stainless steel, and fiberglass, with aluminum being the most popular and hence the most frequently specified.

General Classification

Aluminum Aluminum flagpoles are fabricated from both pipe and tube, the difference being the size and thickness of the material. In both cases, the product is extruded, rather than being formed from sheet. Extruded pipe or tube may be either

Exposed Pole, Height	Flag Size
15	3 x 5
20 or 25	4 x 6
30 or 35	5 x 8
40 or 45	6 x 10
50, 55, or 60	8 x 12
65 or 70	9 x 15
80 to 90	10 x 15
100	12 x 18

Fig. 10-33   Ground-set poles (feet).

Pole Height above Roof	Flag Size
15	4 x 6
20 to 30	5 x 8
35 or 40	6 x 10
45 or 50	8 x 12
60 or 65	9 x 15
70 or 75	10 x 15

Fig. 10-34   Roof-mounted poles (feet).

Pole Height above Top of Wall	Flag Size
12 to 15	4 x 6
16 to 30	5 x 8
35 or 40	6 x 20

Fig. 10-35   Wall-mounted vertical poles (feet).

Pole Length	Flag Size
8	3 x 5
10 or 12	4 x 6
15 or 16	5 x 8
16 to 23	6 x 10

Fig. 10-36   Wall-mounted outrigger poles (feet).

Size, feet	Material	Cost
3 x 5	Nylon	$21.00
	Polyester	25.00
	Acrylic	24.00
	Cotton	14.00
4 x 6	Nylon	27.00
	Polyester	34.00
	Acrylic	33.00
	Cotton	19.00
5 x 8	Nylon	38.00
	Polyester	50.00
	Acrylic	48.00
	Cotton	29.00
6 x 10	Nylon	61.00
	Polyester	75.00
	Acrylic	69.00
	Cotton	44.00
8 x 12	Nylon	92.00
	Polyester	118.00
	Acrylic	108.00
	Cotton	67.00
10 x 15	Nylon	142.00
	Polyester	190.00
	Acrylic	172.00
	Cotton	100.00
12 x 18	Nylon	186.00
	Polyester	278.00
	Acrylic	231.00
	Cotton	128.00

Fig. 10-37   Comparative cost for United States flags (suggested retail price, 1979).

of two types: seamless, which is extruded from a cored or hollow billet, using a mandrel and which, consequently, is a homogeneous product; and structural, which is made from solid billet, using a "port-hole" die. This process produces weld joints that sometimes create difficulty in the subsequent tapering operations.

Alloys and Tempers   In most cases, the product used for flagpoles is the extruded seamless tube or pipe in a 6063 alloy with a T6 temper. For some applications, however, the objective is to develop a structurally sound flagpole in heights and diameters comparable with established industry standards but with lighter wall thicknesses and subsequently lower costs. In such cases, 6005 alloy may be substituted, using a T5 temper. This is a higher-strength material than the 6063, permitting the use of a lighter wall tube or pipe extrusion without sacrifice to structural integrity. The straight and tapered portions of aluminum flagpoles are constructed from the same alloy in the pipe or tube form, with the temper being altered after fabrication.

Before the pipe or tube section is formed into the desired tapered shape, it is in a T4 or "soft" condition. The taper is achieved by utilizing a spin-draw process. This is a cold-forming technique that transforms the uniform diameter extrusion into a conical shape without compromise to its seamless characteristics. After tapering, the section's properties are between T5 and T6, but the temper is stabilized at T6, (T5 for the 6005) through an age-hardening process.

Mechanical Properties   Alloy 6063T6 has a minimum ultimate tensile strength of 30,000 pounds per square inch (psi) and a minimum ultimate yield of 25,000 psi. Alloy 6005T5 has a paucity of association values, but those most commonly quoted are 38,000 psi on tensile and 35,000 psi on yield. These values equate to Alloy 6061T6, which is infrequently used in flagpole construction because of its limited tapering characteristics.

Copper alloys: bronze   Most "bronze" flagpoles are made from red brass (alloy 230), containing 85 percent copper and 15 percent zinc. This alloy is readily available from warehouse stock and is produced by virtually all the copper base alloy tube mills. The larger the diameter, however, the fewer the mills capable of producing the item. The quality standard for reference is ASTMB135. It provides a good color match with architectural bronze (alloy 385), which is not available in these product forms and should therefore not be specified for bronze flagpoles.

Alloy 220, known as commercial bronze, is a 90 percent copper, 10 percent zinc material also available in pipe and tube form, but not so readily as red brass and should not be specified.

Mechanical Properties   The cylindrical straight portion of bronze flagpoles is typically produced from 230 pipe in the "hard nominal temper." Temper is the condition of the metal with regard to mechanical properties as determined by the degree of final anneal, the degree of cold work thereafter, or both. The yield strength of red brass 230 in the "hard" condition runs 58,000 psi, with the tensile at 70,000 psi. The tapered portion of the bronze flagpole is achieved in one of two ways. It can be constructed from hard-temper tubing, in which case a "wedge" is cut out of the pipe section and the pipe is reformed and welded. (In this case, the temper is not materially altered, although some annealing will occur along the longitudinal weld zones.) Or the taper can be formed from pipe in the soft temper by a spin-draw technique. In the process of creating the taper, this technique hardens the material back to a range of between 38,000 and 58,000 psi on the yield. Of course, the greater the degree of taper, the more work hardening goes into the pipe with high subsequent mechanical properties.

Stainless steel   Stainless steel flagpoles are fabricated from pipe, tube, and plate, depending on the method of fabrication employed. The base metal from which stainless steel alloys are made is iron with one important common additive — sufficient chromium to render them corrosion-resistant. There are nearly 100 stainless steel alloys, but flagpoles of this material are almost exclusively constructed from type 304. Occasionally, when extremely high corrosion resistance properties are required, type 316 may be specified.

Composition determines the corrosion resistance of the different grades. It also determines their fabricating characteristics, that is, how they respond to welding, forming, and other shop operations necessary to convert them from their mill condition into the finished product.

Alloy   Chromium gives stainless steel its inherent "stainless" quality. Type 304, the most popular for architectural applications, has a chromium content of 18 percent and a nickel base of 8 percent. This material will not rust even though it is never cleaned, but it eventually will pit when corrosive compounds, such as sea salt, are deposited and allowed to remain on the metal for extended periods. If this type of condition is going to exist, then type 316, which will not pit, should be used. One must consider the cost factor, however, because prices of these alloy forms increase rapidly depending upon chromium content and availability — the lower priced, of course, being the more popular.

Mechanical Properties   The cylindrical, straight portion of a stainless steel flagpole is generally fabricated from type 304 welded pipe with a minimum yield strength of 36,000 psi and an ultimate tensile of 80,000 psi. Seamless pipe can also be used, but the cost is much higher, with no architectural or structural gain. When we talk of welded pipe, the seam is finished and virtually undetectable.

The tapered portions can be constructed in either one of two ways. Using pipe, a "wedge" is cut out of the section, then the pipe is reformed, welded, and finished. Or the taper can be rolled from plate to the desired shape, seam-welded, and finished. Both methods produce a uniformly constructed taper without visible seams and joints. The mechanical properties of both are identical to those noted for the commercially produced, cylindrical pipe sections.

Ferrous metals   The ferrous metals used in building construction are carbon steel, which may be hot- or cold-rolled, high-strength steel, cast steel, cast iron, malleable iron, and genuine wrought iron. Except for the last two, all these forms are used in the construction of "steel" flagpoles and their related accessories.

Iron is the base metal for all ferrous alloys. They all contain carbon and other elements in controlled amounts, the metal thus becoming an iron alloy.

The flagpole sections are most generally made from carbon steel, which is a hot-rolled, all-purpose, structural grade steel.

Both pipe and tubing are made from carbon steel and flagpoles are constructed from both. The product, which, for commercial reasons, is classified as tubing, is manufactured in pipe mills and has essentially the same dimensions and other physical characteristics as pipe. The diameter dimensions of flagpoles are quoted externally rather than nominally, so the primary distinction between a tube-size and a pipe-size flagpole is the manner in which its butt diameter is expressed (for example: pipe: 5⁵⁄₁₆″OD, 6⅝″OD, 7⅝″OD, etc.; tube: 5″OD, 6″OD, 7″OD, etc.).

Grades Traditionally, the butt sections or the lowermost cylindrical portions of good flagpoles have been made from material conforming to ASTMA53 "welded and seamless steel pipe." The mechanical properties of this material typically run 42,000 psi on the yield and 58,000 psi on the tensile. The tapered sections are made from 1020 steel sheet and plate, rolled to the desired configuration, electric resistance-welded and then cold-drawn to produce high-strength mechanical properties. The typical yield strength on these types of constructed pole sections usually runs upward of 60,000 psi.

Fiberglass Fiberglass flagpoles are fabricated from either a woven fiberglass cloth or a filament that is wound over a tapered mandrel to produce the tapered tubular shape—and then impregnated with resin. It eventually emerges as a finished flagpole shaft. These processes produce a seamless plastic flagpole which subsequently is sanded and gel-coated to obtain the desired architectural finish. The mechanical properties thus obtained produce designs that are represented as being capable of withstanding wind velocities of upward of 150 miles per hour. The leading manufacturers claim that the minimum axial tensile strength of their poles will run 40,000 psi.

FINISHES

General Classification of Finishes

Finishes for flagpoles and their accessories range from the protective ones usually associated with ferrous metals to the decorative finishes employed to enhance the natural beauty of aluminum, the bronzes, stainless steel, and fiberglass. They comprise mechanical and chemical finishes, electroplating, and coatings of many types, including anodizing. All finishes commonly used on architectural metals, with flagpoles falling in this family designation, can be classified as one of three principal types:

Mechanical Finish The metal surface is physically affected by some mechanical means.

Chemical Finish The metal itself undergoes a chemical or electrochemical conversion, which has the effect of changing its exterior surface.

Coatings Another material is applied to the metal surface.

All the above finishes are extensively used on aluminum. The carbon steels, on the other hand, most frequently employ coatings, with infrequent use of mechanical or chemical treatments other than for pretreatment purposes. The copper alloys are commonly subject to both mechanical and chemical finishes, while stainless steel utilizes mechanical finishes almost exclusively (see Figure 10-38).

STANDARD FINISHES

Aluminum	Satin-brushed
	Clear anodized
	Bronze anodic
	Black anodic
	Applied coating
	Epoxies
	Urethanes
	Fluorocarbons
	Siliconized polyesters
Steel	Applied coating
	Enamels
	Urethanes
	Fluorocarbons
	Siliconized polyesters
Copper alloys (bronze)	Satin-brushed
	Oxidized
	Statuary antique
Stainless steel	No. 4 satin
	No. 7 reflective
Fiberglass	Color applied
	Color impregnated
	Satin
	Gloss

MECHANICAL FINISHES

Satin: Aluminum Association designation M33
(Coarse satin 80-100 grit) or M32
(Medium satin 180 to 220 grit)

Satin and brushed: M32 satin followed by a brushing operation using a stainless steel wire brush or Scotchbrite wheel.

ANODIC FINISHES

Clear: Aluminum Association designation AA-A41 - Arch. Class I 0.7 mil thickness. Alcoa designation Alumilite 215.

Integral color: Aluminum Association designation AA-A42 - Arch. Class I 0.7 mil thickness

Color	*Range*	*Alcoa Designation*
Bronze	Light	311
	Medium	312
	Dark	313
Black		335

Impregnated color: Aluminum Association designation AA-A43 — Arch. Class I 0.7 mil thickness

Color	*Alcoa Designation*
Gold	4011

Electrolytically deposited color: Aluminum Association designation AA–A44 — Arch. Class I 0.7 mil thickness

Color	*Alcan Designation*
Black	Anolok. Series 5000

Fig. 10-38 **Table of finishes.**

Finishes for Aluminum Flagpoles

Mechanical finishes The mechanical finishes still remain the most popular for flagpoles, with the directional textured finishes far outdistancing the nondirectional ones.

Directional Textured Finishes This finish produces a smooth, satiny sheen of limited reflectivity. The characteristic soft texture results from tiny, nearly parallel, scratches in the metal surface produced by belt polishing or stropping the surfaces with fine abrasives. The fineness is controlled by the size of the grit used in conjunction with the speed of the belt and the pressures exerted. Fine, medium, and coarse satin finishes are all produced by belt polishing and grits of varying degrees. The higher the grit designation, the finer the finish achieved. Most flagpoles, unless otherwise specified, receive a coarse-to-medium satin finish, which is achieved by belt polishing with aluminum oxide grit of 80 to 120 size. In order to attain a medium-to-fine satin finish, a grit size of 180 to 220 is required. The fine calls for a 320- to 400-grit belting sequence.

Sometimes a "brushed" finish is desired. It is usually achieved by following up the medium satin finish with the application of a power-driven, abrasive-impregnated, foamed-nylon-disc treatment. The material commonly used for this application is generally known as Scotchbrite.

Nondirectional Textured Finishes These are matte finishes of varying degrees of roughness produced by blasting. Nondirectional finishes should not be specified for flagpoles. Their principal use in the flagpole industry is on accessory items. Since the surface produced by even the finest abrasive is actually rough, the finished piece tends to show fingerprints, and it collects and retains dirt unless protective coatings of clear lacquer are applied. Anodizing also provides an excellent coating, but this finish would not be applied to fittings unless the poles also were specified to have an anodic finish. The uniformity of the texture of the surface is determined primarily by the positioning and movement of the blasting nozzle. Controlling this element in finishing a round, tapered shaft is extremely problematical, making it unusually difficult to obtain a uniform appearance—especially if the piece is to be anodized.

Chemical finishes Chemical finishes are generally used

- To clean the metal

- To provide a matte-textured surface

- To produce a smooth, bright finish

While the chemical treatments may be used to produce a so-called finish, their primary function is an intermediate step in an overall finishing process requiring a subsequent application of some form of protective coating.

There are four chemical finishes or treatments: non-etch cleaning, matte finishes, bright finishes, and conversion coatings. The first two are treatments preparatory to painting and infrequently used as a final finish. Matte and bright finishes are chemically induced by immersing the product in certain acids or etching solutions. These finishes have very limited application or architectural worth and are generally used on inexpensive commercial flagpole kits where production quantities are involved and the cost of obtaining a visually satisfactory finish prohibits the use of mechanical processes.

Coatings:

Anodic Probably the most important, certainly unique, and the coatings gaining most rapidly in popularity are those finishes achieved by the anodizing process. For flagpoles that will not be regularly maintained, anodic coatings should have at least an 0.7 mil thickness and a minimum coating weight of 27 mg per square inch. For the purpose of identification, these finishes are classified by the Aluminum Association as "Architectural Class I Coatings." There are four subdivisions: clear coating; integrally colored coatings; impregnated color coatings; and electrolytically deposited color coatings.

Clear Coating Ordinarily, clear anodic finishes on architectural products are preceded by a mechanical satin finish and a subsequent chemical etch that imparts a pleasing satinlike texture that is retained after anodizing.

Essentially, the clear anodizing process consists of immersing the item in an acid solution and passing a direct electric current between the metal and the solution with the aluminum pole acting as the anode. The result is the controlled formation of a transparent oxide film on the surface of the metal. This film greatly increases the product's resistance to corrosion and abrasion.

Integrally Colored Coatings The bronze, gray, and black colors familiar to all architects are derived from the characteristics of the aluminum alloy itself. These coatings have excellent colorfastness and durability, making them highly suitable for outdoor applications and accounting for their increasing architectural popularity.

Impregnated Color Coatings The sulfuric acid process has long been the most widely used for clear anodizing, but it also lends itself to the application of a variety of impregnated colors. Only the gold, however, is considered sufficiently colorfast for exterior architectural use.

Electrolytically Deposited Color Coatings This is a newly developed process by which stable pigments are electrolytically deposited in coatings produced by sulfuric acid anodizing in a range of lightfast colors similar to the hardcoats produced by integral color anodizing. For flagpoles, this system finds applicability in producing black anodic finishes that are difficult to obtain on the 6063 alloy in the T6 temper.

Organic and Vitreous Coatings These coatings, although finding their widest use on architectural iron and steel work, also are used on aluminum. In the flagpole industry, certainly the organic finishes are more popular with the vitreous rarely seen, but they both warrant discussion. Because these applied coatings are more frequently associated with steel fabrication, we have reserved comment on them for the section "Finishes for Carbon Steel."

Standard finish designations In 1964 the Aluminum Association published its "Finishes Designation System," which covers all commonly used finishes for architectural metals. This system of course includes flagpoles and is the best reference for specifying a finish. Since the flagpole finish is very often color-coordinated with the building trim, the designer may refer to *Metal Finishes Manual,* prepared by the National Association of Architectural Metal Manufacturers. "Aluminum Finish Designations," Tables 2 through 5, in the Manual, gives a detailed analysis of all available mechanical, chemical, and coating finishes for architectural metals.

The most frequently specified mechanical and anodic finishes for flagpoles are shown in Figure 10-38.

Finishes for Copper Alloys

Mechanical finishes Among the process mechanical finishes for architectural bronze, the only one applicable to flagpoles and accessories is the directional textured finish. The three most popular standard varieties are:

Fine satin	180 to 240 grit
Medium satin	120 to 180 grit
Coarse satin	80 to 120 grit

Because bronze will quickly oxidize if left exposed in its polished state, the satin finishes should be immediately coated with a clear, protective lacquer finish to a 1.0 mil thickness.

Chemical finishes Among the most important finishes for bronze flagpoles are those produced by chemical treatments. In general, these processes may have any of four principal purposes.

- To clean
- To provide a matte surface
- To produce a bright finish
- To convert the surface chemically, changing the color of the metal while also providing a final finish

The chemical treatment is the one of primary concern to flagpole manufacturers because, almost invariably, the architectural community is looking for a dark, chemically induced, statuary finish on their bronze flagpoles. The process essentially is a conversion coating, the purpose of which is to duplicate, by accelerated chemical means, the natural, weathered effect generally resulting after the metal is exposed to the elements for 5 to 12 years. These processes still depend largely upon art and craft techniques. Since they are not automated, controlled processes, one must recognize that variations in color uniformity will inevitably occur. The opinion of many, however, is that this characteristic contributes to, rather than detracts from, the natural beauty of architectural bronze work.

Conversion treatments are of two general types: those producing the patinas, or verde antiques, and those producing the statuary or oxidized colors. Since flagpoles invariably receive the latter, we will confine discussion to the statuary and oxidized finishes.

Statuary bronze finishes are usually obtained by formation of a surface film of cupreous oxide or a mixture of copper sulfides. The ultimate appearance is critically influenced by the natural color of the substrate, the coarseness of the mechanical finish, and the thickness of the conversion film. The most common coloring treatment for flagpoles uses a sulfide treatment by which the statuary brown color is produced by various aqueous sulfide solutions such as potassium sulfide, sodium sulfide, and ammonium sulfide.

Standard finish designation The finishing processes used on the bronzes are basically the same as for aluminum. Consequently, the copper industry has adopted a designation system similar to that established by the Aluminum Association. A detailed analysis of the bronze finishes appears on NAAMM's *Metal Finishes Manual* "Copper Alloys Finish Designation Tables 6–8."

The most frequently specified finishes for bronze flagpoles are:

Statuary conversion coating over satin finish M32-C55, representing

Mechanical finish M32, directional textured medium satin, 120-180 grit, C55'

Chemical finish conversion coating, sulfide (statuary)

Colors: Light, medium, or dark, depending on the repetition of applications of the chemical solutions

Natural satin finish, lacquered M31-06x representing M31—mechanical finish, directional textured, fine satin, 180-240 grit, 06x—coating, clear organic, air-dry (lacquer to be specified).

Finishes for Stainless Steel

Stainless steel finishes for flagpoles are invariably selected from the mechanical finishes applicable to this hard and durable noncorrosive metal. The mechanical finishes fall into three categories—mill, polished, and patterned—but only the polished ones are applicable to stainless steel flagpoles. These are characterized by fine parallel scratch lines and are comparable to the directional textured finishes described for nonferrous flagpoles. These finishes are produced by successive belting operations, and in the case of the highly reflective finishes, perhaps also buffing. They vary in cost depending on the number of sequential operations required and the degree of reflectivity desired.

Standard finish designation   The most frequently specified architectural finish for flagpoles in this group is the No. 4 Polished Finish. It is directionally textured, medium bright, and obtained with 120- to 150-grit abrasives following initial belting with coarser abrasives.

The No. 7 Polished Finish, although less frequently specified, is becoming more popular, especially on outstanding architectural projects. It is a highly reflective finish produced by buffing a finely ground surface with proprietary materials. It is important to note that while highly reflective, this finish will still show evidence of grit lines.

The No. 6 Polished Finish, a soft satin one having lower reflectivity than the No. 4, is rarely specified for flagpoles. The No. 8 finish, the most reflective, is essentially free of grit lines but impractical for application on flagpoles and should not be specified.

Once the desired finish has been achieved, it is essential that the polished surface be thoroughly cleaned with an acid solution to remove all traces of ferrous oxide that may have been deposited on the surface during the grinding and polishing operations. Failing to do so will result in discoloration of the finish after exposure to the elements.

Finishes for Carbon Steel

The chief function of the finishes used on the ferrous metals is to counteract their tendency to rust. The term "finish," when used in reference to steel, most commonly connotes applied coatings rather than a surface treatment, like the finishes for the other flagpole types discussed earlier. Mechanical and chemical processes are used extensively for cleaning and surface preparation but rarely as the final finish.

Since, in the case of steel, determination of the coating usually is initiated at the interface between the coating and the substrate, the preparation of that substrate becomes a critical factor. Before discussing the various coatings used on steel flagpoles, it first is necessary to examine the surface treatments.

Mechanical Cleaning　There are two basic mechanical means of obtaining a surface suitable for painting:

SANDING:　This is a rotary procedure by which scale, rust, dirt, and other contaminants are removed, using coarse abrasive belts or stropping equipment.

BLASTING:　Either with shot or sand, this procedure will remove all contaminants and also produce a surface sufficiently roughened to ensure good coating adhesion.

CHEMICAL TREATMENTS:　In the flagpole industry, their only purpose is to thoroughly clean an already-prepared surface immediately preceding application of the finish coatings. The chemicals used are common cleaning and degreasing agents.

Applied Coatings　By far the most common are the organic coatings, such as paint. The metallic vitreous coatings are also used, but rarely.

Of the metallic coatings, only galvanizing warrants discussion in this book. A number of other metallic coatings for steel have applicability to other types of architectural work, however. They are discussed in detail in NAAMM's *Metal Finishes Manual.*

GALVANIZING, HOT DIP PROCESS:　The steel flagpole is first chemically cleaned and then immersed in a bath of molten zinc. This is by far the most widely used metallic finish. A galvanized finish, however, is rarely used as a final finish, but rather is a pretreatment for painting. Coatings of approximately 1.25 ounces per square foot will provide adequate protection against rust, especially if followed by painting.

Organic Coatings　It is important to note that these finishes are applicable to *both* steel and aluminum flagpoles, but they are discussed here because of their wide use on the ferrous metals.

Organic coatings fall under two functional categories:

- Those providing protection only—namely the primers
- Those serving a decorative as well as a protective function—namely, the pigmented coatings

They are generally grouped as paints, varnishes, enamels, and lacquers. Regardless of their grouping, the first step in the application process is a thorough cleaning of the substrate by methods described earlier. This step is necessary for both steel and aluminum flagpoles.

In nearly every instance, the life of any organic coating is dependent more upon the pretreatment and subsequent priming than upon the protective properties of the final coat. Pretreatment has been discussed. Priming is equally important.

PRIMERS, GENERAL-PURPOSE FINISHES:　The most successful primers are usually compounds of lead or zinc. In the flagpole industry, they generally include red lead and zinc chromate, the former being used on steel and the latter on aluminum.

INTERMEDIATE PAINTS　Frequently only the primer coat is provided by the fabricator with the specifications calling for the subsequent intermediate and finish coats to be applied by the painting contractor. Sometimes, though, the flagpoles may be completely finished in the shop prior to delivery—especially with the epoxy, urethane, and thermal-cured finishes.

In the case of the general-purpose finishes, one or two intermediate coats may be required. These should have essentially the same properties as the primer, and frequently the same paint is used. The field coats also must be compatible and should provide good protection for the primer and intermediate coats.

FINISH PAINTS The finish coat must have good color retention and good resistance to weathering, since recoating flagpoles is not an easy procedure. The variety of suitable materials is vast, ranging from the traditional oil-base paints and marine enamels to the newer and more sophisticated synthetic resin vehicles.

Decorative Coatings The air-dry enamels, applied either by brush or spray, have been the traditional final coatings for steel flagpoles. Under outdoor exposure, 3 years' service for these coatings is considered good. But longer life can be expected from some of the newer materials.

Baking enamels are essentially plastic resins. When applied to correctly prepared metal (steel or aluminum) and properly heated, the resins polymerize and become hard, developing a high-performance finish coating. Unfortunately, length limitations restrict this type of finish to one-piece poles under 35 feet in length and two-piece poles of less than 66 feet.

Other high performance steel and aluminum flagpole finishes include epoxy resins, urethane, and fluorocarbons and siliconized acrylics and polyesters.

Epoxy coatings have exceptionally high resistance to corrosion, abrasion, moisture, and chemicals, and are noted for their excellent adhesion, flexibility, and toughness. They have good exterior-exposure life, with one reservation: Many tend to show surface chalking. Recently, new formulations have been introduced which will not chalk, but, since generalizations may be misleading, the architect should consult reliable manufacturers before specifying a particular epoxy coating for a flagpole application.

Urethanes are exceptionally tough, flexible, and resistant to corrosion, abrasion, moisture, and chemical contamination. They also have excellent color and gloss retention and are more resistant to chalking than the traditional epoxies. One of the excellent features of the urethanes is that they do not require thermal-induced heat curing, so no length limitations are imposed.

Fluorocarbons are organic polymer resins that require high-temperature curing. They display outstanding resistance to weathering, abrasions, and corrosive contaminants and are gaining in popularity for architectural applications. The fluorocarbons offered to manufacturers for architectural uses are: Kynar 500 (PennWalt), Fluropon (DeSoto), Nubelar (Glidden-Durkee), and Duranar (PPG). The industry recommends a two-coat application using a corrosion-resistant primer 0.2 mils thick, followed by a fluorocarbon top coat 0.8 mils thick. *A note of caution to architects:* Oven limitations affect the pole lengths that can be accommodated. The chosen manufacturer should be consulted before these finishes are specified.

Siliconized polymers are available but vary considerably in performance. Only siliconized acrylics and polyesters are suitable for exterior architectural work, and while we see them gaining in popularity for architectural work, they are rarely specified for flagpoles. The Duracons by PPG have been used on flagpole installations and are available in a growing number of colors. These finishes range from low to high gloss in one- and two-coat formulations. Again, oven sizes impose length limitations. Consequently, the factory should be consulted prior to developing a specification for these finishes.

Applications of organic coatings are usually done by brushing, hand-rolling, or spraying. Today, most factory-applied finishes are sprayed. When products are to be supplied with only a primer coat, brush or roller application may be used.

Vitreous Coatings   These are porcelain enamel finishes in which an inorganic coating is bonded to the substrate metal by fusion at a temperature of 800°F or higher. They are used to decorate architectural metals and are applied to either carbon steel or aluminum. Although rarely specified for flagpoles, an architect will occasionally call for vitreous coating when trying to match the flagpole installation to a building trim coated in a porcelain enamel.

Since this is a thermal-induced finish, length limitations must be considered. Furthermore, it is not an "in-house" finish offered by the industry. Accordingly, it is strongly recommended that the architect consult with the chosen flagpole manufacturer before specifying this finish.

RESISTANCE TO VANDALISM

Flagpoles, like almost everything else that is publicly accessible, are subject to vandalism. Since the poles themselves are not generally receptive to the more common forms of graffiti, their operating accessories are more often the target of the vandals. Fortunately, these mechanisms can be effectively protected at modest cost. Several devices to discourage vandalism are illustrated (Figures 10-39 through 10-45).

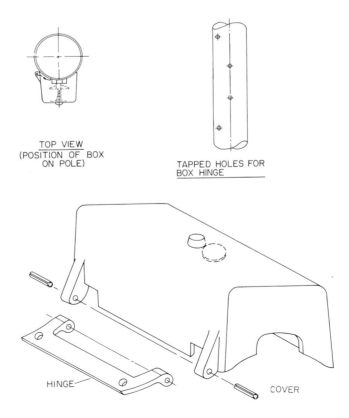

TOP VIEW
(POSITION OF BOX
ON POLE)

TAPPED HOLES FOR
BOX HINGE

HINGE

COVER

Fig. 10-39   Cleat cover and halyard box.

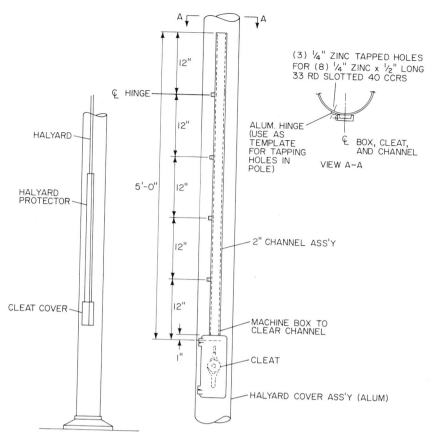

HALYARD

HALYARD PROTECTOR

CLEAT COVER

A ← | → A

12"

℄ HINGE

12"

5'-0"

12"

12"

12"

1"

(3) ¼" ZINC TAPPED HOLES
FOR (8) ¼" ZINC x ½" LONG
33 RD SLOTTED 40 CCRS

ALUM. HINGE
(USE AS
TEMPLATE
FOR TAPPING
HOLES IN
POLE)

℄ BOX, CLEAT,
AND CHANNEL

VIEW A-A

2" CHANNEL ASS'Y

MACHINE BOX TO
CLEAR CHANNEL

CLEAT

HALYARD COVER ASS'Y (ALUM)

Fig. 10-40   Halyard protector.

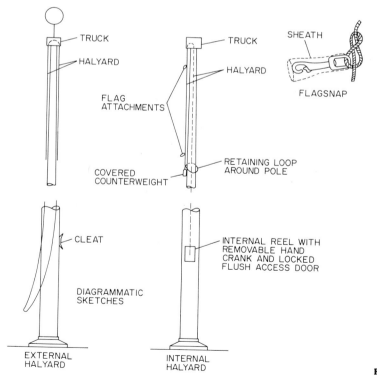

TRUCK

HALYARD

FLAG
ATTACHMENTS

COVERED
COUNTERWEIGHT

TRUCK

HALYARD

RETAINING LOOP
AROUND POLE

SHEATH

FLAGSNAP

CLEAT

DIAGRAMMATIC
SKETCHES

EXTERNAL
HALYARD

INTERNAL REEL WITH
REMOVABLE HAND
CRANK AND LOCKED
FLUSH ACCESS DOOR

INTERNAL
HALYARD

Fig. 10-41   Internal halyard system.

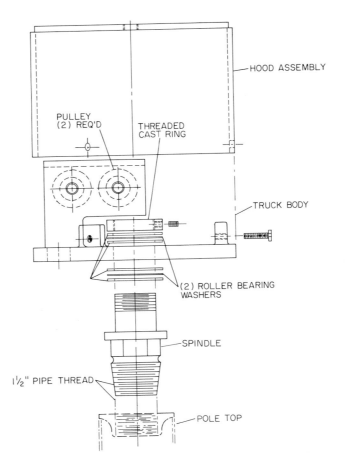

HOOD ASSEMBLY

PULLEY
(2) REQ'D

THREADED
CAST RING

TRUCK BODY

(2) ROLLER BEARING
WASHERS

SPINDLE

1½" PIPE THREAD

POLE TOP

Fig. 10-42 Revolving truck assembly for internal halyard system.

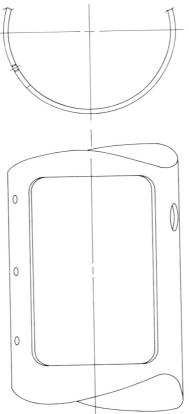

Fig. 10-43 Hole opening for internal winch.

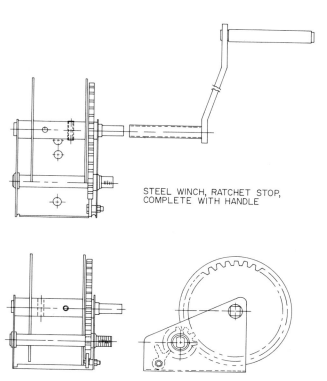

STEEL WINCH, RATCHET STOP,
COMPLETE WITH HANDLE

Fig. 10-44 Winch mechanism.

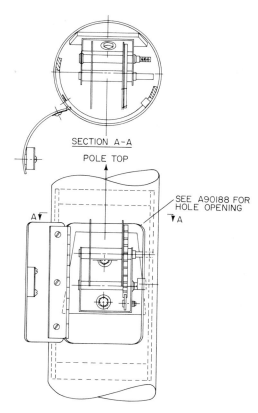

SECTION A-A

POLE TOP

SEE A90188 FOR
HOLE OPENING

Fig. 10-45 Internal winch assembly.

COMPARATIVE COSTS

There are so many variables in the specification and manufacture of flagpoles that it is not possible to publish an accurate list of uniform prices, especially in the light of the steadily increasing inflation to which the economy has been subject since the end of World War II. However, making a large number of reasonable assumptions, a table of comparative cost data has been prepared for use as a guide to relative costs for the various flagpole materials and sizes (Figure 10-46).

Pole Height (feet)	Aluminum	Fiberglass	Steel	Stainless Steel	Bronze
20	$500	$500	$600	$2,500	$2,500
25	600	600	700	2,700	2,700
30	1,000	1,000	1,000	3,500	3,700
35	1,200	1,200	1,200	4,500	4,900
40	1,500	1,500	1,500	5,000	8,000
45	2,000	2,000	1,800	8,500	10,000
50	2,200	2,200	1,900	10,000	12,000
60	3,100	3,000'	3,000	12,000	16,500
70	4,000	3,600	3,600	15,000	25,000
80	5,000	4,000	4,000	18,000	33,000

Fig. 10-46 Comparative cost data. **363**

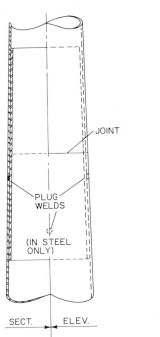

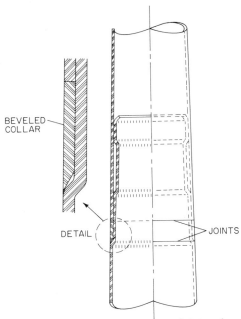

Fig. 10-48 Field joint using formed integral sleeve.

Fig. 10-47 Field joint using plug-welded internal sleeve.

CONSTRUCTION DETAILS AND DATA

Field Joints

To facilitate shipping, poles over 38 feet 6 inches in length are usually manufactured in two or more sections. The length limitations for certain finishing processes (anodizing and thermal cured applied finishes) also require larger poles (over 33 feet) to be made in multiple sections. These sections are designed and produced to be permanently joined in the field before installation.

To facilitate this step, a field joint is provided. There are two popular types, either of which can be located in the cylindrical butt section or the tapered portion of the pole (Figures 10-47 and 10-48).

Field joints in aluminum poles may be either the internal or integral type with a tight, friction-fit hairline joint. No field welding is required on these types of joints when used on aluminum poles. Field joints on steel flagpoles are usually the internal type and are circumferentially welded at the joint line. The weld is then ground flush to provide a smooth continuous appearance.

Stainless steel and bronze flagpoles, because of their comparative higher cost and exceptional nature, are usually manufactured for delivery to the field in one continuous length. In such cases, special transportation, often at an inordinately high cost, must be provided. However, these poles can be provided with field joints with no significant negative impact on aesthetics. Considering the cost savings involved, this alternative should not be arbitrarily dismissed.

Mountings

Throughout this discussion, reference has been made to poles of all types and to numerous mounting methods, such as embedded, surface-mounted, outrigger, wall-mounted, vertical wall-mounted, roof-mounted, and so on. Typical mounting details covering standard installation conditions for ground- and building-mounted installations are shown in Figures 10-49 through 10-55. Unusual conditions should be referred to the manufacturer for appropriate recommendations.

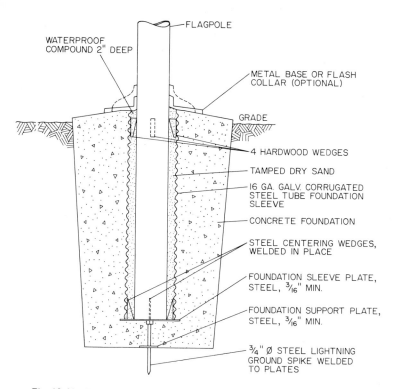

FLAGPOLE

WATERPROOF
COMPOUND 2" DEEP

METAL BASE OR FLASH
COLLAR (OPTIONAL)

GRADE

4 HARDWOOD WEDGES

TAMPED DRY SAND

16 GA. GALV. CORRUGATED
STEEL TUBE FOUNDATION
SLEEVE

CONCRETE FOUNDATION

STEEL CENTERING WEDGES,
WELDED IN PLACE

FOUNDATION SLEEVE PLATE,
STEEL, 3/16" MIN.

FOUNDATION SUPPORT PLATE,
STEEL, 3/16" MIN.

3/4" Ø STEEL LIGHTNING
GROUND SPIKE WELDED
TO PLATES

Fig. 10-49 Typical ground-set mounting detail.

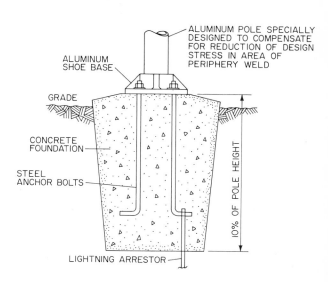

ALUMINUM POLE SPECIALLY
DESIGNED TO COMPENSATE
FOR REDUCTION OF DESIGN
STRESS IN AREA OF
PERIPHERY WELD

ALUMINUM
SHOE BASE

GRADE

CONCRETE
FOUNDATION

STEEL
ANCHOR BOLTS

10% OF POLE HEIGHT

LIGHTNING ARRESTOR

Fig. 10-50 Shoe base type.

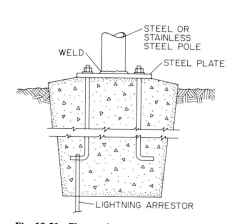

STEEL OR
STAINLESS
STEEL POLE

WELD

STEEL PLATE

LIGHTNING ARRESTOR

Fig. 10-51 Flange plate type.

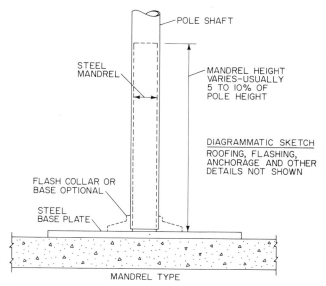

POLE SHAFT

STEEL
MANDREL

MANDREL HEIGHT
VARIES-USUALLY
5 TO 10% OF
POLE HEIGHT

DIAGRAMMATIC SKETCH
ROOFING, FLASHING,
ANCHORAGE AND OTHER
DETAILS NOT SHOWN

FLASH COLLAR OR
BASE OPTIONAL

STEEL
BASE PLATE

MANDREL TYPE

Fig. 10-52 Mandrel type.

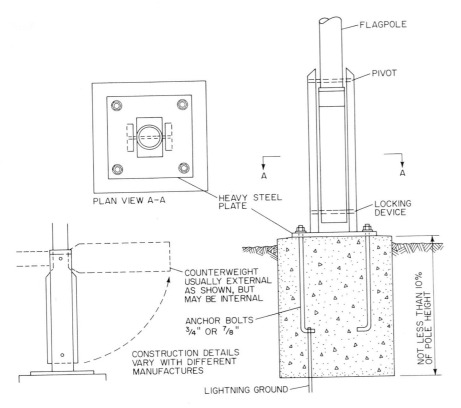

PLAN VIEW A-A

FLAGPOLE

PIVOT

A

A

HEAVY STEEL PLATE

LOCKING DEVICE

COUNTERWEIGHT USUALLY EXTERNAL AS SHOWN, BUT MAY BE INTERNAL

ANCHOR BOLTS ¾" OR ⅞"

CONSTRUCTION DETAILS VARY WITH DIFFERENT MANUFACTURES

NOT LESS THAN 10% OF POLE HEIGHT

LIGHTNING GROUND

Fig. 10-53 Typical counterbalance mounting detail.

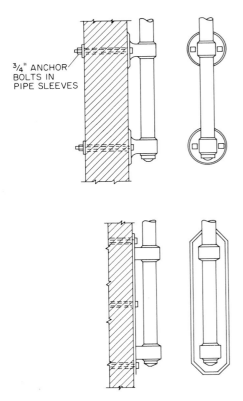

¾" ANCHOR BOLTS IN PIPE SLEEVES

Fig. 10-54 Typical vertical wall-mounting bracket details.

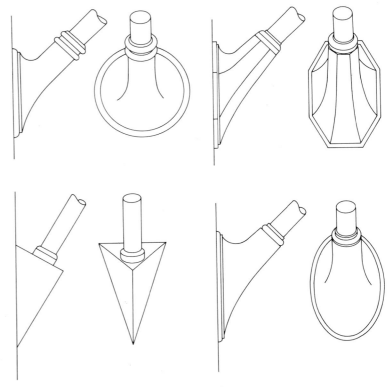

Fig. 10-55 Typical outrigger wall-mounting bracket details.

Lightning Protection for Metal Flagpoles

It is a generally accepted practice to ground metal flagpoles to protect both the flagpole and its anchorage in the event of a lightning strike.

All ground-set flagpoles with an exposed height above 25 feet should be grounded. The most popular method is through the use of a lightning ground-spike attached to the base of the foundation tube. While the length and diameter of the spike will vary among manufacturers, it is usually made of steel rod ranging in length from 18 to 24 inches and in diameter from ⅝ to ¾ inches. Figure 10-49 shows the typical construction. A less popular method, but equally effective, incorporates the use of a separate ground wire and rod which are attached to the pole just below the flash collar and run down into the ground adjacent to the footing. The ground wire is either braided or twisted construction ranging in diameter from ¼ to ½ inch and made of either aluminum or copper. The ground rods range in length from 6 to 10 feet and in diameter from ⅝ to ¾ inch; they are made of either galvanized steel or copper-clad steel rod. A wide range of fittings for attaching the rod to the wire and the wire to the pole are used and will vary among manufacturers.

Flange-mounted poles, utilizing anchor bolts, can be effectively grounded using either of the two procedures. When the ground spike is employed, it is generally welded to one of the anchor bolts. A typical detail showing construction is provided in Figures 10-50 and 10-51.

Ground-set poles set on plazas or over parking garages, where direct grounding is not possible, are generally grounded by tying the anchorage into the building ground system. When this kind of grounding is planned, it should be incorporated into the electrical contract.

Wall-mounted and roof-mounted poles should also be grounded, but they require different treatment that is tailored to the specific anchorage employed. They also are generally tied into the building ground system, a phase of the work that should also be incorporated into the electrical contract.

Fiberglass, not being a conductor, need not be grounded, so all plastic reinforced flagpoles are excluded from this requirement.

Fittings and Accessories

A variety of fittings and accessories are used interchangeably on flagpoles. Many of these appurtenances have already been discussed in detail in earlier sections of this chapter. Details covering some standard fittings that are customarily offered by the industry are shown in Figures 10-56 through 10-60.

Lighting

It has become accepted practice to fly the United States flag at night provided it is adequately lighted. Such lighting can be accomplished by "spotting" the flag with spotlights independently mounted in the ground or on the building.

Increasingly popular are up-lights contained in round or square aluminum canisters mounted to the flagpole and wired internally through the pole shaft. A number of manufacturers offer custom designs and should be consulted for specific applications (Figures 10-61 and 10-62).

In most cases the fixtures can be finished to match the flagpole in both color and configuration so that they provide a symmetrical and integral appearance.

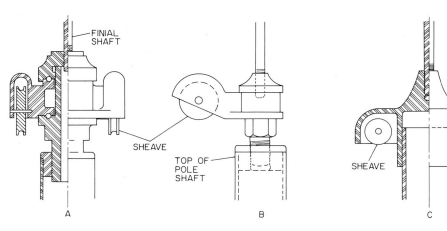

Fig. 10-56 Trucks.

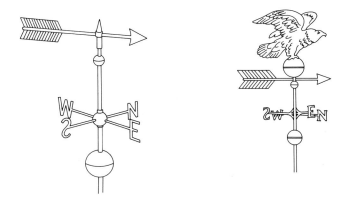

Fig. 10-57 Finials.

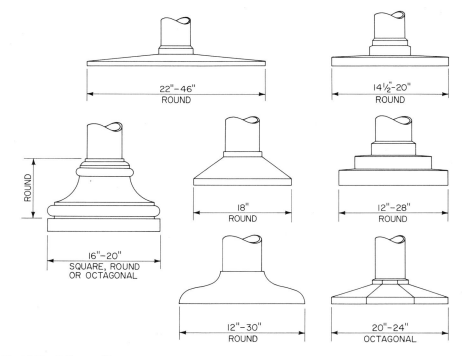

Fig. 10-58 Collars and bases.

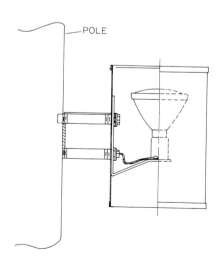

Fig. 10-59 Swivel snap hook.

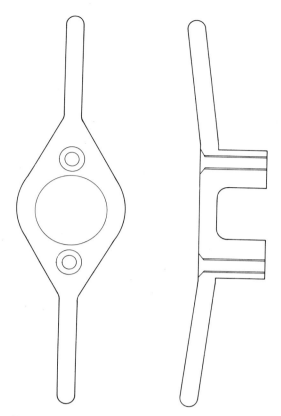

Fig. 10-60 Cleat.

POLE

Fig. 10-61 Lighting.

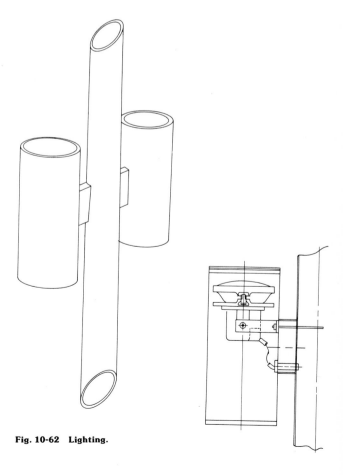

Fig. 10-62 Lighting.

Maintenance

Today's flagpoles require little maintenance. There are, of course, many older wood and steel pole installations that demand frequent care, but this discussion will be confined to modern-day poles, with instructions on the maintenance of the principal fittings given in Figures 10-63 and 10-64.

Aluminum Mechanically finished and anodized flagpole shafts require no maintenance. The fittings and halyards should be checked periodically (every 90 days) for wear and be replaced if necessary. The truck assemblies are maintenance-free,

Item	*Maintenance*
Truck assemblies	None
Finials	None
Halyards	Replace when worn
Snaps	Replace when nonfunctional
Cleats	None
Halyard boxes	None
Collars and bases	None

Note:

If any of the above fittings cease to function or become damaged, they should probably be replaced rather than repaired.

Internal Halyard Systems

Internal halyard systems, more than any other flagpole component or accessory, must be periodically maintained to provide trouble-free operation.

Checklist schedule: Every 30 days

Check winch mounting bolts for tightness
Check dog and spring assembly
Check cable for kinks or frays
Check cable fittings, including snaphooks
Check counterweight and attachment fittings for wear
Check restraining sling for wear
Lubricate winch shaft and dog

Fig. 10-63   Maintenance—fittings.

Item	*Maintenance*
Truck assembly	None
Cable	Replace if kinked or frayed
Cable clamps	Replace when worn or nonfunctional
Shackles	Replace when worn or nonfunctional
Sling	Replace when worn
Weight	Replace when neoprene cover shows excessive wear
Dog and spring	Replace worn parts when necessary
Winch	Replace worn parts when necessary
Lock	Replace if nonfunctional
Snaps	Replace when nonfunctional

Fig. 10-64   Maintenance schedule.

precluding the necessity of having to check them. Shafts with applied coating finishes will eventually require periodic refinishing. The frequency will be a function of the original coating system and environmental conditions.

Steel   Since a steel flagpole shaft is finished with an applied coating, it will eventually require refinishing. The life of the coating will depend on preparation, material, and environmental conditions, but most finishes offered today are expected to provide lives of 2 to 10 years. Periodic maintenance should be provided, including, but not limited to, spot priming and resurfacing chips, peels, blisters, lifts, etc. Fittings should be checked and replaced as noted in the previous section.

Bronze   Statuary bronze finishes should be maintained, although on flagpoles this maintenance is a cumbersome and relatively expensive procedure. Statuary finishes will last from about a year or more up to several years, depending on atmosphere and environmental conditions, but they will eventually break down and develop into a verde patina. If this is the desired effect, then no maintenance of the factory-applied statuary finish is necessary. But should the original statuary finish be desired, periodic maintenance will be necessary. Fittings should be checked and replaced as required.

Stainless steel   The stainless steel flagpole is truly maintenance-free, when specified in the common No. 4 satin finish and the No. 7 and No. 8 mirror finishes. Fittings should be checked and replaced as required.

Fiberglass   Fiberglass flagpoles require no maintenance, but the products of some manufacturers will tend to chalk with age. In these cases, recoating of the shaft surface with a top-grade epoxy or urethane may be desired. The frequency of such a procedure will depend largely on the personal tastes of the owner and the degree of chalking or deterioration of the secondary finishes that will eventually occur with age.

FLAG ETIQUETTE

THE FOLLOWING FLAG LAWS AND REGULATIONS SET FORTH THE EXISTING RULES, CUSTOMS AND ETIQUETTE PERTAINING TO THE USE OF THE FLAG OF THE UNITED STATES OF AMERICA

1. FLAG LAWS AND REGULATIONS PUBLIC LAW 829 AS AMENDED BY THE SEVENTY-SEVENTH CONGRESS OF THE UNITED STATES, CHAPTER 36 OF THE UNITED STATES CODE SECTIONS 173 to 178.

The following codification of existing rules and customs pertaining to the display and use of the flag of the United States of America be, and it is hereby, established for the use of such civilians or civilian groups or organizations as may not be required to conform with regulations promulgated by one or more executive departments of the Government of the United States.

Sec. 2. (a) It is the universal custom to display the flag only from sunrise to sunset on buildings and on stationary flagstaffs in the open. However, the flag may be displayed at night upon special occasions when it is desired to produce a patriotic effect.

(b) The flag should be hoisted briskly and lowered ceremoniously.

(c) The flag should not be displayed on days when the weather is inclement.

(d) The flag should be displayed on all days when the weather permits, especially on New Year's Day, January 1; Inauguration Day, January 20; Lincoln's

Birthday, February 12; Washington's Birthday, February 22; Army Day, April 6; Easter Sunday (variable); Mother's Day, second Sunday in May; Memorial Day (half staff until noon), May 30; Flag Day, June 14; Independence Day, July 4; Labor Day, first Monday in September; Constitution Day, September 17; Columbus Day, October 12; Navy Day, October 27; Armistice Day, November 11; Thanksgiving Day, fourth Thursday in November; Christmas Day, December 25; such other days as may be proclaimed by the President of the United States; the birthdays of States (dates of admission); and on State holidays.

(e) The flag should be displayed daily, weather permitting, on or near the main administrative building of every public institution.

(f) The flag should be displayed in or near every polling place on election days.

(g) The flag should be displayed during school days in or near every schoolhouse.

Sec. 3. That the flag, when carried in a procession with another flag or flags, should be either on the marching right; that is, the flag's own right, or if there is a line of other flags, in front of the center of that line.

(a) The flag should not be displayed on a float in a parade except from a staff, or as provided in subsection (i).

(b) The flag should not be draped over the hood, top, sides, or back of a vehicle or of a railroad train or a boat. When the flag is displayed on a motorcar, the staff shall be fixed firmly to the chassis or clamped to the radiator cap.

(c) No other flag or pennant should be placed above or, if on the same level, to the right of the flag of the United States of America, except during church services conducted by naval chaplains at sea, when the church pennant may be flown above the flag during church services for the personnel of the Navy.

(d) The flag of the United States of America, when it is displayed with another flag against a wall from crossed staffs, should be on the right, the flag's own right, and its staff should be in front of the staff of the other flag.

(e) The flag of the United States of America should be at the center and at the highest point of the group when a number of flags of States or localities or pennants of societies are grouped and displayed from staffs.

(f) When flags of States, cities, or localities, or pennants of societies are flown on the same halyard with the flag of the United States, the latter should always be at the peak. When the flags are flown from adjacent staffs, the flag of the United States should be hoisted first and lowered last. No such flag or pennant may be placed above the flag of the United States or to the right of the flag of the United States.

(g) When flags of two or more nations are displayed, they are to be flown from separate staffs of the same height. The flags should be of approximately equal size. International usage forbids the display of the flag of one nation above that of another nation in time of peace.

(h) When the flag of the United States is displayed from a staff projecting horizontally or at an angle from the window sill, balcony, or front of a building, the union of the flag should be placed at the peak of the staff unless the flag is at half staff. When the flag is suspended over a sidewalk from a rope extending from a house to a pole at the edge of the sidewalk, the flag should be hoisted out, union first, from the building.

(i) When the flag is displayed otherwise than by being flown from a staff, it should be displayed flat, whether indoors or out, or so suspended that its folds fall as free as though the flag were staffed.

(j) When the flag is displayed over the middle of the street, it should be suspended vertically with the union to the north in an east and west street or to the east in a north and south street.

(k) When used on a speaker's platform, the flag, if displayed flat, should be displayed above and behind the speaker. When displayed from a staff in a church or public auditorium, if it is displayed in the chancel of a church, or on the speaker's platform in a public auditorium, the flag should occupy the position of honor and be placed at the clergyman's or speaker's right as he faces the congregation or audience. Any other flag so displayed in the chancel or on the platform should be placed at the clergyman's or speaker's left as he faces the congregation or audience. But when the flag is displayed from a staff in a church or public auditorium elsewhere than in the chancel or on the platform, it shall be placed in the position of honor at the right of the congregation or audience as they face the chancel or platform. Any other flag so displayed should be placed on the left of the congregation or audience as they face the chancel or platform.

(l) The flag should form a distinctive feature of the ceremony of unveiling a statue or monument, but it should never be used as the covering for the statue or monument.

(m) The flag, when flown at half staff, should be first hoisted to the peak for an instant and then lowered to the half-staff position. The flag should again be raised to the peak before it is lowered for the day. By "half staff" is meant lowering the flag to one-half the distance between the top and bottom of the staff. Crepe streamers may be affixed to spear heads or flagstaffs in a parade only by order of the President of the United States.

(n) When the flag is used to cover a casket, it should be so placed that the union is at the head and over the left shoulder. The flag should not be lowered into the grave or allowed to touch the ground.

Sec. 4. That no disrespect should be shown to the flag of the United States of America; the flag should not be dipped to any person or thing. Regimental colors, State flags, and organization or institutional flags are to be dipped as a mark of honor.

(a) The flag should never be displayed with the union down save as a signal of dire distress.

(b) The flag should never touch anything beneath it, such as the ground, the floor, water, or merchandise.

(c) The flag should never be carried flat or horizontally, but always aloft and free.

(d) The flag should never be used as drapery of any sort whatsoever, never festooned, drawn back, nor up, in folds, but always allowed to fall free. Bunting of blue, white, and red, always arranged with the blue above, the white in the middle, and the red below, should be used for covering a speaker's desk, draping the front of a platform, and for decoration in general.

(e) The flag should never be fastened, displayed, used, or stored in such a manner as will permit it to be easily torn, soiled, or damaged in any way.

(f) The flag should never be used as a covering for a ceiling.

(g) The flag should never have placed upon it, nor on any part of it, nor attached to it any mark, insignia, letter, word, figure, design, picture, or drawing of any nature.

(h) The flag should never be used as a receptacle for receiving, holding, carrying, or delivering anything.

(i) The flag should never be used for advertising purposes in any manner whatsoever. It should not be embroidered on such articles as cushions or handkerchiefs and the like, printed or otherwise impressed on paper napkins or boxes or anything that is designed for temporary use and discard; or used as any portion of a costume or athletic uniform. Advertising signs should not be fastened to a staff or halyard from which the flag is flown.

(j) The flag, when it is in such condition that it is no longer a fitting emblem for display, should be destroyed in a dignified way, preferably by burning.

Sec. 5. That during the ceremony of hoisting or lowering the flag or when the flag is passing in a parade or in a review, all persons present should face the flag, stand at attention, and salute. Those present in uniform should render the military salute. When not in uniform, men should remove their headdress with right hand holding it at the left shoulder, the hand being over the heart. Men without hats should salute in the same manner. Aliens should stand at attention. Women should salute by placing the right hand over the heart. The salute to the flag in a moving column should be rendered at the moment the flag passes.

Sec. 6. That when the national anthem is played and the flag is not displayed, all present should stand and face the music. Those in uniform should salute at the first note of the anthem, retaining this position until the last note. All others should stand at attention, men removing the headdress. When the flag is displayed, all present should face the flag and salute.

Sec. 7. That the pledge of allegiance to the flag, "I pledge allegiance to the flag of the United States of America and to the Republic for which it stands, one Nation under God, indivisible, with liberty and justice for all," to be rendered by standing with the right hand over the heart. However, civilians will always show full respect to the flag when the pledge is given by merely standing at attention, men removing the headdress. Persons in uniform shall render the military salute.

Sec. 8. Any rule or custom pertaining to the display of the flag of the United States of America, set forth herein, may be altered, modified, or repealed, or additional rules with respect thereto may be prescribed, by the Commander in Chief of the Army and Navy of the United States, whenever he deems it to be appropriate or desirable; and any such alteration or additional rule shall be set forth in a proclamation.

No person shall display the flag of the United States or any other national or international flag equal, above, or in a position of superior prominence or honor to, or in place of, the flag of the United States at any place within the United States or any Territory or possession thereof: Provided, That nothing in this section shall make unlawful the continuance of the practice heretofore followed of displaying the flag of the United Nations in a position of superior prominence or honor, and other national flags in positions of equal prominence or honor, with that of the flag of the United States at the headquarters of the United Nations.

HOW TO DISPLAY THE FLAG (Figure 10-65)

1. When the flag is displayed over the middle of the street, it should be suspended vertically with the union (the blue field) to the north in an east and west street or to the east in a north and south street.

2. The flag of the United States of America, when it is displayed with another flag against a wall from crossed staffs, should be on the right, the flag's own right, and its staff should be in front of the staff of the other flag.

3. The flag, when flown at half staff, should be first hoisted to the peak for an instant and then lowered to the half-staff position. The flag should be again raised to the peak before it is lowered for the day. By "half staff" is meant lowering the flag to one-half the distance between the top and bottom of the staff. Crepe streamers may be affixed to spearheads or flagstaffs in a parade only by order of the President of the United States.

4. When flags of states, cities, or localities, or pennants of societies are flown on the same halyard with the flag of the United States, the latter should always be at the peak. When the flags are flown from adjacent staffs, the flag of the United States should be hoisted first and lowered last. No such flag or pennant may be placed above the flag of the United States or to the right of the flag of the United States.

5. When the flag is suspended over a sidewalk from a rope extending from a house to a pole at the edge of the sidewalk, the flag should be hoisted out, union first, from the building.

Fig. 10-65   Different ways of displaying the flag.

6. When the flag of the United States is displayed from a staff projecting horizontally or at an angle from the window sill, balcony, or front of a building, the union of the flag should be placed at the peak of the staff unless the flag is at half staff.

7. When the flag is used to cover a casket, it should be so placed that the union is at the head and over the left shoulder. The flag should not be lowered into the grave or allowed to touch the ground.

8. When the flag is displayed in a manner other than by being flown from a staff, it should be displayed flat, whether indoors or out. When displayed either horizontally or vertically against a wall, the union should be uppermost and to the flag's own right, that is, to the observer's left. When displayed in a window it should be displayed in the same way, that is, with the union to the left of the observer in the street. When festoons, rosettes or drapings are desired, bunting of blue, white and red should be used, but never the flag.

9. That the flag, when carried in a procession with another flag or flags, should be either on the marching right; that is, the flag's own right, or, if there is a line of other flags, in front of the center of that line.

10. The flag of the United States of America should be at the center and at the highest point of the group when a number of flags of states or localities or pennants of societies are grouped and displayed from staffs.

11. When flags of two or more nations are displayed, they are to be flown from separate staffs of the same height. The flags should be of approximately equal size. International usage forbids the display of the flag of one nation above that of another nation in time of peace.

375

These guide specifications are identical to those developed by the National Association of Architectural Metal Manufacturers (NAAMM).

They are included here with the permission of NAAMM. A number of revisions and some additions have been made to update the original document, with the approval of the Association. As stated by NAAMM, these guide specifications are intended to be used as the basis for developing a job specification, and must be edited to fit specific job requirements. Inapplicable provisions should be deleted, appropriate information should be provided in the blank spaces and provisions applicable to the job should be added as necessary.

Guide Specifications	*Notes to Specifier*
SECTION 10350—Metal Flagpoles	
PART 1—GENERAL	
1.01 RELATED WORK SPECIFIED ELSEWHERE	
A. Earthwork: Section 02205, Item(s) _____.	
B. Cast-in-place Concrete: Section 03300, Item(s) _____	
C. Rough Carpentry: Section 08100, Item(s) _____	
D. Painting: Section 09900, Item(s) _____	
E. Special Systems: Section 16 ____, Item(s)_____	
1.02 QUALITY ASSURANCE	1.02.A List 3 or more companies that are considered to be reliable and acceptable flagpole manufacturers.
A. Acceptable manufacturers:	
1. _____	
2. _____	
3. _____	
B. Design Criteria: Flagpole and all anchorage devices to be designed to resist 90 mph wind velocity minimum when flying flag of appropriate size.	1.02.B Refer to Section 2 of this manual for recommended appropriate flag sizes. Revise criteria if location requires higher wind resistance.
1.03 SUBMITTALS	
A. Submit shop drawings for all poles, showing:	
1. General layouts, fully dimensioned	
2. Foundation details (ground-set poles only)	
3. Flash collars or bases (ground-set poles only)	
4. Mounting and support systems (wall-mounted or roof-mounted poles)	
5. Finishes	
6. Cleat(s)	
7. Trucks	
8. Finials	
9. Types of Halyard(s)	
10. Flag attachment devices	
11. Any other specified features	
B. Furnish two copies of manufacturer's specifications and installation instructions for each type of pole, base and fittings being provided.	
1.04 DELIVERY, STORAGE AND HANDLING	
A. Spiral wrap each flagpole with heavy kraft paper and/or polyethylene wrap and pack in tube prior to shipment.	
B. Deliver flagpole(s) in original wrappings.	
C. Pending installation, store flagpole(s) in area protected from weather, moisture and damage, as recommended by pole manufacturer.	
D. Handle flagpole(s) so as to prevent damage or soiling.	

PART 2—PRODUCTS

2.01 FLAGPOLES

A. Provide and install each flagpole as a complete unit, furnished by single acceptable manufacturer, including base, anchorage devices and all accessories.

B. Type(s) and Size(s)

   1. Flagpole(s) to be ___(shaft form, metal and type),___ feet exposed length, with butt diameter of____ inches and butt wall thickness of ____ inches.

                              —OR—

   1. Flagpoles to be of types, metals and sizes shown in the following schedule:

No.	Shaft	Metal	Type	Exp. Lgth.	Butt Diam.	Butt Wall Th.

   2. Overall length of embedded ground-set poles to be such as to provide a setting depth of not less than 10% of exposed length.

C. Material

   1. Aluminum:

      a. Seamless extruded tube, ASTM B241 _____.

      b. Alloy: 6063-T6

      c. Heat treat and age harden after fabrication.

   2. Steel:

      a. Standard weight seamless pipe, ASTM A53 _____, Type S, Grade B.

      b. Structural Tubing, ASTM _____

      c. Carbon steel sheet: ASTM A366 _____.

   3. Copper Alloy:

      a. Seamless pipe, ASTM B43 _____.

      b. Seamless tube, ASTM B135 _____.

      c. Alloy: C23000, red brass.

   4. Stainless Steel:

      a. Welded pipe, ASTM 312 _____.

      b. Sheet, ASTM A167 _____.

      c. Alloy: AISI Type 304/302

D. Shaft

   1. Cone tapered

      a. Uniform smooth straight line tapered section above cylindrical butt section.

      b. Manufacturer's standard rate of taper.

   2. Entasis tapered

      a. Smooth Venetian entasis convex curved tapered section above cylindrical butt section.

   3. Workmanship

      a. Fabricate all joints and seams so as to be inconspicuous.

      b. Grind all exposed welds smooth, and finish to match pole shaft.

E. Shaft Finish

   1. Aluminum:

      a. Directional textured mechanical satin finish, _____.

                   —OR—

      a. Clear anodized finish, AA M32-C22-A41.

                   —OR—

      a. Color anodized finish, AA M32-C12-A color _____.

                   —OR—

      a. Factory-applied _____ of color selected, following pretreatment and/or primer recommended by manufacturer of coating.

2.01.B.1 Use first alternative for single pole or any number of identical poles. Shaft form: (cone tapered), (entasis tapered). Type: (ground-set conventional, automatic flag-storing, tilting or nautical), (wall-mounted vertical or outrigger) or (roof-mounted).

Use alternative schedule when two or more sizes or types of pole are required.

2.01.C.1a Fill in year of ASTM Std.

2.01.C.1b Alloy 6005-T5 is possible alternative. See discussion under Materials, Section 3 of this Manual.

2.01.C.2a Fill in year of ASTM Std.

2.01.C.2b Hot-formed tubing (A501); cold-formed (A500). Fill in year of Std.

2.01.C.2c Fill in year of ASTM Std.

2.01.C.3a & b Fill in year of ASTM Standards

2.01.C.4a & b Fill in year of ASTM Standard

2.01.E.1a (AA M32) or (AA M33). Protective coat of clear wax may be specified.

2.01.E.1a (A42) for integral hardcoat: (A43) for impregnated gold only; (A44) for electrolytically deposited color. See Section 3 of this Manual.

2.01.E.1a (air-dry enamel), (epoxy coating), (urethane coating), (fluorocarbon coating), (siliconized polymer coating) or other.

2. Steel:
   a. Minimum one coat of rust-inhibitive primer, _____.

   —OR—

   a. Factory-applied _____ of color selected, following pretreatment and/or primer recommended by manufacturer of coating.

3. Copper Alloy:
   a. Statuary antique, M32-C55, sealed with appropriate sprayed-on clear lacquer.

   —OR—

   a. Directional textured satin finish, M32, and clear lacquer coating.

4. Stainless Steel:
   a. AISI No. 4 bright polished finish.

F. Field Joints
   1. Provide internal splicing, self-aligning sleeves of compatible metal with snug fitting and tightly butted field joints.
   2. Welding permitted only on steel poles.

G. Nautical Flagpole(s)
   1. Provide _____, complete with all necessary connections, pulley blocks and other fittings.

   2. Dimensions:

H. Flag-storing Pole(s)
   1. Fully automatic type, Series ____, complete with motor unit installed in lower section of pole, photo electric control and three-position switch with circuit protection, and pigtail at base for electrical connection.

   —OR—

   1. Manually operated type, Series HC, with geardriven mechanism for operating halyard installed in lower section of pole, removable hand crank and flush cover.
   2. Cast aluminum entry system equipped with two aluminum rollers on Delrin shafts.

2.02 MOUNTING
   A. Ground-set poles, embedded
      1. Flash Collar
         a. Metal: same as pole shaft.
         b. Design similar to design No. ____ as supplied by (name of pole mfr.).

         —OR—

      1. Ornamental Base
         a. Metal: same as pole shaft.
         b. Design similar to design No. ____ as supplied by (name of pole mfr.).

         —OR—

         b. Special design as shown on architect's details.
      2. Ground Protector
         a. Standard weight steel pipe.
         b. One pipe size larger than butt diameter of pole shaft x 18 inches (455 mm) long.
      3. Foundation Sleeve
         a. 16 gauge corrugated galvanized steel tube.
      4. Foundation Sleeve Plate
         a. Square steel plate, ³⁄₁₆ in. (5 mm) minimum thickness, welded to bottom of foundation sleeve.
      5. Centering Wedges
         a. Internal steel wedges, ⅛ in. (3 mm) minimum thickness, welded to support plate for centering of flagpole.

2.01.E.2a (zinc chromate, FS-TT-P-645) or (zinc-rich paint, FS-TT-P-641). Specify finish field coat(s) under Painting, Section 09900.
2.01.E.2a See notes under fourth alternate of 2.01.E.1a.

2.01.F Omit if overall length of any pole specified does not exceed 33'0".

2.01.G.1 [single-mast pole with yardarm (and gaff)] [double-mast pole with yardarm and gaff]. Gaff optional on single-mast pole.
2.01.G.2 Specify lengths of yardarm, upper and lower masts and gaff.

2.01.H.1 (A) for ground-set or roof-mounted poles. (VA) for vertical wall-mounted poles. Specify all electrical work in Electrical Specifications.

2.02.A.1a Select from manufacturer's literature. Other acceptable manufacturers can usually match closely.

2.02.A.2 Ground protector for steel poles only.

2.02.A.4a Size usually 2 to 4 inches (50 to 100 mm) larger than inside diameter of foundation sleeve.

    6. Ground Spike
        a. ¾ inch (19 mm) steel spike, welded to bottom of foundation
           sleeve plate.
        b. Minimum length below concrete foundation to be equal to
           footing thickness below foundation sleeve plate.
    7. Foundation Support Plate
        a. Steel plate, 6 inches (150 mm) square by ⁵⁄₁₆ (5 mm) minimum
           thickness, welded to ground spike at base of concrete
           foundation.
B. Ground-set poles, surface mounted
    1. Shoe base
        a. Provide cast aluminum shoe base properly sized for snug fit.
        b. Furnish complete with galvanized anchor bolts and ground spike
           of sizes recommended by pole manufacturer.
    2. Flange plate
        a. Provide properly sized steel flange plate with four anchor bolt
           holes, welded to bottom end of pole shaft.
        b. Furnish complete with galvanized anchor bolts and ground spike
           of sizes recommended by pole manufacturer.
    3. Mandrel
        a. Provide steel mandrel base of dimensions recommended by pole
           manufacturer and shown on approved shop drawings, complete
           with galvanized anchor bolts and lightning protection device.
C. Tilting Base Assembly
    1. Provide two upright structural steel channels or rectangular steel
       tubes welded to steel base plate
    2. Provide _____ counterbalance weights at bottom of pole.

    3. Furnish complete with pivoting mechanism, vertical positioning
       device _____ lock, galvanized anchor bolts and ground spike.
D. Wall-mounted poles, vertical
    1. Provide, for each pole, _____ of same metal as pole,
       complete with all necessary parts for _____ mounting.
    2. Design similar to design no. ____ as supplied by _(name of pole
       mfr.)_ .
                              —OR—
    2. Special design as shown on architect's details.
    3. Spacing of wall brackets to be not less than 10% of pole length.
E. Wall-mounted poles, outrigger
    1. Provide, for each pole, a mounting base of same metal as pole,
       complete with mounting plate and all necessary parts
       for_____ mounting.
    2. Design similar to design no. ____ as supplied by _(name of pole
       mfr.)_ .
                              —OR—
    2. Special design as shown on architect's details.
    3. Furnish lateral bracing arrangement, complete with collars, rods
       and anchorage devices.
F. Roof-mounted poles
    1. Pole socket: Galvanized steel pipe, sized to fit pole butt diameter,
       welded to steel plate for mounting on roof.
                              —OR—
    1. Flange plate: square steel plate of size recommended by pole
       manufacturer, welded to bottom end of pole shaft.
                              —OR—
    1. Cast aluminum shoe base properly sized for snug fit.
                              —OR—
    1. Steel mandrel base of dimensions recommended by pole
       manufacturer and shown on approved shop drawings, complete
       with galvanized anchor bolts.
    2. Bracing assembly
        a. Material: _____ .

2.02.A.6b Adequate for lightning protection in most cases. If ground conditions require longer spike, so specify.

2.02.B.1 Specify shoe base only for aluminum poles specially designed for this type of mounting.

2.02.B.2 Specify only for steel or stainless steel poles.

2.02.B.3 Mandrel mountings are always custom designed to meet specific requirements.

2.02.C.2 (external) (internal) Consult manufacturer's literature.
2.02.C.3 (with) (without) Omit ground spike if pole is to be mounted on roof.

2.02.D.1 (a bracket mounting) (two wall brackets). (through-wall) or (expansion bolt) mounting. Through-wall mounting recommended whenever possible.

2.02.E.1 (through-wall) or (expansion bolt). Through-wall mounting recommended whenever possible.

2.02.E.3 Specify only when so recommended by pole manufacturer.

2.02.F.1 Specify only for steel or stainless steel poles.

2.02.F.1 Specify only for aluminum poles.

2.02.F.1 Mandrel base is always custom designed to meet specific requirements

2.02.F.2a (steel, hot dip galvanized) or (aluminum)

   b. Braces: _____ of size recommended by pole
      manufacturer, in ____ arrangement.
   c. Assembly to be so designed as to permit adjustment to plumb
      pole and to firmly hold it in that position.
   d. All connections to roof to be properly flashed and watertight.
3. Through-roof mounting
   a. Base of flagpole to be extended through roof sleeve and firmly
      anchored to special framing provided in the building
      construction below. All materials and dimensions to be as shown
      on approved shop drawing.
   b. Roof penetration and all connections to roof to be properly
      flashed and watertight.

2.03 FITTINGS
  A. Finial

   1. Type: _____.
   2. Dimensions:

      a. Ball diameter: ____ inches
      b. Eagle wing span: ____ inches
      c. Weathervane length: ____ inches
   3. Materials:
      a. Ball: flush seam _____.

      b. Eagle: _____.
      c. Weathervane: _____.
   4. Finishes
      a. Aluminum: _____.

      b. Copper: _____.
      c. Stainless steel: finish to match pole shaft.
  B. Truck
   1. _____ revolving, non-fouling _____ sheave truck with
      stainless steel ball bearings.
                              —OR—

   1. Fixed single-sheave truck of metal compatible with pole shaft.
                              —OR—
   1. Truck for internal halyard system.
                              —OR—
   1. Cast aluminum truck with removable top cover, two aluminum
      sheaves with sealed roller bearings on Delrin shafts.
  C. Cleats
   1. Provide one 9 in. (230 mm) cleat per halyard.
   2. Material: _____, with fastenings of compatible metal.
  D. Halyards
   1. Conventional External
      a. Provide ____ halyard(s) per flagpole.

      b. Material: _____.

      c. Size: _____
                              —OR—
   1. Internal System
      a. Stainless steel cable with vinyl- or neoprene-covered weights.
      b. Internally mounted direct drive winch with control stop to hold
         flag in any position on pole.
      c. Removable winch crank.
      d. Flush-mounted winch access door with cylinder lock.
                              —OR—
   1. Flag-storing Type

2.02.F.2b (rod) (pipe) (structural angles). Arrangement may
be "L," "T," "Y" or "X." Type and arrangement of braces
depends on pole height; consult pole manufacturer.

2.02.F.3 Specify only when size of pole is such that this type
of mounting is recommended by pole manufacturer.

2.03.A. Finials not generally recommended on internal halyard systems.
2.03.A.1 (ball), (ball and eagle), (weathervane), (ball, eagle,
and weathervane) or other. Many designs available; consult
manufacturer.
2.03.A.2a Usually about same as butt diameter of shaft.
2.03.A.2b Span in inches usually ½ of pole height in feet.
2.03.A.2c Approximately the same as eagle wing span.

2.03.A.3a (20-oz. copper) (14 ga.spun aluminum) (spun stainless steel)
2.03.A.3b (copper) (aluminum)
2.03.A.3c (copper) (aluminum)

2.03.A.4a (brushed, AA-M35), (clear anodized, AA-A41),
(color anodized, AA-A42) (23-karat gold leaf over 3 coats
waterproof paint and 1 coat waterproof sizing)
2.03.A.4b (23-karat gold leaf over 3 coats waterproof paint
and 1 coat waterproof sizing) (statuary bronze)

2.03.B.1 for aluminum poles, (cast aluminum); for steel poles,
(cast iron, galvanized), (cast bronze), (stainless steel); for
bronze poles, (cast bronze); for stainless steel poles, (chrome-
plated bronze), (stainless steel). (single) or (double) sheave.
2.03.B.1 Fixed truck usually specified only for wall-mounted
outrigger or small ground-set poles.

2.03.B.1—4th alternate for flag-storing poles only.

2.03.C. Cleats not used on internal halyard system.

2.03.C.2 (galvanized cast iron),(cast aluminum),(cast bronze),
(stainless steel).

2.03.D.1a (one) or (two), except on nautical poles three or
more.
2.03.D.1b (braided polypropylene), (nylon),(nylon with metal
core), (cotton with metal core).
2.03.D.1c [5/16 in. (8mm) or No. 10], [3/8 in. (9mm) or No. 12].

2.03.D.1—3rd alternate for flag-storing poles only.

a. Continuous stainless steel cable, with antifurling device and with two aluminum stops mounted on each side of cable to engage or disengage limit switches.

E. Flag Attachment Devices

    1. Provide two _____ flagsnaps on each halyard.

              —OR—

    1. Provide two non-metallic flag holders on each halyard.

F. Cleat Covers

    1. Provide one _____ cleat cover box, complete with hinged cover, tamper-proof fastenings, and _____ over each cleat.

    2. Finish to match pole shaft.

G. Halyard Protector(s)

    1. Provide one aluminum channel halyard protector, ____ feet in length and securely locked in place, for each cleat cover.

H. Other

2.03.E.1 (bronze),(chrome-plated bronze),(aluminum). Bronze is standard with most manufacturers. If snaps are to have vinyl or neoprene covers, so specify.

2.03.F Optional feature

2.03.F.1 (cast aluminum), (cast bronze), (stainless steel), (hasp and staple for padlock) or (cylinder lock)

2.03.G Optional feature, used only with cleat cover.

2.03.G.1 5 feet is standard length, but may be longer, up to 10 feet.

2.03.H Specify any additional fittings or features desired.

PART 3—EXECUTION

3.01 INSPECTION

  A. Inspect foundations for ground-set poles for proper size, depth and construction.

  B. Inspect bracing systems for roof-mounted poles for proper construction and anchorage.

  C. Inspect the location, spacing and anchorage of brackets or bases for wall-mounted poles.

3.02 PREPARATION

  A. Paint portions of ground-set poles to be embedded below grade with heavy coat of bituminous paint.

3.03 INSTALLATION

  A. Install all flagpoles, base assemblies and fittings in compliance with approved shop drawings and manufacturer's instructions.

  B. Provide proper lightning ground for each flagpole.

3.04 ADJUSTMENTS

  A. Check and adjust all installed fittings for smooth and proper operation.

Installation of flagpoles is generally not the responsibility of the pole manufacturer.

3.02.A Painting may be done by pole manufacturer prior to shipment.

3.03.B See Section 4 of Flagpole Manual for information on grounding.

CHAPTER ELEVEN
SIGNAGE
Fred T. Knowles

INTRODUCTION

The practice of architecture and design should be dedicated to the creation of effective and efficient spaces to better serve human needs. Creating environments that enhance motivation and production involve many disciplines working as a team to ensure the best approach to problem solving. One discipline on which little emphasis has been placed involves visual communications systems—signs—to direct, inform, and control both vehicular and pedestrian traffic through architectural sites and spaces, rendering one's passage a totally controlled environmental experience.

All structures require some kind of signing, whether functional signs that depict an important message, or graphics that simply enhance architectural spaces by the tasteful and aesthetic use of various letterforms, designs, shapes, and colors. Regrettably, many architects design, construct, and furnish buildings without giving thought to a signage system, forcing the owner or tenants to purchase any readily available marking devices to apply haphazardly on doors and walls, thereby degrading the efforts of the many talents involved in developing the structure. Architectural control over the sign system is as important as other disciplines required in the development of the structure and its environment.

Frequently, too many marking devices are used on streets and in buildings to communicate messages. The population increase during the last 20 to 30 years has brought with it many scattered shopping districts, places of employment, institutions, and public facilities, resulting in an accompanying proliferation of signs tastelessly conceived and without a "systems" approach to problem solving. A systems approach to signing will help rid our land of the urban blight created by the last quarter-century of thoughtless signing (Figure 11-1).

An effective signage system must be designed carefully and creatively, with equal consideration placed upon design and the selection of materials. Whether the project involves a sports arena, convention center, airport, subway system, shopping center, theater, hospital, or office space, the basic problem is that of controlling and moving people effectively and efficiently without detracting from the environment.

Some architectural firms have expanded their staffs to include graphic design capability; however, most of the firms practicing architecture rely on catalogs sup-

Fig. 11-1

Fig. 11-2

Fig. 11-3

Fig. 11-4

plied by sign manufacturers and other sources for information required in the development of a comprehensive signage system. This time-consuming approach frequently results in a compromised signage program influenced strongly by the most readily available catalog or brochure.

The purpose of this chapter is to present, in a concise format for easy reference, all parameters involved in the execution of a signage program. Aesthetic design philosophy and critique are not included; emphasis is placed upon a systems approach in organizing for the task by providing checklists with relevant details and visual aids, and by evaluating techniques and materials available to the architect.

SIGNAGE SYSTEM DESIGN CRITERIA

Initial consideration should be directed toward determining the basic parameters required in developing the sign system. Each of them merits discussion here. Also—for easy reference, they are included in the checklist at the end of this chapter.

Performance Requirements

Signs usually must be designed to meet specific performance requirements. The good designer will determine how a system is to perform within given space relationships. The sign system may function entirely on its own merit, or it may be supplemented by staff personnel at major decision-making locations, such as the main lobby and reception areas. Sign devices may become decorative amenities to be featured within the environment (Figure 11-2), or they may be subtle and low-key elements of minor importance. Supergraphics may be considered in certain areas simply as an art form (Figure 11-3), or as a functional graphic device presented in large scale for emphasis of context (Figure 11-4). Certainly, a combination of the two is feasible. These are only several performance considerations that should be addressed prior to the development of the signage system. The designer must evaluate the needs of the client, the unique traffic flow requirements and mounting restrictions dictated by the structure, and the basic performance requirements desired of the signing devices to be utilized.

Usage Considerations

The general nature of the building complex often defines how signs are to be used. They may be given an appearance of being fixed and an integral part of the architecture by the appropriate selection of materials, colors, and mountings (Figure 11-5), or they may appear changeable and temporary should need so dictate (Figure 11-6). Some signage requires constant change to properly relate information to people or people to facility, while most sign devices are considered permanent fixtures within a given space (Figure 11-7). The designer is responsible for determining how signs are to be used most effectively, and at the same time, for enhancing the environment.

Fig. 11-5

Durability Requirements

Prior to the selection of materials for a signing system, durability requirements must be considered. The vast assortment of materials available for signs covers a wide spectrum of durability from soft plastics to metals. The sign copy and background material should be evaluated both individually and jointly when considering durability requirements.

Vandalism Considerations

Signs located in controlled spaces are often free from destructive vandalism; however, in many instances vandalism becomes rampant and uncontrolled. There are no materials that may accurately be labeled "vandalproof." However, some materials are more vandal-resistant than others. Where vandalism is of prime importance, only materials and graphic techniques engineered to resist destruction should be considered.

Fig. 11-6

Flexibility to Accommodate Changes and Additions

Modern architectural structures are designed to accommodate inner spacial changes to meet tenant needs. Partition systems, prehung door units, room dividers, and modular furniture have ensured ease of change in officescapes. The sign system may also require alterations to preserve continuity (Figure 11-8). Changes and additions to a sign system should be considered by the designer prior to the selection of materials, graphic techniques, and mounting methods to be used.

Readability Factors

Sign readability is determined by the letter style selected, size of copy, interletter spacing, copy position relevant to background, colors, and angle of observance.

Letter style Letter styles are classified as sanserif and serif. Sanserif letters, such

Fig. 11-7

Fig. 11-8

HELVETICA MEDIUM
CLARENDON

Fig. 11-9

Helvetica Medium
Clarendon

Fig. 11-10

Architectural Signage Systems
Architectural Signage Systems
Architectural Signage Systems

Fig. 11-11

as Helvetica, are more contemporary than serif letters, such as Clarendon (Figure 11-9). Each letter style has its own unique personality and flavor. Printers carry alphabets in most letter styles, including lowercase letters as well as uppercase (Figure 11-10). Test results indicate that messages starting with an initial uppercase letter and followed by lowercase characters are more recognizable than messages formed with uppercase characters only. Lowercase letters have more "personality" because their shape is varied by ascenders and descenders, resulting in characteristic word forms that are much easier to recognize than all-uppercase word forms. Also, people are more accustomed to reading text in upper- and lowercase than in all uppercase. The proper selection of a particular alphabet should be carefully considered, not only from a legibility point of view, but also from a "personality" standpoint. The letter style should make a concise and meaningful impression in the environment it serves.

Readability Readability is directly related to the size of copy. Visibility studies indicate that 1-inch-high Helvetica Medium, for example, is readable from a distance of 40 feet. Using this as a measure for comparison, 1-inch-high Clarendon style would be readable from a somewhat lesser distance, approximately 25 feet. The distance visibility per 1-inch height may be used as a guideline to determine distance readability for larger letters; that is, 2-inch-high Helvetica Medium will be readable at 80 feet, and 3-inch-high at 120 feet. This direct proportion may be helpful for determining copy (text) sizes for signs used in pedestrian situations. However, the direct proportion may not hold true for vehicular traffic applications where many other factors are involved. The designer must exercise caution after selecting the alphabet and copy size to make certain the lettering will fit properly on the sign background. The sign size should be determined using the longest line of copy and the maximum number of copy lines that may be required.

Letter and line spacing Interletter spacing and interline spacing of copy greatly affect the overall readability of a sign. Message legibility and ease of recognition are increased when proper visual relationships are established between individual characters, words, and lines of copy. Copy with spacing too tight becomes very difficult to read; copy with too open spacing tends to break the message down into fragments (Figure 11-11). Proper spacing depends largely on the distance from which the message is to be read. Messages to be read at close distances should employ tighter spacing than messages that will be read at greater distances (Figures 11-12 and 11-13). Spacing is also affected by the angle at which the message is to be viewed: Greater angles of observance require wider interletter spacing to prevent the characters of the message from appearing to run together.

Copy position The position of copy on the sign background influences the overall readability. Signs on which copy occupies most of the background are not as readable as signs that have sufficient background material surrounding the copy to form a visual barrier separating the message from the environment (Figures 11-14 and 11-15).

Emphasis should be placed on selecting an appropriate sign size to best accommodate the sign message. There are nine basic copy placement positions to be considered in determining the important relationship of copy to sign background. They are:

upper left	upper centered	upper right
centered left	centered	centered right
lower left	lower centered	lower right

Normal Letter Spacing / Helvetica-Medium

The table below is provided as a guide for inter-letter spacing. The letters indicated in the column to the left of the chart contain the characters which have already been positioned. The unit distance between the fixed character and the subsequent one is found opposite the fixed character and under the column heading in which the next character is listed.

The graduated unit scale indicating both negative and positive spacing, 3 to 7, found above the chart, provides the actual distance between characters for 1″ lettering. The scale may be photostatically reduced or enlarged so that the unit height corresponds with the desired letter height. The graduated units will thus provide

the actual spacing distance for any letter size.

Positive spacing is the distance between the extreme right hand edge of the initial character to the extreme left hand edge of the subsequent character. An exception to this rule is the lower case "a" where spacing is measured from the straight back of the character rather than its serif

Negative spacing is the overlap distance between two characters as when a "T" is followed by an "a".

Word spacing is to be the equivalent of the width of a lower case "v".

Readability ratio factor, 1:25.

	acde goqs 12	bhijkl	mnpru	vwy 356890	ft 7	x	z 4	
adghijlmnqu	5	6	6	1	3	2	5	
bceops	2	5	5	0	0	0	2	
vwyr	0	2	2	2	2	1	1	
ftz 2356890	2	3	5	2	1	1	2	
kx	0	2	2	0	1	1	1	
GHIJMNU 1	6	7	7	4	4	3	5	
BCDOQRS	2	6	6	3	2	2	3	
VW	-1	2	1	0	0	0	0	
KX	-1	2	2	-2	-2	2	2	
A	0	2	2	-3	-2	2	2	
E	3	6	6	1	1	2	4	
F 4	0	2	2	2	0	0	2	
L	2	3	3	-2	0	2	4	
P 7	0	5	5	0	2	0	-2	
T	-3	3	0	-2	0	-2	0	
Y	-3	2	-1	-1	-1	-1	-1	
Z	2	3	2	0	0	1	2	

Fig. 11-12   Courtesy of E. Christopher Klumb Assoc., Inc., New York.

Distance Letter Spacing / Helvetica-Medium

The table below is provided as a guide for inter-letter spacing. The letters indicated in the column to the left of the chart contain the characters which have already been positioned. The unit distance between the fixed character and the subsequent one is found opposite the fixed character and under the column heading in which the next character is listed.

The graduated unit scale indicating positive spacing, 0 to 7, found above the chart, provides the actual distance between characters for 1" lettering. The scale may be photostatically reduced or enlarged so that the unit height corresponds with the desired letter height. The graduated units will thus provide the actual spacing distance for any letter size.

Positive spacing is the distance between the extreme right hand edge of the initial character to the extreme left hand edge of the subsequent character. An exception to this rule is the lower case "a" where spacing is measured from the straight back of the character rather than its serif.

Word spacing is to be the equivalent of the width of a lower case "x".

Readability ratio factor, 1:40.

	bhikl mnpru	cdegoq	vwxy	asz	ft	j		
	1		7	356890			4	2
adghijlmnqu	7	6	4	5	4	6		
bcest	6	5	4	5	4	6		
vwxy 7	5	3	4	3	4	6	0	2
fpz	6	4	4	5	4	6		
k 3568	6	3	3	4	4	6	4	3
o	6	5	3	5	4	6		
r	5	4	4	4	4	6		
EGHIJMNU 1	7	6	5	6	7	7	6	6
BCDOS	6	5	4	5	4	6		
TVY	4	0	0	0	1	0		
FP	5	4	4	4	4	6		
A	5	3	3	4	3	6		
K	5	3	3	3	3	5		
L	6	4	4	4	3			
Q	6	6	5	5				
R	6	5	5	5	5	6		
W	4	1	1	1	1	4		
X 290	5	4	3	4	3	3	4	4
Z	6	5	4	5	4	6		
4		2	3	4			4	4

Fig. 11-13 Courtesy of E. Christopher Klumb Assoc., Inc., New York.

Architectural Signage Systems

Fig. 11-14

Architectural Signage Systems

Fig. 11-15

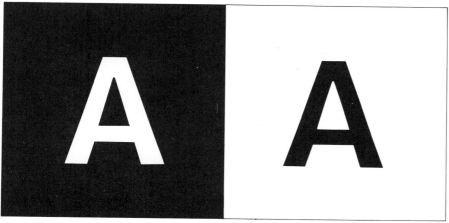

Fig. 11-16

Traditionally, the most popular placement selections have been the centered and upper left positions.

Color   Color of copy and sign background greatly affect readability. Strong contrasting colors are more readable than less dramatic color combinations. White copy on a black background offers the greatest contrast and readability. Color also influences the apparent relationship between the copy size and the background. For example, white copy on a black field appears larger than black copy on a white field, although letter height, sign size, and copy position remain the same in both examples (Figure 11-16).

Colors in a signage system should also relate harmoniously with the pallet of colors selected for the building and its environment. The designer may choose to select colors that blend with the environment or vibrant primary colors that accent the sign system and perhaps contrast with the architectural color scheme.

The viewing angle   The angle of observance is influential in the design of a signage system, since it affects interletter spacing and overall readability. Normally, interior signs are viewed chiefly from a straight-on position; however, exterior signs are frequently seen from more than one angle. Signs to be read from vehicles moving at varying speeds with different angles of observance may require a compromise in letter spacing to best communicate the message.

Multilingual Needs

The jet age is a contributing factor in bringing people together from all over the world to visit and transact business. Transportation terminals and public facilities that may be used by visitors unaccustomed to reading English should employ sign systems that bridge any visual communication gap. Multilingual messages in English and the dominant foreign languages used by visitors may be combined and presented on one sign background. However, sign design and graphic formats become very critical to prevent confusion. A more popular solution involves the use of pictorial symbols as word substitutes. Pictographic signs are bold, recognizable images not bound by language barriers (Figures 11-17 through 11-22).

Regulatory Considerations

The designer should become aware of regulations governing signs. Federal regulations concerning safety signs are enumerated in Occupational Safety and Health Administration (OSHA) publications. American National Standards Institute (ANSI) publishes standards concerning signage for the physically handicapped. Underwriters' Laboratory (UL) issues standards applicable to illuminated signs. State and local codes contain regulatory information concerning sign sizes, mounting locations and heights, quantities of signs allowable in various zoning areas, and other restrictions relating to exterior signs. These rules, and those of other regulatory bodies, should be taken under advisement prior to completing a comprehensive signage program.

Need for Illumination

Many signs are required to relate their messages after dark as well as during natural daylight. The careful designer will determine which signs require artificial illumination and decide on the method of illumination. Signs can be externally illuminated by readily available stock fixtures produced by many manufacturers, or they can be internally illuminated. Fluorescent lighting is the most common source of internal illumination, although metal arc lamps, incandescent lamps, and neon are frequently employed.

Need for a Graphics Manual

Many signage programs are developed for institutions that have a continuing need not only to maintain, but also to augment or change, their signage systems. The preparation of a signage manual containing all the information required to create additional signs or components would benefit the client and ensure continuity in the system as changes and additions are made. The designer should determine this potential need and include the manual with other documents developed for the signage program (Figure 11-23).

Budget Considerations and Cost Effectiveness

Prior to the selection of materials, the designer should establish budget parameters with the owner if cost is of prime importance. Many materials and graphic techniques span a wide range of initial costs. The designer should evaluate initial cost compared with long-term cost to properly determine the cost effectiveness of a signage system since the most inexpensive system might very well become the most costly for the

Universal

Applicable to any building or facility

Picto'grafics not shown:

1.110	Children	1.372	Playroom
1.144	Man with boy	1.410	Church
1.340	Fragile	1.472	Synagogue
		1.469	Police

1.493	Smoke
1.516	Parking
1.488	Keep Dry
1.155	Janitor

Entry
Exit
Ramp up
Ramp down

1.403

1.404

1.461

1.462

Emergency
Women's Toilet
Men's Toilet
Stairs

4.412

1.189

1.143

1.377

Handicapped
No Smoking
Telephone
Escalator

1.188

3.316

1.365

1.328

Elevator
Down
No Parking
Drinking fountain

1.311

1.402B

3.516

1.139

Mail Box
Check Room
Up
No Entry

1.326

1.317

1.402A

3.463

Shower
Waiting Room
Telegraph Office
Information

1.376

1.151

1.327

1.530

Fig. 11-17

Medical

Nursing Homes
Medical Complexes
First-Aid Centers

Picto'grafics not shown:
1.516 Parking   1.413 Health
1.372 Playroom   2.531 Warning
1.150 Library or Reading 1.147 Chest

Hospital
Pharmacy
Dental Care
Wheelchair

1.508   1.518   1.184   1.188

X-Ray
Physiotherapy
General Medicine, Female
General Medicine, Male

1.146   1.148   1.440   1.450

Coronary Care
Hematology
Urology
Eye

  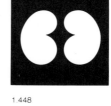 

1.446   1.417   1.448   1.123

Podiatry
Mental Health
Ear, Nose & Throat
Oxygen

1.129   1.473   1.137   1.368

Shower
Isolation
Nursery
Laboratory

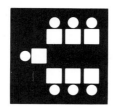   

1.376   1.411   1.302   1.359

Conference
Occupational Therapy
Rehabilitation
Ambulatory Patients

1.406   1.347   1.483   1.152

Fig. 11-18

Commercial

Picto'grafics not shown:

1.218	Concrete Mixer	1.226	Flatbed Truck	1.314	Vegetable Produce
1.219	Cushman Vehicle	1.250	Pickup Truck	1.363	Newspaper Vendor
1.222	Dump Truck	1.304	Basket	1.370	Record Store
				1.394	Cooking

Cocktail Lounge
Pub
Coffee Shop
Liquor Store

1.344

1.361

1.360

1.307

Mens' Furnishings
Furniture
Cinema
Camera Store

1.352

1.315

1.126

1.338

Gift Shop
Florist
Dress Shop
Shoe Store

1.339

1.393

1.321

1.375

Restaurant
Soda Fountain
Grocery Store
Tobacco Shop

1.354

1.341

1.337

1.316

Bookstore
Record Shop
Fuel
Toy Shop

1.305

1.455

1.336

1.372

Theater
Van
Beauty Salon
Barber Shop

1.449

1.290

1.192

1.149

Fig. 11-19

Travel

Picto'grafics not shown:

1.350 Motel
1.266 Seaplane Base

Airport
Departures
Arrivals
Car Rentals

1.253

1.255

1.254

1.202

Bus
Subway
Train
Taxi

1.208

1.268

1.278

1.203

Monorail
Ferry
Cable Car
Automobile

1.239

1.225

1.215

1.201

Lost & Found
Porter
Locker
Fuel

1.310

1.319

1.308

1.336

Baggage Claim
Customs
Immigration
Money Exchange

1.303

1.125

1.464

1.532

Motorcycle
Moving Sidewalk
Lodging
Ice Cubes

1.241

1.145

1.173

1.353

Fig. 11-20

Recreation and Sports

**Sports Arenas
Parks
Recreation Facilities
Amusement Parks**

Picto'grafics not shown:
1.112 Curling
1.115 Dancing
1.140 LaCrosse

1.138 Hockey
1.183 Tobogganing

1.471 Wintersports
1.387 Outdoor Recreation

Campers
Picnic Area
Midway
Trailer Train

1.276

1.366

1.313

1.185

Water
Swimming
Canoeing
Sailing

1.492

1.177

1.217

1.265

Marina, Boating
Life Preserver
Snowmobiling
Camping

1.401

1.357

1.267

1.385

Judging
Bicycling
Women's/Girl's Toilet
Fishing

1.370

1.211

1.910

1.334

Skiing
Soccer
Ice Skating
Football

1.172

1.176

1.181

1.130

Hunting, Shooting
Golf
Baseball
Tennis, Badminton

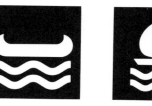
1.170

1.133

1.105

Fig. 11-21

395

SAFETY

Safety Signs for:
Factories
Industrial Parks
Industrial Complexes

Complying with
OSHA Regulations

Picto'grafics not shown:
2.306 Safety Boot
1.320 Drain
4.489 Shut-off-valve

2.531 Warning
4.331 Fire Axe
5.376 Safety Shower
4.365 Emergency Phone

Caution
High Voltage

2.420

Caution
Overhead
Crane

2.362

Danger
Explosives

2.425

Caution
Men
At Work

2.154

Caution
Crosswalk

2.153

Caution
Wet Floor

2.155

Caution
Wear
Goggles

2.343

Caution
Wear
Hard Hat

2.346

Caution
Wear
Earmuffs

2.325

Caution
Chemical
Burn

2.136

Alarm Bell

4.301

Caution
Wear Gloves

2.342

Danger
Radiation

2.460

Caution
Wear
Gas Mask

2.335

Eye Wash

5.124

Fire
Extinguisher

4.332

Fire Hose

4.333

No
Open Flame

3.358

Stretcher
Station

5.378

First Aid

5.135

Fig. 11-22

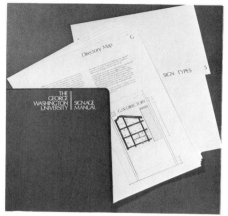

Fig. 11-23

Fig. 11-24

client on a long-term basis. A reasonable preliminary budget for signage might be 0.25 percent of the projected total project budget.

SIGN TYPES CATEGORIZED BY FUNCTION

Signage systems should be logically broken down into various types of signs to be utilized on a particular project. Many categories of sign types may be developed, but one of the most conclusive listings is based on function. The following discussion of signage system components, including sign requirements for specific applications, covers these functions.

Fig. 11-25

Exterior Signs

Exterior sign system components are normally viewed from vehicles or by pedestrians who have parked their vehicles and are walking toward their destination.

Primary identification All architectural projects require some form of identification that is both easily readable and recognizable (Figure 11-24). A person's first association with a building is the identifying device selected to "label" the structure. The importance of the first impression created by this device should be recognized. A sign that produces an image in keeping with the environment it serves reflects the quality of the people associated with that environment. Major corporations spend large sums of money on corporate identity programs to ensure the visual image presented to the public best reflects corporate philosophy and product desirability. Equal emphasis should be placed upon the image presented by the device employed to identify an architectural structure.

Secondary identification Many complexes containing more than one basic structure require secondary identification signs to properly identify the various elements within the complex (Figure 11-25). A systems approach to design will provide continuity in the relationship of primary to secondary identification signs.

Vehicular advance notice A system of road signs suitably located in advance of decision-making points will allow vehicular traffic to execute the proper decisions smoothly and safely at the appropriate times (Figure 11-26).

Fig. 11-26

Fig. 11-27

Fig. 11-28

Fig. 11-29

Fig. 11-30

Vehicular directional Intersections and parking facility entrances are major decision-making locations requiring directional devices to guide drivers toward their destination (Figure 11-27).

Traffic regulatory and control Vehicular traffic can be systematically controlled by employing signing devices. Traffic codes are usually clear as to what signs are required, where they are to be located, and the height at which they are to be mounted. Usually, colors, sizes, and shapes are standardized by the traffic authorities. Stop, yield, and speed limit signs are representative of this classification of signs (Figure 11-28).

Instructional Frequently, signs are required to instruct vehicular and pedestrian traffic. These notices must be properly installed in carefully selected locations to be effective. Examples include parking procedures, delivery and service directions, and the like (Figure 11-29).

Informational Some signs are required to present information that is both relevant to the location and important to the viewer. This information may pertain to parking rates, hours of operation, and security, or it may relate to items of interest within the environment (Figure 11-30).

Decorative Decorative graphics may be employed to enhance the beauty or decor of a particular area; form, color, and design may be utilized to create interest and to become features of the exterior landscape (Figure 11-31).

Interior Signs

Interior sign system components should assist visitors to travel from the building entrances throughout the complex until they reach their desired destination.

Identification Multiple-occupancy buildings require tenant identification; frequently, buildings with only one tenant will also utilize identification in the main lobby or reception areas to reinforce the corporate signature (Figure 11-32). Criteria for

398

Fig. 11-31

Fig. 11-32

multiple-tenant signage are very important and should be included in lease documents to provide for visual continuity and architectural harmony. When individuals are allowed to implement their own desires concerning signage, each will attempt to outdo the other, resulting in clutter, confusion, and visual pollution. Signs that are too big, too gaudy, too competitive, and poorly conceived and executed will become commonplace unless controls on tenant identification are established and enforced.

Primary directory   Information relevant to one's location within a complex should be clearly enumerated on the primary directory, usually located in a very visible area of the main lobby (Figure 11-33). Alphabetized listings of tenants, departments, and individuals should be concise and should designate the floor and room numbers. Such directories may be flush or recessed wall mounts, horizontal projected wall mounts, or pedestal or kiosk mounts, and internally illuminated or not, depending upon the ambient lighting conditions.

Fig. 11-33

Elevator lobby floor directory   High-rise structures require well-positioned signage that not only identifies each individual floor, but also serves as a secondary directory system for that floor (Figure 11-34). Frequently, the floor identification, directory, and corridor directional signage may be included in one device. When a visitor exits from an elevator on a chosen floor, a sign showing the floor number and also the direction of the office or room number sought is both helpful and reassuring.

Pictorial "you are here" indicators   Pictorial schematic maps may become an integral part of directory systems, or they may be utilized separately as visual aids in depicting one's intended passage through a complex (Figure 11-35). Hospitals, sports complexes, and transportation centers, are good examples of structures that may require pictorial maps to supplement word messages. Caution will be exercised by the expert designer to keep the pictorial map simple and correctly oriented in the building according to where the viewer is standing, and to evaluate the need of color coding as part of the visual aid. Too frequently, designers employ a complicated color-coded system that becomes very confusing to the viewer and, in fact, compromises the effectiveness of the system.

Fig. 11-34

Primary directional   The maze that often results from interior corridor layouts creates many decision-making points for a visitor (Figure 11-36). Primary directional

399

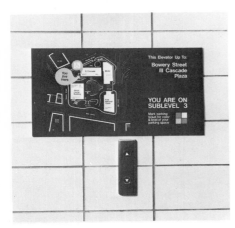

Fig. 11-35

Fig. 11-36

Fig. 11-37

Fig. 11-38

Fig. 11-39

Fig. 11-40

signs may be ceiling-mounted, wall-mounted, or floor-mounted as kiosk-type units in open areas. Areas with heavy pedestrian traffic should have directional signs located so that people do not obstruct the line of sight to the sign device. Normally, ceiling-suspended or kiosk-type units are the best choice to enhance visibility.

Secondary directional Directional signs should be considered in locations where traffic flow and corridor layouts do not demand primary directional devices but do require some guidance for direction control (Figure 11-37). Corridors within suites of offices and corridors that change direction should be considered as decision-making points that may require a secondary directional signage device.

Area identification Specific areas within a complex should be properly identified (Figures 11-38 through 11-40). These areas may be tenant spaces, divisions, or departments. When occurring along main corridors, they are usually designated by wall-, door-, or transom-mounted devices. Ceiling-suspended signs are a good solution in open office spaces.

Room identification Wall- or door-mounted room identification signs are required to "label" the function of a particular room (Figures 11-41 and 11-42). Work functions are properly identified within tenant areas, while service and maintenance functions should be suitably designated in most situations.

400

Desk identification Reception areas may require a sign device located on a desk or counter to identify a particular service or individual rendering assistance to visitors (Figure 11-43). Such signs may be permanently affixed or removable, and may provide for changeable name inserts.

Personnel identification Persons rendering a service to the public, such as nurses, maintenance personnel, and food service personnel, generally are identified by name badges or pins (Figure 11-44).

Regulatory and control signs Signs that authorize or prohibit certain functions are required, frequently by law or code, to inform people using the facility (Figure 11-45). Examples include signs for the handicapped and signs relevant to no smoking areas, elevator capacities, "no entry" areas, fire control, and "authorized personnel only" areas. These signs are usually mounted on doors or their adjacent walls; they may employ colors which deviate from the standard colors used in the comprehensive signage system to emphasize a dangerous situation or the need for caution.

Fig. 11-41

Fig. 11-42

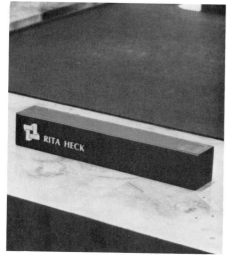

Fig. 11-43

Fig. 11-44

Fig. 11-45

Fig. 11-46

Fig. 11-47

Fig. 11-48

Exits   Exit signs are required by codes to designate exits effectively in times of emergency (Figure 11-46). Supplemental devices are used to give additional information pertaining to a particular exit such as "Emergency Exit Only" and "Alarm Sounds When Door Is Opened." OSHA-approved exit signs are standard items manufactured by many lighting companies, and are generally provided by the electrical contractor.

Information exhibit cases   Notices, posters, attractions, and promotional pieces should be contained within an appropriately designed case to control the display of this type of information (Figure 11-47). Standard units featuring vinyl-covered cork panels housed within extruded aluminum frames with lockable doors are available from many directory manufacturers.

Decorative features   Decorative designs may be reproduced on walls as interior features (Figure 11-48). Reproduction processes include appliqués, painting, and screen printing on location; or mural processes, which are applied much like wall-coverings, may be considered. Doors may also receive supergraphic treatments in which copy may become an integral part of the design.

Dedicatory plaques Building dedication plaques should be carefully conceived and implemented, using materials that reflect favorably upon the talents involved in the realization of the project (Figure 11-49). Historically, these plaques have been bronze or aluminum castings. However, modern technology has provided photographic methods and photochemical processes which offer the designer a freedom of size, format, letterform, and color not available in the casting operation.

Donor recognition Buildings constructed in part by contributions from donors require special recognition for the donors (Figures 11-50 and 11-51). Hospitals, performing arts centers, and service institutions rely on gifts to assist in financing buildings, additions, and furnishings, and usually stipulate that donors will be remembered and recognized in some prestigious location in the building. The designer is responsible for establishing controls and developing a system that fulfills promises made by those soliciting funds, while allowing flexibility to expand the system as future needs may dictate. Location selection is very important in the overall effectiveness of the donor recognition signage.

Mechanical, instrumentation, and control system markings Many industrial and mechanical installations require equipment, control, and pipe markings to meet codes, assist maintenance and service personnel, and ensure safety (Figure 11-52). Often, these locations are not public spaces, and require an industrial, rather than an architectural, approach to signage. Elevator floor-indicator panels, however, should receive special attention and be considered in a comprehensive signage program.

Fig. 11-49

Fig. 11-50

Fig. 11-51

LEXICON OF SIGNAGE SYSTEM COMPONENTS

Many signing devices are produced to meet specific needs. Graphics reproduction techniques and available materials cover a wide spectrum of choice. The designer will want to become both familiar with standard devices produced by manufacturers and knowledgeable about the methodology utilized in the various signage system components. Each of the sign devices discussed in this section may be subdivided and expanded upon to include every signing device required in a comprehensive system.

Elevated Pylons

Primary identification signs and product promotional signs used in commercial applications customarily are exhibited as internally illuminated, metal sign cabinets with embossed acrylic plastic faces, mounted on structural elevated posts (Figure 11-53). Too frequently this type of sign contributes to the visual pollution and clutter prevalent along streets and highways because of lack of controls. These signs are usually too large, too garish, too bright, and lacking design sensitivity. The architect rarely has the opportunity to become involved in the design and execution of commercially oriented, elevated pylon signs. But when the occasion does present itself, careful consideration should be given to criteria for the sign, determination of size and mounting height, material and color selections, and local codes controlling such signs.

Exterior elevated pylon-type signs may be engineered with one or two poles as desired. These support columns are structural steel members engineered for the sign-loading conditions, and penetrate through the bottom of the sign cabinet up through the sign to the top filler. Internal structural supports within the cabinet are mechanically fastened to the support columns.

All plastic sign faces must have tolerances for expansion and contraction within the retainer to prevent cracking and breakage. Large exterior sign faces must have internal-face wind braces or tiebacks to prevent loss due to wind loading.

Fig. 11-52

Fig. 11-53

Fig. 11-54

Fig. 11-55   **Fig. 11-56**

Monolithic Sign Structures

Advances in materials technology and methods of graphic reproduction have resulted in the development of sign structures that appear "monolithic" and that offer the designer a great deal of freedom in selecting shapes, sizes, colors, and graphics. These monoliths may be fabricated from steel or aluminum plate with continuous welds that are ground smooth prior to finishing (Figure 11-54). Copy may be in dimensional applied letters, or in painted or die-cut pressure-sensitive letters for non-illuminated signs; the words or symbols may be precision-cut out of the metal face and backed up with translucent acrylic for internally illuminated monoliths. Letterforms are precision-cut to fit exactly into the letter cutout in the metal face, and are chemically bonded to a clear acrylic back panel which is secured into the sign structure. Care must be exercised in specifying the attachment method to allow for the difference in the expansion and contraction of the dissimilar materials.

Monoliths are also fabricated from fiber-reinforced plastic. The designer may select sculptural shapes and have them reproduced as molded fiberglass structures in which the graphics may be an integral part of the sign, subsurface-embedded, screen-printed, or surface-applied (Figures 11-55 and 11-56). Polyurethane coatings are used to achieve a large variety of colors and to offer a tough, vandal-resistant finish. A unique advantage of this construction technique is the repairability feature not available in other signing mediums. Ultraviolet inhibitors used in the polyurethane coatings prevent excessive fading, and the monoliths maintain a good appearance for an exceptional period of time. Clear glass strands and translucent colors ensure an internal illumination capability, yielding smooth, evenly illuminated surfaces.

These seamless monoliths are internally reinforced with fiberglass pultrusions, and a system of "ribbing" is used to control the "oil canning" effect prevalent in metal monolithic structures (Figure 11-57). Fiber-reinforced plastic monoliths, while relatively new in the sign industry, are exceptional structures with features not available in most other materials.

Interior monolithic signs may be constructed of plywood, acrylic plastic with chemically bonded edges, or particle board covered with plastic laminate. The designer

Mounting Details
Ground, Slab

Drawings
A Elevation-Section
B Mounting Detail
  Ground-Mounted
C Mounting Detail
  Slab-Mounted

Notes
1 Fiberglass Shell
2 High Output Fluorescent Lamps
3 Electrical Raceway
4 Welded Steel Frame
5 800 MA High Power Factor Ballast
6 Fiberglass Straps
7 Disconnect Switch
8 Anchor Bolts with Leveling Nuts
9 Grout
10 Poured Concrete Foundation
11 Anchor in Shield
12 Concrete Slab
13 Primary Wiring
14 Earth

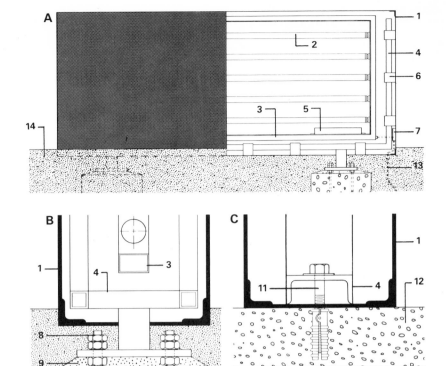

Access Panels, Inserts

Aluminum panels for access to electrical
components, and for re-lamping purposes
are located in one side of the monolith.
Panels located on the top of a unit must be
mechanically fastened to the fiberglass shell,
while panels located on a vertical surface
may be hinged. Extruded aluminum cases for
the display of posters, schedules or diagrams, may also be incorporated into the
monolithic structure.

Drawings
A Access Panel
B Hinged Access Panel
C Inset Directory Case
D Inset Panel

Notes
1 Fiberglass Shell
2 Fiberglass Reinforcing Angle
3 Aluminum Plate, 1/8" Thick
4 Countersunk Screw with Perimeter Gasket
5 Stainless Steel Cam Lock
6 Stainless Steel Continuous Hinge
7 Aluminum Framed Directory Case
8 Fiberglass Removable Panel

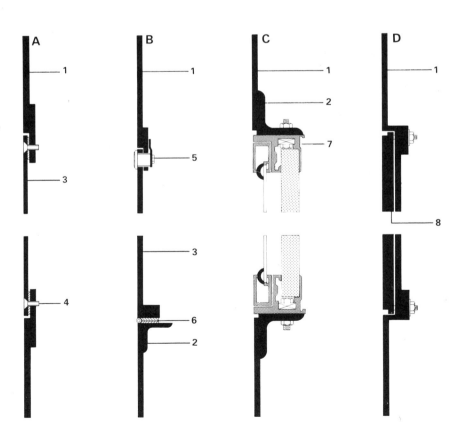

Fig. 11-57

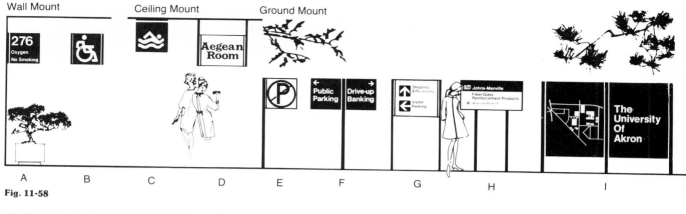

Fig. 11-58

Fig. 11-59

Fig. 11-60

should evaluate the advantages of each possible method of construction and graphic application technique to best meet the criteria established for the system.

Monolithic structures, offering a contemporary approach with many design alternatives, should be considered for identification signs, informational kiosk units, and primary directional signs.

Panel and Post Systems

Exterior signs that are used to identify, direct, control, and inform vehicular traffic consist of sign panels mounted mechanically to one or more support posts (Figure 11-58). Panel sizes usually range from 1 square foot to 40 square feet in area, secured to posts of adequate section modulus to withstand prevalent wind loading— usually 30 to 35 pounds per square foot. Panels may be flat sheet material utilizing aluminum, steel, fiber-reinforced plastic, acrylic plastic, or exterior plywood. Greater strength and durability, especially for large sign panels, may be obtained by selecting dimensionally reinforced panels constructed of fabricated or molded fiber-reinforced "pans" that encapsulate a fibrous core material for structural integrity (Figures 11-59 and 11-60). Other systems include aluminum extrusions designed to hold flat

407

Illuminated
2 Post Mount

Aluminum panels for access to electrical components, and for relamping purposes are located on either the top or the bottom of internally illuminated signs. Service panels located on the top of a unit must be mechanically fastened to the fiberglass shell, while panels located on the bottom may be hinged.

Drawings
A Partial Elevation
B Section

Notes
1 Aluminum Post
2 Aluminum Channel
3 Fiberglass Shell
4 Wood Blocking
5 Bolt and Nut
6 Electrical Raceway
7 High Output Fluorescent Lamp
8 Plastic Plug at Bolt Location

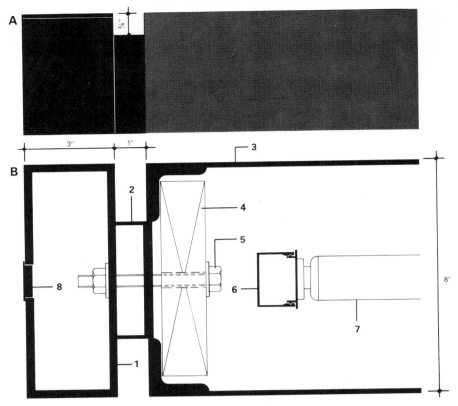

Non-Illuminated
2 Post and Flag Mount

Panels for non-illuminated signs may be either 2″ or 3″ thick, with a corresponding aluminum post. A number of variable factors such as sign panel size, overall sign height, wind load requirements and mounting conditions should be taken into consideration when determining panel thickness. Please contact the factory directly, or your local sales representative, for specific applications.

Drawings
A Partial Elevation
B Section
C Section

Notes
1 Aluminum Post
2 Aluminum Connector
3 Fiberglass Panel with Honeycomb Core

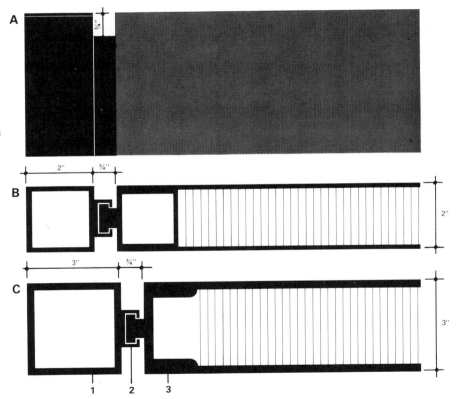

Fig. 11-61

408

sheet faces, giving a dimensional panel effect that may also be internally reinforced for added strength. Many sign manufacturers offer standard panel and post assemblies with a variety of features. The designer may specify those that will best meet the design criteria selected for the particular project (Figure 11-61).

Illuminated Sign Cabinets

Most national manufacturers of illuminated sign cabinets for architectural applications employ aluminum extrusions in the construction of the sign cabinet (Figure 11-62). Components include the sign filler, face retainers, and raceway extrusion, which are engineered to snap together or lock in position by the use of mechanical fasteners. Some cabinets feature concealed fasteners exclusively and are designed with narrow depth fillers for a slim-line, contemporary appearance; others are engineered to withstand severe exterior loading conditions and require much deeper fillers and other structural components. Standard systems have been developed for sign sizes up to 240 square feet in area, utilizing aluminum extrusions.

Several manufacturers have patented designs for sign cabinets for use in interior spaces. The filler depth is only 3⅝ inches and consists of a one-piece extrusion that serves as the filler, face retainer, and raceway (Figure 11-63). Each system features ease of access for service and mountings for flush or projected wall or ceiling conditions.

Most exterior applications receive an acrylic enamel paint or polyurethane coating, while most interior cabinets are finished in the standard duranodic colors.

Internal illumination consists of T12 high-output fluorescent lamps properly spaced for even illumination, powered by a 800-milliampere, high-power-factor ballast properly engineered for the temperature requirements of a given locality. Smaller interior units often utilize incandescent or fluorescent lighting with rapid starters in lieu of ballasts.

Sign faces may be embossed or debossed custom-decorated acrylic, silk-screen-printed acrylic, or acrylic panels with pressure-sensitive messages or dimensional graphics surface applied. Film negatives may be inserted between two pieces of acrylic—a translucent acrylic back panel and a lens of matte colorless acrylic, solar gray or solar bronze acrylic. Theatrical gels of red, green, blue, yellow, and amber may be inserted behind the negative into the "sandwich," should colored lettering be desired when using this film negative system.

Faces may also be fiber-reinforced plastic featuring subsurface graphics (Figure 11-64), or they may be aluminum panels with cutout copy backed up with translucent acrylic. Some manufacturers offer stained glass and etched glass faces for decorative applications (Figure 11-65).

The method of holding the face to the filler depends upon the extrusion selected and the face material. Normally, the face will be held in position by a retainer, which may be an integral part of an extruded filler, or a separate retainer that snaps and locks into the filler with spring clips or mechanical fasteners (Figures 11-66 through 11-68).

Directory and Information Systems

The type of information to be exhibited determines the style of the directory unit to be specified. Directory units consist of a housing and inserts, selected to define the usage requirements of the directory most effectively.

Fig. 11-62

Fig. 11-63

Fig. 11-64

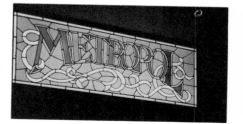

Fig. 11-65

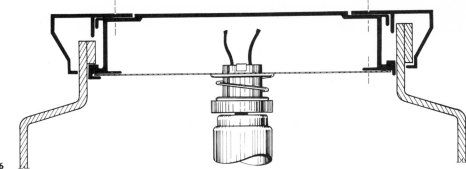

Fig. 11-66

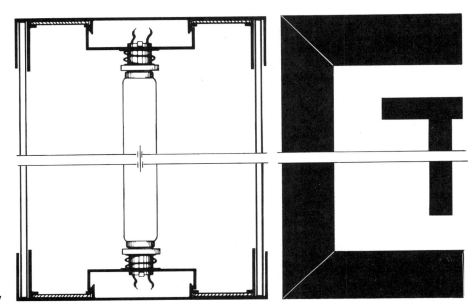

Fig. 11-67

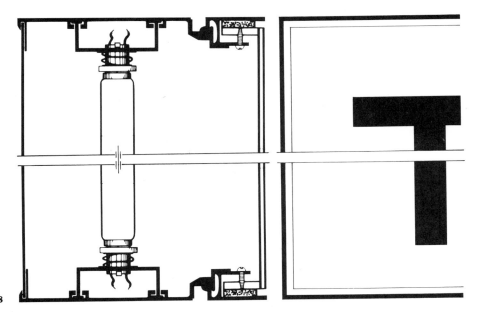

Fig. 11-68

The specifier will first consider the standard assortment of available inserts that clearly display the information to be presented. Directory inserts may be:

Changeable strips

1. Acrylic plastic strips with engraved, imprinted, or silk-screen-printed lettering, which are individually stacked and friction-held at each end for ease of changeability, are the most commonly used directory inserts.

2. Metal strips with pressure-sensitive applied, silk-screen-printed, or transfer-type lettering are held in position on the back panel with magnetic tape and are easily removed.

3. Film negative strips, consisting of a molded plastic carriage which receives the film negative strip and support liner and interlocks with each adjacent carriage to prevent light leaks, are easily replaced (Figure 11-69).

Changeable letters

Injection-molded plastic letters are individually positioned onto a grooved background to form the copy required (Figure 11-70). The background may be grooved plywood covered with felt in a variety of colors, or molded rubber (available in black, brown, and gray only). Individual molded characters are available in several styles in white, red, yellow, orange, green, blue, and black, and in ⅜-, ½-, ¾-, 1, 1¼-, 1½-, 1¾-, and 2¼-inch sizes. They are shipped in compartmentized storage boxes that are indexed to facilitate easy utilization.

Cork bulletin panels

Paper inserts may be tacked to a cork bulletin panel using thumbtacks, tack pins, or map pins (Figure 11-71). The panel may be natural

Fig. 11-70

Fig. 11-69

Fig. 11-71

Fig. 11-72

exposed cork, or it may be vinyl-covered, using the standard patterns and colors available in the industry, to produce a more durable, longer-wearing tack surface.

Pictorial maps   Silk-screen-printed acrylic panels or film negative inserts may be utilized as "You Are Here" pictorial maps or schematic diagrams that provide visual aid in complicated architectural corridor patterns.

Combination inserts   A combination of any number of the above inserts may be utilized within the same directory frame system where multiple usage is desired (Figure 11-72).

Directory housings   Aluminum extrusions, acrylic plastic, bronze, and hardwood such as oak, walnut, or teak, may be used for directory housing.

Aluminum Extrusions   Designed to serve as an overall outer frame and as an inner door frame, aluminum extrusions are available from manufacturers specializing in the production of directories and bulletin boards. They offer a wide range of designs, sizes, and finishes to meet most requirements. The aluminum extrusions are precision-mitered at the corners and reinforced with concealed angle brackets to prevent "racking" and to ensure structural integrity. Doors are held secure to the outer frame by a continuous piano hinge and either a cam lock, spring latch, or magnetic catch, depending on the design of the directory unit. Glazing is usually double-strength glass as standard, with an extruded vinyl moulding, set into the door frame extrusion. Tempered glass and Lexan polycarbonate sheet are available from most manufacturers upon request. Standard aluminum finishes include satin natural anodized, dur-anodic bronze, and black. Three designs are typical of units available from directory manufacturers: Style A; Style B; and Style C (Figures 11-73 through 11-75).

Style A features individual modular panels which may be grouped to form as many directory modules as required with a separate header panel to span the number of modules selected, or multiple panels may be contained within one master outer frame. Inserts may be changeable, or permanent pictorial map inserts can be used (Figure 11-76).

Style B features an aluminum extrusion with an outer frame separated from an inner frame by an acrylic reveal (Figure 11-77). The entire frame swings on concealed pivot hinges with a lock located on the side of the frame. All inserts may be utilized in this style.

Style C frames feature a door frame set into the master frame. It swings on a full-length piano hinge, locked with a disc tumbler-type lock (Figure 11-78). This type of

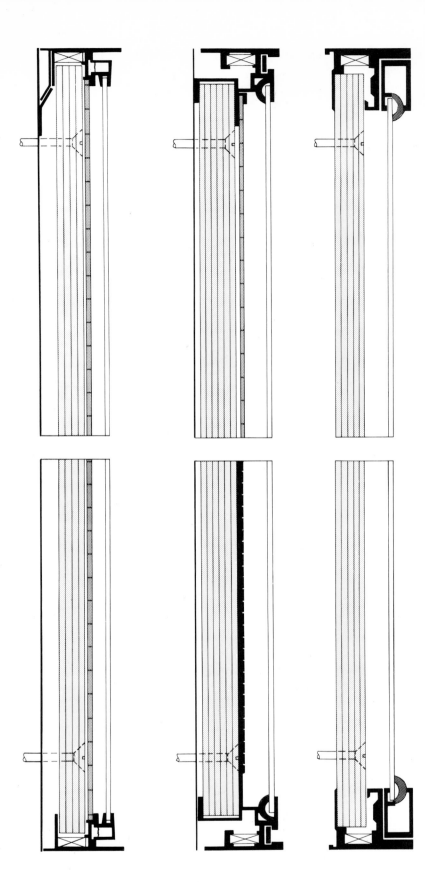

Fig. 11-73

Fig. 11-74

Fig. 11-75

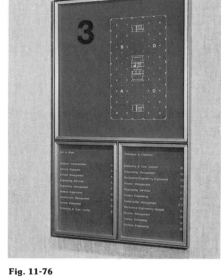

Fig. 11-76

Fig. 11-77

Fig. 11-78

design is required where strength considerations are a factor. Any insert may be selected.

Standard frame heights for the aluminum-framed styles A, B, and C with corresponding acrylic name-strip capacities are:

Frame height	24 in	30 in	36 in	42 in	48 in
Strip capacity	45	56	68	80	92

Units are available with a 5-inch high integral header panel which, if used, will decrease by 10 the number of strips shown. All units are available in any of the heights shown with the following frame widths, determined by the number of panels selected. All sizes are predicated upon the standard acrylic strip size of 7⅛ inches by ½ inch.

Number of Panels	***Style A***	***Style B (in inches)***	***Style C***
1	8½	9¼	9⅞
2	17	16½	12½
3	25½	23¾	24⅜
4	34½	31	31⅝
5	42½	38¼	38⅞

Changeable letter and cork bulletin inserts are available in the following standard sizes:

Styles B and C (single door)	***Style C (double door)***	***Style C (triple door)***
18 × 24 inches	48 × 36 inches	90 × 36 inches
20 × 30 inches	60 × 36 inches	108 × 36 inches
36 × 36 inches	72 × 36 inches	108 × 48 inches
36 × 48 inches	72 × 48 inches	

All units may be flush wall-mounted or recessed-mounted; however, style B must have a reveal around the directory large enough to allow the door to open fully. Styles A and B may be mounted on free-standing aluminum standards. All units feature a metal housing containing the electrical requirements for internal illumination.

Style D aluminum extrusions are also utilized for directories designed for "in-house" strip maintainability (Figures 11-79 and 11-80). This concept features a back panel containing mounting pins and a spring-loaded device, and a front assembly holding the name strips to which heat-resistant transferable lettering is applied. Using a name-strip guide and a preprinted lettering sheet, names may be quickly burnished onto the name strips. Removal of obsolete copy is easily accomplished with cellulose tape, leaving the name strip clean for reuse. The metal strips are held in position by magnetic sheeting laminated to the back panel. The anodized aluminum frame is available in natural satin, dark bronze, and black. Name strips are available in bronzetone or matte black. Glazing may be ⅛-inch glass or acrylic plastic. White transfer lettering sheets are available in ¼-inch and ½-inch Helvetica Medium, Clarendon,

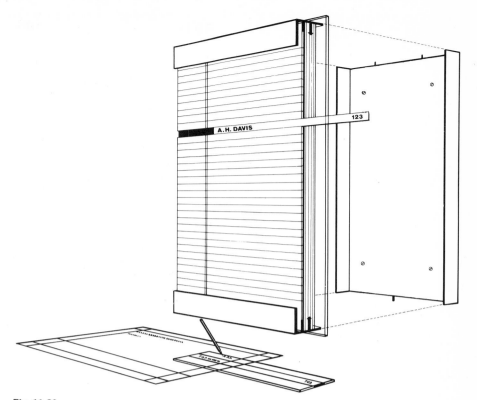

Fig. 11-80

Fig. 11-79

Fig. 11-81

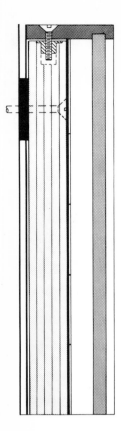

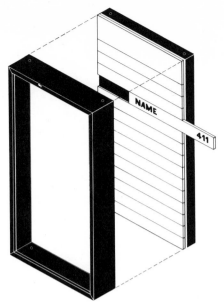

Fig. 11-83

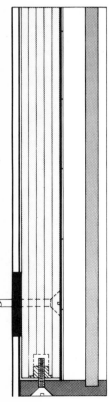

Fig. 11-82

Craw Modern, and Eurostile upper- and lowercase. Standard sizes are 12⅜ inches by 24½ inches, with 40 name strips 12 inches by ½ inch, and 12⅜ inches by 12⅜ inches, with 10 name strips 12 inches by ¾ inch (Figure 11-81).

Directory Modules   These may be fabricated with an acrylic or hardwood frame, complete with acrylic or glass glazing to form a single-piece case that is mechanically fastened to a plywood back panel (Figures 11-82 and 11-83). Inserts may be painted metal magnetic strips with transfer or die-cut pressure-sensitive lettering, or acrylic strips attached to the back panel with double-faced tape. Pictorial maps, plans, or schematic diagrams may be screen-printed on acrylic sheets and inserted into the system. Changeable letters for cork bulletin inserts are also available. Cases may be fabricated with depths suitable for the display of exhibit pieces, art collections, etc. Cases may be fabricated in any size up to 48 inches square from acrylic plastic or select woods. Glazing for both is clear, bronze, or gray acrylic (Figure 11-84).

Die-Cut Pressure-Sensitive Lettering

Individual characters are die-cut from pressure-sensitive elastomeric film, prespaced and prealigned on a transfer carrier, and applied to the sign substrate as a single unit. They may be applied to any sound, clean, smooth, and dry surface, and will withstand exterior conditions (Figures 11-85 through 11-87). The film is produced by several national manufacturers as roll goods in a variety of standard colors, in .003-inch thickness. Reflective material is also available. The letterforms are die-cut, using steel rule-edged dies, or they may be reproduced from photographic dies. A large selection of styles and sizes is offered by firms specializing in this technique. The following offering is representative:

Name	Size in inches
Avant Garde Medium	¾, 1, 1¼
Avant Garde Bold	¾, 1, 1¼,

Fig. 11-84

Fig. 11-85

Fig. 11-86

Fig. 11-87

Name	Size in inches
Blippo	1, 1½, 2, 3, 4
Caslon Regular	¼, ⅜, ½, ⅝, ¾, 1, 1⅜, 1½, 2, 3
Clarendon Bold	⅜, ½, ¾, 1, 1½, 2, 3, 4
Clarendon Condensed (caps)	½, ¾, 1, 1½, 2, 3, 4
Craw Clarendon	½, ¾, 1, 1½, 2, 3, 4
Eurostile Normal	½, 1
Eurostile Bold	1¼
Futura Medium	¾, 1, 1½, 2, 3
Helvetica Light	⅜, ½, ¾, 1, 1½, 2, 2½
Helvetica Medium	¼, ⁵⁄₁₆, ⅜, ½, ⅝, ¾, 1, 1¼, 1½, 2, 2½, 3, 4, 5, 6, 8, 10, 12, 14, 16, 18, 20, 22, 24, 30, 36, 48
Microgramma Bold Extended	⅛, ½, ¾, 1, 1½, 2, 3, 4

Tight Letterspacing
Normal Letterspacing
Wide Letterspacing

Fig. 11-88

Optima	¾, 1, 1½, 2, 3
Optima Semi Bold (caps)	½, ¾, 1
Optima Semi Bold (caps and lowercase)	1½
Palatino	¾, 1, 2
Rhonda Bold	½, ¾, 1, 1½, 1¾, 3
Times Roman	⅜, ½, ¾, 1, 1½, 2, 3½
Univers 55	⅛, 1, 1½, 3
Univers 63	½, ¾, 1½, 1¾, 2, 3½
Univers 65	½, ¾, 1, 1½, 2
Univers 67	½, ¾, 1, 1½, 2

The designer is free to specify interletter and word spacing. Standard spacing usually specified is "tight," "normal," or "wide" (Figure 11-88).

Standard colors available include white, orange, red, blue, green, gold, silver, bronze, copper, chrome, and brushed aluminum. Special colors such as tan or dark bronzetone may be silk-screen printed on white film and clear-coated. Any color may be custom-color-matched.

Several manufacturers produce die-cut letters as individual units mounted on a self-alignment tile, packaged in compartmentized boxes. Letter styles and sizes are limited, but the advantages of an "instant sign making" capability for replacement lettering are obvious (Figures 11-89 through 11-92).

Characters may be reverse-cut for application to the inside of glass. Normally, only white and black are offered as color selections for this purpose, and only in selected letter styles, such as Helvetica Medium.

Dimensional Graphics

Individual graphic elements applied to a wall, transom, parapet, or other vertical surface are used primarily for identification purposes.

Precision-cut elements

Aluminum Plate   Lettering is precisely hand-cut from aluminum plate material on a band saw (Figure 11-93).

Letterforms:	Any letterform or logotype
Finishes:	Natural satin, bright satin alumilite, duranodic, baked enamel, and porcelain enamel
Heights:	2 to 48 inches
Thicknesses:	⅛, ³⁄₁₆, ¼, ⅜, and ½ inch

Bronze Plate   Lettering is precisely hand-cut from bronze plate material (Figure 11-94).

Letterforms: Any letterform or logotype

Fig. 11-89

Fig. 11-90

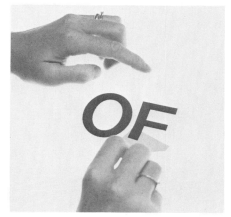

Fig. 11-91

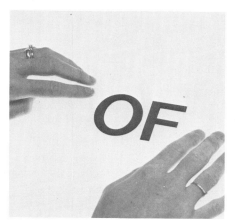

Fig. 11-92

Fig. 11-93

Fig. 11-94

Finishes: Natural satin, oxidized, and polished. Special finishes, including polished or satin chrome, silver plate, gold plate, and nickel plate.

Heights: 2 to 24 inches

Thicknesses: ⅛, ³⁄₁₆, ¼, ⅜, and ½ inch

Metal Laminate Thin metal sheeting is bonded to acrylic or tempered hardboard; letterforms are precisely cut out, using a set of master fonts on a pantograph machine. The edges of the letters may have sharp 90° returns, or they may be beveled, depending on the cutting tool used in the cutting process (Figure 11-95).

Letterforms: The following represent standard styles available from manufacturers specializing in this process

Condensed Block
Condensed Clarendon
Copperplate
Copperplate Extended
Craw Clarendon
Craw Clarendon Book
Craw Modern
Eurostile Bold Extended
Eurostile Normal
Hellenic Wide Extended
Helvetica Medium
Helvetica Regular
Microgramma Bold Extended
Optima
Venus Bold Extended

Finishes: Face finishes include natural satin, anodized aluminum, polished aluminum, duranodic bronze, satin bronze or brass, polished bronze or brass. Edges of the letters are painted in the color desired.

Fig. 11-95

Fig. 11-96   Fig. 11-97   Fig. 11-98

Heights: ¾ to 9 inches
Thicknesses: ⅛, ¼, and ½ inch

Metal-Faced Wood   Metal laminate is bonded to wood and cut to desired letterforms on a band saw. The edges are sanded smooth, primed, and painted in the color desired (Figure 11-96).

Letterforms: Any letterform or logotype.
Finishes: Face finishes include natural satin anodized aluminum, polished aluminum, duranodic bronze, satin bronze or brass, polished bronze or brass. Special finishes are mirror-finish gold and silver. Edges of the letters are painted in the color desired.
Heights: 4 to 24 inches
Thicknesses: ½, ¾, 1, 1½, 2, and 4 inches, or any other standard wood thickness.

Wood   Seven-core marine plywood letters are cut on a band saw (Figure 11-97).

Letterforms: Any letterform or logotype
Finishes: Painted in any color required
Heights: 4 to 48 inches
Thicknesses: ½, ¾, 1, and 1½ inches

Plastic Laminate   Countertop material is precision-cut to a variety of letterforms using a pantograph engraving machine (Figure 11-98). Since engraving master fonts are required, lettering styles are limited. Manufacturers specializing in this technique offer the following styles as representative:

Letterforms:

Americana	Hellenic Wide	Peignot Demibold
Amelia	Helvetica Medium	Playbill
Blippo	Helvetica Regular	Standard Extended
Craw Clarendon Book	Libra	Stymie Medium
Craw Clarendon Condensed	Melior	Tribune
Eurostile Bold Extended	Microgramma Bold	Venus Bold Extended
Eurostile Extended	Microgramma Normal	
Fortuna Extra Bold	Optima	

421

Finishes: Any standard plastic laminate color or texture produced by firms specializing in laminates may be selected.
Heights: ½ to 6 inches
Thicknesses: ¹⁄₁₆ inch

Fiberglass Sheeting   Fiber-reinforced sheet material is precision cut on a band saw (Figure 11-99).

Letterforms: Any letterform or logotype
Finishes: Any standard colors offered by producers of the sheet material.
Heights: 4 to 48 inches
Thicknesses: .060, .090, and .125 inch

Acrylic Plastic   Letters are cut out with a pantograph engraving machine. Edges are normally beveled 2° or 3°, but some manufacturers offer the letters with 90° returns (Figure 11-100).

Letterforms: Standard letter styles for which engraving masters are available.
Finishes: Standard finish is gloss, and a satin or matte face is obtainable. All standard acrylic colors are available, including gold and silver metallic. Letters may also be painted, if desired.
Heights: ½ to 9 inches
Thicknesses: ¹⁄₁₆, ⅛, ³⁄₁₆, ¼, ⅜, and ½ inch

Fabricated elements

Aluminum   Letterforms are reproduced by cutting the desired shape out of aluminum sheet and welding a return around the letter perimeter to the depth desired (Figure 11-101).

Letterforms: Any letterform or logotype.

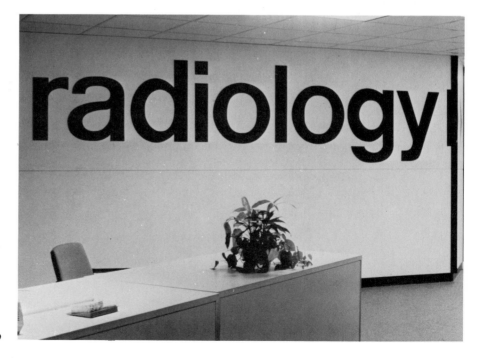

Fig. 11-99

Fig. 11-100

Fig. 11-101

Fig. 11-102

Finishes:	Baked enamel, clear satin anodized, duranodic bronze, and porcelain enamel.
Heights:	6 to 72 inches
Thicknesses:	1, 2, 3, 4, 6, 8, 10, and 12 inches. Letters up to 24 inches high may be fabricated from .063 gauge aluminum, while .087 gauge is standard for letters up to 72 inches in height.

Stainless Steel   Letters are custom-fabricated from Type 302, 18-8 alloy stainless steel sheeting. Faces are 18-gauge and returns are 22-gauge (Figure 11-102).

Letterforms:	Any letterform or logotype.
Finishes:	Satin or polished mirror finish
Heights:	8 to 60 inches
Thicknesses:	2, 2½, 3, and 4 inches

Paint Grip Steel   Letters are fabricated from paint grip steel and are available with 18-gauge faces and 22-gauge returns (Figure 11-103).

Letterforms:	Any letterform or logotype
Finishes:	Letters are painted with baked enamel or polyurethane in many standard colors.

Fig. 11-103

Fig. 11-104

Fig. 11-105

Heights: 8 to 60 inches
Thicknesses: 2, 2½, 3, and 4 inches

Bronze Muntz Metal   Letterforms are fabricated from 20-gauge Muntz metal (Figure 11-104).

Letterforms: Any letterform or logotype
Finishes: Satin bronze, light statuary and dark oxidized, all protected with clear lacquer coating.
Heights: 8 to 48 inches
Thicknesses: 2, 2½, 3, and 4 inches

Formed elements   Acrylic plastic is available, molded from sheet acrylic plastic employing a heating and vacuum forming process (Figure 11-105).

Letter styles: Catalogs indicating styles, sizes, stroke widths, and average character widths and depths are available from each manufacturer specializing in this process.
Finishes: Any standard acrylic color may be specified.

Heights and Depths:	Height (in inches)	Depth
	6–9	⅝
	12–15	⅞
	18	1
	24	1½
	36	2

Thicknesses: Plastic .125 inch thick is used for letters up to 24 inches high, and .187 inch thick is used for larger sizes.

Molded elements   Injected molded acrylic plastic letters are available with beveled edges, and may be decorated with mylar foils in metallic finishes (Figure 11-106).

<dl>
<dt>Letterforms:</dt>
<dd>Catalogs indicating styles, sizes, stroke widths, and average character widths and depths are available from each manufacturer specializing in this process.</dd>
<dt>Finishes:</dt>
<dd>Standard colors include black, white, red, and blue; many decorative-foil stamped finishes—silver, copper, and gold metallics, and cherry, oak, and maple woodgrains—are offered by several manufacturers.</dd>
<dt>Heights:</dt>
<dd>½ to 12 inches</dd>
<dt>Thickness:</dt>
<dd>.125 inch</dd>
</dl>

Cast elements

Polyester Decorative letters are cast in molds using polyester resins (Figure 11-107).

Fig. 11-106

Letterforms: Catalogs indicating styles, sizes, stroke widths, and average character widths and depths are available from each manufacturer specializing in this process.

Finishes: Letters are painted any color desired, or may be plated bronze, gold, pewter, or bright chrome, using a special metalizing process.

Heights: 1 to 18 inches

Thicknesses: Letter thicknesses range from ⅛-inch for 1-inch-high letters to 1½ inches for letters 18 inches in height.

Aluminum Cast aluminum characters are cast from #43 alloy ingots for letters receiving a baked enamel, natural satin, or porcelain finish, and from F-214 alloy ingots for letters receiving a satin Alumilite finish (Figure 11-108).

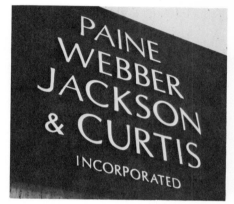

Fig. 11-107

Letterforms: Catalogs indicating styles, sizes, stroke widths, and average character widths and depths are available from each manufacturer specializing in this process.

Finishes: Baked enamel, natural satin or porcelain enamel, satin Alumilite.

Heights: 1 to 16 inches

Thicknesses: Letter depth depends on the style and height of the letter, and also varies from manufacturer to manufacturer.

Bronze Cast bronze characters are cast from architectural bronze ingots containing 85 percent copper, 5 percent tin, 5 percent lead, and 5 percent zinc (Figure 11-109).

Fig. 11-108

Letterforms: Letters are available in the same alphabet selections as offered for cast aluminum.

Finishes: Satin, oxidized, or polished finish as standard satin and polished chrome, and silver, gold, and nickel plate are special offerings.

Heights: 1 to 16 inches

Thicknesses: Letter depth depends on the style and height of the letter, and also varies from manufacturer to manufacturer.

Other custom processes may be employed for the reproduction of dimensional graphics. The above listing is representative of the major product offerings available, however.

Dimensional graphics may be flush-mounted or projected from the wall surface, using mechanical studs and spacer sleeves, or they may be flush-mounted, using

Fig. 11-109

Drawing Key

A Vertical cross section of precision cut letter with adhesive mount
B Vertical cross section of precision cut letter with concealed threaded stud flush mount
C Vertical cross section of precision cut letter with concealed threaded stud and spacer project mount
D Vertical cross section of fabricated metal letter with concealed flush mechanical mount using expansion screw anchors
E Vertical cross section of fabricated metal letter with concealed threaded stud project mount
F Vertical cross section of internally illuminated metal letter with a plastic face showing concealed mount using lag screw expansion shields and a PK housing

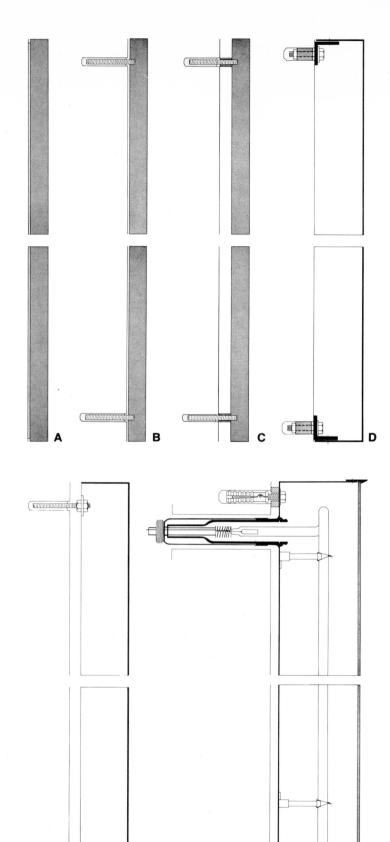

Fig. 11-110

Fig. 11-111

Fig. 11-112

Fig. 11-113

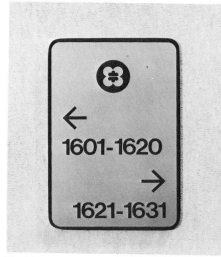

Fig. 11-114

Fig. 11-115

Fig. 11-116

adhesive or double-sided neoprene tape. Size, weight, and design intent must be considered in specifying the proper mounting technique (Figure 11-110).

Plaque Signage

Architectural plaques may be manufactured from acrylic and phenolic plastic, fiber-reinforced plastic, aluminum, bronze, brass, stainless steel, Muntz metal, wood, or vinyl in any desired size and many colors. Legend techniques include engraved, imprinted, screen-printed, etched and dimensional applied (Figure 11-111 through 11-117).

Custom plaques, unframed or framed with aluminum, wood, or cast polyester frames, are in any material and legend technique applicable to that material. Mounting brackets, desk bases and bars, milled insert slots, etc., may be utilized with most plaque selections.

The following planning system chart may aid in the selection of plaque materials (A through K), legend techniques (1 through 9), frames, brackets, and mounting techniques (Figure 11-118).

Fig. 11-117

427

Planning System

Plaque Material / Legend Technique / Frames / Bases & Brackets / Mounting

Plaque Material	1	2	3	4	5	6	7	8	9	10a	10b	11	12	13	14	15	16	17	18	19	20	21
A Acrylic Plastic	•	•	•	•	•		•			•	•	•	•	•	•	•	•	•	•	•	•	•
B Phenolic Plastic	•		•	•			•			•	•	•	•	•	•	•			•	•	•	•
C Fiberlite (FRP)				•	•		•			•	•	•	•	•	•	•			•	•	•	•
D Aluminum	•		•	•		•	•													•	•	•
E Bronze	•		•	•		•	•													•	•	•
F Brass	•		•	•		•	•													•	•	•
G Stainless Steel	•		•	•		•	•													•	•	•
H Muntz Metal						•						•								•	•	•
I Wood	•	•	•	•		•	•			•		•	•	•						•	•	•
J Vinyl		•	•	•	•					•	•	•	•	•	•	•	•	•		•	•	•
K Photographic Film								•	•				•							•	•	•

Legend (columns 1–21):
1 Engraved, 2 Imprinted, 3 Silk Screened, 4 Die-cut Legends, 5 Subsurface Printed, 6 Etched, 7 Dimensional Applied, 8 Negative Exposure, 9 Positive Exposure, 10a Aluminum Frame (1/16"), 10b Aluminum Frame (1/8"), 11 Wooden Frame (5/16"), 12 MultiFrame, 13 UniFrame, 14 Slanted Desk Base, 15 Vertical Desk Bar, 16 Desk Bar, 17 Molded Desk Unit, 18 Project Bracket, 19 Neoprene Tape, 20 Panel Adhesive, 21 Mechanical

Fig. 11-118   1   2   3   4   5   6   7   8   9   10a 10b 11   12   13   14   15   16   17 18   19   20   21

Plaque materials and sizes Sign sizes are limited only by the standard sheet sizes available from the manufacturers as follows: (thickness and size in inches)

A. Acrylic plastic (1/16, 1/8, 3/16, 1/4)	48 × 96
B. Phenolic plastic (1/16 or 1/8)	36 × 84
C. Fiber reinforced plastic (.020, .040, .060, .125, .187, .250)	48 × 144
D. Aluminum (.040, .063, .090, .125, .187, .250)	48 × 144
E. Bronze (.040, .125)	24 × 120
F. Brass (.040, .125)	24 × 120
G. Stainless steel (.040, .125)	48 × 144
H. Muntz metal (.043, .063, .090, .125, .187, .250)	36 × 96
I. Wood (1/4, 1/2, 3/4, 1 1/2)	48 × 96
J. Vinyl (.015)	21 × 50
K. Photographic film (.004)	20 × 24

Plaque colors Materials with integral color cast into the sheet are available in standard colors manufactured by the supplier; e.g., acrylic, phenolic. Materials which are painted—aluminum, clear acrylic, wood, and vinyl—may be sprayed in any color desired.

Legend techniques and letter sizes

  1. Engraved, 1/4 inch through 6 inches—Precision-incised into the plaque surface, using a pantograph machine.

2. Imprinted, ⁵⁄₁₆ inch through 1 inch—Mylar film .003 inch thick, impressed into the plaque surface under heat and pressure.

3. Silk-screened, no size limitation—Durable inks surface-applied, employing screen-printing techniques.

4. Die-cut legends, ½ inch through 6 inches—Elastomeric film .003-inch thick, with pressure-sensitive backing surface applied.

5. Subsurface printed, no size limitation—Silk-screened inks printed on second surface with background color oversprayed.

6. Etched, no limitation—Acid bath yields raised or recessed copy approximately .006 inch deep in Muntz metal. Aluminum is photo-etched, and wood is mechanically milled or sand-blasted.

7. Dimensional Applied, ¾ inch through 9 inches—Precision-cut with aluminum, brass, bronze, or acrylic faces and bonded to plaque surface.

8. Negative Exposure, 20 by 24 inches—Photographic exposure on film .004 inch thick, inserted into message frame.

9. Positive Exposure, 20 by 24 inches—Photographic exposure on film .004 inch thick, inserted into message frame.

Custom art or corporate marks may be reproduced by all nine techniques enumerated above.

Letter styles   The following styles are standard for the legend techniques (1 through 9) enumerated in the planning system chart:

Americana	1,3,5,6,8,9
Americana Italic	3,5,6,8,9
Avant Garde Medium	3,4,5,6,8,9
Baskerville Bold Italic	3,5,6,8,9
Bodoni	3,5,6,8,9
Bookman	3,5,6,8,9
Century Schoolbook	2,3,5,6,8,9
Columbus	3,5,6,8,9
Copperplate Gothic Light	3,5,6,7,8,9
Craw Clarendon	2,3,4,5,6,7,8,9
Craw Clarendon Book	1,2,3,5,6,7,8,9
Craw Modern	2,3,5,6,7,8,9
Eurostile	3,4,5,7,8,9
Eurostile Bold	2,3,4,5,6,8,9
Eurostile Bold Extended	1,2,3,5,7,8,9
Eurostile Extended	1,3,5,6,8,9
Firmin Didot	3,5,6,8,9
Folio Medium	3,5,6,8,9

Fig. 11-119

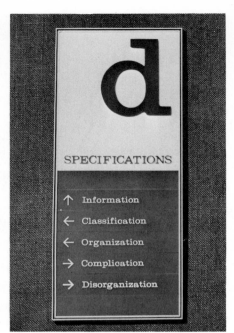

Fig. 11-120

Fig. 11-121

Fig. 11-122

Franklin Gothic	3,5,6,8,9
Garamond Bold	3,5,6,8,9
Helvetica Light	3,4,5,6,7,8,9
Helvetica Medium	1,2,3,4,5,6,7,8,9
Helvetica Outline	3,5,6,8,9
Helvetica Regular	1,2,3,4,5,6,7,8,9
Lutetia	3,5,6,8,9
Melior	1,2,3,5,6,8,9
Melior Semi Bold	3,5,6,8,9
Microgramma	1,2,3,5,6,8,9
Microgramma Bold	1,3,5,6,8,9

Microgramma Bold Extended	3,4,5,6,7,8,9
Optima	1,3,4,5,6,7,8,9
Optima Semi Bold	2,3,4,5,6,8,9
Palatino Semi Bold	3,4,5,6,8,9
Standard Medium	3,5,6,8,9
Univers 53	3,5,6,8,9
Univers 55	3,4,5,6,8,9
Univers 56	3,5,6,8,9
Univers 63	3,4,5,6,8,9
Univers 65	3,4,5,6,8,9
Univers 67	3,4,5,6,8,9
Univers 83 Outline	3,4,5,6,8,9
Vanguard Medium	3,5,6,8,9
Venus	3,5,6,8,9
Venus Bold Extended	1,3,5,6,8,9
Venus Extra Bold Extended	3,5,6,8,9

Plaque frames Plaque frames are fabricated from aluminum angle extrusions, milled hardwood shapes, and acrylic (Figures 11-119 through 11-122). Some manufacturers produce cast polyester frames in limited sizes. The following frames are indicative of standards available within the industry. (Figure 11-123).

1. Aluminum frames with either a ⅟₁₆-inch or a ⅛-inch wall thickness are available with square or radiused corners. The interchangeable plaque insert is separated from the frame by a ³⁄₃₂-inch reveal. Frame finishes include clear satin, duranodic bronze, and black.

2. Hardwood frames with ⁵⁄₁₆-inch wall thickness are available only with square corners in any size required. The interchangeable plaque insert is separated from the wood frame by a ¼-inch reveal. Frames may be stained or painted any specified finish.

3. Name-plate holders fabricated from aluminum extrusions 1½, 2, 2½, 3, or 4 inches high by lengths required are available with satin natural, duranodic bronze, and black finish. Milled acrylic face lens may be clear, solar bronze, or solar gray acrylic, ¼-inch thick. Message inserts may be photographic paper or film positives or negatives, as desired.

4. Interlocking aluminum extrusions 3 inches high by the length required are available for application of pressure-sensitive die-cut legends, surface screen-printed graphics, or acrylic plaques laminated to face plates as desired. Back panels may be mechanically mounted, and matching face panels slide onto the back panel and lock into place with a set screw. Finishes include clear satin, duranodic bronze, and black.

Bases and brackets Bases and brackets are normally fabricated from extruded aluminum parts and assembled into a variety of shapes to provide the necessary

Fig. 11-123

Fig. 11-124

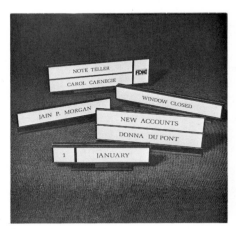

Fig. 11-125

Fig. 11-126

fixture to display the plaque insert at desk and counter locations (Figures 11-124 through 11-127).

1. Desk bases feature an aluminum support and base secured to an aluminum frame. Plaque inserts may be held in the frame with double-faced neoprene tape, double-faced foam tape, or special magnetic tape to allow rapid change. Finishes include clear satin, duranodic bronze, and black.

2. Vertical support with base is more legible for counter-height applications and may be double-faced, if desired.

3. Desk bars consist of aluminum bar extrusions normally 1½ inch by 1½ inch by the length required. The graphics may be pressure-sensitive die-cut legends or subsurface printed vinyl laminated to the face of the bar. Standard finishes are clear satin, duranodic bronze, and black.

4. Injection-molded acrylic frames 9 inches by 2 inches by ⅜ inch thick contain plastic plaques held magnetically into the frame. Graphics may be pressure-sensitive die-cut letters or screen-printed graphics. Frames are attached to one or both sides of weighted plaque bases to form the completed desk unit. Matte black and dark bronzetone are standard colors available.

5. Project brackets consist of two aluminum extrusions, concealed mounting base "T" bracket for project-mounting framed or unframed plaques on one or both sides. Brackets may be used for project-ceiling or project-wall installations. Finishes include clear satin, duranodic bronze, and black.

Mountings Plaque signage may be mounted to walls and doors with double-faced neoprene tape, double-faced foam tape, panel adhesive, or mechanical fasteners. A combination of double-faced tape and adhesive is advisable in some installations (Figure 11-128). The careful designer will consider the material to which the sign is to be mounted and the need for removability before specifying the best mounting attachment for a particular application.

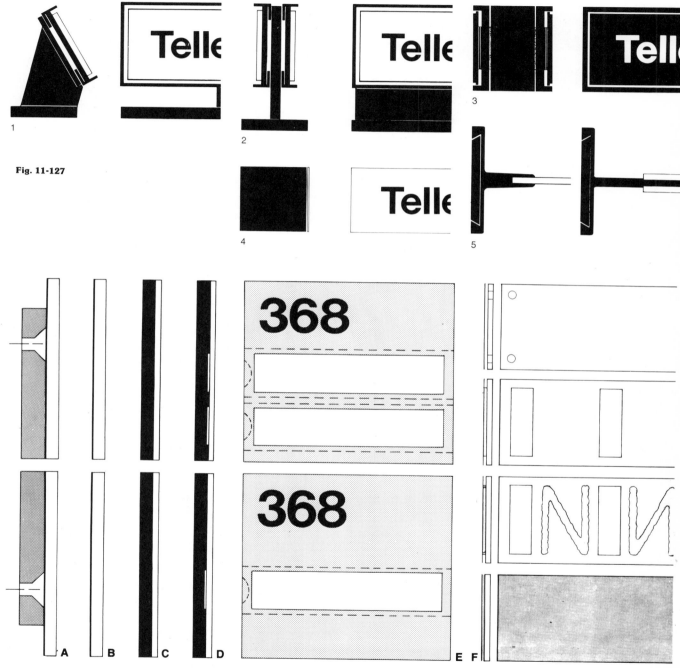

Fig. 11-127

Fig. 11-128

Drawing Key

A Cross section of a reverse screen printed acrylic plaque with ¼" thick mounting shim plate

B Cross section of a reverse screen printed acrylic plaque ⅛" thick

C Cross section of a reverse screen printed acrylic plaque 1/16" thick laminated to a ⅛" thick acrylic mounting base

D Cross section of a reverse screen printed acrylic plaque 1/16" thick laminated to a ⅛" thick acrylic mounting base with milled name slots to receive changeable inserts

E Elevations of acrylic insert type plaques showing one and two slots

F Plaque mounting details including (top to bottom) drilled holes for screw mounting, double sided tape, double sided tape and silicon adhesive, and magnetic sheeting

Letterstyles	Sizes												Case	
	¼"	5⁄16"	3⁄8"	½"	5⁄8"	¾"	7⁄8"	1"	1¼"	1½"	1¾"	2"	Caps	C/lc
CHATHAM		•	•	•	•			•	•	•		•	•	
Craw Clarendon			•	•	•	•		•		•			•	•
DEEP BLOCK CONDENSED	•	•	•	•	•	•	•	•	•	•	•	•	•	
Futura	•	•	•	•	•	•	•	•	•	•		•	•	•
GOTHIC	•	•	•	•	•	•	•	•	•	•		•	•	
Helvetica Regular			•	•	•	•		•	•	•		•	•	•
Helvetica Medium			•	•	•	•		•	•	•		•	•	•
Microgramma Bold Extended			•	•	•	•		•		•			•	•
ROMAN CLASSIC	•	•	•	•	•	•	•	•	•			•	•	
ROMAN CLASSIC CONDENSED			•	•	•	•	•	•	•	•	•	•	•	
ROMAN CLASSIC OVAL FACE	•	•	•	•	•	•	•	•	•	•		•	•	

Fig. 11-129

Cast plaques may be made from aluminum or bronze ingots, but their design must conform with the restraints of the industry concerning letter styles, sizes, and inter-letter spacing. Castings do not graphically offer the visual aesthetics available in photographic reproduction processes. Standard letter styles and sizes are available (Figure 11-129).

Standard borders, background textures, and mounts are available from manufacturers specializing in this process (Figure 11-130).

Environmental Graphics

Architectural spaces can become alive with well-designed and -executed decorative and colorful signs, supergraphics, murals, and banners. Graphic designs may be reproduced on aluminum, fiber-reinforced plastic, wood, acrylic, or canvas, or they may be surface-painted on location, using paints and inks that are compatible with the substrate to which they are applied. The accompanying photographs are examples of various materials methodology and graphic reproduction techniques (Figures 11-131 through 11-136).

This listing of signing devices may be further expanded or subdivided. But the lexicon covers the majority of the product considerations for comprehensive signage programs. The designer and the specifier will need to develop a working knowledge of these products and the manufacturers producing them. *Sweet's Architectural File,* sections 10.11a and 10.11b, contains catalog inserts of many of the nation's leading suppliers of signing devices and systems; also, many manufacturers provide catalogs not shown in Sweet's but available on direct request to the supplier. Such catalogs provide the nucleus of an invaluable resource library for the signage specifier.

Border Styles
Standard

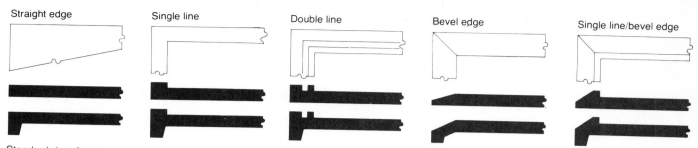

| Straight edge | Single line | Double line | Bevel edge | Single line/bevel edge |

Standard sizes for the above 5 border styles:
Size: 14" x 10," 16" x 10," 16" x 12," 18" x 12," 18" x 15," 24" x 12," 24" x 16," 24" x 18," 24" x 20," 28" x 18," 30" x 18," 30" x 20," 30" x 24," 36" x 24"

Special

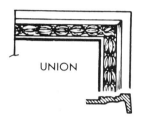
UNION

IVY LEAF

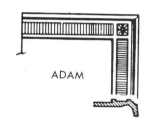
ADAM

Background Textures

Leatherette   Pebbled

Mounts

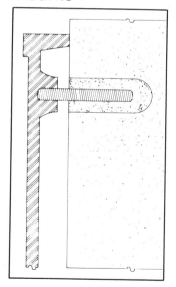

Bosses and studs BS-1 for concealed mounting to brick or stone walls.

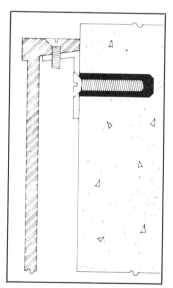

Invisible frame IF-2 Angle frame used with wood screws, toggle bolts, or machine screws and expansion sleeves for concealed mounting to any surface. Not available on plaques smaller than 14" x 10."

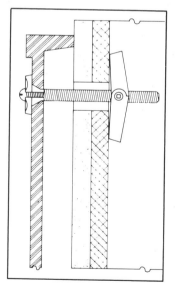

Rosette covers and toggle bolts RT-3 for plaster, hollow tile, or cement block walls.

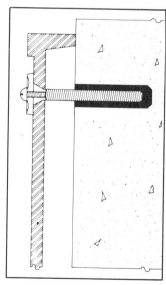

Rosette covers and expansion bolts RE-4 for brick, stone, or concrete walls.

Fig. 11-130

Fig. 11-131

Fig. 11-132

Fig. 11-135

Fig. 11-133

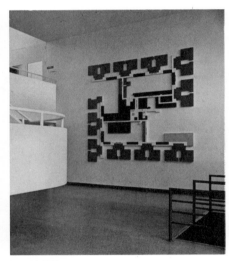

Fig. 11-134

Fig. 11-136

The correct selection of a signing device to fulfill each signage requirement on a project is paramount to a successful program. A project may have excellently defined design criteria with appropriately selected sign types. If the designated signing devices do not satisfy the criteria, however, the program will not be totally satisfactory. Materials technology and sign methodologies must be studied, learned, and understood prior to their application in the development of a rewarding comprehensive signage program.

DETERMINATION OF SIGN LOCATIONS

Exterior

A careful review of traffic flow patterns and procedures is essential, using the site plan as a reference. Field surveys to determine special conditions and visibility restrictions are helpful prior to establishing final sign locations. Each decision-making point should be defined on the site plan, and the need for "advance notice" signs should be determined. Traffic regulatory and control signage requirements will have to be defined as a function of the site utilization and management policy.

Interior

Architectural floor plans or furniture location plans are necessary in order to locate all the signs needed at decision-making intersections and areas requiring identification.

A symbol should be selected to represent the location of each signing device, indicating the exact location in plan view, the sign reference number, and the type of sign by function. Typical designs for this symbol are shown (Figure 11-137). The number above the line represents the consecutive sign number and the letter below the line indicates the sign type by function. The leader line is drawn to the exact sign location on the plan. Double-faced signs must have an additional identifier indicating faces (a) and (b) of the sign. All the sign locations should be determined and the location symbol drawn on the plan prior to adding the nomenclature. Each sign type is assigned an alphabetical letter, which then is inserted on the location symbol. Then the sequence in which the signs will be installed is methodically determined and a sequential number is assigned to each of the location symbols. The location plans will now be complete, showing the sign reference number, sign type, and location in a systematic order that greatly expedites the production and installation process, and also simplifies the checking process (Figure 11-138).

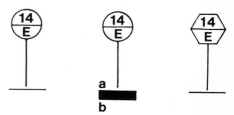

Fig. 11-137

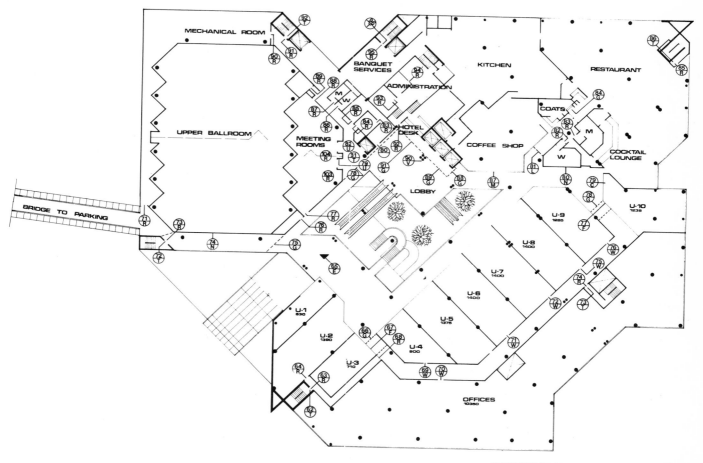

Fig. 11-138

SECOND LEVEL

Alternate GOTHIC NO. 3	Futura MEDIUM	Quorum MEDIUM
Americana	**Futura** DEMIBOLD	Romana NORMAL
Americana ITALIC	**Garamond** BOLD	**Schadow** ANTIQUA SEMIBOLD
Aster	Gerstner Program MEDIUM ™	Serif Gothic REGULAR
Avant Garde GOTHIC MEDIUM	Gill Sans	**Serif Gothic** BOLD
Baker Danmark 2 ™	**Harry** FAT ™	Solitaire BOLD ™
Baker Sans MONO REGULAR ™	**Hellenic** WIDE	Souvenir LIGHT
Baskerville BOLD ITALIC	Helvetica LIGHT	*Souvenir* MEDIUM ITALIC
Bodoni	Helvetica	**Standard** MEDIUM
Bookman	**Helvetica** MEDIUM	**Stymie** BOLD
Caledonia BOLD ITALIC	Helvetica MEDIUM OUTLINE	Times ROMAN
Caslon BOLD	Horizon MEDIUM	**Times** ROMAN BOLD
Century SCHOOLBOOK	**Karen** BOLD	Trooper ROMAN LIGHT ™
Century SCHOOLBOOK BOLD	Korinna	**Trooper** ROMAN ™
Cheltenham MEDIUM	**Korinna** BOLD	Univers 55
Columbus	Lydian	*Univers 56*
COPPERPLATE GOTHIC LIGHT	Melior	**Univers 65**
Craw Clarendon BOOK	**Melior** SEMIBOLD	**Univers 67**
Craw Clarendon	MICROGRAMMA NORMAL	Univers 53
Craw Modern	**MICROGRAMMA** BOLD	**Univers 63**
Delta MEDIUM ™	**MICROGRAMMA** BOLD EXTENDED	Univers 55 OUTLINE
Eastern Souvenir MEDIUM ™	Modula MEDIUM ™	Univers 65 OUTLINE
Eurostile	**News Gothic** BOLD	Univers 83 OUTLINE
Eurostile BOLD	Olive ANTIQUE	Venus MEDIUM
Eurostile EXTENDED	Optima	**Venus** EXTRABOLD
Eurostile BOLD EXTENDED	**Optima** SEMIBOLD	**Venus** EXTRABOLD CONDENSED
Firmin Didot	Palatino	**Venus** BOLD EXTENDED
Folio MEDIUM	**Palatino** SEMIBOLD	**Walbaum** MEDIUM
Folio MEDIUM EXTENDED	**Permanent** MEDIUM	Weiss ROMAN EXTRABOLD
Fortuna LIGHT	Perpetua ROMAN	**Windsor**
Franklin Gothic	Plantin	Windsor OUTLINE

Fig. 11-139

Architectural Signage Systems
Planning · Design · Implementation

Fig. 11-140

Fig. 11-141

These Doors Should
Not Be Opened
Except During
An Emergency

Fig. 11-142

Emergency
Exit Only

Fig. 11-143

CONCEPTUAL DESIGN OF THE SIGN FACE

Emphasis will not be placed on the graphic design of each sign required in a comprehensive signage program. However, the following considerations will help to ensure continuity, correctness, and aesthetic acceptability.

Alphabet selection   An alphabet must be carefully chosen that best exemplifies the graphic image to be portrayed to the public without compromising legibility and performance requirements. More than one alphabet may be selected should need dictate. However, good design practices should be maintained in choosing the family of alphabets to be employed (Figure 11-139).

Interletter, word, and line spacing   Each alphabet has its own "personality" and visual impact; therefore, spacing between characters, words, and lines of copy must be carefully developed to give the best legibility and visual harmony possible (Figure 11-140).

Arrow selection   Directional arrows should be designed to reflect the "personality" of the letterform selected. Stroke width and size relationships are important considerations (Figure 11-141).

Copy determination   The message for each sign must be accurately determined and the copy condensed to the fewest words that will still relay the desired message. Wordy signs are frequently misread or not read at all. The message must be concise, clear, and informative (Figures 11-142 and 11-143).

Copy placement format   The placement of copy on a sign face may take one of the nine basic positions or a custom format for special situations (Figure 11-144).

Fig. 11-144

439

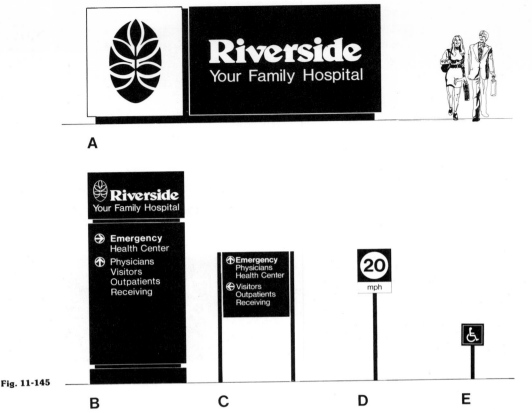

Fig. 11-145

Size determination of the sign face After the copy for each sign is in final form, the sign with the greatest amount of copy is selected from each of the sign types utilized and the desired copy height is determined for each type. This height should be based upon the distance from which the sign will be read and the graphic design portrayed. Using this letter height, the message should be laid out with photographic type or transfer lettering to scale, incorporating the copy placement and spacing requirements. The most pleasing shape and size for the message to be contained are then determined, realizing that this particular layout is for the maximum copy required for that particular sign type. A shape and size format should be chosen that works well as a module which can be proportioned and become applicable to the entire family of sign types. While this may be ideal, frequently the proportional system is not applicable. An example of each sign type should be drawn to scale and fully dimensioned to serve as a production guide for all signs within that type (Figure 11-145).

Color selections Selection is then made of the copy and background colors that offer good contrast and harmoniously blend with the prominent colors in the environment. It is also wise to consider any corporate colors required by the client.

PREPARATION OF THE SIGN SCHEDULE

All information relevant to each sign is then organized into a sign schedule. This schedule may be a numerical listing by sign number, or a more useful organization

Sign Schedule — Courthouse Plaza - First Floor — Architectural Graphics Inc.

No.	Type	Qty.	Material	Letter Size	Letter Color	Sign Size	Sign Color	Face s	Face d	Copy	Remarks
1	A	2	Cast Bronze	12"	Oxidized	-	-	x		Courthouse Plaza	1) Project mount from cast concrete panels 3/4" using non corrosive threaded studs and spacers. 2) Center copy over east and west main entrances horizontally and vertically. 3) Copy shall be Optima Semibold.
2	B	1	Plastic Laminate covered particle board	2"	White	60" x 12"	#1608 Bronze	x		Administration Judicial Chambers Recorder's Court	1) Copy shall be die-cut pressure sensitive lettering in Optima Semibold. 2) Core shall be 1½" thick particle board covered with plastic laminate. 3) Mounting shall be by 2" x 2" x ¼" continuous angles at each end, into the back of the sign and the precast concrete wall with shields and lag screws.
3	M	1	Plastic Laminate covered particle board	1½"	Brown	23"x12"x23"	#1480 White		4	(North Face) Elevators → (East Face) Recorder's Court → (South Face) Elevators ← (West Face Blank)	1) Core shall be 5/8" particle board covered with plastic laminate on four sides and bottom. 2) Copy shall be die-cut pressure sensitive lettering in Optima Semibold. 3) Mount units flush with ceiling tile in exact grid alignment as shown on location plan. 4) Through bolt sign units to treated 1" x 3" predrilled wood strips cut 30" long. Use four bolts per sign.

Fig. 11-146

Sign Schedule — Courthouse Plaza - Sign Type N — Architectural Graphics Inc.

No.	Type	Qty.	Material	Letter Size	Letter Color	Sign Size	Sign Color	Face s	Face d	Copy	Remarks
27	N	1	.125" Acrylic	1½" 1" 1"	White	12" x 12"	#2418 Brown	x		← Information Collections	1) All Type N are reverse screen printed on matte colorless acrylic .125" thick, and oversprayed background color. 2) Copy is Helvetica Regular upper and lower case as typed. 3) Copy position is upper left with 1½" margins and ½" inter line spacing. 4) All edges are square; corners shall have ½" radius. 5) Mounting shall be with double faced neoprene tape. 6) See Sign Type drawings for other details.
36	N	2	.125" Acrylic	1½" 1"	White	12" x 12"	#2418 Brown	x		→ Courtroom B	
51	N	1	.125" Acrylic	1½" 1" 1"	White	12" x 12"	#2418 Brown	x		↑ Central Records B1 Lounge	
52	N	1	.125" Acrylic	1½" 1" 1" 1" 1"	Brown	12" x 12"	White	x		Maintenance B5 Microfilm Processing B8 Restrooms Printing B3	
67	N	2	.125" Acrylic	1½" 1"	Brown	12" x 12"	White	x		→ Courtroom F	
76	N	1	.125" Acrylic	1½" 1"	Brown	12" x 12"	White	x		← Courtroom E	
77	N	1	.125" Acrylic	1½" 1"	White	12" x 12"	#2418 Brown	x		← Courtroom D	
97	N	2	.125" Acrylic	1½" 1"	White	12" x 12"	#2418 Brown	x		→ Courtroom C	
102	N	1	.125" Acrylic	1½" 1" 1"	White	12" x 12"	#2418 Brown	x		↑ Judicial Chambers, Superior & State Court	
114	N	1	.125" Acrylic	1½" 1" 1" 1"	White	12" x 12"	#2418 Brown	x		→ Attorney Conference Rooms Courtooms C, D & F Jury Assembly	

Fig. 11-147

441

may be utilized that lists the signs by sign type, in which the sign numbers are in an ascending, rather than sequential, order.

Figure 11-146 shows a schedule prepared in numerical order.

Figure 11-147 shows a schedule prepared by sign type.

CONSTRUCTION DRAWINGS

Detailing a comprehensive signage program is an important step on competitive bid projects to ensure proper interpretation by the bidders and to eliminate inaccurate judgments or conclusions that may have a significant impact on the bid. Most designers rely on shop drawings for this phase. However, bid documents with insufficient detailing will frequently result in compromised implementations (Figure 11-148).

Fig. 11-148

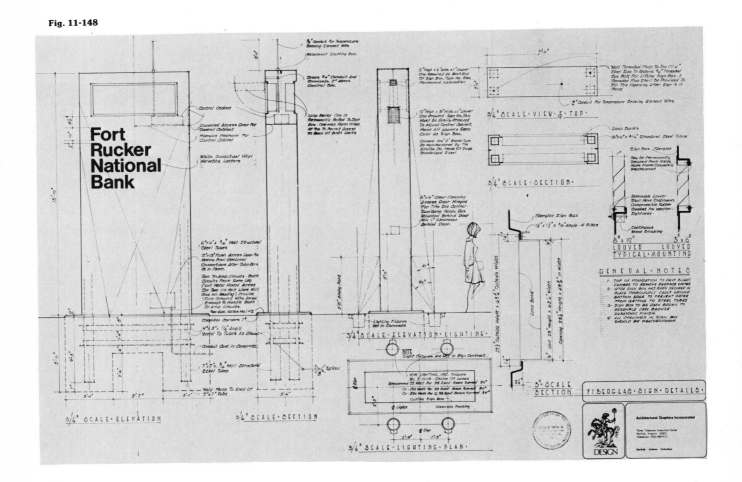

SIGNAGE SYSTEM DEVELOPMENT CHECKLIST

The completed sign schedule, location plans, scaled drawings of typical examples from each sign type, construction or assembly details or both, mounting details, and specifications form the documents required to bid competitively or to negotiate signage projects. Well-prepared documents prevent individual interpretation by vendors and result in comparable competitive bids.

The following systematic approach to the design and development of a comprehensive signage program will serve as a guideline to problem solving, employing the concepts contained in this chapter. This checklist may be expanded or condensed to meet individual project parameters. The basic systematic thought process, however, is applicable to all projects.

1. Develop the signage system design criteria based on:

   a. Performance requirements

   b. Usage considerations

   c. Durability requirements

   d. Vandalism considerations

   e. Flexibility to accommodate changes and additions

   f. Readability factors

   g. Multilingual needs

   h. Regulatory considerations

   i. Need for illumination

   j. Need for graphics manual for ongoing implementation and system maintenance

2. Study the traffic flow patterns, determine all sign locations, and draw the location symbols on the site and floor plans.

3. Evaluate and select the sign types required from the following list, categorized by function, that meet the design criteria:

   a. Exterior sign types
   Type A—Primary identification
   Type B—Secondary identification
   Type C—Vehicular advance notice
   Type D—Vehicular directional
   Type E—Traffic regulatory and control
   Type F—Instructional
   Type G—Informational
   Type H—Decorative

   b. Interior sign types
   Type I—Primary identification
   Type J—Primary directory
   Type K—Elevator lobby floor directories
   Type L—Pictorial "You Are Here" indicators
   Type M—Primary directional
   Type N—Secondary directional
   Type O—Area identification
   Type P—Room identification

Type Q—Desk identification
Type R—Personnel identification
Type S—Regulatory and control
Type T—Exit
Type U—Information exhibit cases
Type W—Dedicatory
Type X—Donor recognition
Type Y—Mechanical, instrumentation, and control system markings
Type Z—Other (to be specified by designer)

4. Select the best signing devices for each sign type designated above from the following lexicon of signage system components that most effectively satisfy the design criteria established:

a. Elevated pylons

b. Monolithic sign structures

c. Panel and post assemblies

d. Illuminated sign cabinets

e. Directory and informational systems

f. Die-cut pressure-sensitive lettering

g. Dimensional graphics

h. Plaque signage

i. Environmental graphics

j. Other (to be defined by the designer)

5. Conceptually design the sign face for each sign type selected, indicating:

a. Alphabet selection

b. Interletter, word, and line spacing

c. Arrow selection

d. Copy determination

e. Copy placement format

f. Size determination of copy and sign face

g. Color selections

6. Complete the location plans by filling in the symbol indicating sign number and type.

7. Prepare scaled drawings of typical examples from each sign type.

8. Prepare the detailed sign schedule.

9. Prepare typical construction and assembly details, mounting details, and engineering drawings for wind loading, foundations, and illumination.

10. Prepare detailed specifications for all materials, techniques, and components required in the system.

A FINAL WORD

A handbook on signage can only serve as an introductory reference for understanding the many aspects in developing a comprehensive signage program. Many good books and materials included in the following bibliography contain detailed information on the many aspects of signage and should become a part of a resource library for study and ready reference.

Organizing for the task, using a systems approach to problem solving as defined in this chapter, will aid the designer in the development of a signage program that will best serve the needs of people and complement the environment it serves.

BIBLIOGRAPHY

Claus, Karen E., and **R. James Claus,** *Handbook of Signage and Sign Legislation,* 2nd ed., The Institute of Signage Research, Palo Alto, Calif., 1976

———— and ————, *Signage: Planning Environmental Visual Communication,* The Institute of Signage Research, Palo Alto, Calif., 1976

———— and ————, *Visual Communication through Signage,* Vol. 3, Design of the Message, The Signs of the Times Publishing Co., Cincinnati, 1976

———— and ————, *Street Graphics: A Perspective,* The Signs of the Times Publishing Co., Cincinnati, 1975

———— and ————, *Visual Communication through Signage,* Vol. 2, Sign Evaluation, The Signs of the Times Publishing Co., Cincinnati, 1975

———— and ————, *Visual Communication through Signage,* Vol. 1, Perception of the Message, The Signs of the Times Publishing Co., Cincinnati, 1974

Claus, R. James, *Some Policy Considerations for Sign Legislation,* The Signs of the Times Publishing Co., Cincinnati, 1973

Constantine, Mildred, and **Egbert Jacobson,** *Sign Language,* Reinhold Publishing Corporation, New York, 1961

Ewell, William R., Jr., and **Daniel R. Mandelker,** *Street Graphics,* American Society of Landscape Architects Foundation, Washington, D.C., 1971

Fitzgerald, Bob, *Electrical Signs in the Commercial Shop,* The Signs of the Times Publishing Co., Cincinnati, 1965

Gray, Mildred, and **Ronald Armstrong,** *Lettering for Architects and Designers,* Reinhold Publishing Corporation, New York, 1962

Kepes, Gyorgy, Ed., *Module, Proportion, Symmetry, Rhythm,* George Braziller, Inc., New York, 1966

————, *Sign, Image, Symbol.* George Braziller, Inc., New York, 1966

Oliphant, Robert M., Karen E. Claus, and **R. James Claus,** *Psychological Considerations of Lettering for Identification,* The Signs of the Times Publishing Co., Cincinnati, 1971

Patty, C. Robert, and **Harvey L. Vredenburg,** *Electric Signs, Contribution to the Communications Spectrum.* Rohm and Haas Company, Philadelphia, 1970

Signs/Lights/Boston, *City Signs and Lights,* A Policy Study Prepared for The Boston Redevelopment Authority and the U.S. Department of Housing and Urban Development, Boston, 1971

U.S. Department of Transportation and the Federal Highway Administration, *Manual on Uniform Traffic Control Devices,* Government Printing Office, Washington, D.C., 1970

CHAPTER TWELVE
DESIGNING FOR THE DISABLED
Robert James Sorensen

INTRODUCTION

Successful design for accessibility by the handicapped requires concern for those with handicaps other than the obvious confinement to a wheelchair. They include blindness, loss of hearing, loss of strength, reduced ability to move or manipulate parts of the body, and deformity of limbs and hands.

The designer must take into account all three major classifications of the handicapped: blindness, deafness, and problems with physical movement and dexterity. Generally, design to accommodate those in wheelchairs will allow for use of the designed space by most of the movement-impaired population. Provision for persons with hearing and sight impairments requires careful attention to the removal or guarding of potential hazards and provision of additional or special information systems. A list of state agencies with access regulations for the handicapped is given in Table 12-1.

HANDICAPS OF MOVEMENT

For those disabled in their ability to move and manipulate their bodies, space allowances beyond the customary ones must be made, along with the location of all controls and handles between approximately 24 inches and 40 inches above the floor level. Clearances for the wheelchair will generally provide for sufficient space for maneuvering with other types of appliances as well.

The basic operation in the use of a wheelchair is entering and leaving the chair. The preferred method is to place the wheelchair alongside the stationary seat, facing in the same direction as the seat. The wheelchair arm is lowered and the user can slide sideways from the seat to the chair. The less desirable method is to place the wheelchair facing the seat from or to which the person will transfer, or at a 45° angle to it. By the use of grab-bars, the user rises and pivots his or her body, for example, from the stationary seat onto the wheelchair.

Grab-bars are necessary for the front approach for those with malfunctioning lower limbs, since they must rise to pivot the body. These grabs should preferably

Table 12-1   GOVERNMENT AGENCIES REGULATING HANDICAPPED ACCESS

Federal	U.S. Department of Health and Human Services, Office of Civil Rights, Office of New Programs, Washington 20201
State	
Alabama	State Building Commission 800 South McDonough Montgomery 36104
Alaska	State Department of Transportation and Public Facilities, Division of Design Review and Construction; Pouch 6900, Anchorage 99501
Arizona	State Department of Administration, Finance Division, Planning Office; 605 West Wing, Capitol Building, Phoenix 85007
Arkansas	Arkansas Department of Health; 4815 West Markham Street, Little Rock 72201
California	Office of the State Architect; 1500 5th Street, Sacramento 95814
Colorado	State Buildings Division; State Service Building; 1525 Sherman Street, Room 617, Denver 80203
Connecticut	Department of Administrative Services, Bureau of Public Works; Room 523, State Office Building, Hartford 06115
Delaware	Department of Administrative Services, Division of Facilities Management; O'Neil Building, P.O. Box 1401, Dover 19901
District of Columbia	Bureau of Building and Zoning Administration; 614 H Street, Washington 20001
Florida	Department of Community Affairs, Division of Technical Assistance; 2571 Executive Center Circle East, Tallahassee 32301
Georgia	Georgia State Fire Marshal's Office; 7 Martin Luther King Drive S.W., Atlanta 30334
Hawaii	State Department of Accounting and General Services; 1151 Punchbowl Street, P.O. Box 119, Honolulu 96810
Idaho	Department of Labor and Industrial Services, Safety Division; 317 Main Street, Room 400, State House, Boise 83720
Illinois	Illinois Capitol Development Board; William Stratton Office Building, Springfield 62706
Indiana	State Building Commissioner; 215 North Senate Avenue, Room 300 Graphic Arts Building, Indianapolis 46204
Iowa	Office of Planning and Programming, Building Code Commission; 523 East 12th Street, Des Moines 50319
Kansas	State Department of Administration, Division of Architectural Services; State Office Building, Topeka 66612
Kentucky	State Fire Marshal's Office; 127 Building, Frankfort 40601
Louisiana	Department of Public Safety, Office of Fire Protection; 9131 Interline Drive, Baton Rouge 70809
Maine	Bureau of Public Improvements; Room 119, State Office Building, Augusta 04333
Maryland	Governor's Office for the Handicapped; Old Armory Building, 11 Bladen Street, Annapolis 21401
Massachusetts	Architectural Barriers Board; McCormick State Office Building, 1 Ashburton, Room 1319, Boston 02108
Michigan	Michigan Department of Labor, Bureau of Construction Codes; State Secondary Complex, 7150 Harris Drive, P.O. Box 30015, Lansing 48909
Minnesota	State Department of Administration, Building Code Office; 408 Metro Square, Saint Paul 55101
Mississippi	Mississippi State Board of Health, Division of Food and General Sanitation; P.O. Box 1700, Jackson 39205

Missouri	Office of Administration, Division of Design and Construction; P.O. Box 809, Jefferson City 65101
Montana	State Building Code Office; 1509 6th Avenue, Capitol Station, Helena 59601
Nebraska	State Fire Marshal's Office, Public Safety Advisory Committee; 301 Centennial Mall South, 6th Floor, Lincoln 68509
Nevada	State Public Works Board; 505 East King Street, Carson City 89710
New Hampshire	State Department of Public Works, Public Works Architect; John O. Morton Building, 85 Loudon Road, Concord 03301
New Jersey	State Department of the Treasury, Division of Building and Construction; P.O. Box 1243, Trenton 08625
New Mexico	State Construction Industry Bureau; P.O. Box 5155, Santa Fe 87115
New York	Housing and Building Codes Bureau, Division of Housing and Community Development; 2 World Trade Center, New York 10047
North Carolina	State Department of Insurance, Engineering and Building Code Division; P.O. Box 26387, Raleigh 27611
North Dakota	State Construction Superintendant; State Capitol Building, Bismark 58505
Ohio	State Industrial Relations Department, Division of Factory and Building Inspection; 2323 West 5th Avenue, P.O. Box 825, Columbus 43216
Oklahoma	State Board of Public Affairs, Engineering Division; 306 State Capitol Building, Oklahoma City 73105
Oregon	Department of Commerce, Building Codes Division; 401 Labor and Industry Building, Salem 97310
Pennsylvania	Bureau of Occupational and Industrial Safety, Building Division; Room 1514 Labor and Industry Building, 77th and Forster Streets, Harrisburg, 17120
Rhode Island	State Building Code Commissioner; 12 Humbert Street, North Providence 02911
South Carolina	Chief Engineer, Finance Division, Budget Control Board; P.O. Box 11333, Columbia 29211
South Dakota	State Engineer's Office; Suite 205, Foss Building, Pierre 57501
Tennessee	State Architect; Suite 1100, 1 Commerce Place, Nashville 37219
Texas	State Board of Control, Prevention of Architectural Barriers Division, Box 13047 Capitol Station, Austin 78711
Utah	State Building Board; Room 124, State Capitol, Salt Lake City 84114
Vermont	Architectural Barriers Compliance Board; 2 West Avenue, Montpelier 05602
Virginia	Division of Engineering and Building; 209 9th Street Office Building, Richmond 23219
Washington	State Department of Administration, Engineering and Architecture Division; 106 Maple Parkway, Olympia 98504
West Virginia	Division of Vocational Rehabilitation; 1427 Lee Street East, Charleston 25301
Wisconsin	Safety and Building Division; 201 East Washington Avenue, P.O. Box 7946, Madison 53707
Wyoming	Division of Fire Prevention and Electrical Safety; 720 West 18th Street, Cheyenne 82002

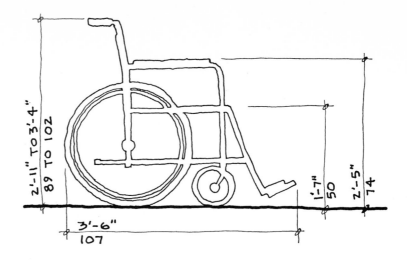

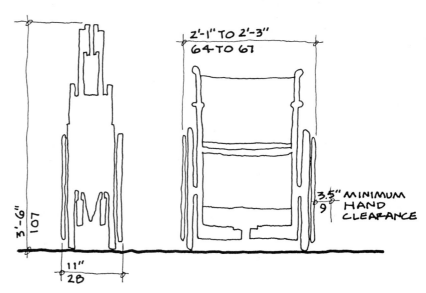

Fig. 12-1   'Standard' collapsible wheelchair.

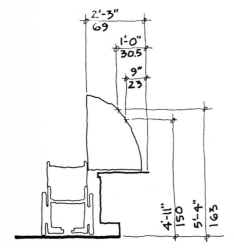

Fig. 12-2   Maximum reach over an obstruction 2
feet 9 inches high.

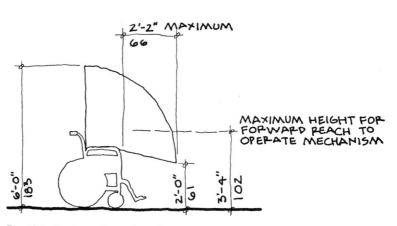

Fig. 12-3   Maximum forward reach.

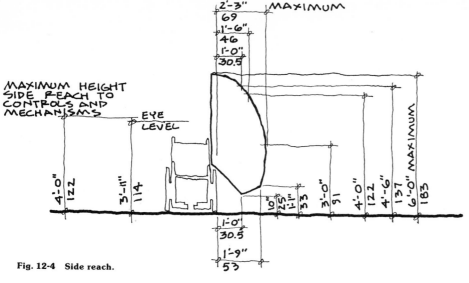

Fig. 12-4 Side reach.

Fig. 12-5 Minimum clearance through door or between obstructions.

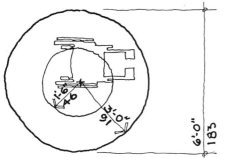

Fig. 12-6 One-wheel pivot.

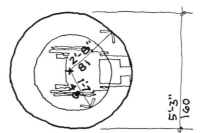

Fig. 12-7 Center pivot.

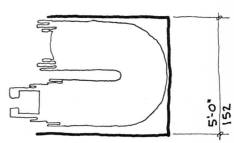

Fig. 12-8 Minimum 180° turn space.

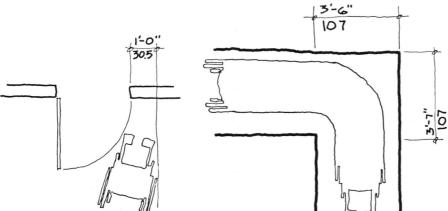

Fig. 12-9 Minimum latch side clearance to open door without maneuvering.

Fig. 12-10 Minimum 90° turn space.

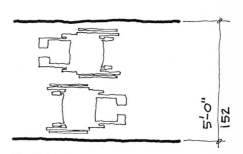

Fig. 12-11 Minimum passing space.

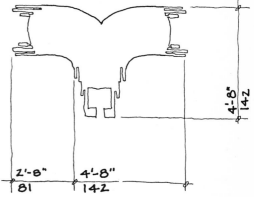

Fig. 12-12 Standard wheelchair three-point turn.

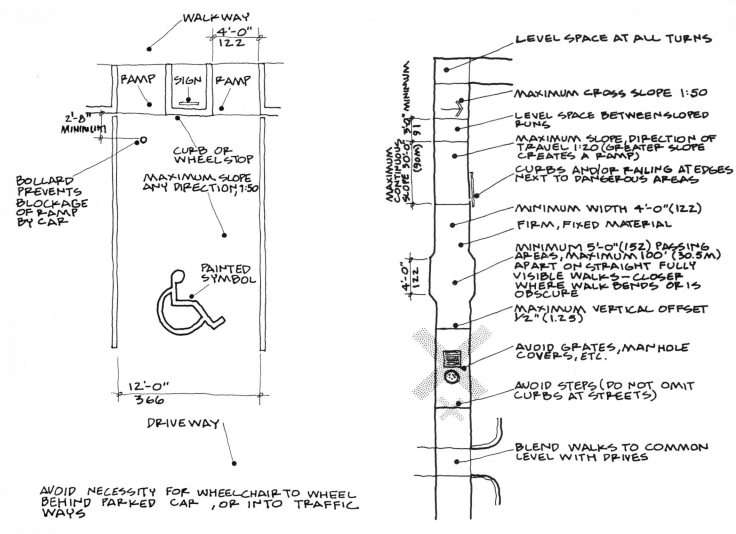

Fig. 12-13 Typical parking space.

Fig. 12-14 Sidewalk

be the horizontal and vertical "L" type. Where possible, bars should be provided at both sides of seats to enable the person to balance his or her weight on both sides. Diagonal bars should not be used in place of the "L" type, since the diagonal bar affords the possibility neither to lift nor to pull. If a diagonal bar is provided on one side, however, another *must* be installed on the other side to provide balance, or the person may lose his or her grip and fall.

While it is possible for some persons to lift a wheelchair up one step, it is quite difficult, and the necessity to do so should be avoided. It is also quite difficult to drive the small front wheels of a chair over any obstruction higher then ½ inch, so such a barrier also should be avoided.

Overhanging stair risers that can "trap" the rigidly held toes of a person in leg braces should be avoided in favor of inclined risers.

BLINDNESS

The blind can maneuver better in small, acoustically "live" spaces than in large ones. Fixed elements, located so as not to create hazards, provide orientation.

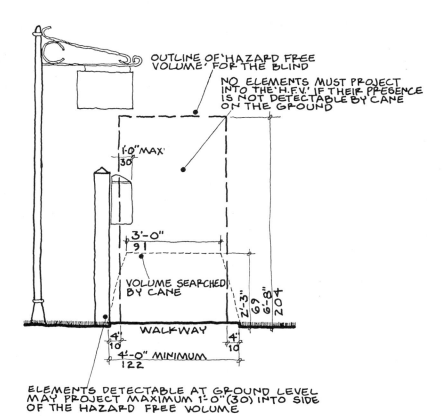

OUTLINE OF 'HAZARD FREE
VOLUME' FOR THE BLIND

NO ELEMENTS MUST PROJECT
INTO THE 'H.F.V.' IF THEIR PRESENCE
IS NOT DETECTABLE BY CANE
ON THE GROUND

1'-0" MAX
30

3'-0"
91

VOLUME SEARCHED
BY CANE

2'-3"
69

6'-8"
204

WALKWAY

4"
10

4"
10

4'-0" MINIMUM
122

ELEMENTS DETECTABLE AT GROUND LEVEL
MAY PROJECT MAXIMUM 1'-0" (30) INTO SIDE
OF THE HAZARD FREE VOLUME

Fig. 12-15   Volume of space that must be free of hazards.

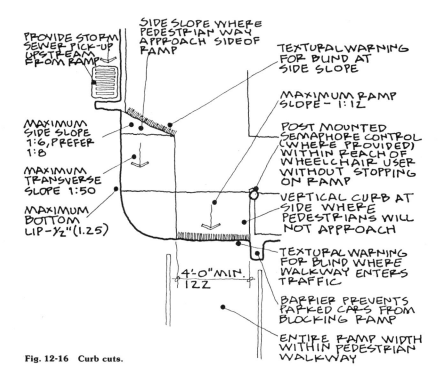

PROVIDE STORM
SEWER PICK-UP
UPSTREAM
FROM RAMP

SIDE SLOPE WHERE
PEDESTRIAN WAY
APPROACH SIDE OF
RAMP

TEXTURAL WARNING
FOR BLIND AT
SIDE SLOPE

MAXIMUM
SIDE SLOPE
1:6, PREFER
1:8

MAXIMUM RAMP
SLOPE - 1:12

POST MOUNTED
SEMAPHORE CONTROL
(WHERE PROVIDED)
WITHIN REACH OF
WHEELCHAIR USER
WITHOUT STOPPING
ON RAMP

MAXIMUM
TRANSVERSE
SLOPE 1:50

VERTICAL CURB AT
SIDE WHERE
PEDESTRIANS WILL
NOT APPROACH

MAXIMUM
BOTTOM
LIP - ½" (1.25)

TEXTURAL WARNING
FOR BLIND WHERE
WALKWAY ENTERS
TRAFFIC

4'-0" MIN.
122

BARRIER PREVENTS
PARKED CARS FROM
BLOCKING RAMP

ENTIRE RAMP WIDTH
WITHIN PEDESTRIAN
WALKWAY

Fig. 12-16   Curb cuts.

Generally, those born blind will be more likely to know braille without knowing the forms of written letters, while those blinded later—the majority of the blind—will more likely not know this writing system. Individual raised letters and small groups of letters can be "read" by touch by many blind persons. Larger or longer groups will become confusing, however. Audible signals for the blind should be in the lower frequencies, since they are most easily heard by the elderly.

Most blind people are taught to use a cane in the "long cane technique." This technique will detect obstructions at ground level within about 18 inches in front of the person and 12 inches to either side of the line of travel. Because of this area of detection, it is important that nothing hang or project into the path of travel that is not detectable by the cane at ground level.

DEAFNESS

Because many legally deaf persons can hear somewhat in favorable circumstances, it is desirable to provide a good aural environment, especially where many deaf per-

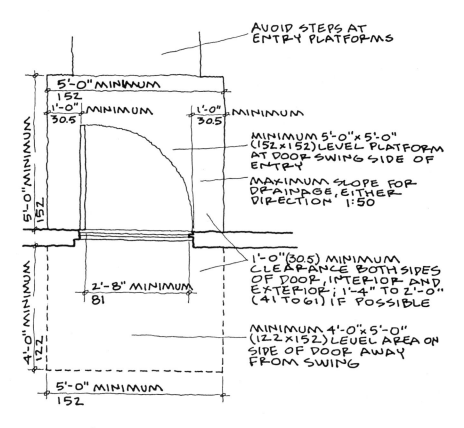

Fig. 12-17 Accessible exterior entrance conditions.

sons will be present. Ideally, this environment will entail having a space that is acoustically fairly "dead" and that has a low level of background noise.

It is desirable (mandatory, where many deaf persons will be present) that emergency and warning signals be visible, and flashing if at all possible.

EXTERIOR ELEMENTS

Consideration of "architectural access" to any facility should begin at the point of vehicular arrival. No barriers should exist in the path from the point of arrival to the actual entrance. An adequate vestibule, traffic-circulation provisions, and appropriate doors are essential to the facility. In particular, there must be no vertical offsets greater than ½ inch and no grills or grates in the path of travel. Textural "warnings" for the blind should be provided to warn them that they are approaching stairs or ramps. Special care must be taken, however, to avoid coarse textures and loose surfaces on floors where wheelchairs will be operated.

In northern climates where freezing occurs, walks and ramps should not exceed

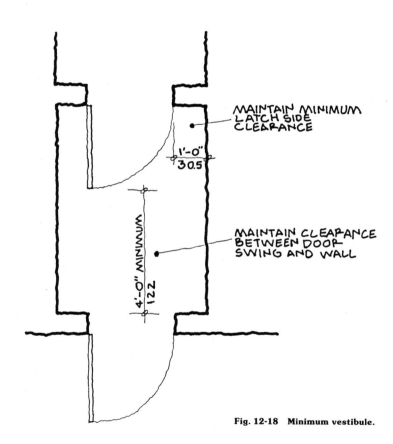

Fig. 12-18 Minimum vestibule.

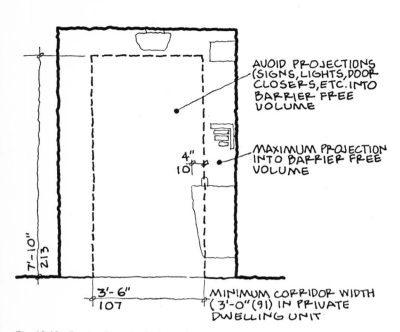

AVOID PROJECTIONS (SIGNS, LIGHTS, DOOR CLOSERS, ETC. INTO BARRIER FREE VOLUME

MAXIMUM PROJECTION INTO BARRIER FREE VOLUME

4" 10

7'-10" 213

3'-6" 107

MINIMUM CORRIDOR WIDTH (3'-0" (91) IN PRIVATE DWELLING UNIT

Fig. 12-19   Barrier-free circulation volume.

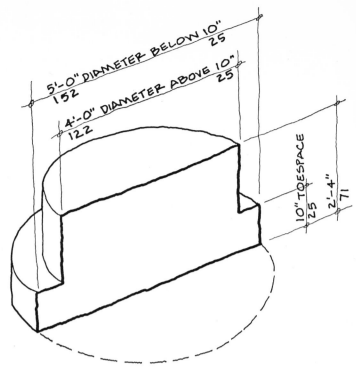

5'-0" DIAMETER BELOW 10" 25 152

4'-0" DIAMETER ABOVE 10" 25 122

10" TOESPACE 25

2'-4" 71

Fig. 12-20   Wheelchair turning volume.

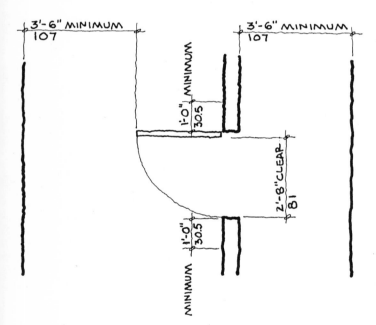

3'-6" MINIMUM 107

3'-6" MINIMUM 107

1'-0" MINIMUM 30.5

2'-8" CLEAR 81

1'-0" MINIMUM 30.5

PROVIDE CLOSERS (PART OPEN DOORS ARE HAZARDOUS TO THE BLIND)
NOTE THAT A 2'-8" (81) DOOR DOES NOT GIVE THE REQUIRED 2'-8" (81) CLEAR OPENING

MINIMUM DOOR WIDTH =
    2'-8" (81.25) + DOOR THICKNESS +1" (2.5)
MAINTAIN 1'-0" (30.5) SIDE CLEARANCE ON LATCH SIDE, EVEN WHERE SMALLER DOOR (DOWN TO 2'-8" (81) MINIMUM CLEARANCE) MUST BE USED

Fig. 12-21   Typical interior door.

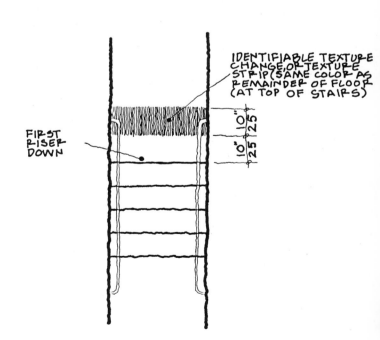

IDENTIFIABLE TEXTURE CHANGE, OR TEXTURE STRIP (SAME COLOR AS REMAINDER OF FLOOR (AT TOP OF STAIRS)

FIRST RISER DOWN

10" 25

10" 25

Fig. 12-22   Corridor stair warning.

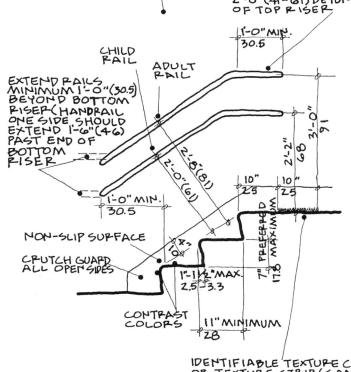

LIGHTING MINIMUM 10 F.C.
(108 LUX), ENTIRE STAIRS

EXTEND RAILS MINIMUM
1'-0" (30.5), PREFER 1'-4"—
2'-0" (41-61) BEYOND LINE
OF TOP RISER

1'-0" MIN.
30.5

CHILD RAIL

ADULT RAIL

EXTEND RAILS
MINIMUM 1'-0" (30.5)
BEYOND BOTTOM
RISER (HANDRAIL
ONE SIDE SHOULD
EXTEND 1'-6" (46)
PAST END OF
BOTTOM
RISER

3'-0"
91

2'-2"
68

2'-8" (81)
2'-0" (61)

10"
25

10"
25

1'-0" MIN.
30.5

7" PREFERRED MAXIMUM
17.8

NON-SLIP SURFACE

CRUTCH GUARD
ALL OPEN SIDES

4"
10

1'-1½" MAX.
2.5—3.3

CONTRAST
COLORS

11" MINIMUM
28

IDENTIFIABLE TEXTURE CHANGE,
OR TEXTURE STRIP (SAME
COLOR AS FLOOR) AT TOP
OF STAIR

PREFER MAXIMUM RISER HEIGHT OF 7" (17.8)
CONTRAST COLOR OF TREAD/RISER
AVOID STAIRS OF 1 OR 2 RISERS (PROVIDE RAMPS)
MORE THAN 1 RISER IS IMPASSABLE BY
WHEELCHAIR

Fig. 12-23 Typical stair.

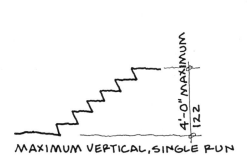

4'-0" MAXIMUM
122

MAXIMUM VERTICAL, SINGLE RUN

Fig. 12-24 Exterior stair.

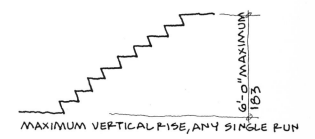

6'-0" MAXIMUM
183

MAXIMUM VERTICAL RISE, ANY SINGLE RUN

PROVIDE PLATFORM IN CENTER OF SINGLE
RUN STAIR WHERE VERTICAL RISE
EXCEEDS MAXIMUM

Fig. 12-25 Interior stair.

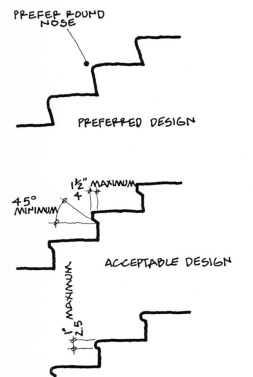

Fig. 12-26 Stair riser profiles.

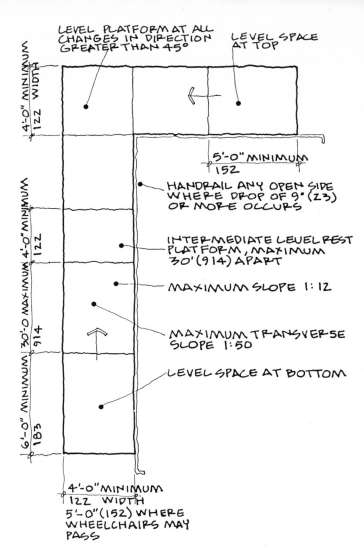

Fig. 12-28 Typical ramp.

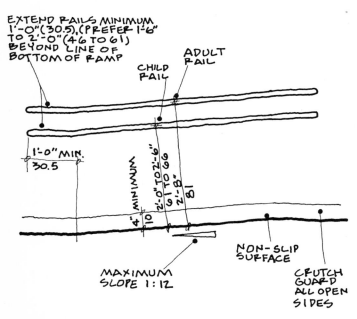

Fig. 12-27 Ramp section.

Fig. 12-29 Ramp criteria.

RAMP SLOPE	MAXIMUM RISE OF A SINGLE RUN	MAXIMUM LENGTH OF A SINGLE RUN	MAXIMUM TOTAL (AGGREGATE) LENGTH OF RUN
1:8	3"(7.5)	2'(61)	2'(61)
1:10	9"(23)	8'(244)	8'(244)
1:12	2'-6"(76)	30'(914)	60'(18.3M)
1:16	2'-6"(76)	40'(12.2M)	160'(49M)
1:20	2'-6"(76)	50'(152M)	—

a slope of 1 foot in 20; textures and materials which will retain water that can freeze into ice are to be avoided.

There should be no signs, posts, and similar items that project into the path of travel unless they are detectable at ground level by a cane.

BUILDING AREAS

Entry for the handicapped to buildings should be provided at locations where normal entry occurs—not at "back door" or service locations. The architect or designer must also consider the need to provide at least two accessible fire exits from the building, even though they may not be required by code.

Equal attention should be given to the appropriate design of elevators, their doors, and the elevator call buttons. A 32-inch door does not provide the requisite 32-inch clear opening required for accessibility in a wheelchair. A minimum clearance of 12 inches between any door-latch edge and the nearest obstruction will allow operation of the door without the need to move the chair while opening the door.

In accessible toilets, it is highly desirable that one water-closet compartment be at least 4 feet 6 inches wide to provide for lateral (alongside) transfer from a wheelchair. Ideally, two such compartments should be installed, one arranged for right-handed transfer and the other for a left-handed one, since some physically handicapped persons can operate from only one side or the other.

Some persons with disabilities of movement can be extremely sensitive to heat and cold, so surfaces that naturally feel cold (ceramic tile or enameled metal) should not be placed where they may contact a person's body. Many handicapped persons, on the other hand, may have lost all, or a large part of, their sensitivity to heat or cold. The designer should take great care to avoid putting such persons into a situation where they may be injured by contact with a very hot surface of which they may not be aware.

Because of the inability of many handicapped persons to move quickly out of danger, all hot-water supply sources must be thermostatically (not volumetrically) guarded against extreme heat.

The kitchen to be used by the physically handicapped is an area where the designer will want to pay great attention to the reduction of potential hazards. In addition to guarding for extreme temperatures at the sink, the dangers present at the range and oven must be guarded. All controls should be "up front" to avoid the necessity of reaching over heating elements; almost as important, flush countertops and cooking tops allow the sliding of utensils containing hot liquids. Kitchens with abundant food-storage space will minimize the need for shopping trips.

The thoughtful designer will provide bedrooms of sufficient size to allow for access (including turning) between at least the bed and the closets. Closets should be wide and shallow, with folding partitions or bifolding doors in place of conventional swinging doors.

Work and assembly areas should of course be arranged to provide for passage between all fixed elements, including the projections of doors, drawers, and other jutting elements. Assembly locations should allow for a choice of seating places, as well as provide several "paired" handicapped locations to allow for companionship. Facilities for the use of amplified hearing devices should be installed at several locations for people with impaired hearing.

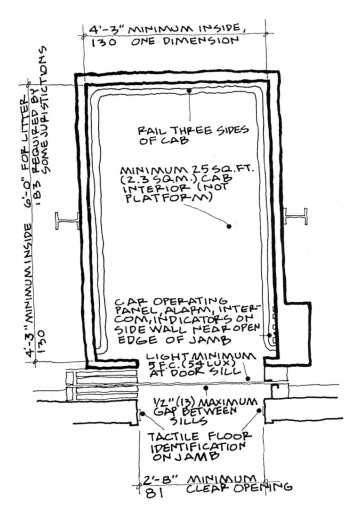

RAIL THREE SIDES OF CAB

MINIMUM 25 SQ. FT. (2.3 SQ.M.) CAB INTERIOR (NOT PLATFORM)

4'-3" MINIMUM INSIDE, 130 ONE DIMENSION

4'-3" MINIMUM INSIDE 130

6'-0" FOR LITTER '83 REQUIRED BY SOME JURISDICTIONS

CAR OPERATING PANEL, ALARM, INTERCOM, INDICATORS ON SIDE WALL NEAR OPEN EDGE OF JAMB

LIGHT MINIMUM 5 F.C. (54 LUX) AT DOOR SILL

½" (13) MAXIMUM GAP BETWEEN SILLS

TACTILE FLOOR IDENTIFICATION ON JAMB

2'-8" MINIMUM 81 CLEAR OPENING

VARIABLE SPEED MOTORS WITH LESS INITIAL ACCELERATION ARE BETTER FOR THE ELDERLY AND AMBULATORY HANDICAPPED

Fig. 12-30 Elevator plan.

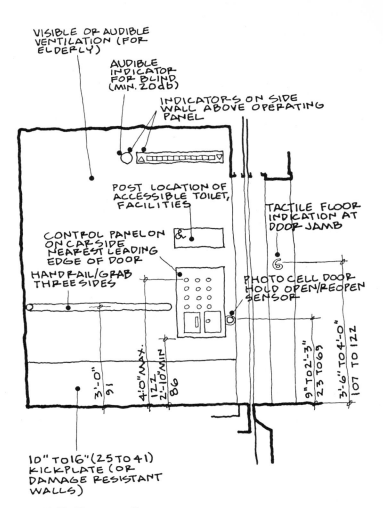

VISIBLE OR AUDIBLE VENTILATION (FOR ELDERLY)

AUDIBLE INDICATOR FOR BLIND (MIN. 20 db)

INDICATORS ON SIDE WALL ABOVE OPERATING PANEL

POST LOCATION OF ACCESSIBLE TOILET, FACILITIES

CONTROL PANEL ON CAR SIDE NEAREST LEADING EDGE OF DOOR

HANDRAIL/GRAB THREE SIDES

TACTILE FLOOR INDICATION AT DOOR JAMB

PHOTO CELL DOOR HOLD OPEN/REOPEN SENSOR

3'-0" 91

4'-0" MAX. 122 2'-10" MIN. 86

9" TO 2'-3" 23 TO 69

3'-6" TO 4'-0" 107 TO 122

10" TO 16" (25 TO 41) KICKPLATE (OR DAMAGE RESISTANT WALLS)

Fig. 12-31 Elevator section.

MINIMUM FULL OPEN TIME 3 SEC., PREFER 5-6 SEC. FOR AMBULANT, 7 SEC. FOR WHEELCHAIR

MINIMUM CLOSING TIME 3 SEC.

MAXIMUM CLOSING SPEED 80 FPM (24.4 M/SEC.) FOR AMBULATORY HANDICAPPED, 40 FPM (12.2 M/SEC.) FOR ELDERLY

Fig. 12-32 Elevator doors.

460

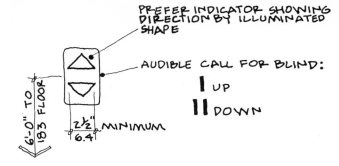

PREFER INDICATOR SHOWING DIRECTION BY ILLUMINATED SHAPE

AUDIBLE CALL FOR BLIND:

I UP

II DOWN

6'-0" TO 183 FLOOR

2½" MINIMUM 6.4

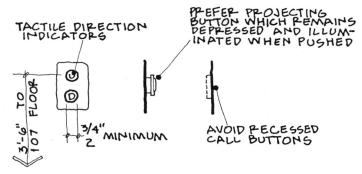

TACTILE DIRECTION INDICATORS

PREFER PROJECTING BUTTON WHICH REMAINS DEPRESSED AND ILLUMINATED WHEN PUSHED

AVOID RECESSED CALL BUTTONS

3'-6" TO 107 FLOOR

¾" MINIMUM 2

Fig. 12-33   Elevator indicator and call buttons.

	MINIMUM NUMBER OF FIXTURES			NUMBER OF FIXTURES			
	W.C.	LAV.	BATH	W.C.	LAV.	BATH	UNITS/REMARKS
RESIDENTIAL^A (WITH PRIVATE FACILITIES)	1	1	1	⅓ 4%	⅓ 4%	⅓ 4%	PER RESIDENT PER D.U. OR SLEEPING ROOM
RESIDENTIAL^A,D (WITH COMMON OR CENTRAL FACILITIES)	2^B	2^B	2^B	½ 2%	½ 2%	¼ 2%	PER RESIDENT PER D.U. OR SLEEPING ROOM
INSTITUTIONAL/ COMMERCIAL^E (WITH PRIVATE TOILET ROOMS)	2^B	2^B	—	10%	10%	—	% OF TOILET FACILITIES
INSTITUTIONAL/ COMMERCIAL^E (WITH COMMON OR CENTRAL FACILITIES)	2^B,C	2^B,C	—	10%	10%	—	% OF TOILET FACILITIES

A. RESIDENTIAL D.U. OR INSTITUTIONS FOR THE HANDICAPPED

B. ONE FOR EACH SEX

C. MINIMUM ONE IN EACH BANK OF FIXTURES

D. MAXIMUM 3 MINUTE (ONE WAY) TRIP FROM ANY LOCATION

E. MAXIMUM 5 MINUTE (ONE WAY) TRIP FROM ANY LOCATION

WHERE TOILETS ARE SIZED FOR LATERAL TRANSFER, PROVIDE ½ FOR RIGHT HAND, ½ FOR LEFT HAND

WHERE ELEVATOR SERVICE IS AVAILABLE, ACCESSIBLE TOILET SHOULD NOT BE MORE THAN 2 FLOORS AWAY

Fig. 12-34   Toilet-planning criteria.

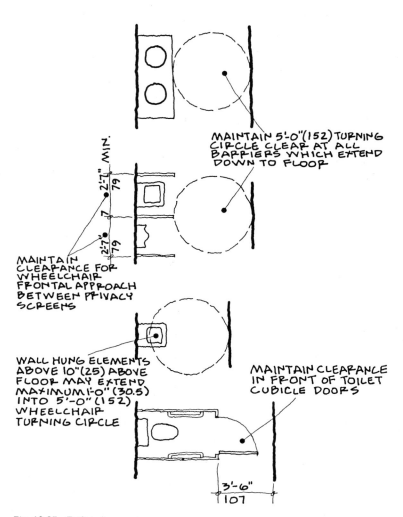

Fig. 12-35   Toilet clearances.

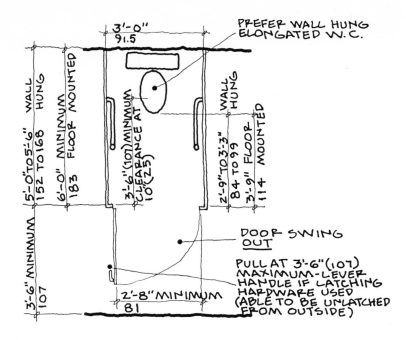

PREFER WALL HUNG
ELONGATED W.C.

3'-0"
91.5

5'-0" to 5'-6" WALL
152 TO 168 HUNG

6'-0" MINIMUM
183 FLOOR MOUNTED

3'-6" (107) MINIMUM
CLEARANCE AT 10" (25)

2'-9" TO 3'-3" WALL
84 TO 99 HUNG

3'-9" FLOOR
114 MOUNTED

3'-6" MINIMUM
107

2'-8" MINIMUM
81

DOOR SWING
OUT

PULL AT 3'-6" (107)
MAXIMUM-LEVER
HANDLE IF LATCHING
HARDWARE USED
(ABLE TO BE UNLATCHED
FROM OUTSIDE)

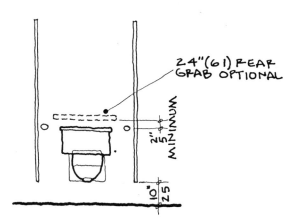

24" (61) REAR
GRAB OPTIONAL

2" MINIMUM
5

10"
25

NOTE: 3'-0" (91.5) WIDTH NOT PERMITTED UNDER
ANSI 117.1

Fig. 12-36 Minimum toilet.

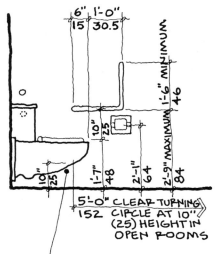

6"   1'-0"
15   30.5

1'-6" MINIMUM
46

10"
25

10"
25

1'-7"
48

2'-1"
64

2'-9" MAXIMUM
84

5'-0" CLEAR TURNING
152 CIRCLE AT 10"
(25) HEIGHT IN
OPEN ROOMS

PREFER DEEPLY RECESSED FRONT
WALL HUNG WATER CLOSET

PROVIDE LATERAL TRANSFER IF POSSIBLE
FRONTAL TRANSFER DIFFICULT/IMPOSSIBLE
FOR SOME HANDICAPPED

Fig. 12-37 Typical toilet stall.

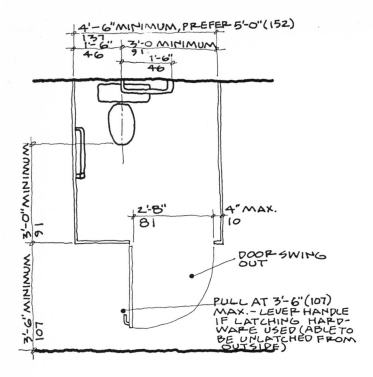

4'-6" MINIMUM, PREFER 5'-0" (152)
137
1'-6"   3'-0 MINIMUM
46   91
              1'-6"
              46

3'-0" MINIMUM
91

3'-6" MINIMUM
107

2'-8"   4" MAX.
81   10

DOOR SWING OUT

PULL AT 3'-6" (107) MAX.- LEVER HANDLE IF LATCHING HARD-WARE USED (ABLE TO BE UNLATCHED FROM OUTSIDE)

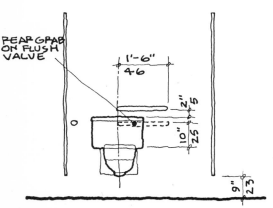

REAR GRAB ON FLUSH VALVE

1'-6"
46

2" 5

10" 25

9" 23

MINIMUM SIZE COMPARTMENT ALLOWED BY ANSI 117.1

Fig. 12-38 Side and lateral transfer com-partment.

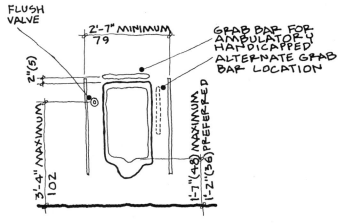

FLUSH VALVE

2'-7" MINIMUM
79

2" (5)

GRAB BAR FOR AMBULATORY HANDICAPPED ALTERNATE GRAB BAR LOCATION

3'-4" MAXIMUM
102

1'-7" (48) MAXIMUM
1'-2" (36) PREFERRED

URINALS ARE DIFFICULT FOR THE BLIND, AND ARE LITTLE USED BY THOSE IN WHEEL CHAIRS

Fig. 12-39 Typical urinal.

464

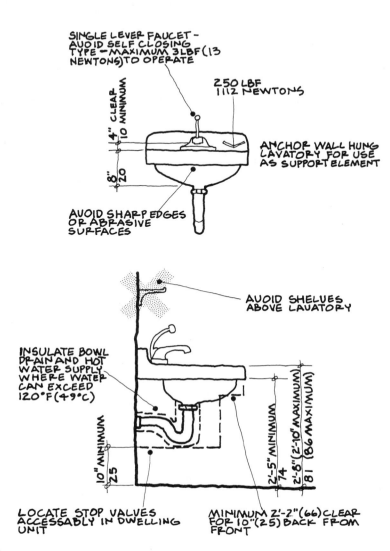

SINGLE LEVER FAUCET –
AVOID SELF CLOSING
TYPE – MAXIMUM 3 LBF (13
NEWTONS) TO OPERATE

250 LBF
1112 NEWTONS

4" CLEAR
10 MINIMUM

8"
20

ANCHOR WALL HUNG
LAVATORY FOR USE
AS SUPPORT ELEMENT

AVOID SHARP EDGES
OR ABRASIVE
SURFACES

AVOID SHELVES
ABOVE LAVATORY

INSULATE BOWL
DRAIN AND HOT
WATER SUPPLY
WHERE WATER
CAN EXCEED
120°F (49°C)

10" MINIMUM
25

2'-5" MINIMUM
74

2'-10" (2'-10" MAXIMUM)
81

2'-6" (2'-10" MAXIMUM)
86 MAXIMUM)

LOCATE STOP VALVES
ACCESSABLY IN DWELLING
UNIT

MINIMUM 2'-2" (66) CLEAR
FOR 10" (25) BACK FROM
FRONT

Fig. 12-40 Typical lavatory.

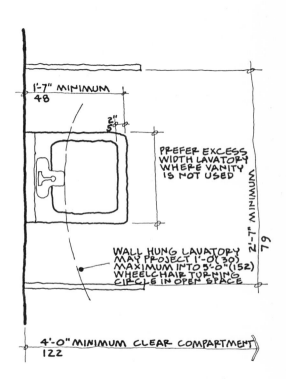

1'-7" MINIMUM
48

2"
5

PREFER EXCESS
WIDTH LAVATORY
WHERE VANITY
IS NOT USED

2'-7" MINIMUM
79

WALL HUNG LAVATORY
MAY PROJECT 1'-0 (30)
MAXIMUM INTO 5'-0" (152)
WHEELCHAIR TURNING
CIRCLE IN OPEN SPACE

4'-0" MINIMUM CLEAR COMPARTMENT
122

Fig. 12-41 Typical lavatory.

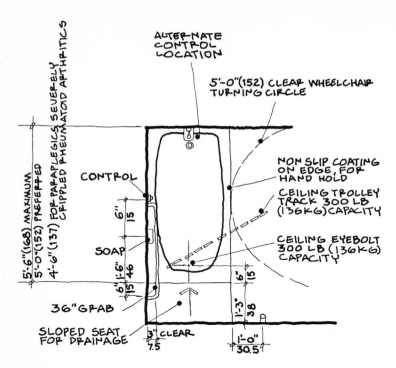

ALTERNATE CONTROL LOCATION

5'-0"(152) CLEAR WHEELCHAIR TURNING CIRCLE

5'-6"(168) MAXIMUM
5'-0"(152) PREFERRED
4'-6"(137) FOR PARAPLEGICS SEVERELY CRIPPLED RHEUMATOID ARTHRITICS

CONTROL

NON SLIP COATING ON EDGE, FOR HAND HOLD

CEILING TROLLEY TRACK 300 LB (136KG) CAPACITY

CEILING EYEBOLT 300 LB (136KG) CAPACITY

6" / 15

SOAP

6"-1'-6" / 15-46

36" GRAB

6" / 15

SLOPED SEAT FOR DRAINAGE

3" CLEAR / 7.5

6" / 15

1'-3" / 38

1'-0" / 30.5

PROVIDE TUB SEAT 15"(38) BY FULL WIDTH, MAXIMUM 17"-20"(43-51) ABOVE BOTTOM OF TUB

ALL WATER CONTROLS SINGLE LEVER, THERMOSTATICALLY GUARDED

HAND HELD SHOWER SHOULD HAVE SHUT OFF; MIX VALVE IN HANDLE IS DESIRABLE

AVOID DOUBLE HANDLE MIX VALVES

ALL MIX VALVES SHOULD BE OPERATED BY GROSS HAND MOVEMENTS ONLY

AVOID SHOWER DOORS ON TUB

ALL GRABS SHOULD HAVE NON SLIP SURFACES

PROVIDE LEVER TYPE DRAIN PLUG CONTROL

AVOID COLD (TILE/ENAMELED CAST IRON) SURFACES

DO NOT USE DIAGONAL GRABS (EXTREMELY DANGEROUS)

Fig. 12-42 Wheelchair tub with seat (plan).

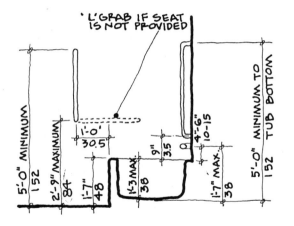

33"(84) GRAB MINIMUM

ADJUSTABLE/HAND SHOWER HEAD WITH MINIMUM 6'(183) HOSE AND 4'(122) ADJUSTABLE LENGTH

1'-3" / 38

2'-6" MAXIMUM / 76

6" / 15

4'-6" / 10-15

1'-8" MAX / 51

9" / 23

1'-7" / 48

SEAT

36" GRAB (91)

SOAP NO GRAB

CONTROL VALVE

'L' GRAB IF SEAT IS NOT PROVIDED

5'-0" MINIMUM / 152

2'-9" MAXIMUM / 84

1'-0" / 30.5

1'-7" / 48

9" / 3.5

1'-3" MAX / 38

4'-6" / 10-15

1'-7" MAX / 38

5'-0" MINIMUM TO TUB BOTTOM / 152

Fig. 12-43 Wheelchair tub with seat (sections).

466

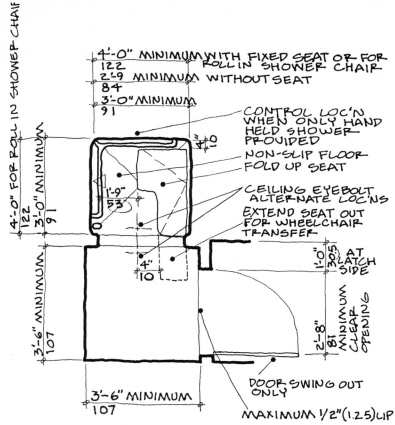

4'-0" MINIMUM WITH FIXED SEAT OR FOR
122   ROLL IN SHOWER CHAIR
2'-9 MINIMUM WITHOUT SEAT
84
3'-0" MINIMUM
91

4'-0" FOR ROLL IN SHOWER CHAIR

4'-0" FOR ROLL IN SHOWER CHAIR
122

3'-0" MINIMUM
91

1'-9"
53

CONTROL LOC'N
WHEN ONLY HAND
HELD SHOWER
PROVIDED
NON-SLIP FLOOR
FOLD UP SEAT
CEILING EYEBOLT
ALTERNATE LOC'NS
EXTEND SEAT OUT
FOR WHEELCHAIR
TRANSFER

4"
10

1'-0" 305 AT
LATCH
SIDE

2'-8" 81 MINIMUM CLEAR OPENING

3'-6" MINIMUM
107

3'-6" MINIMUM
107

DOOR SWING OUT
ONLY

MAXIMUM 1/2" (1.25) LIP

Fig. 12-44 Wheelchair shower (plan).

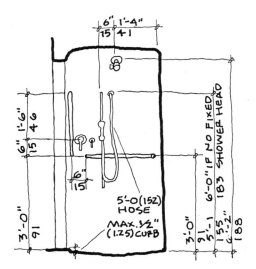

6" 1'-4"
15 41

6" 1'-6"
15 46

6"
15

6"
15

3'-0"
91

6'-0" IF NO FIXED
183 SHOWER HEAD

3'-0"
91

5'-1"
155

6'-2"
188

5'-0 (152)
HOSE

MAX. 1/2"
(1.25) CURB

Fig. 12-45   Wheelchair shower (section)

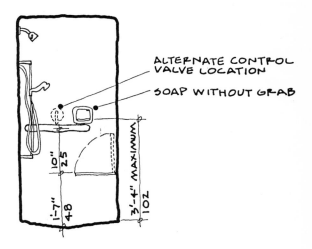

ALTERNATE CONTROL
VALVE LOCATION
SOAP WITHOUT GRAB

10"
25

1'-7"
48

3'-4" MAXIMUM
102

Fig. 12-46   Wheelchair shower (section).

SECOND MIX VALVE LOCATION ON SIDE WALL
AND ACCESSIBLE FROM SEAT WITH LIMITED
ARM REACH

ALL WATER SUPPLY – SHOWER HEAD AND
HOSE MUST BE THERMOSTATICALLY
GUARDED

PROVIDE SINGLE LEVER MIXING VALVE ONLY

HAND HELD SHOWER SHOULD HAVE SHUT OFF;
IF ONLY HAND SHOWER IS PROVIDED, IT
SHOULD HAVE MIX VALVE IN HANDLE

AVOID SLATTED BOARD SEAT

SEAT SHOULD BE SELF DRAINING

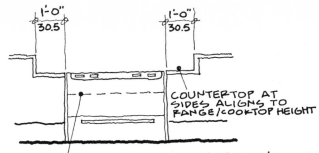

ALTERNATE: ADJUSTIBLE HEIGHT 'DROP IN'
COOKTOP (BLANK PANEL BELOW TO
AVOID WHEELCHAIR KNEESPACE: ADJUSTIBLE
TO 2'-4", 2'-8", 3'-0" (71.5, 81, 91) HEIGHTS

GAS:

CAN BE HEARD BY BLIND
HEAT CEASES QUICKLY - FOOD CAN BE LEFT ON
RANGE WHEN DONE
PROVIDE AUTOMATIC SHUT OFF CONTROL FOR
FLAME/PILOT LIGHT NON FUNCTION
GENERAL USE; RESIDENCES FOR THE BLIND
RANGE SHOULD HAVE EASILY SEEN CONTROLS:

ELECTRIC:

MORE EASILY SHUTOFF BY THOSE WITH HAND
DISORDERS
MANY ELDERLY AND DISABLED PERSONS CANNOT
SMELL GAS
RESIDUAL HEAT IN ELECTRIC COILS IS DANGEROUS
FOR THE BLIND AND SENSORY DISABLED
PREFER FOR THE RESIDENCES FOR THE ELDERLY,
THOSE WITH OLEFACTORY DISORDERS, THOSE
WITH HAND DISORDERS

Fig. 12-47   Range and cooktop.

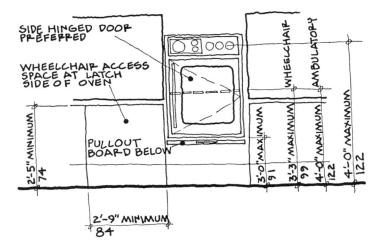

OVEN SHELVES: NON TIP
                NON PULL OUT

OVENS WITHOUT SIDE WHEELCHAIR SPACE FOR
ACCESS SHOULD BE SELF CLEANING

OVENS SHOULD HAVE INTERIOR LIGHT

Fig. 12-48   Oven.

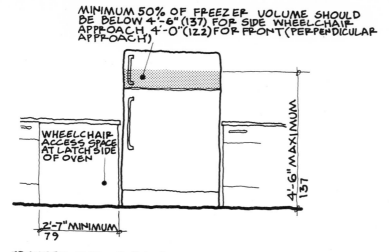

MINIMUM 50% OF FREEZER VOLUME SHOULD
BE BELOW 4'-6" (137) FOR SIDE WHEELCHAIR
APPROACH 4'-0" (122) FOR FRONT (PERPENDICULAR
APPROACH)

WHEELCHAIR
ACCESS SPACE
AT LATCH SIDE
OF OVEN

4'-6" MAXIMUM
137

2'-7" MINIMUM
79

FREEZER SHOULD BE SELF DEFROSTING TYPE

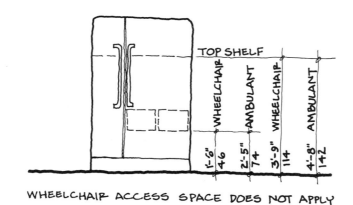

TOP SHELF

WHEELCHAIR 1'-6" 46
AMBULANT 2'-5" 74
WHEELCHAIR 3'-9" 114
AMBULANT 4'-8" 142

WHEELCHAIR ACCESS SPACE DOES NOT APPLY

Fig. 12-49   Refrigerator and freezer.

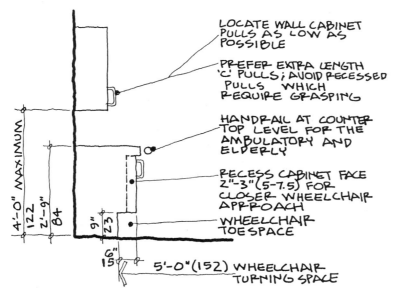

LOCATE WALL CABINET
PULLS AS LOW AS
POSSIBLE

PREFER EXTRA LENGTH
'C' PULLS; AVOID RECESSED
PULLS WHICH
REQUIRE GRASPING

HANDRAIL AT COUNTER
TOP LEVEL FOR THE
AMBULATORY AND
ELDERLY

RECESS CABINET FACE
2"-3" (5-7.5) FOR
CLOSER WHEELCHAIR
APPROACH

WHEELCHAIR
TOE SPACE

4'-0" MAXIMUM 122
2'-9" 84
9" 23
6" 15

5'-0" (152) WHEELCHAIR
TURNING SPACE

Fig. 12-50   Typical cabinets.

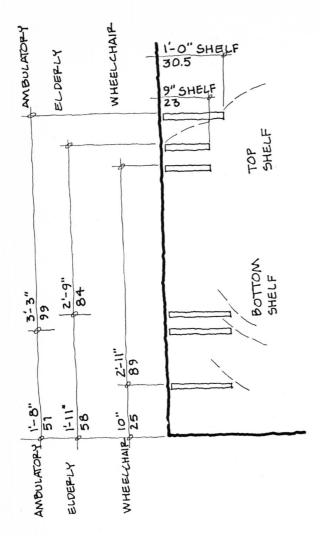

AMBULATORY
ELDERLY
WHEELCHAIR

1'-0" SHELF
30.5

9" SHELF
23

TOP SHELF

BOTTOM SHELF

3'-3"
99

2'-9"
84

2'-11"
89

1'-8"
51

1'-11"
58

10"
25

AMBULATORY
ELDERLY
WHEELCHAIR

Fig. 12-51 Storage shelving.

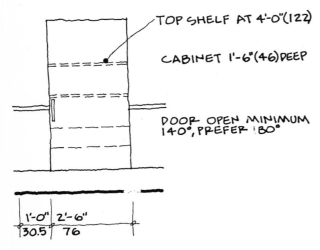

TOP SHELF AT 4'-0"(122)

CABINET 1'-6"(46)DEEP

DOOR OPEN MINIMUM
140°, PREFER 180°

1'-0"   2'-6"
30.5   76

Fig. 12-52 Storage cabinets.

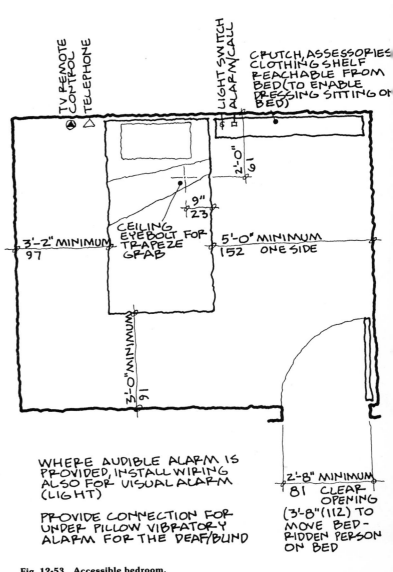

TV REMOTE CONTROL
TELEPHONE

LIGHT SWITCH
ALARM/CALL

CRUTCH, ASSESSORIES
CLOTHING SHELF
REACHABLE FROM
BED (TO ENABLE
DRESSING SITTING ON
BED)

2'-0"
61

CEILING
EYEBOLT FOR
TRAPEZE
GRAB

9"
23

3'-2" MINIMUM
97

5'-0" MINIMUM
152   ONE SIDE

3'-0" MINIMUM
91

WHERE AUDIBLE ALARM IS
PROVIDED, INSTALL WIRING
ALSO FOR VISUAL ALARM
(LIGHT)

PROVIDE CONNECTION FOR
UNDER PILLOW VIBRATORY
ALARM FOR THE DEAF/BLIND

2'-8" MINIMUM
81 CLEAR
OPENING
(3'-8"(112) TO
MOVE BED-
RIDDEN PERSON
ON BED)

Fig. 12-53 Accessible bedroom.

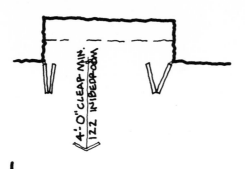

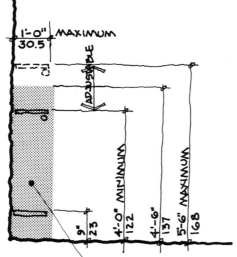

4'-0" CLEAP. MIN.
122 IN BEDROOM

1'-0" MAXIMUM
30.5

(ADJUSTABLE)

4'-0" MINIMUM
122

4'-6"
137

5'-6" MAXIMUM
168

9"
23

MINIMUM 75% OF CLOSET STORAGE VOLUME
SHOULD BE WITHIN 4'-6" (137) OF THE
FLOOR

Fig. 12-54 Closets.

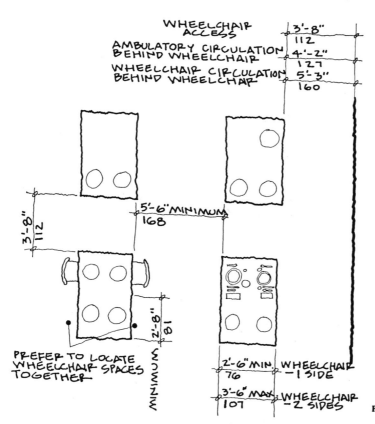

WHEELCHAIR
ACCESS   3'-8"
                                    112
AMBULATORY CIRCULATION   4'-2"
BEHIND WHEELCHAIR   127
WHEELCHAIR CIRCULATION   5'-3"
BEHIND WHEELCHAIR   160

5'-6" MINIMUM
168

3'-8"
112

MINIMUM 2'-8"
81

PREFER TO LOCATE
WHEELCHAIR SPACES
TOGETHER

2'-6" MIN. WHEELCHAIR
76   -1 SIDE

3'-6" MAX. WHEELCHAIR
107   -2 SIDES

Fig. 12-55 Dining room.

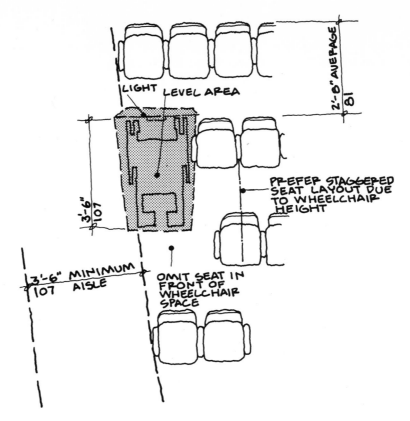

Fig. 12-56 Wheelchair space in auditorium.

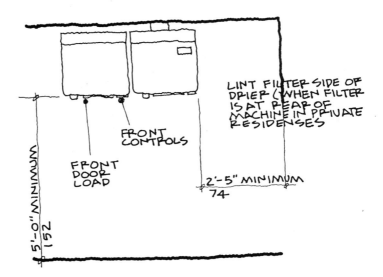

MINIMUM 1 WASHER, 1 DRIER IN EACH GROUP
TO BE WHEELCHAIR ACCESSIBLE (FRONT
CONTROLS, FRONT LOAD

PREFER FRONT LOADING WASHER/DRIER
COMBINATION FOR WHEELCHAIR USE
WHERE POSSIBLE

Fig. 12-57 Washer/dryer criteria.

BUILDING ELEMENTS

Doors for access to building areas must be wider than 32 inches to provide the required 32 inches for clear access by wheelchairs. Where doors are wider than 36 inches and solid or heavy, ball-bearing hinges should be used. For storage and similar locations, bifolding, folding, or sliding doors are essential; pocket folding doors are to be avoided.

Generally, all hardware should be surface-mounted rather than recessed, and should be oversized. Handles should be shaped to enable use by those who cannot grasp or squeeze. Lever-handles for doors and "C" pulls for cabinets are most appropriate.

Telephones, drinking fountains, and other such facilities should be located so that a wheelchair can be brought alongside for access if it cannot fit beneath these facilities. All controls should be placed at the front, and within 40 inches of the floor. Even tables should be designed for easy access.

All electrical controls and accessible elements should also be within the 40-inch limitation from the floor level. Switches mounted on projecting boxes make it much easier for the elderly or palsied to grasp and to steady their hands while operating the control device. Electrical convenience receptacles should be no closer to the floor than 24 inches for wheelchair-occupant accessibility.

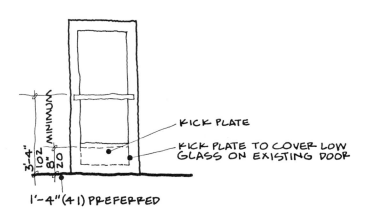

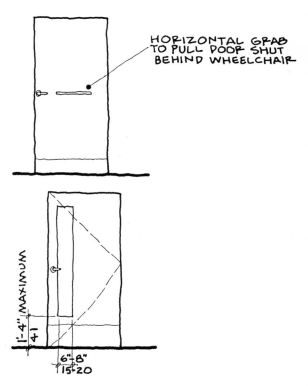

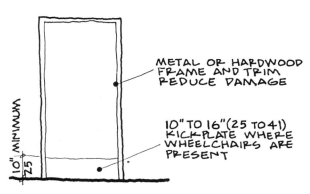

Fig. 12-58 Doors.

Fig. 12-59 Doors.

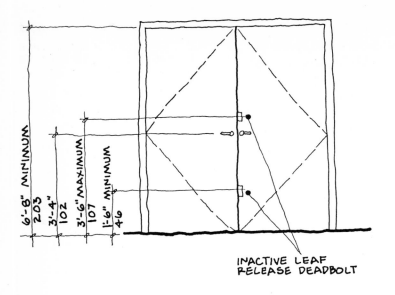

EACH LEAF OF DOOR PAIR SHOULD
MEET ACCESSIBILITY STANDARDS

Fig. 12-60   Door pairs.

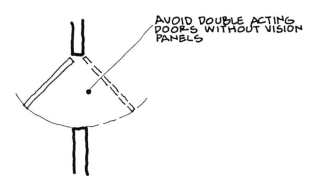

Fig. 12-61   Double-acting door.

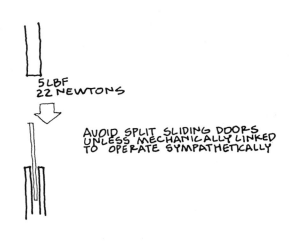

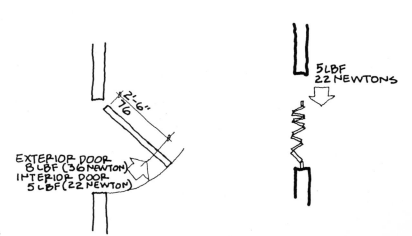

Fig. 12-62   Door force.

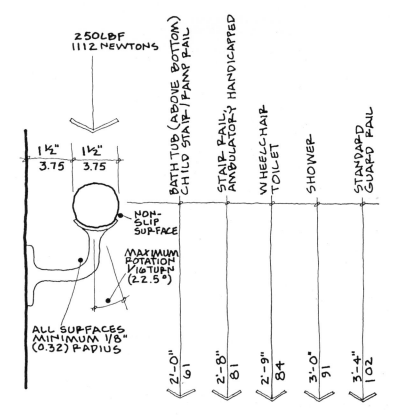

Fig. 12-63   Typical handrails.

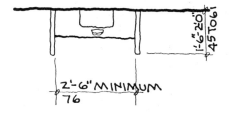

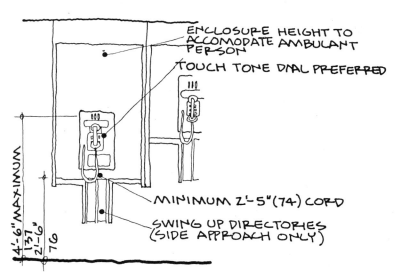

ENCLOSURE HEIGHT TO
ACCOMODATE AMBULANT
PERSON

TOUCH TONE DIAL PREFERRED

MINIMUM 2'-5" (74) CORD

SWING UP DIRECTORIES
(SIDE APPROACH ONLY)

FOR SHALLOW ENCLOSURE, BOOKS MAY
HANG BELOW PHONE

FOR DEEP ENCLOSURE OR BOOTH WHICH
REQUIRES 'HEAD IN' APPROACH, SEAT,
SHELF, AND/OR DIRECTORIES MUST NOT
EXTEND BELOW 2'-5" (74)

Fig. 12-64   Telephone enclosure.

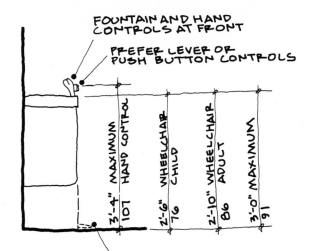

FOUNTAIN AND HAND
CONTROLS AT FRONT

PREFER LEVER OR
PUSH BUTTON CONTROLS

3'-4" MAXIMUM HAND CONTROL 107

2'-6" WHEELCHAIR CHILD 76

2'-10" WHEELCHAIR ADULT 86

3'-0" MAXIMUM 91

FOOT OPERATED FOUNTAINS
MUST ALSO HAVE HAND CONTROL

PROVIDE ALTERNATE FOUNTAINS WHERE
RIM OF EXISTING FOUNTAIN IS HIGHER
THAN 3'-0" (91)

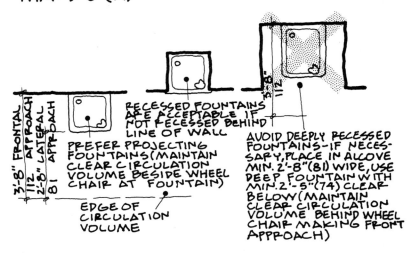

3'-8" FRONTAL APPROACH 112

2'-8" LATERAL APPROACH 81

RECESSED FOUNTAINS
ARE ACCEPTABLE IF
NOT RECESSED BEHIND
LINE OF WALL

PREFER PROJECTING
FOUNTAINS (MAINTAIN
CLEAR CIRCULATION
VOLUME BESIDE WHEEL
CHAIR AT FOUNTAIN)

EDGE OF
CIRCULATION
VOLUME

AVOID DEEPLY RECESSED
FOUNTAINS—IF NECES-
SARY, PLACE IN ALCOVE
MIN. 2'-8" (81) WIDE, USE
DEEP FOUNTAIN WITH
MIN. 2'-5" (74) CLEAR
BELOW (MAINTAIN
CLEAR CIRCULATION
VOLUME BEHIND WHEEL
CHAIR MAKING FRONT
APPROACH)

Fig. 12-65   Drinking fountains.

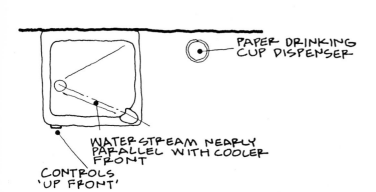

PAPER DRINKING
CUP DISPENSER

WATER STREAM NEARLY
PARALLEL WITH COOLER
FRONT

CONTROLS
'UP FRONT'

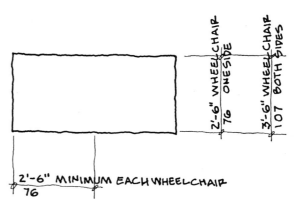

2'-6" WHEELCHAIR ONE SIDE
76

3'-6" WHEELCHAIR BOTH SIDES
107

2'-6" MINIMUM EACH WHEELCHAIR
76

SPOUT LOCATION, HEIGHT, DIRECTION
SUCH AS TO ALLOW FOR USE OF
4"(10) HIGH PAPER CUPS

CONTROLS SHOULD BE AT FRONT OR
FRONT SIDE OF FOUNTAIN

AVOID CONTROLS REQUIRING GRASPING,
PINCHING OR TWISTING

Fig. 12-66   Drinking fountains.

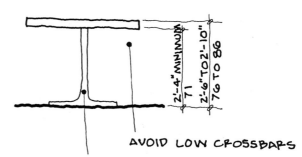

2'-4" MINIMUM
71

2'-6" TO 2'-10"
76 TO 86

AVOID LOW CROSSBARS

AVOID CORNER LEGS, PREFER
CENTER PEDESTAL

CENTER PEDESTAL SHOULD BE HEAVILY WEIGHTED
TO OFFSET USE OF CORNERS OF THE TABLE AS
SUPPORT POINTS BY THE HANDICAPPED

Fig. 12-67   Accessible table.

BIBLIOGRAPHY

American National Standards Institute. *Proposed Specifications for Making Buildings and Facilities Accessible to, and Usable by Physically Handicapped Persons* (proposed standard ANSI A 117.1), with 1977 and 1978 revisions, Syracuse University, Syracuse, N.Y. 1977, 1978

American Society of Landscape Architects, *Barrier Free Site Design,* U.S Department of Housing and Urban Development, Washington, D.C. 1975

Dreyfuss, Diffrient, Tilley, and **Bardagjy,** *Humanscale 1-2-3,* The MIT Press, Cambridge, Mass., 1974

Goldsmith, Selwyn, *Designing for the Disabled,* rev. ed., Royal Institute of British Architects, London (1963), 1976

Harkness and **Groom,** *Building without Barriers for the Disabled,* Watson-Guptil, New York, 1976

New Jersey Easter Seal Society, *Comprehensive Barrier-Free Standards,* New Jersey Easter Seal Society, Trenton, N.J., 1975

New York State University Construction Fund, *Making Facilities Accessible to the Physically Handicapped,* New York State University Construction Fund, Albany, N.Y., 1967

North Carolina State Department of Insurance, *An Illustrated Handbook of the North Carolina State Building Code,* North Carolina State Department of Insurance, Raleigh, N.C., 1974

Ohio Governor's Committee on Employment and **Schooley Cornelius Associates,** *Access for All,* The Governor's Office, Columbus, Ohio, 1977

Sorensen, R. J., *Design for Accessibility,* McGraw-Hill Book Company, New York, 1979

Tice and Shaw, *Barrier-Free Design: Accessibility for the Handicapped,* Institute for Research and Development in Occupational Education, New York, 1974

U.S. Department of Housing and Urban Development, *Housing for the Physically Impaired,* A Guide for Planning and Design, Washington, D.C., 1972

————, *Manual of Acceptable Practices for the HUD Minimum Property Standards,* Washington, D.C., 1973

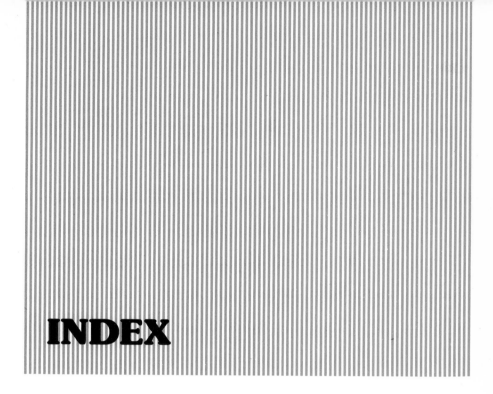

INDEX